MENTAL TESTS AND CULTURAL ADAPTATION

Psychological Studies

7

Mouton . The Hague . Paris

Mental Tests
and
Cultural Adaptation

edited by

L.J. CRONBACH and P.J.D. DRENTH

Mouton . The Hague . Paris

Library of Congress Catalog Card Number: 72-79985

© 1972, Mouton Publishers, Herderstraat 5, The Hague, Netherlands

Printed in the Netherlands

Foreword

The title under which these proceedings appear is deliberately ambiguous, for the themes of the papers and discussion were diverse. The meeting was initially planned as a 'conference on mental tests', and all participants were interested in practical use of tests or in pursuing basic research with the aid of tests. But the sentiment of the meeting was clearly opposed to reliance on mental tests in isolation, for either scientific or practical purposes. Thus, while many of the papers demonstrated how tests can be used effectively, limitations of tests received equal emphasis.

'Adaptation' was very much in the minds of the participants, but the term was used in many different contexts. Some papers addressed themselves to the specific difficulties in adapting an established testing procedure when collecting data outside the culture of its origin. Some writers introduced 'adaptability' as a property of the person tested, in order to escape both the misleading connotations of the term 'intelligence' and the common emphasis on tests that measure crystallized, school-acquired knowledge. While it was agreed that tests measure adaptive processes, it was also stressed that the test-successful subject is likely to be one who employs the concepts and tactics that help in adapting to the particular culture that is currently dominant in Western nations. Is it good social planning to ask individuals to adapt to such a culture? Or should the effort not be to adapt the culture so as to fit it better to the characteristics of its population? Such broad issues are not resolved within these pages, but the fact that the questions are raised in itself sets the stage for new sophistication in future work.

The adjectives 'mental' and 'cultural' in the title likewise need some explanation. To avoid an unmanageable spread of topics, the plan for the conference restricted attention to intellectual measures. Participants, however, find the old division between 'cognitive' and 'affective' activities an impediment to interpretation. They see task performance as social, motivational, and temperamental, as well as 'cognitive'. As for 'cultural', it must be admitted that 'culture' emerged as the ubiquitous undefined term of the meeting. Perhaps it has been sufficient in the past to identify crosscultural research as research that collects data in two or more nations. But research is equally crosscultural when it tests two distinct populations within the same nation. Even within a single community or district there may be different cultures at work, if different homes use different language patterns and teach different lifestyles. The conference participants were as much interested in the gradations of experience 'within a culture' as they were in dramatic contrasts between South Sea Islanders and Londoners.

All papers presented to the conference are included in these proceedings, but it has been necessary to shorten papers wherever possible. Papers originally written gracefully have sometimes been reduced to a telegraphic style that we hope conveys the same message, less elegantly. Tables and figures were reduced to a minimum. Our authors were generous in citing predecessors, but we have restricted bibliographies to works dated later than 1960 except for an unfamiliar source or one about which a pointed comment was made.

L.J.C.
P.J.D.D.

Contents

LEE J. CRONBACH, CONFERENCE DIRECTOR
Stanford University

Introduction

This volume constitutes the proceedings of a conference held in Istanbul, Turkey on July 19-23, 1971, under the sponsorship of the NATO Advisory Group on Human Factors and the Turkish Scientific and Technical Research Council. For the purpose of encouraging exchange of ideas and promoting scientific work within its member countries, NATO sponsors many meatings where scientific advances are discussed. The proposal leading to the present conference was made by Hasan Tan of Middle East Technical University, who pointed out the spreading demand for tests and the need for each nation to profit from the experience of others that have been developing, adapting, and interpreting tests.

A program committee consisting of Drs. Arıcı, Drenth, Lévy-Leboyer and myself was appointed, and this group suggested an agenda for the conference that would cover not only practical testing but also basic studies of cognitive development from psychological and anthropological perspectives. Survey papers were solicited from experienced persons, and an invitation to contribute communications was widely distributed. Fortunately it was possible to open the conference to persons from all nations, and some 30 nations are represented in the program, making it an unusually far-ranging survey of current thinking.

Dr. Tan served as President of the meeting. Much help with regard to matters both large and small was given by the organizing committee under his chairmanship; the other members were Drs. Arıcı, Kagıtçibaşı, Pekintürk, and Turgut.

The smooth operation of the conference owed a great deal to the administrative officer, Mehmet Okuturlar, and to my secretary, Jenny Cloudman. Considerable help was given by M.A.G. Knight and B.A. Bayraktar, scientific affairs officers of NATO.

We acknowledge with thanks the basic financial support from NATO which made the conference possible, a special grant from the Turkish Scientific and Technical Research Council, and a grant from the Social Science Research Council of the USA which supported travel for three Latin American participants.

HASAN TAN, CONFERENCE PRESIDENT
Middle East Technical University, Ankara

Development of psychology and mental testing in Turkey

The developmental status of psychology in Turkey may be representative of the efforts in this discipline in many developing countries. Therefore, it seems reasonable to take a look at some important stages in its process of development in Turkey, so that its main problems in this process may be understood better.

HISTORICAL DEVELOPMENT

Ideas of past centuries

The land of Anatolia has been the cradle of many civilizations — Hittites, Lydians, Phrygians, and Ionians in the early centuries, and Byzantines, Moslems, Seljuk Turks, and Ottoman Turks later. Each culture in the land certainly contributed something to the other. Present-day Turkey had in a sense inherited something from each. Psychological treatment of mental patients took place as early as the fifth century B.C. in the Asclopion in Bergama, Western Turkey. It was a famous mental hospital of the time where mental disturbances were accepted as disease and the patients were treated through hydrotherapy, music therapy, suggestion, activity treatments, and the like.

As in many great religions, Islamic thought believed that the soul was eternal where the body was mortal. Many Mohammedan philosophers and scientists were concerned with the problem of soul in relation to the body. They developed certain philosophical constructs which were taught in the Medressahs – the higher educational institutions of the day in the Moslem countries. Their beliefs in human behavior were used in education and medicine, the most famous being, I believe, Ibn Sina's teachings.

Ibn Sina (980-1037), a well-known physician and philosopher of his days, was famous for his treatment of mental patients through suggestion, as well as for his books on medicine, logic, philosophy, natural sciences, and psychology. He explained his ideas on psychology that he classified among the higher sciences (metaphysics), in his famous book *Science of soul (Ilm el Nefs)*. He identified three levels of soul: the vegetative soul which directs nourishment, growth, and reproduction, the animal soul which involves motor movement and performance, and the human soul which embodies the intellectual powers or faculties from the simplest form of perception to higher mental functions. These faculties, from the lowest to the highest level, are fantasy, mediation, imagination, cognition, motivation, memory, and thinking.

Soul (self) is not material. When something can be thought of, it exists. You can think of the soul, therefore the soul exists. The soul is the essential spirit because it can control and change the primary function of any organ of the body. Faculties other than thinking are not able to recognize themselves. Those other faculties become tired, but thinking even improves after age 40 (Ülken, 1951).

Turkish culture in Asia Minor had such a background in psychology. At the time of Seljuks and Ottomans the teaching of psychology continued in Medressahs in a philosophical context. It is especially interesting to note that in the middle of the fifteenth century, Sultan Mehmet the Conqueror ordered the establishment of a mental hospital within the complex of the academic institutions named after him in Istanbul. There mental disease was considered to be like any other disease and mental patients were treated through kind human interaction, music, gymnastics, and the like. Specific kinds of melodies were prescribed for specific types of mental disorder (Bayülkem, 1970, pp. 14-17). Hunting parties were regularly scheduled in order to offer specific kinds of meat to the patients with specific types of disturbance. At the time of such a progressive view regarding mental diseases and such psychological treatment in Istanbul, mental patients were being handled by demonology in Europe. There are also some indications that crude performance tests were employed in evaluating the students in the palace school *(Enderun mektebi)* as early as the sixteenth century (Ergin, 1939, pp. 1-20).

Modern events

There have been three important attempts since the beginning of the present century to establish psychology as a modern experimental science in the universities. In 1909 Istanbul University, under the influence of Ziya Gökalp, a famous Turkish sociologist, and his friends such as I. H. Baltacıoğlu, reformed its program and teaching procedure on the model of European institutions. It was decided to invite foreign professors in experimental pedagogy and psychology; Anschutz came from Germany to Istanbul to teach experimental psychology in 1915, bringing some laboratory equipment with him. He left for his country at the end of the war in 1918 (Birand, 1956). After his departure the work stopped. A Turk who had his training under Claparède in the Institute Jean-Jacques Rousseau took over the chair of psychology in 1919. He published a number of books and articles and translated a number of works including some of James and Freud.

Despite the difficulties of the war years and thereafter, it is interesting to see that some important developments in Europe were also followed in Turkey. For instance, the famous Binet test was published in Turkish in 1915, a year earlier than its American version. Psychology was taught in teacher-training institutions, and a textbook on child psychology was published in 1915. Topics of psychology under logic and philosophy were introduced into the curriculum of Istanbul Sultanisi, a Western-type high school, as early as 1912 (Yücel, 1938, pp. 159 and 186). A decade later psychology occupied an independent place in the ninth-grade curriculum (o.c. p. 170). Despite these reform activities, psychology could not free itself from the philosophical characteristics and could not extend itself from the walls of the university classrooms to the everyday problems of the country during the years 1909-1933.

The second attempt began with the reorganization of Istanbul University in 1933 and continued up to the 1950's. The government closed down the University to make changes in its organization and staff, and reopened it in 1933. Some foreign authorities in various scientific fields were invited in, and some young persons were sent abroad for postgraduate training. William Peters, formerly a professor at Jena, came to Turkey in 1937 and established the Institute of Pedagogy, which included chairs for pedagogy and psychology as experimental disciplines. The chair of general psychology continued independently under Tunç. Peters established the first psychology laboratory and directed some 80 minor experimental studies and half-a-dozen doctorates during this period (Birand, 1956; McKinney, 1960).

This period witnessed some increase in psychological publications, some well-known names in teaching of psychology in higher educational institutions, and the establishment of Ankara University. For instance the late Egon Brunswik, an Austrian, came to teach in Gazi Teacher Training Institute in the early 1930's. Muzafer Sherif, now a leading name in social psychology, started teaching in the same institute in 1936 after completing his Ph.D. at Columbia. Mümtaz Turhan, with a Ph.D. from Germany, and Refia Semin, Ph.D. from Switzerland, were included in the staff of Istanbul University in the late 1930's. Some young people were sent abroad by the Ministry of Education for graduate study in psychology and education. Some important books by leading figures of the time were translated into Turkish (see Gündüzalp, 1951, vol. 2). Sherif translated the Stanford-Binet into Turkish. A college (faculty of letters) with a chair in psychology was established in Ankara in 1937. Pratt of Princeton University formally organized and headed the institute of philosophy in 1945, when Sherif left for the United States, psychology being within this institute. A number of visiting psychologists occupied teaching positions or were active in research in Istanbul and Anakara. All these activities, however, were not yet enough to develop a strong interest and desirable tradition in psychology. My third period covers the years from 1950's to the present. Many significant attempts were made in various branches of psychology, not just for the implementation of psychology as an experimental and empirical discipline of instruction but also for its practical use. New psychology courses were added in the higher educational institutions. New universities with psychology departments based on Ango-Saxon tradition were established. Psychology started to be used in personnel selection, classification, counseling, and therapy.

In Istanbul University the chair of experimental psychology separated itself from pedagogy as an independent department in 1952 (Birand, 1956). Gazi Teachers' College, then a leading teacher training institution in Ankara, in the early 1950's introduced new courses such as educational psychology, differing from the old pedadogy by its scientific and experimental approach, adolescent psychology, clinical psychology, test construction, statistics, and counseling and guidance. Middle East Technical University was established in Ankara in 1956. An independent psychology department with a curriculum in the Anglo-Saxon tradition was formally organized in 1960. The curriculum, scientific and experimental on one hand, and concerned with the needs of the country on the other, has been influential on curricula of sister institutions. Such courses as psychology of learning, psychology of counseling, industrial and personnel psychology, test construction and measurement, and research methods were offered. Industrial psychology was offered in 1958 for the first time in Turkey. Another newly established University in Ankara, Haçettepe, has a good psychology curriculum with a modestly equipped laboratory. The psychology curriculum in high schools was revised, in a more empirical direction, in 1965.

During this period important public and private organizations became interested in using psychological services. The Ministry of Education established a Test and Research Bureau in 1953, of which more will be said below. Attempts to inaugurate counseling and guidance in schools were made. Selection and classification of military personnel became increasingly important. The Armed Forces started employing some American tests in classification of reserve offices and soldiers, but did not find these adaptations fully satisfactory. Some large companies — Sümerbank, Istanbul Bus and Electricity Service, Turyağ, etc. — became interested in selection programs after 1960. Some of them established psychotechnical laboratories while others depend on the help of psychologists from the universities. Also, psychiatrists recently realized the need for clinical psychologists in their clinics.

The number of psychologists with doctoral degrees has increased, especially since the late 1950's. The number of research publications has been rapidly increasing. The Turkish Psychological Association, affiliated with APA, was established in 1956. It has not yet been very influential in creating a fertile professional atmosphere for psychologists and in popularizing psychological services.

THE PRESENT OUTLOOK

Psychology has just recently been able to divorce itself from its philosophical past and is barely on the way to becoming an applied science.

At present, four of the seven universities in Turkey have psychology departments. Some 300 students are majoring in psychology. However, a large proportion of them are girls, who mostly terminate their active interest in psychology by marriage. At present there are 25 Ph.D.'s working in universities or university affiliated institutions.

Three of the four universities offering a psychology major have psychology departments independent from philosophy. They have laboratory accommodations and equipment, although the laboratories are not yet very productive of research, being more suited for classroom demonstrations. Haçettepe and Middle East Technical Universities in Ankara have counseling laboratories. The lack of adequate undergraduate reading material in psychology in Turkish is still a problem. Middle East Technical University has a good library for psychological literature in English, French, German, and Turkish, plus all leading professional journals. Two universities (Istanbul and Ankara) offer a doctoral program. There is a shortage of instructors in all psychology departments, and visiting instructors are employed whenever conditions permit. The number of publications in psychology is increasing.

The main consumer of psychology is still education. Some schools last year started installing guidance and counseling programs formally, and more schools will do so in the coming academic year. Mental-health problems in schools are seen as important. The Ministry of Education is operating its Testing Bureau and a number of guidance and counseling centers. A number of schools have classes for children who need special education. The selection of students to various schools and colleges has been made through achievement and aptitude tests for many years. Mental clinics and hospitals are crying for the professional help of psychologists. Some public organizations such as the State Planning Department, National Security Agency, and Police Department are either realizing the need for or using the services of psychologists. The Armed Forces now have a psychotechnical laboratory in an officer training school.

TESTING AND MEASUREMENT

There was some interest in measuring the performance of the students in Enderun, a special school for talented youth and children of the elite in earlier centuries of the Ottoman Empire. Scientific testing in Turkey began with the translation of the Binet test in 1915. Its translation was not the result of practical aims but rather of scientific curiosity. It was not standardized on a Turkish population. As increased interest in testing began in the 1930's and continued to 1945. I could locate 11 books on testing from 1930 to 1950, 6 of which were published before 1940. Eight of them are translations from English, French, or German.

More serious attempts started with the establishment of the Testing and Research Bureau by the Ministry of Education in 1953. The Bureau has been established for the purpose of helping the schools to identify special students and student problems, to increase systematic and objective evaluation in schools, to train personnel in testing, to render advisory services on testing to other organizations, and to provide psychological instruments for guidance and manpower planning.

Since its establishment the Bureau has prepared a number of achievement tests for elementary and high schools. It also developed some group aptitude tests. However, I have not been able to locate any validity studies or standardization activities on the tests the Bureau has developed. The Bureau has been preparing the selection batteries and directing entrance examinations for various schools at all levels. A number of people from various organizations has been trained in test application and interpretation, which also increased interest in testing. One of the most significant contributions of the Bureau besides publication on testing has been in increasing the number of test specialists in the country by sending its staff members abroad for graduate studies.

The Pedagogical Institute of Istanbul University carried out a standardization study of the Stanford-Binet under Prof. Şemin. Gazi Teacher's College developed the Gazi-Beier Test, a projective test, under Dr. Beier of the University of Indiana. Middle East Technical University has an experimental adaptation of the 1960 rivision of the Stanford-Binet and the WAIS. Haçettepe and Istanbul Universities are working on the WISC. Construction of original tests has just begun. Some were prepared for university entrance examinations.

The standardization of an interest test is already under way (Tan, Newspaper Headings Test).

SOME PROBLEMS

As has been seen, psychology in Turkey has mostly been a teaching subject in the Continental tradition. It has been philosophical in nature until recently, and is still in the developmental stage. There are some reasons for this. Not enough psychologists were fully trained in psychology as behavioral scientists in the early quarter of the present century, so that the field has lacked strong and effective leadership to publicize the discipline as a utilitarian science. There were no adequate publications in Turkish, hence a professional atmosphere for psychology has not been formed in the country. Professional contacts among psychologists are still on the personal basis to an extent. The best brains among youth are still attracted by more prestigious technical fields. The number of psychologists is still short to fill the vacancies and meet the needs at present. Why?

Some writers have speculated that the Moslem religion might have blocked such scientific development (McKinney, 1960). As a matter of fact, the Koran has many sections valuing knowledge and encouraging new learnings. It is true that Islamic countries are underdeveloped but this does not seem to be because of the religion. Major Islamic countries lived prosperously and had advanced civilizations in the past under the same religion.

Bowra (1958) observed that the Eastern cultures are fonder of poetry than Western cultures. McKinney (1960) hypothesized that the love of poetry in Turkish culture led the people to understand human behavior from an emotional standpoint instead of objectively and it is true that in the past centuries more poetry books were written in Turkish than science books. Thus the hypothesis may find partial support, but there are other factors that can be mentioned.

One of the main causes seems to be that the science of psychology did not and still does not have enough consumers. The best customer of psychological services has been education, but it could not pay much. Thus, youth still prefers the financially more promising technical fields (Tan, 1966). Industry has newly found an interest in using the services of psychology to promote efficiency and productivity. Turkey has still not completed its industrialization, despite its serious efforts over almost two centuries. It seems to me that Turkey has overemphasized the technical aspects of the West, missing cultural aspects in its efforts of Westernization. I think this is the most basic cause in the slow development of psychology as a basic and applied science in Turkey.

REFERENCES

Bayülkem, F. (1970) *Some views in the application of rehabilitation and a summary of the historical evaluation of rehabilitation in Turkey.* Istanbul.

Birand (Toğrol), Beğlan (1956) Psychology in Turkey. *Istanbul Univer. studies in exper. psychol.,1,* 3-5.

Bowra, C. M. (1958) Poetry and tradition. *Diogenes, 22,* 16-26.

Ergin, O. (1939) *History of Turkish education,* Vol. I. Istanbul.

Gündüzalp, F. (1951) *Bibliography of teachers' professional books,* Vols. I & II. Istanbul: Milli Eğitim Bakanliği.

McKinney, F. (1960) Psychology in Turkey: Speculation concerning psychology's growth and area culture. *Amer. Psychologist, 15,* 717-723.

Tan, H. (1966) Foreign students in USA: Developing countries and Turkey. *Türk Kültürü, 42,* 548-556.

Ülken, H. Z. (1951) Ibn Sina, in *Encyclopedia of Islam.* Istanbul. Pp. 807-824.

Yücel, H. A. (1938) *Secondary education in Turkey,* Ministry of Education, Istanbul.

PART I

Testing in its social framework

To introduce the general discussion, Arıcı and Drenth were asked to point out both the potentialities for constructive use of tests and the issues that need to be faced if that potential is to be realized. Both of them emphasize the resistance to tests that arises from legitimate and illegitimate sources. Arıcı calls for a higher level of responsibility among testers. Drenth amplifies by showing that different questions are raised according as the test developer and research workers focus on the test *per se,* the criterion, or the decision to be made. Blake shows more concretely how tests are put to practical use, treating tests to be examined in later sections, from other points of view, by Biesheuvel, Reuning, and Grant. He describes the use of job analysis in NIPR work and reviews validity studies.

Alongside these practical concerns is the attempt to develop psychological interpretations of tests and explanations of intellectual performance. Biesheuvel examines what crosscultural studies can contribute to this understanding. He questions the usefulness of 'intelligence' as a construct and introduces 'adaptability' as a target for investigation. He applies the concept to experience with tests in South Africa. Dague employs a similar concept in his invited review of research in Africa, and notes the importance of measuring how well the person responds when given an opportunity to learn the test task.

HÜSNÜ ARICI
Haçettepe University, Ankara

Laying the groundwork for test application in less-developed countries

From the earliest beginnings of human society, men have tried to evaluate the abilities of one another. They had noticed individual differences not only in physical appearance and physical strength but also in mental functioning. As their experience in social interaction became richer, they noticed the relation between man's performance in different activities and his physical and mental characteristics. Therefore, it seems justified to assume that man's interest in evaluating his fellows is as old as his history. But only in the last hundred years or so have attempts been made to systematically evaluate the mental abilities of men.

THE NEED FOR APTITUDE TESTS

The philosophy of psychological measurement and evaluation has not changed for years. Today we are concerned with human beings either as individuals or as groups of individuals, because we want, or we are forced, to make decisions about them. We want each decision to be as sound as possible, and we know that relevant information is of prime importance for sound decisions. Aptitude tests are one means of gathering relevant information.

Aptitude tests, as I use the expression, are designed to evaluate the mental capacity to acquire proficiency either in many activities or in a given area. In many countries, information gathered through aptitude tests plays a vital role in determining who should be accepted to a certain school, job, etc., what kinds of

changes are needed in school programs, and what line of education a given person should follow to use fully his potentialities
and to fulfill his needs and interests? Consequently, aptitude tests
have become the basis for student and personnel selection, curriculum change, evaluating school programs, and determining
young people's futures.

However, the practice of aptitude testing has been beset with
some basic problems. For example, through hard experience we
have come to learn that describing mental status is more difficult
and less successful than describing physical characteristics. Devices for measuring of mental characteristics are far from fully
satisfactory. I do not undervalue the achievements of psychologists in their efforts to develop adequate measuring devices, but
the work is far from a complete success. Part of the difficulty
stems from the fact that mental characteristics cannot be directly
observed.

If we define a test as 'any method of observing and measuring
human behavior for comparative purposes', then the idea and the
practice of testing, in one form or another, has long existed in all
the less-developed countries. However, the idea of using 'objective tests' and conducting the observation and measurement procedures in a systematic manner is relatively new.

The basic areas of need for aptitude tests in less-developed
countries are almost the same as those in developed countries:
selection of students for different educational programs and of
personnel for various kinds of jobs; placement or classification of
students and of personnel; guidance and counseling; and evaluating the effectiveness of treatments such as school programs and
the like.

All societies must train their citizens to perform the tasks
required for the continuation and development of the society.
Furthermore, every society must provide for allocation of its
citizens to positions in the society. No nation seems to wish to
leave the development and allocation of its manpower to chance,
but a great variety of means have been used to accomplish these
ends. The quality of the means used seems to be rather consistent
with the general developmental level of the country concerned.
In developed countries individuals are most often channeled into

one treatment or another on the basis of their potentialities, achievements or performances, whereas in some of the less developed countries such channeling is done mainly on the basis of ascribed characteristics. The situation has been changing rapidly, because in such countries the importance of educated manpower and effective utilization of human resources in achieving national goals is being recognized. Since less-developed countries have limited resources and cannot provide everyone with extensive education, selection and placement for educational and vocational training and for jobs is crucial.

Among the alternative ways of carrying out selection and placement is trial and error; initial selection or placement is based on ascribed characteristics. The individual's performance in the position is the basis for the final decision. Those regarded as successful are retained and those considered unsuccessful are replaced. It is impossible, however, to give every likely candidate a chance to try himself out in every position.

The resources of less-developed countries are too limited for large-scale trial and error. Such an approach is uneconomical, resulting in a high proportion of misplacement and rapid turnover of personnel. This demoralizes the people, and wastes the country's manpower, money, and time. Consequently, it has become urgent for less-wealthy countries to develop sounder ways of predicting success in different treatments (in school, on jobs, etc.) before making assignments and providing training.

Another alternative is to use school performance as a general criterion for the allocation of further opportunities. This has been a rather common practice in many less developed countries, but here again the situation has been changing rapidly. As such countries are not as yet able to provide all of their citizens with the appropriate educational opportunities; only a small portion of the population can benefit from the available opportunities. Yet the need and the desire to extend opportunities to all sectors of the society is growing. Also, as in many developed countries, it has been recognized that teachers' judgments of pupils are somewhat subjective and based in part on characteristics completely unrelated to aptitude. Standards vary from school to school as well as from teacher to teacher.

As mentioned earlier, another purpose of aptitude testing is guidance and counseling. It is difficult to accept the position that for less-developed countries guidance and counseling services are a luxury. Less-developed countries cannot and should not tolerate wasteful use or loss of their human resources. Relevant and adequate information about the individual is ·essential for guidance. The developed countries have found adequately developed and properly used aptitude tests invaluable in collecting some of the information needed.

CRITICISMS OF TEST APPLICATION

Despite the precautions taken by some psychologists, the rapid expansion of test application in less-developed countries has led to certain problems, which are sometimes so great that one wonders whether the use of tests could continue. In some countries, tests have been misunderstood and misused. As a result, the public, scholars in various disciplines, and some politicians have developed misgivings about tests and their use for decision-making. In Turkey, for example, sensation-seeking politicians and columnists have exploited these feelings to the extent of arousing public boycotts and protest demonstrations. Some question the constitutionality and the technical and ethical value of 'American-inspired tests', ignoring the fact that neither the concept nor most of the techniques of testing are peculiar to any specific culture.

Many times the critics have good cause to attack tests and testing, because many of those who use and talk about tests do not themselves know anything about testing and its techniques. There is no question that such people do more harm than those who make no use of testing.

A common criticism is that the tests emphasize memory of facts, names, terminology, and superficial details. This criticism, too, is right on the target, for very often the tests used indeed measure nothing but simple knowledge. In some of the less-developed countries anyone who can write a statement after which he can put a question mark supplying 4 or 5 words, numbers, figures or statements as possible answers, regards himself a test expert. His test is very often one which measures only simple knowledge (if it measures anything at all). We, of course, know that, if properly constructed, tests can measure behaviors well beyond simple knowledge.

In the final analysis, many of the criticisms can be characterized as half-truths, personal bias, or misunderstanding of testing principles and its objectives. Our most important concern in judging the concept of testing is not quantity, but the way tests are developed, their appropriateness for a particular purpose, and the way they are used. Attacks should not be directed at the idea of using tests, but at the way they are developed and used. It appears that the way to deal with such criticisms is to put our own kitchen in order first by combating the misusers. The best strategy of combat probably would be to develop technical standards and professional ethics. This can be done through professional organizations. I believe the time has come to establish common international standards and ethics to facilitate better testing practices throughout the world.

There is nothing wrong with using aptitude tests so long as we know what we are doing with them and realize their limitations. If the scores on an aptitude test become the only basis for making decisions, however, we supply ammunition to those who are waiting eagerly to attack tests and testing.

SOME SUGGESTIONS FOR SOUND TESTING

There is hardly any job or activity for which just one test is an adequate predictor. Jobs and educational activities are more complex than they seem. Aptitude tests ought to be supplemented with measures of achievement, interest, and even personality. Having the pertinent mental capacity and the skill does not guarantee that the individual will be successful. Other characteristics such as personality may be the determining factor. Therefore due consideration should be given to the development and use of 'typical performance' tests not only for guidance and counseling but also for possible use in selection and placement. Moreover, test scores should be supplemented with other information. Let us not forget that the basic function of testing is to improve decisions. Too often teachers, administrators, and pupils find themselves working to master what the test demands of them. Those who manage testing programs in less-developed countries should see to it that tests serve educational and training activities rather than dominate over them.

As cultural factors affect an individual's behavior in many ways, behavior cannot be measured or analyzed independent of culture. Every test is developed and validated within a specific cultural framework. Even the so-called 'culture-free' and 'culture-fair' tests reflect cultural differences. Despite the considerable amount of work by psychologists to create culture-free or culture-fair tests, the results are still not consistent and valid. Differences between cultures and differences among subcultures within a culture should always be given due attention in developing tests or adapting instruments from other cultures.

If a test is to contribute to our understanding of the individual, it should be appropriate for the purpose of testing and for the individuals to be tested, and there should be information about how persons similar to these examinees have performed on the test. The first criterion will require information about validity and the second about the norms of the test.

The application of an aptitude test must not be based on subjective confidence that the instrument works. Validity must be empirically established in relation to each use.

Norms are frequently neglected. Many times, raw scores are used as if they are a true indication of the characteristics of interest. Psychologists in less-developed countries should not forget that one of their fundamental problems is making sense out of test data. Appropriate norms play an important role in handling such problems.

Public relations of testing are often neglected. As mentioned earlier, the increasing use of tests in less-developed countries has already started to affect the behavior of pupils, teachers, administrators, patients, and the public in general. Since we could not carry out our activities without the approval of those who determine policies and of those who are directly effected by tests, it is essential that we establish good public relations. It is our duty to educate all concerned about the need for better testing practices.

In summary, the growth of psychological testing as an aid to important decisions calls for an increasing sense of professional responsibility among psychologists in less-developed countries. As it became possible to administer tests to large groups of people, relatively untrained people (who also have less concern for professional ethics) began using tests too widely too soon. The quality of the tests, the interpretation of the scores, and the decision based on test results are often of questionable value. Psychologists in less-developed countries must recognize their responsibility to educate teachers, administrators and others to a more effective use of tests.

Despite the advantages of testing, it has some disadvantages as well. It must be the policy of professionals everywhere to maximize the advantages of testing. As Tyler (1966, p. 49) puts it: '. . . the problem cannot be met by denying the existence of the double-edged sword and by claiming that tests are neutral and are not in themselves agents for good or bad'. Psychologists working in less-developed countries should seek wise action rather than no action, and set examples instead of being an agency only for suggestions and advice.

Despite the problems mentioned, psychologists in less-developed countries should continue to use tests because the consequences of not using tests seem to be more serious and dangerous than the hazards in using them. As Ebel (1966, p. 28) says, 'If the psychological tests were abandoned, the distinction between competence and incompetence would become more difficult to discern . . . Educational opportunities would be extended less on the basis of aptitude and merit and more on the basis of ancestry and influence; social class barriers would become less permeable.'

We psychologists in less-developed countries all know that we have a difficult job before us. But we could benefit from the experiences of other countries, as well as each other's, and avoid some mistakes that have been made. This of course requires dedication, technical competence, a well-established and well-functioning organization, and good public relations.

REFERENCES

Ebel, R. L. (1966) The social consequences of educational testing. In Anne
    Anastasi (Ed.), *Testing problems in perspective.* Washington, D.C.: Amer.
    Council on Educ. Pp. 18-28.
Tyler, R. W. (1966) What testing does to teachers and students. In Anne
    Anastasi (Ed), *Testing problems in perspective.* Washington, D.C.: Amer.
    Council on Educ. pp. 46-59.

Note: *Thrane remarked that resistance to testing is not confined to
developing countries. Something close to a revolt against comparative evaluation of students is to be found among Norwegian youth.* (Eds.)

PIETER J. D. DRENTH

2

Free University of Amsterdam

Implications of testing for individual and society

The psychological test influences many facets of life in the USA and many European countries. Government, schools, industry, counseling facilities, and clinics use tests extensively in order to reach decisions about people. These decisions are in many cases aimed to benefit the future behavior or future achievements of the person taking the test. Therefore, test usage has a strongly predictive character. This contrasts with test usage in the USSR, where tests are almost exclusively used for educational evaluation. Testing is most extensive in the USA, where according to Goslin (1966) more than 150,000,000 tests per year are taken in the schools alone.

Whatever one's views about the desired role of testing, the correctness of the decisions reached (from both the technical and ethical viewpoints), and the advantages and disadvantages for the individual and for society, the fact remains that the test can hardly be eliminated from the Western social system. Testing has contributed to more effective use of manpower, to more equal distribution of educational and professional opportunities, and to identification of talents that might otherwise remain hidden. In criticizing testing – and criticism will be offered in this paper – one must not ignore its benefits. Ebel (1963) ends a critical article with the comment that our concern for the social consequences of testing must be offset against concern for the social consequences of *not* testing. This paper criticizes testing so that we may sooner realize the benefits of proper testing.

In less-industrialized countries, testing will undoubtedly increase. It appears that in these countries the road to general application of psychology in society will run via test psychology, as it has in Western countries. This test psychology will probably develop much as it has in the countries where testing is well established, and it runs the risk of repeating the mistakes and shortcomings of Western test psychology.

This can perhaps be prevented if we become aware of the societal, ethical, human consequences of test usage, consequences that have been underestimated, misjudged, or overlooked in the past. After all exaggerations and simple malevolence in public judgments of testing are set aside, much justified and realistic criticism remains (see Drenth, 1968, Ch. 7).

As testing practice has developed, thinking has broadened. An initial phase that we may call test-oriented broadened into a criterion-oriented phase, and this is now supplemented by a decision orientation. Each orientation directs attention to different matters, and advances certain interests of individual or society while neglecting others. (For an expanded treatment, see Drenth, 1971.)

THE TEST ORIENTATION

When the test orientation was dominant, attention was primarily directed towards the nature and construction of the test, and toward methods of interpretation and evaluation. Much energy and inventiveness were invested, resulting in a large variety of tests and a highly developed psychometrics. We shall take up five inadequacies of work done under the test orientation.

First of all, the creativity of psychologists with this orientation has been (with a few exceptions) directed more towards methodological refinement and data-theoretic sophistication than towards a search for relevant aspects of ability or personality. There was too strong an emphasis on classical intelligence factors and scholastic aptitude. This has led to insufficient utilization of specific talents (with consequences for individual and society), and to a narrow concept of talent. One starts with an attempt to predict achievement in school or society. The tests for this gradually begin to lead a life of their own, and finally may come to determine what is judged to be of importance in school or society. Thus the roles are reversed! Instead of being 'derivative', the test concept becomes normative. One can easily see, in a country such as the USA, how this stimulating but restricting influence has come from the classical intelligence test.

Second, intelligence and general ability are too often seen as inherited attributes rather than as performances that can be modified by learning. The test then acquires too much power to determine decisions. This can damage the individual's self-esteem and interfere with his educational motivation, so that the test actually causes failure in his educational and professional career. For society, the same misconception can lead to neglect of talent and to waste of educational investment.

Intelligence tests measure the result of a learning process. Many factors have been of influence, including the quality of education and the diversity of stimulation in the child's environment. Inferences made about inherited learning capacities from test results rest upon uncertain grounds, and it seems wise to place less emphasis on the genetic or hereditary aspects of intelligence. This hazard is perhaps especially grave in the developing countries. Verhaegen and Laroche (1958, p. 249) conclude, on the basis of extensive experience in Africa, that 'the notion of aptitude as a hereditary disposition exercising a limiting effect on some defined behavior, becomes even less valuable, when it concerns peoples who suffer from lack of education as in the case of indigenous African populations.'

A third problem is that the culture-bound character of tests is too easily ignored in practice. Although textbooks warn against this, practice is careless. In countries where testing is just beginning, foreign tests are likely simply to be translated and put directly to use. Or, at best, research on a test may go no further than a tabulation of the distribution for cases on hand. This has happened in Europe, and Asia and Africa are following suit.

Test form, content, and meaning are culture-bound, often more than anticipated. The low reliabilities and validities repeatedly found by thorough evaluation studies can be attributed to this primary misconception about the cultural transferability of test data.

The whole time-consuming and painstaking process of item-
and test-analysis must be performed when a test is translated;
some items or tasks must be dropped and new ones added. The
advantage of translation, as opposed to construction of a new
test, is then limited to the use of test ideas contained in the
nature of the items – and even these can lose their significance in
another culture. One cannot make use of the 'same' test in two
cultures. The desire to do so often originates from the much-too-
simple design: 'translate a test and compare mean scores'.
Thorough item analysis and revision diminishes the 'equivalence'
of the tests and the possibility of straight comparisons.

Fourth, it is to be noted that testing within a country is
equally culture-bound. Within one nation there are many differences in environmental influences and educational possibilities;
the test psychologist must take these into account to guard
against discrimination.

A test is validated with respect to a certain population. Strictly
speaking, this test may only be used for decisions for which its
interpretation has been verified, and for the population on which
it is validated; its use for other populations or subpopulations is
unsupported.

A test that shows differences between cultural or racial groups
is not *ipso facto* biased. There can be true differences in the
characteristic measured. Strictly speaking, a test can never be
biased; it only indicates differences. What can be biased is the
way the test results are used. Test usage can be termed biased
when predictions or criterion scores for a certain demographic
subgroup, derived from the user's regression formula or expectan-
cy tables, are constantly too low or too high. O'Leary, Farr, and
Bartlett (1970), among others, describe instances in which validities for subgroups of a population differ in size and direction;
many of these instances can be subsumed under the definition of
bias.

The issue of whether to prefer mental-ability tests or achievement tests in educational selection embodies the test-bias problem. An achievement test can be viewed as an objective registration of what the person knows *or* as an indication of the 'learning
ability' that has influenced his attainment of that knowledge. A

person whose education has been of poor quality is then at a disadvantage, since that determines his level of knowledge as much as actual learning ability does. The emphasis on learning ability in interpretation is more likely to lead to straight select-or-reject decisions. The more operational view might lead to an earlier recognition of the discrimination against persons who have been subjected to education of poor quality. Seen from this viewpoint, low achievement-test scores could sooner indicate the need for compensatory programs or extra training, or for reconsidering the application after supplementary education.

This problem is complex. It is related to the issue of 'ability grouping', with both psychological and moral aspects (right to equal opportunity). Whether selection in education, business, and occupational choice should be so strongly based on differences in ability (intelligence) is open to question. Genetically determined capacities perhaps should not weigh more strongly than actual achievements which are sometimes the result of great effort and sacrifice.

Even a valid test or item may contribute to discrimination against a minority group, when a correlation exists between the test or item and race or sex or religion. This can occur in subtle and disguised forms. The simplest example is to be found in items in biographical questionnaires, with, e.g., questions like 'Were you living with both your parents when you were in high school? ', or 'Did you have an own room at home? ' Lovell (1967) comments that if empirical validity is the only concern, one could ask 'Are you a Negro? ', which in the USA would correlate strongly with school achievement, promotion in corporations, and even criminality.

Finally, the public impression of testing and the reaction of the individual tested have received too little attention among psychologists.

It is remarkable that objective testing consistent with the rules of psychometrics appears to the public as deterministic, freedom-limiting, impersonal, and mechanistic. Even those people who think objectively and quantitatively about nonpsychological matters prefer to have persons assessed by subjective and rather unscientific methods (impressions, references, grades). Probably this is one of the important causes of the popularity of clinical, impressionistic methods of psychology in many countries. It is a challenge for psychology to retain the advantages of objective testing and simultaneously to reduce the resistance of the public.

With the public increasingly critical of testing procedures, the examinee has also become more critical. This criticism is largely justified. The tested individual has long been seen by the psychologist as passive; he is subjected to a process whose purpose remains unclear to him and to a decision about which he has nothing to say. He has to submit to unchallenging and often infantile test items; he has to answer intimate questions that invade his privacy. The purpose of testing and the way in which the psychologist comes to his conclusions remain unexplained. The examinee has no guarantee that the test data and psychological report will remain confidential and he is usually given no feedback beyond the final accept-or-reject decision. The situation has purposely been described a little too harshly, to emphasize that the tested individual is a responsible human being who brings rights and desires to the test situation. This is too often forgotten.

The examinee must be able to acquire insight into the testing procedure and the decision-making process. He must be guaranteed that the data will remain confidential. He must have the right to get information from the test, if possible with an opportunity to discuss the results. To the classical psychometric requirements of reliability and validity must be added another desideratum, what de Groot (1970) has called 'acceptability for the testee'.

Another kind of acceptability is related to the quality of the test. It is paradoxical that to the extent that tests have improved, they may have become more threatening. When tests give a more valid indication of someone's abilities, moderate or poor results are more difficult to rationalize or deny. The test will therefore cause tension and anxiety in the person tested; a good test will be quicker to engender resistance. Gardner (1961, p. 72) says it aptly: 'If a society sorts people out efficiently and fairly according to their gifts, the loser knows that the true reason for his lowly status is that he is not capable of better. That is a bitter pill for any man'.

THE CRITERION ORIENTATION

Test psychologists extended their attention to the study of criteria and their improvement when they found that energy and ingenuity devoted to the tests themselves could not raise correlations with typical criteria above a moderate level. Attention to the criterion brought new problems to light. We mention only some of the most important ones.

First, we point to the confusion due to the failure to distinguish the criterion as psychometric problem from the criterion as objective. For example, whether to use grades, teacher evaluations, or advancement in validating a school entrance test is largely a psychometric problem. Each operationalizes, in some form, learning achievements. The most important consideration is the reliability of the measure to be chosen, when all operations reflect the same outcome.

Whether one should use performance in training or in actual work as criterion in validating a selection procedure depends on the aim of selection. Tests correlated with one of these criteria often do not correlate with the other (Ghiselli, 1966). The criteria themselves are apparently not sufficiently in agreement. Which criterion should be chosen is no longer a psychometric problem, but rather one of policy.

It has been argued in the past (even by me) that the psychologist should only concern himself with locating the most reliable operation to fit a policy decision handed down by the sponsor (director of the corporation, or the school). But the psychologist cannot properly evade responsibility for the objective of selection. The sponsor is sometimes hardly conscious that he is choosing between alternative goals of selection, and it is the task of the psychologist to stimulate this awareness. A proposed criterion sometimes includes unacceptable elements that the psychologist can recognize and take into consideration. We shall return to this point.

The second difficulty is the vagueness of the task assigned to the psychologist. Often the psychologist is asked to select 'a good secretary', 'a good representative', or 'a good manager'. In the past, the psychologist simply accepted the question; he directly began to look for – or worse, he simply chose – a 'single overall criterion'. Without hesitation, he took up his tests to predict these overall criteria.

This is an important cause of the limited success of classical validations. Criteria used in practice are complex and multidimensional (see, e.g., Ronan & Prien, 1966). It is impossible for a test series to predict whether someone will be 'good', if 'being good' has many facets and can be realized in many ways.

A reversal also occurs here. Because a single overall criterion is assumed, a test series is chosen to reflect this supposedly unidimensional concept 'good performance'. This test series will measure a restricted ability and will select only people who possess this ability. This way it affects the view of performance in practice. The vicious circle is closed and the erroneous assumptions are thus justified.

Third, the approach is too empirical. Attention to the criterion, for all its benefits, has unfortunately fostered the idea that the greatest good in test psychology is prediction of the criterion. This had led to a strong accent on validation of the test-should-predict-criterion type.

Purely correlational studies are hardly interesting for theory. Nor are they of much interest for practice! I do not agree that 'why it works' is more an academic question than a practical problem. If it is not known why a relationship exists, improvement becomes impossible. Furthermore, with a new criterion a large series of predictors must be tried haphazardly, without the guarantee that a sufficient number will survive the validation process. This method leaves us helpless when we come to a rare or unique situation; we cannot even formulate hypotheses. A final argument is that with the purely correlational approach, one misses the possibility of drawing conclusions about the criterion on the basis of the test (see below). The question of 'why it works' certainly should be asked, even in practically motivated work. This means more construct validation and more analysis of test meaning, and less exclusive emphasis on prediction.

We have already referred to the task, often forgotten by the psychologist, of analyzing the criterion before forming the criterion-related tests into a selection battery. Correlations between tests (of known meaning) and criteria can tell much about the determinants of the criteria! A study of the reasons for the correlations is needed before deciding which of the valid tests are acceptable for inclusion in the test series. There may be determinants unacceptable to the psychologist, and possibly unacceptable also to the decision-making authority once it is made aware of them.

This analysis and evaluation *of the criterion* from its correlations with tests is what Hofstee (1970) calls 'inverted diagnostics'. It is really a form of discriminant validity. We have here the requirement that a test not correlate with something other that it is intended to measure. In this case the requirement does not concern something outside the given criterion, but something it embraces that is unwanted or unacceptable. A selection battery for Marine officer candidates (Hofstee, personal communication) serves as an example; data are explicitly collected on 'appearance' and 'socioeconomic status of father'. The results allow one to assay to what extent these unintended 'discriminators' may influence the practical evaluation (criterion). Where there is such influence one can eliminate these discriminators from the selection process by means of partial correlations.

THE DECISION ORIENTATION

Since the first publication of the Cronbach-Gleser monograph in 1957, the decisions made with tests have gradually received more and more attention. Wickert (1962) helped to popularize this viewpoint and has applied it to developing countries.

The advantages of a systematic and explicit decision orientation are that the assumptions and elements in the decision process are exactly identified, and that the place and contribution of the test become much clearer than before. A clear distinction is made between several decision strategies in which the test plays different roles and fulfills different demands on different occasions.

Consequently, the decision orientation identifies more exactly what the test contributes to the decision-making process; it makes more likely the choice of the right type of test for a certain decision; and it leads to a better statement of the requirements a test must fulfill. Tests for simple selection differ markedly from those needed when people are to be distributed over several qualitatively different jobs. Likewise, whether or not to continue with college education is very different from an 'open' question such as 'What kind of profession shall I choose? '

The decision approach makes it clear that the test is 'responsible' only for determining probability of success. Since much besides the test has to be taken into consideration in order to reach decisions about people, the role and contribution of the test becomes more realistic and modest. Making decisions is certainly more than using tests.

The decision orientation also poses problems – questions that are not new now become explicit. It appears that often the wrong tests are chosen for certain decisions (e.g., using tests of general ability such as the Wechsler tests for differentiation and for placement decisions, or using typical broad-band procedures like observation tests and projective techniques for specific decisions).

The contribution of the test is often compared with chance results and not with the results under an a priori strategy. Tests may be used in situations where testing is unnecessary or even wrong (e.g., where the base rate is very low, or where a slight increase in utility is purchased at high testing expense). Training that takes individual differences into consideration can increase utility just as selection can, and a combination of the two (called 'selection with adaptive treatment' by Cronbach and Gleser) yields the greatest output. This possibility is seldom taken into account.

A most important distinction is made between individual and institutional decisions. In the former the choice of courses of action is that of the individual. The expected payoff from a course of action may vary between individuals even when they have the same chance of a certain outcome, as they value this outcome differently. Examples of such individual decisions are occupational, career, and school choice as well as individual career planning within a company.

In the institutional decision it is the institution whose interests are served. The value placed on the outcomes is that of the institution (the school, company, or society) and is the same for every person considered. The utility of the whole decision-making strategy is determined by the average payoff over all decisions, and the strategy is to maximize this total yield. Examples of institutional decisions are admission to a school. selection for a company, examination for military service.

This distinction is important because most ethical and social problems refer to it. The problems of confidentiality, invasion of privacy, use of misleading techniques, making the subject defenseless, restriction of his freedom, the concerned individual's having insufficient voice in a decision made about him – these problems hardly occur in the case of individual decisions, properly made. There the ultimate goal is the well-being of the individual, and his value system is used as guide. However, these problems become significant when the decisions are taken for the institution (school, business firm, insurance company, profession, traffic system), according to *its* value system.

Some ethical codes for psychologists state or imply that the primary concern of the psychologist is the client, i.e. the subject of investigation. In practice, however, the psychologist identifies himself with the institution. This is of course not to say that all institutional decisions are detrimental to the individual. But a conflict of interests can definitely occur. And in that case, the psychologist all too easily chooses the side of the institution at the cost of the client's interest. Solutions to this problem should be sought. One step is to make selection integral with other personnel work. Selection especially emphasizes differences. If one sees selection as part of a process that also includes placement, training, and development, one can sooner realize both goals. The proposal of selection with adaptive treatment is an extension of this idea.

Second, the psychologist, even one connected with an institution, could take a more independent stance; his professional responsibility should at times prevail over his identification with the institution. He should be able to decide or advise in the interest of the individual even when this does not coincide with the interest of the institution.

A step in this direction is seen in the attempts of the Dutch Psychological Association to broaden the concept of 'client', (NIP, 1971). They would not refer solely to the individual studied or to the institution for which the individual is tested, but to a client system, embracing both the individual and the institution. The psychologist does not serve exclusively the interests of one of the two parties; rather, he serves both. This concept suggests an attempt to find a 'match' to which both parties agree. Both have the right to confidential treatment, information about decision procedures, and openness about matters influencing the decision.

A most radical proposition made in the Netherlands by Hofstee (1971) is to nationalize personnel selection. A national bureau, it is suggested, could function as servicing agency allowing for democratic control of procedures. The selection psychologist is employed and paid by the community. A side advantage is that such concentration and coordination of manpower releases time for research that is now too often neglected.

These attempts to solve the individual-vs.-institution controversy are commendable. They conform to the basic principles of a sound psychological relationship between tester and examinee.

This paper has brought up many controversies about test usage. To repeat what was said in the beginning: the intent is not to bring testing into discredit, but rather to consider social and ethical consequences so as to guarantee the important benefits that can come from tests.

REFERENCES

Cronbach, L. J. & Gleser, G.C. (1957) *Psychological tests and personnel decisions,* Urbana: Univ. of Illinois Press. (2nd ed., 1965).
Drenth, P. J. D. (1968) *De psychologische test.* (2nd ed.) Arnhem: Van Loghum Slaterus.
Drenth, P. J. D. (1971) Theory and methods of selection. In P. A. Warr (Ed.) *Psychology at work,* London: Penguin. Pp. 169-193.

Ebel, R. L. (1964) The social consequences of educational testing. In *Proceedings, 1963 invit. confer. testing problems.* Princeton: ETS. Pp. 130-143.

Gardner, J. W. (1961) *Excellence.* New York; Harper.

Chiselli, E. E. (1966) *The validity of occupational aptitude tests.* New York: Wiley.

Goslin, D. A. (1966) *The search for ability.* New York: Wiley.

de Groot, A. D. (1970) Some badly needed non-statistical concepts in applied psychometrics. *Ned. Tijdschr. v. Psychol., 25,* 360-376.

Hofstee, W. K. B. (1969) Individuele verschillen en averechtse toepassing. *Ned. Tijdschr. v. Psychol., 24,* 482-493.

Hofstee, W. K. B. (1971) Selectie van personeel nationaliseren. *Ruim Zicht, 20,* 1.

O'Leary, B. S., Farr, Z. C. & Bartlett, C. J. (1970) Ethnic group membership as a moderator of job performance. Silver Spring, Md.: Amer. Inst. for Res.

Lovell, V. R. (1967) The human use of personality tests: A dissenting view. *Amer. Psychologist, 22,* 383-393.

N.I.P. (1971) Aanbevelingen herziening beroepsethiek N.I.P. *De Psycholoog, 6,* 364-373.

Ronan, W. W. & Prien, E. P. (1966) Toward a criterion theory. Greensboro, N.C.: Richardson Foundation. (Mimeographed)

Verhaegen, P. & Laroche, J. L. (1958) Some methodological considerations concerning the study of aptitudes and the development of psychological tests for African natives. *J. soc. Psychol., 47,* 249-256.

Wickert, F. R. (1962) Some implications of decision theory for occupational selection in West Africa. In A. Taylor (Ed.) *Educational and occupational selection in West Africa.* London: Oxford Univer. Press. Pp. 127-138.

Note. *The idea of nationally centralized personnel testing was unacceptable to members of the conference who saw this as a possible political instrument. Drenth stated that he was not endorsing the proposal but introduced it as one of many alternatives. It could succeed only if brought under genuinely democratic control.* (Eds.)

R. HILTON BLAKE

National Institute of Personnel Research, Johannesburg

3

Industrial application of tests developed for illiterate and semiliterate people

In Southern Africa, although the picture is changing fairly rapidly, many in the indigenous population have no more than a primary-school education (if any), are of rural-agricultural background and orientation, and lack industrial experience. Orthodox bases for selection, classification, and placement (educational standard, kind and length of industrial experience) often cannot be used.

Psychological testing as the basis for these decisions offers an alternative to the usual trial-and-error process in which a man's occupational fate often depends on criteria no more relevant to job demands than facial features. At the least, the use of tests offers the opportunity for consistent decisions based on criteria directly relevant to job demands, *provided* these are expressed as qualities which relate to variables which can be measured, and measured fairly easily, accurately, and with confidence. It follows that the jobs themselves must be analyzed and evaluated in terms of factors which relate directly to cognitive processes.

ANALYSIS, EVALUATION AND CLASSIFICATION OF JOBS

The method of describing, analyzing, and evaluating jobs developed at NIPR in South Africa is a combination of factor comparison and point-rating. Its flexibility is demonstrated by its effective and successful application in a wide variety of industries including farming, mining, building construction, sugar milling, heavy and light engineering, and diverse manufacturing concerns (e.g. motor vehicles, textiles, Portland cement, and domestic ceramic ware). Its reliability is indicated by the agreement of descriptions and evaluations of the same job produced independently by different analysts.

Understanding of the system of analysis is readily gained from a self-instruction manual. The description prepared for each post begins with a general outline in which is presented a clear and concise account of the individual tasks or functions an incumbent performs. This is followed by an analysis in terms of four job-demand factors: decisions and vigilance, controls and checks, education, and experience. Each factor is defined in operational terms. For example, a *decision* is defined as 'the commitment to action arising from a situation (either in the normal flow of work or when a specific problem arises) in which there are alternative courses open to resolve an issue, the one most appropriate to the issue being selected.' *Vigilance* is defined as 'the alertness and sharpness of perception involved in recognising the development of a situation where a decision will need to be made.' Perceptual cues may involve any sense modality.

The central factor is 'decisions and vigilance'. It is believed that decision complexity is determined by the number of alternative courses of action open in a situation, the kind and number of data to be considered in making a decision, and the ease with which they are obtained. At the simplest level, alternatives are limited to two, with relevant cues readily apparent and unequivocal. At higher levels, the process involves the recognition of cues (visual, auditory, tactile, kinaesthetic) and their interpretation in terms of a background of education and experience, rules and regulations, knowledge of similar decisions made in the past, current situational factors, and the like. Welch (1971) found that perceptual load is the key factor in acquiring skill in a simple motor task.

For each of the four factors, six levels of complexity are described. The example which follows relates to 'decisions and vigilance'.

Degree 4

Detecting deviations from set standards. Involves various skill elements in their perception and is based on knowledge of one or more specific processes.

Problem situations are semirepetitive in nature and involve interpretation, coordination, and integration of clues giving rise to the situations.

Alternatives are governed generally by set standards and regulations, but unspecified alternatives based on knowledge of the processes involved may have to be generated to cope with situations of minor scope not encountered before.

Advice is readily available from higher authority, and the consequences of an incorrect decision may involve the department in limited costs.

The analyst must obtain and record examples of actual decisions made, controls and checks exercised, etc., as in the 'critical incidents' technique first described by Flanagan. The evaluation of each job consists largely of comparing the critical incidents with the described rating points, interpolating between 'degrees' if necessary. Examples culled from previously completed exercises are available as guidelines. A numerical value is then ascribed to each factor, and the values are totaled over factors. When a frequency distribution is made of these totals (ungrouped), job groupings are revealed. Careful examination of these groupings leads to the identification of separate grades of skill. For example, the job of machine operator is rated at or above 45, and the job of machine tender is rated 29-44.

The range of jobs filled by those with low literacy is seldom divided into more than three grades, typically laborer, machine tender, and machine operator. The range of jobs open to people at this level is distinctly limited, as more complex positions generally require a greater degree of literacy. Another very important reason is that the limited number of items in the tests applicable at this level and the standard error of measurement of each makes it unrealistic to expect the tests to discriminate reliably between a greater number of grades. Combining tests into batteries allows greater flexibility, but increases testing time.

THE GAB TESTS

It is essential that the nature of the problems set in a test be grasped by Ss. In Southern Africa, the variety of racial groups and tribes encountered, each with its own language or dialect, presents special problems to conveying test instructions to illiterates and semiliterates. Two, three or more unrelated languages may be represented in a group of 25 Ss and conveying instructions orally becomes cumbersome. Administration by mime or silent film is the solution, although it is difficult to keep mimed instructions completely standard, especially over long periods.

It is equally essential that Ss have had the opportunity to acquire the skills and knowledge entering into the test assignments. As suggested by Biesheuvel (1952), it is best to avoid scholastically acquired skills, the conventions of pictorial representation, and logical reasoning characteristic of Indo-European language habits. Satisfactory results, he suggested, are likely to be obtained 'from manipulative tests involving adaptability and learning.'

Pioneer work conducted by Biesheuvel and his team at NIPR between 1948 and 1952 resulted in the by-now widely known General Adaptability Battery (GAB). Intended for administration to those with no more than a primary-school education (7 or 8 years in the local systems), these are group tests administered by silent 16 mm. film. The four tests involve the sorting of objects (e.g. numbered and lettered discs) and the assembly of various components into simple constructions (e.g. cubes of various sizes). Perception and reasoning are required. A correctly sorted object, or a component correctly placed (with reference to the model), scores one point. Time limits are strictly enforced. Testing time (including administration and scoring) for the four tests plus an unscored buffer test is approximately 2½ hours. The tests produce relatively flat distributions of scores, are reliable, and have had their validity demonstrated in a variety of situations. This battery has been in constant use in the South African gold-mining industry since its development, and has also been adapted by a variety of manufacturing enterprises; it has been administered to 2½ million people. The tests are reliable (p. 54).

Biesheuvel gives score statistics for three categories of job families. Incumbents were all experienced workers who had progressed by a trial-and-error process to what might be termed their natural job level; a direct relationship is expected between an individual's cognitive ability and the complexity of the job to which he has risen. For each test the means differed significantly, although not every pairwise difference reached significance. The tests correlate with each other and with education.

THE CLASSIFICATION TEST BATTERY

A new generation of tests for this level was developed between 1964 and 1966 by various workers at NIPR. All are group tests administered by mime or silent film; the majority involve the manipulation of material, but some are in paper-and-pencil format. The tests involve reproduction of patterns varying in kind and difficulty, and the continuation of given patterns made up of various symbols; reasoning and perceptual and conceptual levels is involved. Scoring is similar to that of the GAB.

Studies conducted in the gold-mining industry and originally reported by Grant (1970) yielded the information contained in the following tables. Reliabilities are high (Table 1), and validities obtained for several of the tests are encouraging. In the validation

Table 1. Statistics for the 'second generation' tests (N = 149)

Test	Score range	Mean	s.d.	Reliability	s.e.m.
Pattern reproduction	0 − 39	25.85	9.66	.79	4.4
Form perception	0 − 27	19.36	6.60	.79	3.0
Fret repetition	0 − 10	8.66	2.27	.93*	0.6
Fret continuation	0 − 10	7.36	3.32	.95*	0.7
Form series	0 − 18	8.64	5.21	.91*	1.6
Circles	0 − 48	34.03	9.08	.84	3.6

* Starred reliabilities are obtained by Formula KR21 (with Tucker's correction), others by KR20 in Ferguson's extension.

exercise, 12 carefully constructed training criteria were used (produced by the Human Sciences Laboratory of the South African Chamber of Mines). The KR20 reliabilities of 8 of the measures were in excess of 0.80, one was as low as 0.34, while the remaining three ranged from 0.61 to 0.74. In Table 3, 'theoretical' refers to criteria assessing retention of knowledge conveyed, demonstrated by verbal responses to questions; 'practical' refers to criteria assessing understanding of knowledge conveyed, demonstrated by performance on practical tasks; 'composite'

Table 2. Intercorrelations of 'second generation' tests (N = 149)

	1	2	3	4	5	6	7	8
1. Pattern reproduction								
2. Form perception	.49							
3. Fret repetition	.55	.36						
4. Fret continuation	.66	.44	.68					
5. Form series	.51	.34	.43	.56				
6. Circles	.74	.49	.66	.70	.58			
7. Age	.14	.12	.02	.06	.14	.11		
8. Education	.42	.25	.37	.47	.46	.47	.20	

Levels of significance: .05 = .159, .01 = .208, .001 = .247.

Table 3. Product-moment correlations of tests with criteria

	Criterion		
Test	Theoretical	Practical	Composite
Pattern reproduction	.47	.57	.55
Form perception	.36	.44	.42
Fret repetition	.38	.37	.41
Fret continuation	.39	.46	.46
Form series	.53	.45	.54
Circles	.52	.60	.59
CTB, unweighted	.56	.61	.63
CTB, regression wt'd	.60	.63	.65

refers to a combination of weighted 'theoretical' and 'practical' assessments. Criterion measures were obtained by individual testing.

The tests cease to discriminate effectively if administered to *S*s who have more than an elementary education. The use of separate norms for urban and rural groups is advisable.

Tests 1, 5, and 6, as a battery, yield the highest correlations with the criteria. This battery, named the Classification Test Battery or CTB, gave the validities at the bottom of Table 3. Total testing time is approximately 2 3/4 hours.

A Form Series Test (FST) more difficult than that included in the CTB has proved to be most useful in the context of secondary industry where the labor force tends to be better educated than that in the gold mines.

Parallel forms of this version were constructed and produced a test-retest reliability of 0.85. KR20 reliabilities for the two versions were 0.90 and 0.89. The sample was 1000 mine recruits (Grant, 1965). In a very recent study in an engineering works, version A was administered twice to 86 *S*s, the two administrations being separated by three months. The test-retest reliability was 0.81. Scores increased by more than 1/4 s.d. on the average.

In addition to these tests of general cognitive functioning, more specific tests are being developed. One of these is the Abstract Spatial Relations Test (ASRT), a measure of the perception of space. It, with paper-and-pencil format, is somewhat more difficult to administer than the other tests referred to, but it also functions satisfactorily. For a sample of 300 persons, the range was 0-15, the KR20 reliability was 0.80, and the standard error of measurement 1.6.

In a study incomplete at the time of writing, this test and the 'secondary industry' version of FST (among others) were used to investigate differences between a randomly selected control group and incumbents in a highly skilled task involving the molding of asbestos cement. While no difference emerged on FST, that on the ASRT was highly significant. The ASRT mean for controls was 6.9 while that for incumbent workers was 8.4.

SOME CASE STUDIES

In attempting to assess the effect of this system of job classification and test-based selection, the question of what to use as
criteria presents perhaps greater problems than in many other
areas. Labor stability and productivity are attractive; the purpose
of the installation of the system is, after all, to improve these by
matching people's basic ability better to job demands. It is
recognized, however, that selection is by no means the only
factor affecting the stability and productivity of workers.

Bearing this reservation in mind, several follow-up studies have
been conducted with these two criteria. In three of the four cases
reported here, a high rate of labor turnover had prompted the
organization to approach NIPR; in each case a survey by NIPR
showed selection and placement to be of a trial-and-error nature,
and this was judged to have major influence in producing the
symptom. In example 3, however, a qualified psychologist had
been employed by the organization concerned and NIPR action
was restricted to supplying relevant tests, and guidance on the
installation of the system. The first two cases will be disposed of
briefly. For a manufacturer of ceramic ware, monthly turnover
dropped from 5-6 per cent to 2 per cent after job classification
and testing were installed. For a paint manufacturer, turnover
dropped from 16.5 to 8.3 per cent. As much production as 200
workers formerly turned out is now given by 157.

Case 3 is a heavy engineering shop. The data are as follows:
June, 1968. Turnover averaging 7.2 per cent in a force of 900
    male African employees.
January, 1969. Job classification and test installation completed.
June, 1969. Turnover averaging 3.5 per cent.
Reduction in turnover in certain departments has been dramatic:

	June, 1968	*June, 1969*
Plate Shop	7.5%	0.9%
Machine Shop	4.3%	0.5%
Blacksmith Shop	3.5%	1.2%

In these three cases, although the introduction of tests formed
the major part of the exercise, some attention was also paid to

other factors such as transport, protective clothing, and canteen facilities. In Case 3 the wage structure was revised. Thus, although the system is suspected to be a major cause of the improvement observed, this is not proven in these cases. In one case, however, the action taken was restricted to the installation of the system, and similar results were produced.

Case 4 is another heavy engineering shop. The data are as follows:

August, 1967. Average monthly turnover of 7.5 per cent in a force of 700 male African employees.

May, 1968. Job classification/test installation completed.

May, 1969. Turnover averaging 4 per cent.

While the complexities of the situation make difficult the unequivocal demonstration of the role that rationalization of selection and placement procedures can have in reducing rates of labor turnover, the indications are that this role is a major one.

It is, then, possible to produce cognitive tests specifically for illiterates and semiliterates which satisfy the usual criteria for reliability and validity. They function well in practical situations and when used as the basis for selection and classification of novice employees, in conjunction with an analysis and evaluation of jobs in terms of factors which relate to cognitive functioning, they help to increase labor stability and productivity.

REFERENCES

Biesheuvel, S. (1952) Personnel selection tests for Africans. *So. Afr. J. Sci.,* 49, 3-12.

Blake, R. H. (1966) *The restandardization of the General Adaptability Battery.* Confidential contract report to the South African Chamber of Mines, Johannesburg.

Grant, G. V. (1965) *Construction of a non-verbal test of reasoning ability for African industrial workers.* Unpublished master's thesis, Univer. of the Witwatersrand, Johannesburg.

Grant, G. V. (1970) *The development and validation of a classification test battery designed to replace the General Adaptability Battery.* Confidential contract report to So. Afr. Chamber of Mines, Johannesburg.

Trethewey, N. D. (1970) *Job description and job evaluation training manual*. S.A.C.S.I.R. Guide K7.27. Johannesburg: NIPR.

Welch, P. O. (1971) *Learning patterns and relationships between movements comprising a simple motor task*. Unpublished master's thesis, Univ. of the Witwatersrand, Johannesburg.

Note: *In this paper (as in Biesheuvel's report on the GAB, and in several other papers in this volume) internal-consistency coefficients (Kuder-Richardson, split-half) are given as estimates of reliability. Such coefficients however have little meaning for timelimit tests.*

In Blake's judgment, the fact that about 80 per cent of Ss complete each test or trial in CTS and CAB blunts the force of this criticism. Of the tests in his paper, only Form Series is wholly unspeeded. (Eds.)

S. BIESHEUVEL   4
Johannesburg

Adaptability: its measurement and determinants

PROGRESS IN CROSSCULTURAL MEASUREMENT

Crosscultural testing has advanced considerably in volume, sophistication, and practical usefulness since Haddon, Rivers, and their coworkers measured the physiological, sensory, perceptual and memory capacities of Torres Straits islanders in 1899. Progress has been greatest in test administration and in our awareness of the extrinsic factors affecting test performance. We have become more concerned with qualitative differences in score patterns, as revealed particularly by differential factor spectra. We have given up the futile attempt at finding culture-free or culture-fair measuring devices, belatedly realizing that the objects of our measurement are all to a greater or lesser extent the product of interaction with the cultural environment. There is now a substantial body of knowledge about the variety and potency of environmental and cultural circumstances that can measurably influence mental growth. We have produced some very useful devices, useful for predicting vocational and educational achievement even in cultures far removed from the Western societies in which contemporary scientific psychology originated. There are now a number of texts available which summarize this development, and at least three more are known to be in preparation. For the time being, Vernon's *Intelligence and cultural environment* (1969) presents in the writer's view the most authoritative, comprehensive, and considered statement.

There is less satisfactory progress in developing a systematic body of theory and practice which one could call 'crosscultural psychology'. This is well illustrated by the present position of vocational and educational testing, which is still very largely governed by empirical considerations and where predictive validity remains the determining factor in what is done. As a first approach this is quite admirable, but the scientist cannot remain content with useful results, with merely knowing what to do. He must seek causal relationships that will enable him to improve on his results, to generalize from them and to derive the theory and laws which are the ultimate objectives of scientific effort in any field. To illustrate with an extreme example: a test might validly predict job performance because the ability to understand instructions and to adjust to a novel situation are the common elements determining success in both. The content of the test might be relatively unimportant, if not irrelevant.

With regard to procedure, the necessity of familiarization with the test situation, elaborate demonstration, use of vernacular or mime, some means of ensuring adequate motivation, and control of the race of the tester are recognized. But on other and possibly more important matters practice still varies considerably, often failing to recognize the desirability of prolonged pre-test practice in dealing with the material which constitutes the content of the test, and of introducing a learning element in the test itself.

The theoretical controversy as to the extent, if any, to which group differences can be accounted for on genetic, or at least constitutional grounds, is still with us. We know little about the significance of developmental stages and the critical nature of appropriate environmental interaction during these stages, as factors in the emergence of group differences. We have barely started to reexamine psychological concepts and categories in the light of what we have learned, or could learn, about behavioral development in different cultures.

OBJECTIVES OF CROSSCULTURAL MEASUREMENT

An important first requirement in working towards a definitive conceptualization and methodology in crosscultural psychology is to formulate the purposes of crosscultural research and measurement. Originally it may have arisen from a desire or need to study the psychology of primitive peoples. Today the first and foremost purpose of crosscultural measurement is to measure individual differences in cultures other than those in which the measuring devices and the taxonomic or analytic concepts had their origin. Measurement of individual differences is needed mainly for vocational and educational prediction. This calls for considerable modification of standard tools and procedures.

The second objective is to study the influence upon behavior, and on the origin of individual differences, of a wider range of environmental variation than is available within a single culture or than could be experimentally manipulated in any culture, for obvious practical and ethical reasons. This includes effects of specific child-rearing practices, cognitive deprivation, malnutrition, and tropical diseases. Crosscultural settings provide natural social and general laboratory situations for studying the limits of modifiability of behavior.

Thirdly, crosscultural psychology leads on to an examination of the generality of explanatory constructs and concepts that constitute the body of psychological knowledge.

The fourth objective is the description of group differences, by they ethnic, cultural, or subcultural. This has its uses in gaining an understanding of the cultural process itself, and serves as a starting point for analytic studies. It is becoming less important, however, as change wrought by culture contact and technology blurs more and more the cultural demarcation lines. These descriptive 'folk' psychological studies, insofar as they are analytic at all, should confine their analysis to the cultural process, and should not attempt to deal with the causes of a particular group difference. The complex reasons for this cannot be examined in detail in this paper. Suffice it to state that the constructs in terms of which the comparison is being carried out may not be equally valid for the two cultures. Also the methods of measurement whereby the distribution of individual differences in the two cultures is being analyzed may not be culturally equivalent. Furthermore, in straight comparisons of this type it is virtually impossible to control all the factors that have influenced the variable being measured. Even if one were to succeed in doing so, he would end up either with nonrepresentative samples or with a comparison so remote from reality that the experiment becomes virtually meaningless. In fact, analytic studies of this kind properly belong under the second heading of crosscultural psychological objectives.

From the analysis of the objectives of crosscultural psychology, the following propositions can be inferred:

1. The problem of culture-free or culture-fair testing need not concern us. It is irrelevant for the measurement of individual differences and the achievement of predictive validity within cultures. It is equally irrelevant for the study of limits of modifiability of behavior, which we recommend as the basis for intergroup comparisons as well as for remedial programs. All that one needs is tests that produce a wide range of meaningful individual differences.

2. The nature-nurture problem, insofar as it concerns group differences, can be shelved until limits of modifiability have been fully determined within homogeneous cultures. Only then will it be feasible to set up and test genetic hypotheses, to account for any remaining disparities.

3. The theme of adjustment to change is central to crosscultural psychology. Interest centers on the ways in which both individuals and groups meet the new demands made upon them by acculturation, technology, and the spirit of the times, and on the environmental factors that influence their capacity for adjustment to change.

The implication of these propositions for crosscultural testing is that our efforts should be directed towards the construction of tests to measure potentiality to meet educational, vocational, and social demands and also towards studying the factors that influence modifiability of behavior. These could be called 'tests of adaptability'.

ADAPTABILITY TESTING

The concept of 'adaptability' has considerable advantages over 'intelligence' or 'mental ability' as a basis for crosscultural test construction and procedure. 'Intelligence' is very much identified with 'that which makes for success in Western culture'. It is frequently thought of as an attribute, something that resides in an individual and is largely static by nature. As a concept it still lacks definition, with the unfortunate result that there is no generally agreed-upon method of measuring it. Operationally, it changes its character with every test and every criterion. This is even more unsatisfactory in crosscultural work than in general psychometric practice, because conventional tests presuppose modes of thought of the noëgenetic type. These are characteristic of Western linguistic behavior and are typified by test content involving eduction of relations and correlates. These constructs are quite inappropriate, for example, to Bantu languages. The constructs measured by any test very likely differ from culture to culture. 'Intelligence' is, moreover, the subject of persistent controversies about the extent to which it is or can be a function of environmental, constitutional, and genetic factors. These controversies follow it into crosscultural contexts, to the point where it becomes difficult to keep scientific and emotional considerations apart in the interpretation of any 'intelligence-test' results.

In contrast with 'intelligence' as an abstract function of behavior, 'adaptability' is an essential characteristic of all behavior, considered operationally and as a whole. Psychologically it is not an individual attribute or trait, nor is it a construct that can be factorially defined. Its affinity to culture is particularly close, for culture is the embodiment of man's past adaptations to his environment, transmitted to successive generations with such new developments as changing circumstances may demand. In Dubos' (1967) phrase, culture signifies 'what people do as a result of having been so taught'. The scientific heterogeneity of the concept of adaptability is an advantage in measuring what people can learn to do; it provides scope for the recognition of genetic, constitutional, and cultural involvements without prejudgment of the relative importance of any one determinant. Nor is adaptability linked with any cultural feature which evokes value judgments. Its only assumption is that man must adapt to survive, and that behavior that serves this end in a particular society is 'better', relative to the circumstances, than behavior that does not. It applies as much to the Bushman boy acquiring the skills of tracking down game as it does to the Western youth learning to solve problems by means of calculus.

From the point of view of test procedure, the holistic nature of adaptability is an advantage. If it is behavior as a whole that is adaptive, it does not matter that we are inevitably measuring a total response to the test situation. 'Intelligence' testing, on the other hand, demands that cognitive functions be the principal if not the only source of variance in the test results. The kind of control over noncognitive elements that this implies is extremely difficult to achieve, whatever we may do to put subjects at ease, to allay their anxiety and suspicion, to gain their cooperation, and to neutralize other cultural sources of error. These elements are generally too deeply rooted in culturally conditioned habits, needs, values, and attitudes to yield to superficial and shortterm manipulation of the kind practicable in test situations. This is well illustrated by some aspects of Poortinga's work (1971; see his paper in this volume).

If control cannot be achieved in the measurement of simple behavioral processes (presumably because of the artificiality of the experimental situation), how likely is it that it will be accomplished in the measurement of higher mental functions? In any case, would we not be creating a totally artificial situation if we did phase out the motivations and attitudes that will also be operative in the vocational or educational performance we are attempting to predict? Realistically as well as practically, the advantage lies with adaptability testing.

CHARACTERISTICS OF ADAPTABILITY TESTING

The distinction between intelligence and adaptability testing is more than a terminological quibble; it can genuinely be reflected in tests and test procedures.

1. Because adaptability is concerned with learning whatever it is that one's culture requires one to know or to do, and with modification of knowledge and skills to meet changing circumstances, tests should involve a learning component. This does not

mean that they should be tests of rote-learning, psychomotor learning, or concept-formation. After reviewing the results obtained with a variety of such tests, Vernon (1969, p. 109) concluded that 'the likelihood of obtaining meaningful information from short-term measures of learning, lasting an hour or so, is extremely thin'. He also points to the specificity of all learning tasks. What in fact is intended is that the subject should have ample opportunity to learn to do the task involved in the test by preliminary exercises, in other words, to adapt to the requirements of the test situation. The test should also provide scope for the insight gained and experience acquired in the course of testing to progressively improve performance. This means that the subject must get some feedback on how he is doing.

The General Adaptability Battery (GAB) of the NIPR was deliberately constructed with these ends in view as far back as 1950.* Its administration is preceded by a film demonstration of the test procedure and of what Ss are required to do in the first test; this test serves as a buffer and is not scored. Results on this first test are inspected and wrong responses are pointed out. Each test in the battery is preceded by its own film demonstration. Most of the tests provide for a number of trials, or for a succession of tasks which increase in difficulty. In some tests, the film demonstration is very briefly repeated between trials. The Ss thus have opportunities to try out different strategies, to get a reminder of the required responses and the end results to be achieved, and to become aware of their errors.

They can also apply experience gained in one test to the next. Thus a test of sorting mechanical objects was introduced mainly to familiarize examinees with the sorting task, i.e., with the notion of placing like with like, so as to prepare for a second sorting task in which the ability to distinguish letters and numbers is the required feature. This happens to be important for the illiterate or barely literate worker who must learn to recognize signs and instructions on the job.

---

* GAB is a series of performance tests involving sorting, assembling and design reproductions; in practice, a short battery of 5 tests, though a longer series of 9 tests was also developed.

Classifying mine workers for the gold-mining industry into training groups for laboring, semiskilled and supervisory tasks on the basis of the GAB encountered formidable difficulties. The recruits are adults from numerous tribes and linguistic groups from all over Southern and Central Africa. They have no knowledge of any European language, little or no schooling, and very limited or no contact with industrial activities, apart from previous stints on the mines. They are tested daily at numerous testing centers, in large groups – sometimes of more than 100 *S*s at a sitting. Equipment had to be used which could be cheaply mass-produced, would stand up to rough handling, and would remain standard despite prolonged use. The task had to lend itself to immediate and rapid scoring. These problems were overcome; the battery achieved acceptable split-half reliabilities which have been maintained over 20 years of use without any material change in procedures or in the design of the equipment (see Table 1; the 1969 data are from Grant).

Table 1. Split-half reliabilities of tests in the short battery in two studies

	1952	1969
Sorting I (Mechanical objects)	.88	.89
Sorting II (Discs)	.91	.94
Cube construction	.79	.78
Tripod assembly	.83	.83

More remarkable still is the way validities have held up, despite the fact that hundreds of thousands of subjects have been tested, many of them more than once. Coefficients are not strictly comparable, as different criteria were used. In 1952, the short battery yielded these validities: 0.48 against a rather crude criterion of occupational classification; 0.68 and 0.59 against trade tests for winch drivers and support workers, respectively; 0.67 against pass-fail in a first-line supervisors course; and 0.60 against an objective rating by supervisors on job performance. The latter two coefficients were multiples in which a leaderless group test was included with the short battery (Biesheuvel, 1952). In 1969, the product-moment coefficient was 0.54 for a practical criterion, performance on a variety of tasks, 0.50 for a theoretical criterion, knowledge of procedures, and 0.56 for a composite criterion. The outstanding success achieved by the GAB testifies to the validity of the methodological principles incorporated in it.

Two other instruments that have stood the test of time and have proved generally useful in crosscultural testing are the Porteus Maze and the Kohs Blocks, both recommended in the IBP Handbook (see p. 180). In both these tests, one can gain experience as he goes along, which will help in the similar, but more difficult tasks that follow. In both, *S* is able to judge the success of his performance, and the Kohs presents models to work from. Porteus has said of the Maze test that it 'purports to measure . . . capacity to improve with experience, or to make adjustments of response within the framework of the test itself.' (Porteus, 1969, p. 286). To a lesser extent this also applies to the Progressive Matrices, which can be given with a more or less elaborate introductory learning session using a variety of aids, and with some correction of performance in the initial stages. It too offers scope for applying insight acquired in the solution of the earlier problems to the later and more difficult ones.

2. The inevitable involvement of noncognitive elements in cognitive test performance, especially in crosscultural testing, is recognized both in the procedure and in the test-content of adaptability testing.

It is primarily concerned, not with level of performance (which only becomes important when intergroup comparisons are to be made), but with obtaining an adequate spread of individual differences, corresponding approximately to those in the criterion to be predicted. The procedure must ensure interested participation, in a reasonably relaxed frame of mind. It does not mean that motivation must be raised to the competitive level characteristic of achievement-oriented Western culture. It does not mean that we should attempt to induce the hustling approach which derives from *our* consciousness of time and addiction to speed. Nor need we presuppose the pitch of concentration and the detached scientific attitude required for adequate

performance in laboratory tasks, of which threshold measurements are a typical example. These are culturally determined
characteristics, too deeply embedded in the personality structure
to be induced or changed by whatever manipulation one may
choose to employ in the test procedure.

The GAB demonstrates the kind of arrangements that have
proved practicable. Recruits take the tests as part of the normal
induction process. The novelty of the situation is of a piece with
getting settled in the compounds, being issued with their kit,
undergoing a medical check, and getting acquainted with tools
and the underground workings in a surface mock-up. All are part
of a general adaptive process. There are of course individual
reactions. Some liken the test center to a school. Others find a
resemblance in the tests to the popular and widely known game
of *maraba-raba* and link its name with the test center, thereby
indicating that the activities there were found interesting and
pleasurable. For the majority, motivation is keen, as acceptance
and placement is known to depend on test performance. A test
setting has thus been created in which motivation is not materi-
ally different from what it is in the initial stages of the work
situation. This does not mean that some of the usual procedural
precautions taken in crosscultural testing can be ignored. Anything that contributes to a better understanding of the task set
by the test will give a more valid range of individual differences.
Measures that induce interest are preferred to those that create
anxiety. Schwartz's prescriptions (1963; or in Vernon, 1969, pp.
112-115) provide a useful guide.

A few tests are available with built-in noncognitive components conducive to adaptability. The veteran Porteus Maze
test, in continuous use for half a century, can again be considered
under this heading. It was designed to cover qualities not greatly
involved in the Binet, such as foresight and planning ability
which Porteus (1969, p. 45) called 'prehearsal', or the ability to
concentrate on what one is doing and to keep a purpose in mind.
It was held to provide a better measure of the use an individual
could make of his intellectual capacity, and thus of adaptability,
than tests purporting to measure cognitive elements only.

Another test which enables the subject to plan strategies and which, furthermore, involves a flexibility element, is Elithorn's Perceptual Maze (Elithorn, 1960). It too has possibilities for crosscultural research, though it is too early to determine its value for applied measurement. Other measures of adaptability are the tests of adaptive perceptual integration, including the Birch Intersensory Modality Test, the Witkin Rod and Frame, and the Gottschaldt Embedded Figures. The latter two in particular are concerned with the concept of 'field-dependence' which has lately been prominent in crosscultural research (Witkin, 1962; Dawson, 1967; Campbell, 1964; Segall, Campbell & Herskovits, 1963; Berry, 1966; Wober, 1967).

The perceptual tests involve processes having to do with flexibility of attention, of response and of gestalt formation. These processes are held to determine personality attributes such as autonomy, self-reliance and resourcefulness. Research indicates the possibility that childrearing practices, the rigidity of the culture, and the extent to which it permits individuality and initiative determine the life styles associated with field dependence and independence. The observations of Berry (1966) and Dawson (1967) on the Temne in Sierra Leone, and Berry's comparisons of the upbringing, personality, and test performance of Temne with those of Eskimo children are particularly relevant. It should be noted in passing that the Kohs Blocks test, which is particularly suited for crosscultural measurement on other grounds, also calls for perceptual flexibility (Vernon, 1969, pp. 57-58). The field-dependence concept is therefore relevant for adaptability towards new cultural demands; tests which measure it should be useful in predicting to what extent cognitive capacity will be effectively utilized in meeting educational and vocational demands.

3. The concept of adaptability testing does not require any specific content in the tests, apart from the learning component. Content can be chosen according to what it is that the individual has to adapt to. There is little occasion to test for adaptability towards a traditional way of life because this way of life is everywhere changing, and it is adaptation to change that we are principally interested in. However, such a test could be devised if it were needed. In *The African child* Camara Laye gives a delight-

ful account of what education was like in Guinea, both in the
community and in the school. Clearly those with the greatest
capacity to do exactly what they were told, to ritualize, to
memorize, and to shun deviation for fear of dire punishment
adapted best. For such conditions, a test involving rote learning
and memorizing, or following instructions, would work better
than one requiring conceptual reasoning.

This is borne out by Vernon's observations (1969, p. 164) in
Jamaica. In the elementary schools 'the methods of teaching are
sadly mechanical. Learning is regarded as doing or saying what
the teacher wants and getting the right answers through chanting
and drill, not finding out something by one's own efforts . . . The
frequency of corporal punishment at home or at school is greater
than in any other country known to the writer'. A battery of five
tests including Matrices, WISC Block Design, and Porteus Mazes
gave a multiple R of 0.74 with achievement in English and
arithmetic, whereas a simple group test based on the rote learning
of a list of monosyllables gave a correlation of 0.83 (p. 119).

Adaptability testing is mainly concerned with adjustment to
educational and vocational requirements, but also to a lesser
extent with acculturation in general, as for instance in measuring
the ability spectrum of immigrant groups. Test content can be
varied according to the specific objectives. It should be noted
that the distinction between intelligence, aptitude, and achievement tests, which involves conceptual difficulties in conventional
testing programs, ceases to present a problem in adaptability
testing.

Tests merely differ in the amount and type of past experience
involved, and the relevance of this experience to what one is
attempting to predict. One may even use the attitude-test technique; this Dawson (1971) has demonstrated with his Sierra
Leone T-M (traditional-modern) scale. It predicts work performance as effectively as an intelligence test based on the
indigenous culture, with validity coefficients of the order of
0.60. It proved more useful than standard cognitive tests designed for use in the West. The observed statistical relationship is
perfectly understandable. The attitude of mind which appreciates
how one conducts oneself in the Western type of work situation

is just as important as the possession of certain basic skills, for without this attitude, these skills are unlikely to be used to advantage.

4. The question may, however, be raised whether there exists entity of 'general adaptability' related to capacity to meet cultural change. (One might call this 'acculturability'.) Vernon raises this question when he suggests that 'it is reasonable to recognize a general dimension of civilisation which tends to be associated with complexity and intellectual processes' and that 'for change and progress, some members (in traditional societies) at least must develop an intelligence based on seminal flexible linguistic and numerical symbols' (1969, p. 91). This of course takes us right back to the measurement of g and $v{:}ed$ as the best determinants of success in meeting Western educational and vocational requirements, and to all the controversies associated with this approach.

'Adaptability' as used in this paper is unlikely to reduce to a unique factor structure, essential to all adaptive action no matter what and where. This is not only because learning, which plays such an important part in it, does not yield a general factor, but mainly because there is something unique in every adaptive act and in the pattern of adaptation in various cultural circumstances. This uniqueness depends on what the culture has to contribute, both positively and negatively, on what kind of change is demanded, and on the total personality make-up of the individual undergoing change. What Dawson has called 'bio-social change' is the phenomenon we have in mind, and obviously it is too complex and diverse to be measured by a test or battery of tests appropriate to all acculturation circumstances.

THE DETERMINANTS OF ADAPTABILITY

Despite its generality as an attribute of behavior and the diversity of processes it may represent — genetic, physiological. anthropological, developmental, social, educational, etc. — there is nevertheless scope for studying the determinants of adaptability. This is important both theoretically — to clarify psychological constructs — and practically — to throw further light on the nature of individual and group differences. It is also important as a means of providing a basis for remedial action where there are maladaptations. Adequate discussion of this vast subject is beyond the scope of this paper, but insofar as it involves cross-cultural measurement, some brief comments are called for.

Research concerns the effect of a variety of environmental and cultural factors on the range of individual differences in responsiveness to change, particularly cultural change. Such research can in the first instance be conducted within homogeneous cultural groups. Its objective should be to determine the limits of modifiability of behavior in response to experimental variables such as nutrition, diversity of interaction with the material environment, parent-child relations, child-rearing practices, and the like. The concept of limits of modifiability and the problems that arise in their determination have been discussed elsewhere (Biesheuvel, 1958). Insofar as measurement takes place within a culture, the major problem is not to find a measure which is functionally equivalent and thus comparable across cultures, but to find one which yields an adequate range of relevant individual differences in response to the experimental variable.

Interpretation of any differences in limits of modifiability across cultures in order to arrive at psychological generalization is of course a different matter. At this stage there is unlikely to be a substitute for subjective judgments which will take into account interactions among factors which can be only partially controlled in real situations. We have a long way to go before attempting to determine the cause of a difference in limits of modifiability; one reason is that only longitudinal developmental studies are likely to yield scientifically acceptable conclusions. To compare experimental and control groups at one point in time ignores the possibility of significant developmental differences between them at earlier stages.

Suppose, for example, that children in two ethnic groups A and B — matched in respect of age, sex, number of years of primary schooling, and other contemporary environmental factors — differ on the average in an adaptability test like Kohs Blocks, after an experimental period in which solicitous individual attention and enriched tuition are applied equally to both. We can draw no conclusion about any basic, unalterable difference between them in the limits of modifiability as measured by the Kohs test. We do not know whether, during very early childhood or during some other significant developmental stage, the ability was irreversibly impaired by lack of appropriate stimulation or by parental attitudes adverse to development of the skills concerned.

There is no doubt, for example, that in apparently healthy African children the neural damage caused by kwashiorkor in early infancy can adversely affect behavior. Yet this causative factor would not show up in a crosssectional, control-group study. The importance of longitudinal studies derives particularly from the notion, for which there is as yet insufficient experimental evidence, that for a variety of behavioral functions there are critical developmental periods. If the requisite stimulation or interaction is lacking during such a period, or if some adverse environmental influence intervenes, the potentiality for later growth may be permanently impared.

REFERENCES

Berry, J. W. (1966) Temne and Eskimo perceptual skills. *Intern. J. Psychol.,* *1,* 207-229.

Biesheuvel, S. (1952) Personnel selection tests for Africans. *So. Afr. J. Sci.,* *49,* 3-12.

Biesheuvel, S. (1958). Objectives and methods of African psychological research. *J. Soc. Psychol., 47,* 161-168.

Biesheuvel, S. & Linhart, H. (1961) Some aspects of psychomotor learning ability of African mineworkers. Paper read at SAPA Congress, published in Congress abstracts.

Campbell, D. T. (1964) Distinguishing differences of perception from failures of communication in crosscultural studies. In F.C.C. Northrop & H. H. Livingstone (Eds.) *Crosscultural understanding.* New York: Harper & Row. Pp. 308-336.

Dubos, R. (1965) *Man adapting.* New Haven: Yale Univer. Press.

Dawson, J. L. M. (1967) Cultural and physiological influences upon spatial-perceptual processes in West Africa. *Intern. J. Psychol., 2,* 171-185.

Dawson, J. L. M. (1971) Psychological effects of bio-social change in West Africa. Unpublished MS., Univer. Hong Kong.

Elithorn, A. et al. (1960) A group version of a perceptual maze test. *Brit. J. Psychol.*, *51*, 19-26.

Poortinga, Y. H. (1971) Cross-cultural comparison of maximum performance tests: Some methodological aspects and some experiments with simple auditory and visual stimuli. *Psychol. Afr. Monogr. Supp.*, No. 6.

Porteus, S. D. (1969) *A psychologist of sorts.* Palo Alto, Calif.: Pacific Books.

Schwarz, P. A. (1963) Adapting tests to the cultural setting. *Educ. psychol. Measmt.*, *23*, 673-686.

Segall, M. H., Campbell, D. T. & Herskovits, H. J. (1963) Cultural differences in the perception of geometric illusions. *Science, 139*, 769-771.

Vernon, P. E. (1969) *Intelligence and cultural environment.* London: Methuen.

Witkin, H. A. et al. (1962) *Psychological differentiation.* New York: Wiley.

Wober, M. (1967) Adapting Witkin's field independence theory to accommodate new information from Africa. *Brit. J. Psychol.*, *58*, 29-38.

PIERRE DAGUE 5
Centre National d'Education de Plein Air, Suresnes

Development, application and interpretation of tests for use in French-speaking black Africa and Madagascar

Psychological – or, more precisely, psychometric – research on French-speaking black Africans commenced only at a relatively recent date: immediately after the Second World War and especially after the states achieved independence. First of all was the Pales mission (with Barbe) in French West Africa between 1946 and 1949, as well as the first works of Ombredane in 1951 and of Maistriaux in 1953 in the former Belgian Congo (now Kinshasa). In passing, one may note that Anglo-Saxon studies were undertaken earlier, by Fick in 1929 and Oliver in 1932; and Biesheuvel's *African intelligence* is dated 1943. After 1950 the number of publications on these matters grew logarithmically. There are more than 50 in the French language on the specific problem of psychological examination of children and adolescents (Dague, 1970).

To better understand the findings along with the failures of these studies, and so to reach the most positive conclusions one can, it will surely be useful to place them in an historical context and in a methodological perspective.

THE ANTHROPOLOGICAL APPROACH

In these works one notes two influences, one of a cultural inspiration, the other responding to the requirements of industry and education.

The first falls into the rubric of cultural anthropology, of which Zempleni (1970) has pointed out the limits. These include the studies of Knapen on the Mukongo child (1962), Balandier on the Lebou child (1948), and Thomas on the Diola (1963, 1965). Recently they have taken a psychoanalytic turn, looking for the Oedipus complex in the African setting. These authors seek above all to record for a given culture the specific nature of affective, intellectual, and social behavior, and to relate them to educational and especially family factors. In this perspective, while tests of intellectual level or personality augment observational data, they have to be applied in their original form and with their original criteria in order to permit valid comparison with findings on Europeans and Americans.

However, it quickly became apparent that this methodological goal could not be reached because the questions and tasks often did not correspond to the past experiences or the current concerns of the *S*s, which prevented interpretations on the basis of criteria derived from European populations. For example, Peiffer et al. (1963) and Thomas (1963) could not give real meaning to the Rorschach responses thus obtained, particularly the marked frequency of records with constricted *Erlebnistypus.*

Some have sought to adapt the material to the culture of the *S*s. The most interesting example is Ombredane's Congo TAT (2nd ed, 1969), intended for 'exploration of the mentality of the blacks.' The author kept three of Murray's original plates and had new ones drawn by a Belgian artist in a style derived from Congolese Tschokwe sculpture. Leblanc (1958) criticized this test strongly, on the basis of experience with her own adaptation of it among the Bantu. The pseudo-African drawings induced numerous hypochondriacal, dysphoric, or anxious responses which were not found with other material. The situations portrayed did not always fit the local scene; for example, a picture with persons facing each other produced no story of marital conflict because in Bantu culture one of them should be behind the other. The tests did not at all permit an analysis of 'the mentality of blacks'; there was a great risk of wrong interpretations. One can never take too many precautions when adapting test materials to cultures other than the original. The psychologist who attempts this requires training as an ethnologist.

One encounters no fewer difficulties in interpreting the classical tests of mental development. Authors such as Falade (1955), Geber (1950), and Masse (1969) have established that the black infant is considerably ahead of the European on Gesell's psychomotor tests during the first year of life, but the advantage gradually disappears. Likewise, intellectual development measured by a slightly modified Stanford-Binet seems to be about normal at 3 years but drops behind thereafter (Moreigne & Sénécal, 1962; Masse, 1969). In Congo-Kinshasa, Maistriaux used nonverbal tests based on the Kohs Blocks and others, and interpreted the results according to the stages of Piaget. Illiterate adults did barely as well as white 5 year olds, or white mental defectives. Children entering first grade did not exceed a mental age of 5 even though they were 7 to 9 years old.

The authors suggested that the relative drop in sensorimotor performance after 1 year resulted from abrupt weaning and the nutritional lacks it produced and, above all, from the breaking-off of the symbiotic relation with the mother. But such an explanation is placed in doubt by studies of weaning, especially among the Wolof (Zempleni-Rabain, 1966, 1968). The decline in mental level after age 3 is generally explained by the educational poverty of the environment and above all by the fact that in traditional cultures nothing prepares or stimulates the child to 'manipulate abstractions'. For Maistriaux (1956) this explains all the behavior of blacks in a traditional setting, producing an irreversible formation of adult character.

Maistriaux begs the question when he says: 'la sous-évolution du Noir ... peut être attribuée, partiellement au moins, à son ignorance des exigences de la pensée abstraite de la civilisation moderne ... Ainsi, si nos expériences devraient révéler que le Noir éprouve de grandes difficultés à manier l'abstractions, pourrions-nous y trouver une cause suffisante sinon exclusive de sa sous-évolution.' In the light of this postulate, he assembled a battery of strongly intercorrelated tests which would measure one factor thoroughly. Maistriaux did not ask if the tests suited the Ss, if they called upon mental operations with which the Ss were familiar, or if the tests recalled situations like those encountered in the Ss' daily lives. The white child, *his* mental structure, and *his* behavior remained the sole criteria.

Comparison of African populations with those of Europe and North America show the former at a disadvantage because the tests all are put forward by Europeans and Americans. Must one renounce all comparisons and all use of traditional tests?

WHAT TESTS SHOULD BE USED WITH BLACK AFRICANS?

The question poses itself as soon as one turns from comparison of groups to intragroup comparisons as in selection. At the outset of such selection the colonialists needed to develop inter-mediate-level administrators, then workers and foremen for min-ing and local industry. More recently, the extension of schooling has posed demands for guidance and educational selection, hence for objective evaluation of intellectual potential.

Traditional tests

It was quickly seen that traditional tests could not be applied to blacks, especially blacks of traditional background, without ma-jor modifications. Verbal tests raised many problems. Many children could not speak the language of the tester, nearly always a European; translation into the local language was not always possible because of a lack of corresponding words and concepts; recourse to an interpreter introduced a variable hard to control. The tests were strongly saturated with educational and cultural factors.

It was natural to turn to nonverbal or performance tests. But their material was often strange to the children. Furthermore, pencil and paper are practically unknown in the bush. Forms so simple as the square do not exist (or at least the name does not) in certain cultures where cylindrical, conical, and hemispherical forms prevail. Such tasks as assembly, construction, and drawing do not always correspond to familiar activities or games. Finally, Africans lack the European's concept of competition in speed, and one cannot use speed of execution as a criterion of success.

The performance tests most commonly used report average mental levels will below those normal for the same age in Western society.

This was the case for several applications of the Kohs Blocks in the original version (Barbe; Verhaegen, 1956) or in the adaptations following Goldstein and Scheerer (Maistriaux, 1956; Berbaum, 1969; Doucet, 1969; Etté, 1969). It held equally for the Goodenough Draw-a-Man (Bardet, Moreigne & Sénécal, 1960; Berbaum, 1969; Doucet, 1969; Etté, 1969), which causes one to doubt whether the schema of a man is universal. These authors emphasized that the test results correlated strongly with school success and agreed better with level of education reached than with age.

The use of formboards (Verhaegen, 1956), the battery for deaf children of Borelli and Oléron (Etté, 1969), the Gille blocks, and the lathe test (Laurent, 1963) led to similar conclusions and again indicated the importance of schooling (especially of literacy) on the scores. Two solutions were proposed.

Culture-fair tests

The first proposal never got beyond theoretical discussion. The thought was to use culture-fair tests in which the material used, the tasks, and the problems would be drawn from the daily life of the *S*s, a new set being chosen for each group to be examined.

Many writers (among them Verhaegen, 1956) were easily able to show that there would be no correspondence between the extensive work demanded by such an undertaking and its practical utility. To be frank, the utility would be negligible. Such tests could tell us the level of competence of a subject in familiar situations but is it necessary to use tests for that? One could not infer from success on these tasks anything about capacity for other tasks, whether educational or industrial. As Fontaine put it (1963), 'We are not selecting blacks to make bows and construct pirogues.' Finally, such local task samplings allow no comparison between ethnic groups and would quickly be rendered obsolete by the rapid cultural evolution among many of these groups.

For the same reason, there was no interest in carefully standardizing traditional tests, because the norms would have to be continually revised as the culture changes.

Culture-free tests

There were those who thought that 'culture-free' tests would escape all the difficulties of the tests so far discussed. Alas, we must now recognize that this idea constitutes one of the greatest deceptions psychologists have known.

Among these tests the Raven Matrices in their 1938 and 1947 forms were made the object of many studies. Berlioz (1955), Laroche (1956), Maistriaux (1956), Ombredane et al. (1957), Dormeau (1959), and Laurent (1963) all found that the test distinguished sharply between educated and uneducated persons of the same age. The uneducated showed certain characteristic bad responses. Scores were generally proportional to the length of schooling and inversely proportional to the time elapsed since leaving school. Illiterate adults did not get beyond the 5- or 6-year level. The diversity of samples excluded the hypothesis that the educated *S*s differed by virtue of preselection. The studies of Xydias (1960) on the Cattell Culture Free Test, and of Maistriaux (1956), Durand (1960), and Boppe (1961) on tests inspired by the Matrices produced the same results.

Allegedly culture-free tests are not independent of cultural factors, in particular of literacy (as one must 'read' the matrices from left to right and from high to low). The correlation with scholastic success − even in arithmetic − is usually weak if not zero, at least in primary school (Mertens de Wilmars, 1958; Erpicum, 1959; Durand, 1960). In brief, no test of intelligence could be independent of cultural factors.

A SOLUTION: MEASUREMENT OF ADAPTABILITY

At this point, must we accept our impotence and abandon the task? No. Let me suggest a way to bypass the contradictions noted above.

The transcultural situation

The chief obstacle to application of European tests to Africans resides in the unfamiliar or even incomprehensible nature of the tasks they present. Mertens de Wilmars (1958) is right to say, 'Ces tests représentent plutôt une mesure du degré de familiarité avec les objets et les symboles usuels d'une culture, une évaluation de l'amplitude de l'information culturelle de l'indigène que l'estimation d'une pseudo-aptitude.'

Any test situation requires the native – as Reusch, Jacobson, and Loeb (1948) quoted by Laurent (1963) emphasized – to 'introduce himself to a novel culture', and condemn him to function at an inferior level of integration, carrying out partial and mechanical functions without grasping fully the new value system. In a word, the test situation constitutes a *'situation expérimentale de transculturation aiguë'* (Laurent, 1963). (In French *acculturation* is reserved for the process of bringing a child into command of the culture into which he is born.)

Today the Africans and especially the children and adolescents are living in a transcultural situation. There have been many descriptions of the process of change in African societies: development of a monetary economy as required by industrialization and salaried employment; rapid urbanization breaking up the structures of village life and often creating difficult conditions of existence; great extension of media of communication and information; unprecedented demand for schooling; deep modification of family and interpersonal relations. Some writers retain their nostalgia for traditional cultures and denounce the hazards of rapid evolution. But this evolution is a fact that one cannot ignore.

What appears essential for the individual is his ability to adapt to this change, to assimilate new techniques and modes of thought, without renouncing his own culture and his originality. The tests thus ought to allow us to evaluate not 'innate' aptitudes or acquired skills but the capacity for learning – i.e , educability.

Measuring learning potential

Ombredane made a noteworthy distinction between acculturation and transculturation – between 'le conditionnement de l'individu dans son milieu traditionnel' and 'la plasticité dont il

peut témoigner en regard de configurations différentes de conditionnement et d'apprentissage auxquelles il peut être conduit à
s'adapter plus tardivement.' As early as 1951 he stressed the need
to use tests of adaptability – more precisely, to employ traditional tests to measure that educability.

A large number of studies have followed that lead. On a first
occasion Ss are familiarized with the materials and task through
explanations, demonstrations, and preliminary exercises. On a
second occasion, the test is given two or even three times (without reporting scores to the Ss). The gains from trial to trial are
taken to measure learning potential.

These studies were almost without exception done with Progressive Matrices. Laroche (1959) tested young Congolese of ages
10-14 repeatedly, after demonstration. There were marked gains
from first to second testing. Among those with low initial scores,
some made spectacular gains and some made none. A retest a
year or two later correlated much better with the last test of the
series than with the first. But Laroche found the validity against
educational criteria quite poor; paradoxically, the least unsatisfactory correlations were those of the first testing. This causes
one to doubt the predictive value of this adaptability measure.
The Ss of Laroche had had some years of schooling.

Ombredane, Robaye, and Plumail (1956) used Matrices with
the backward Asalampasu group in Kasaï, demonstrating and
then giving three testing trials. Ss with more education earned
higher scores than others on the first testing; moreover, the gains
on the second and third trials were directly proportional to
duration of schooling. It appears, then, that educability is in part
a function of previous schooling.

As for work with other tests, Doucet and Etté have recently
tested pupils on the Ivory Coast with a Draw-a-Man procedure.
First they compare a spontaneous drawing with a copy of a
model. They then ask for a second free drawing. The comparison
of the first and second spontaneous drawings is evidence of gain
from the copying experience.

Without doubt the measurement of mental plasticity through
learning on tests opens richer perspectives than research on
aptitude scores as such, or on level of mental development. It

appears to be an elegant solution to the dilemma in which psychologists find themselves in Africa. As Richelle said (1959), 'la voie d'approche la plus féconde devrait, nous semble-t-il, partir du principe que la différenciation de la mécanique intellectuelle se définit plus par ses possibilités d'acquisition que par un niveau de performance. En d'autres mots, au lieu de se borner à enregistrer des rendements, il conviendrait d'analyser les processus d'apprentissage eux-mêmes.'

Limits of the approach

Some reservations and criticisms are to be noted.

First, such studies seem most pertinent with young children. Among adults who are illiterate or little educated, one finds little improvement after demonstrations, especially when the tasks call for abstract ideas or logical reasoning.

Learning ability is not independent of education. Does there exist a 'capacity for learning' independent of all prior learning, at least outside what Montessori called the 'sensitive period'? This leads us to stress the importance of early education – prior to 6 years – a salient problem with young African.

The studies deal solely with learning in the tests. Can this be extrapolated to school learning and vocational training? We find no study on this. If we speak of learning potential it is necessary to make clear precisely what task is learned; lacking that, one makes of 'learning potential' an abstract and formal notion which will have no manifest relevance to situations other than the test. One cannot think of ability to learn independent of the mental operations required by the content taught and the methods of instruction. That is to say that psychology cannot ignore pedagogy, and vice versa.

To sum up: Black, French-speaking Africans usually obtain scores on conventional tests that fall below the mean for Europeans and Americans, largely because even the performance tests do not correspond to the experience of the *S*s. But, given the rapid change of these societies, there is no practical value in developing tests of intellectual level that fit the local experience. Capacity to learn in new situations is very likely what one should measure, amid the rapid transculturation that is taking place in Africa. Much research will be needed to clarify the relations between tested learning potential and subsequent school learning. The prognostic value of the measure of learning potential requires investigation.

Throughout Africa there is need for close association of psychologists, ethnologists, sociologists, educators, and physicians. Only a multidisciplinary approach and long-term validation can cope with what, despite the findings to date, remains an open question.

REFERENCES

Abbreviations:
AUDECAM − Assn universitaire pour le développement de l'enseignement et de la culture en Afrique et à Madagascar.
CEPSI − Centre d'études des problèmes sociaux indigènes.
CERP − Centre d'études et de recherches psychotechniques.
IFAN − Inst. français d'Afrique noire.
SOPED − Service d'orientation professionnelle et de documentation.

Balandier, G. (1948) L'enfant chez les Lébou du Sénégal. *Enfance, 4,* 285-303.
Bardet, J., Moreigne, F. & Sénécal, J. (1960) Application du test de Goodenough à des écoliers africains de 7 à 14 ans. *Enfance, 2,* 199-208.
Berbaum, J. (1969) Conditions de la réussite de l'apprentissage de la lecture au Cours préparatoire (1ère année de scolarité). Abidjan: Ecole normale supérieure. (Mimeographed, limited circulation.)
Berlioz, L. (1955) Etude des Progressive Matrices faite sur les Africains de Douala. *Bull. CERP, 4,* 33-44.
Boppe, P. (1961) Deux tests 'papier-crayon' d'intelligence éductive à l'usage de populations illettrées. *Travail hum., 24,* 143-153.
Dague, P. (1970) *Psychologie de l'enfant et de l'adolescent en Afrique et à Madagascar.* Paris: AUDECAM. (Limited circulation.)
Dormeau, G. (1959) L'oeuvre africaine du professeur Ombredane. *Bull. CERP, 8,* 5-12.
Doucet, L. (1969) Esquisse d'une méthode d'examen des enfants du Cours

préparatoire. SOPED, Ministère de l'Education nationale de la République de Côte d'Ivoire. (Mimeographed, limited circulation.)

Durand, R. (1960) Formation et adaptation professionnelle du jeune africain. *Travail hum.*, *23*, 81-92.

Erpicum, D. (1959) Tests mentaux et résultats scolaires chez les enfants congolais. *Rev. Psychol. appl.*, *9*, 11-21.

Ette, L. (1969) Premier essai d'étalonnage de la batterie Borelli-Oléron. SOPED, Ministère de l'Education nationale de la République de Côte d'Ivoire. (Mimeographed, limited circulation.)

Faladé, S. (1955) *Contribution à une étude sur le développement de l'enfant d'Afrique noire. Le développement psycho-moteur du jeune africain originaire du Sénégal au cours de sa première année.* Paris: Foulon.

Fontaine, C. (1963) Notes sur une expérience d'application de tests au Mali. *Rev. Psychol. appl.*, *13*, 235-246.

Geber, M. (1960) Problèmes posés par le développement du jeune enfant africain en fonction de son milieu social. *Travail hum.*, *23*, 97-111.

Knapen, M. T. (1962) *L'enfant mukongo.* Louvain: Publications Universitaires.

Laroche, J. L. (1956) L'analyse des erreurs sur le Matrix 38. *Bull. CERP*, *6*, 161-172.

Laroche, J. L. (1959) Effets de répétition du Matrix 38 sur les résultats des enfants katangais. *Bull. CERP*, *8*, 85-89.

Laroche, J. L. (1960) Recherches sur les aptitudes des écoliers du Katanga industriel. *Travail hum.*, *23*, 69-81.

Laurent, A. (1963) Rapports entre l'instruction scolaire et le développement intellectual en Afrique. Thesis, Faculty of letters and humanities of Paris. (Mimeographed.)

Leblanc, M. (1958) La problématique d'adaptation du T.A.T. au Congo Belge. *Rev. Psychol. appl.*, *8*, 265-274.

Maistriaux, R. (1955-56) La sous-évolution des noirs d'Afrique: Sa nature. Ses causes. Ses remèdes. *Rev. Psychol. Peuples*, *10*, 167-189; *10*, 397-456; *11* 80-90; *11*, 134-173.

Masse, G. (1969) *Croissance et développement de l'enfant à Dakar.* Paris: Centre International de l'Enfance.

Mertens de Wilmars, C. (1958) Vers une étude plus systématique des variables psychologiques de l'acculturation. *Rev. Psychol. appl.*, *8*, 1-23.

Moreigne, F. & Sénecal, J. (1962) Résultats d'une groupe d'enfants africains au Terman-Merrill. *Rev. Psychol. appl.*, *12*, 15-32.

Ombredane, A. (1951) Principes pour une étude psychologique des Noirs du Congo Belge. *Année psychol.*, *50*, 521-547.

Ombredane, A. (1969) *L'exploration de la mentalité des Noirs. Le 'Congo T.A.T.'* (2d ed.) Paris: Presses Universitaires de France.

Ombredane, A., Robaye, F., & Plumail, H. (1956) Résultats d'une application répétée du Matrix couleur à une population de Noirs congolais. *Bull. CERP, 6,* 129-147.

Ombredane, A., Robaye, F., & Robaye, E. (1957) Analyse des résultats d'une application expérimentale du Matrix 38 à 485 noirs Baluba. *Bull. CERP, 6,* 235-255.

Ombredane, A., Robaye, F., & Robaye, E. (1957) Résultats d'une application, selon une technique nouvelle, du test des relations spatiales de Minnesota à une population de Noirs Asalampasu. *Bull. CERP, 6,* 379-395.

Peiffer, E. (1959) Données obtenues au test de Rorschach chez des Noirs d'Afrique Occidentale Française. *Bull IFAN,* II, *21* B, 21-60.

Peiffer, E., Pelage, S. (1963) Quelques résultats obtenus au test de Rorschach chez les Bamiléké du Cameroun. *Bull. IFAN, 25* B, 454-457. 454-457.

Richelle, M. (1959) Contribution à l'étude des mécanismes intellectuels chez les Africains du Katanga. *Bull. CEPSI, 45.*

Thomas, L. V. (1963) Le test de Rorschach comme mode d'approche de la psychologie noire. Aperçus sur la personnalité Diola. *Bull. IFAN, 25* B, 288-350.

Thomas, L. V. (1965) Education traditionnelle et éducation moderne en Afrique Noire. L'exemple du Sénégal. In *Transformations et difficultés actuelles des relations et de l'éducation familiales dans les différents pays.* Brussels: Ministry of Education and Culture. Pp. 41-70.

Verhaegen, P. (1956) Utilité actuelle des tests pour l'étude psychologique des autochtones congolais. *Rev. Psychol. appl., 6,* 139-151.

Xydias, N. (1960) Les Africains du Congo Belge: Aptitudes, attitudes vis-à-vis du travail. *Travail hum., 23,* 41-55.

Zempleni, A. (1970) Milieu africain et développement. Report presented to meeting of l'Association de psychologie scientifique de langue française, Lille. (Mimeographed.)

Zempleni-Rabain, J. (1967) Modes fondamentaux de relations chez l'enfant wolof du sevrage à l'intégration dans la classe d'âge. 1. Les relations de contact physique et de corps à corps. *Psychopathol. Afr., 2,* 143-177.

Zempleni-Rabain, J. (1968) L'alimentation et la stratégie de l'apprentissage de l'échange avec les frères chez l'enfant wolof. *Psychopathol. Afr., 4,* 297-310.

PART II

Crosscultural research strategy

This set of papers have in common a strong emphasis on the cultural context. The authors deal with the logic, methods, and values that enter research on ability, sharing a belief that observations can be interpreted only in the light of cultural demands and norms. Berry's paper is closely related to those of Biesheuvel and Dague in Section I. He is more radical than they in arguing that adaptability takes on qualitatively different forms in different cultures, and that abilities emerge in response to cultural demands. Sanday is concerned with quantitative differences between cultural groups, regarding such differences as environmental in origin and explainable as a function of cultural diffusion. Eckensberger examines the logic of crosscultural comparisons, advocating a search for conditions that explain cultural variables.

J. W. BERRY

Queen's University at Kingston

Radical cultural relativism and the concept of intelligence*

This paper is concerned with two of the most basic problems confronting the crosscultural psychologist: ethnocentrism, and the possibility of behavioral comparisons across ethnic boundaries.

Although we would probably all agree that it has been our recognition of the ethnocentrism inherent in Western psychological science which has led us to seek more generality crossculturally (and thence to the problems of comparison), we would also have to admit that few psychologists have shaken off even a portion of their ethnic-relative assumptions. Further, most of us would probably agree that until we do divest ourselves of these biases, our *raison d'être* mocks us instead of supporting our endeavors. This paper is a call for a radical stripping-away of our ethnic-relative assumptions surrounding one specific concept intelligence.

Of course behavioral comparison is possible within any single ethnic-assumptive framework; if we wish to comment on behavior only within that cultural system, we do not have to make

* Support for the empirical portion of this paper has been provided by grants from the Canada Council, the Government of Quebec, University Research Committees of the University of Sydney and of Queen's University, and the Australian Research Grants Committee.

The financial support of these agencies should not be taken in any way as support for the interpretations offered here; nor should the offering of this paper be taken as in any way implying support for the existence or aims of NATO.

explicit our ethnic-relative assumptions (although we may wish to). If, however, we wish to comment on behavior as seen across ethnic boundaries, we must not only make our assumptions explicit, but attempt to comprehend their influence on the behavior (and, as importantly, the measures of the behavior) which we wish to study.

Anthropologists have attempted to solve the problem of ethnocentrism in their science by adopting a stance of 'cultural relativism'. (See Segall, Campbell, & Herskovits, 1966, pp. 17-18, for a brief overview of the position). In essence, the stance attempts to avoid descriptions based on the investigator's culture, and attempts to describe the culture from the point of view held within, and hence relative to, the culture under study. Psychologists working crossculturally have made similar attempts, but largely because of a comparative perspective is lacking in our education and because we search for behavioral generalities, we have not succeeded in that stance. Regarding this cultural confinement of psychology, Biesheuvel has said (1952, p. 48): 'The fact that the investigators were themselves part of the culture which determined the course of development and the character of the phenomenon which they studied must have influenced the formulation of laws, the description of typical processes and the setting of developmental norms.'

One attempt to formally reduce this inherent ethnocentrism has been made by Berry (1969a). In that framework, an approach is made to another cultural system by way of a concept or instrument already possessed (imposed *etic*); this is gradually modified during experience within the new cultural system (an *emic* modification) until a concept or instrument suitable to both cultural systems is developed (derived *etic*).

An alternative to this gradual approach is a radical one; rather than attempt to modify or merge our assumptions, we can conceptually wipe the slate clean and approach the problem from a nihilistic stance. This position accepts the statement: 'We can assume no psychological universals across cultural systems.' It may be termed a position of *radical cultural relativism*.

This drastic alternative is advocated only for concepts which have firm roots in Western psychological science (and thus are likely to have been firmly imposed on other peoples) *and* are having great impact on non-Western peoples (and thus are potentially very harmful). One such concept is 'personality'. Hsu (1971) suggests that its prominence in Western psychology has obscured alternative concepts of individual humanity which may serve scientific needs better. Another such concept is 'intelligence'; it may be obscuring alternative conceptions of cognitive competence.

If there is a single, universal dimension corresponding to our concept of intelligence, then we may compare quantitative levels on that dimension. If there is not — that is, if there are many cognitive dimensions, qualitatively different — then we have no basis for crosscultural (crossdimensional) comparisons of levels of cognitive competence.

Let us wipe the slate clean, and search for the possibility of qualitatively different 'intelligences', developing in differing cultural contexts. Although the prototype of this quest has been well studied intraculturally (single- versus multi-factor theories), the ground is still fresh interculturally.

This search might be made in three ways:

1. Psychologists socialized within non-Western ethnic groups should explore their own intellectual systems for concepts traditionally used to refer to general cognitive ability. This approach, which may be termed *ethnopsychology* (following the anthropological study of indigenous sciences known as *ethnoscience;* Sturtevant, 1964), must be left to my more competent colleagues.

2. Western psychologists should search the historical roots of their own concept, in an attempt to discover previous insights about and justifications for the notion of qualitatively different 'intelligences'.

3. Psychologists should attempt to demonstrate that cognitive functioning is adaptive to qualitatively differing cultural (and associated ecological) demands. Although such a demonstration would not unequivocally support the notion of qualitative intellectual differences, it would support the *possibility* and so make worthwhile the empirical search for such differences. If such a demonstration is made, there are two possible interpretations:

a) Differences in test performance represent *qualitatively* different 'intelligences'. Or,
b) Differences in test performance represent quantitatively different levels on a universal dimension of intelligence, different patterns of cognitive abilities (on a number of tests) developing as a function of qualitatively different cultural demands.

If evidence supports the former, then our search has been successful; if the latter, then at least we will have met Goodnow's (1969, p. 259) challenge to demonstrate cognitive differences across ethnic groups that are related to the ecology and the culture, and we will have opened the possibility of and justified the empirical search for qualitative differences.

What follows are attempts to extract suggestions of qualitative differences from the history of our own concept and to demonstrate the adaptation of cognitive functioning to ecological and cultural requirements.

HISTORICAL ROOTS OF THE WESTERN CONCEPT

This history of our concept of intelligence has been authoritatively traced by Sir Cyril Burt (1969), who was, so to speak, present at the birth. Its early definition (by Galton, and accepted by others) as an 'innate general cognitive factor' has now generally been termed 'Intelligence A' (following Hebb), and the result of growth of this factor in a particular environmental context has been termed 'Intelligence B'. An estimate of 'Intelligence B', which is some degree of sampling from it, is now generally termed 'Intelligence C' (Vernon, 1969). These definitions grew largely in the context of intracultural research, although the extensions B and C reflect the concerns of the crosscultural worker.

At much the same time, however, anthropologists were commenting on the possibility of multiple kinds of intelligent behavior. Boas argued that apparent cognitive differences across cultures could be explained in two ways (1911, p. 102): 'It may be that the minds of different races show differences of organization; that is to say, the laws of mental activity may not be the same for all minds. But it may also be that the organization of mind is practically identical among all races of man; that mental activity follows the same laws everywhere, but that its manifestations depend upon the character of individual experience that is subjected to the action of these laws.' He concluded that the second was the more probable, and Wundt (1911) came to a similar conclusion.

The existence of a universal cognitive dimension was challenged by Lévy-Bruhl (1910), who claimed that 'the mental processes of "primitives" do not coincide with those which we are accustomed to describe in men of our own type' (p. 14), and concluded that 'the rational unity of the thinking being, which is taken for granted by most philosophers, is a *desideratum*, not a fact' (p. 386). It is not difficult to criticize the extremity of Lévy-Bruhl's assertions. However, he did provide some academic legitimacy for the notion of varieties of cognitive competences; without him, the possibility would probably not be alive today.

Some of the first field work on the question was carried out by Nadel (1937) who made 'qualitative comparative analyses of the higher mental processes' of the Yoruba and Nupe. He concluded that there were different 'types' of psychological traits and characteristics ('psychological differentiation') and that they were in 'essential correspondence' with the organization of the cultures (p. 210). Elsewhere, Nadel noted that the early hope of researchers was 'to arrive ultimately at a universal scale of innate human faculties, on which the different racial and ethnic groups could each be assigned a more or less definite place' (1939, p. 184), but that these aims were thwarted by the very diversity of cultures.

Goodenough (1936, p. 5) addressed herself to the same concerns. When we 'endeavor to classify individuals or races on the basis of some presumably general trait that cannot be measured directly, we are faced with another and much more difficult problem of sampling. Not only must we be sure of the adequacy of our sampling of subjects, but we must also be sure that the test-items from which the total trait is to be judged are *representative and valid samples of the ability in question, as it is displayed within the particular culture with which we are concerned.'*

Further on (p. 8-9) she asked,

'If we are to look upon intelligence tests as samples of the intellectual requirements of a given culture-group, what basis is there left for applying such a sample of tasks to individuals from another group whose cultural patterns differ widely from those of the original group for whom the test was designed? Very little, I think. About all that can be learned from such a procedure is that the cultures are different; in other words that the tasks chosen are not representative of the abilities of the subjects. In this way we may be able to find out a little about what these people can not do, but it is not likely that we shall learn much about what they can do.'

These themes appeared in the literature again, when Ferguson (1954, p. 99) argued that 'presumably children reared in different environments, which demand different types of learning at different ages, develop different patterns of ability'; he claimed that the mass of anthropological data supported such a notion. He further called for an assault on the basic task of 'describing the patterns of ability which are characteristic of individuals reared in different cultural environments' (p. 104).

Most recently, four statements have commented on the possibility of qualitative differences. Berry (1969a), following an earlier argument (1966), claimed that indigenous conceptions of intelligent behavior often differ widely (cf. the *ethnoscience* approach) and hence differences cannot be considered merely as quantitative levels on a single, universal cognitive dimension; further, typical studies to date have considered only 'a scrap of the emic' range of these intelligent behaviors. Irvine (1969, 1970) has similarly argued for recognition of the 'value' inherent in our concept, noting that indigenous 'modes of thought' are not adequately sampled by the usual Western tests. Wober (1969), as well, has distinguished between the two questions: 'How well can *they* do *our* tricks? ' and 'How well can *they* do *their* tricks? '. Vernon (1969, p. 10) too has acknowledged the usefulness of such an approach:

'We must try to discard the idea that intelligence (i.e. Intelligence B) is a kind of universal faculty, a trait which is the same (apart from variations in amount) in all cultural groups. Clearly it develops differently in different physical and cultural environments. It should be regarded as a name for all the various cognitive skills which are developed in, and valued by, the group. In western civilisation it refers mainly to grasping relations and symbolic thinking, and this permeates to some extent all the abilities we show at school, at work, or in daily life. We naturally tend to evaluate the intelligence of other ethnic groups on the same criteria, though it would surely be more psychologically sound to recognise that such groups require, and stimulate, the growth of different mental as well as physical skills for coping with their particular environments, i.e. that they possess different intelligences.'

In summary, over the past 70 years there have been sporadic but recurrent assertions of the notion that people raised in different cultures are different intellectually, have different cognitive competences. These assertions appear to go beyond the usually accepted notion of *quantitative* differences on a single, universal cognitive dimension, to the notion that there are *qualitatively* differing cognitive competences appropriate to the requirements of a particular culture. Whether all peoples have access to all dimensions (but produce a different *pattern* of scores on them), or some peoples have access to some *unique* dimensions, is immaterial; what matters is the assertion of more than a single universal dimension called (in the West) 'intelligence'.

COGNITION AS ADAPTIVE TO ECOLOGICAL AND CULTURAL DEMANDS

In 1966 data and arguments were presented in support of the claim that perceptual development is adaptive to the ecological demands facing a cultural group, and mediated by the cultural supports available to them (Berry, 1966). Aspects of this argument have been followed up more recently (Berry, 1967, 1968, 1969b). Since these original reports, more data have been collected and the model has been elaborated; only an overall view will be presented here since many of the arguments have been reported in the earlier papers.

Briefly the model considers individual behavior (including cognition) as a function of ecological demands, mediated to a large extent by aspects of culture which are themselves adapted to the ecology:

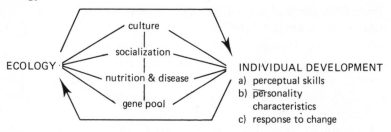

Data in support of this model, using spatial-perceptual development as the relevant behavior, are presented graphically below. A 'traditional' and a 'transitional' sample was tested on four variables in four culture areas: Baffin Island Eskimo, Temne of Sierre Leone, Australian Aborigines. and New Guinea indigenes (for numbers, see Figure 1). Samples included men and women, young and old, and were randomly selected from the 8 regions. In the graphs that follow, samples are arranged on the horizontal axis according to the degree of ecological demand and cultural support for the development of spatial-perceptual skills; test-score means are indicated on the vertical axis. A *high* score on discrimination indicates poor performance; on the three spatial tasks, higher scores indicate better performances.

The interpretation placed on these data (Berry, 1971; Berry, undated) is that perceptual skills are developed to predictable extents in response to the ecological demand for them and the concomitant cultural support. The argument that cognitive functioning is similarly adaptive may be made on the basis of the cognitive content of both Kohs Blocks and Matrices. As noted earlier, it is not possible here to distinguish whether these samples are quantitatively different on a single dimension, or qualitatively different on a number of dimensions, especially since functional equivalence may not have been attained. What can be

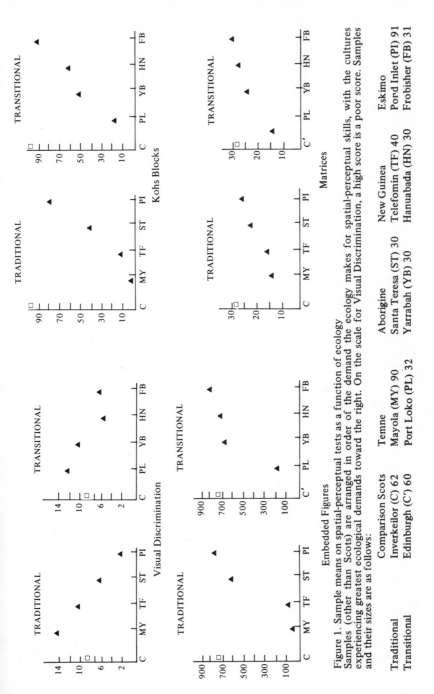

Figure 1. Sample means on spatial-perceptual tests as a function of ecology Samples (other than Scots) are arranged in order of the demand the ecology makes for spatial-perceptual skills, with the cultures experiencing greatest ecological demands toward the right. On the scale for Visual Discrimination, a high score is a poor score. Samples and their sizes are as follows:

Comparison Scots	**Temne**	**Aborigine**	**New Guinea**	**Eskimo**
Inverkeilor (C) 62	Mayola (MY) 90	Santa Teresa (ST) 30	Telefomin (TF) 40	Pond Inlet (PI) 91
Edinburgh (C') 60	Port Loko (PL) 32	Yarrabah (YB) 30	Hanuabada (HN) 30	Frobisher (FB) 31

Traditional
Transitional

asserted is this: the development of perceptual-cognitive competence can be considered within a functional framework, and insofar as ecologies and cultures differ qualitatively, we may accept the possibility of qualitatively different cognitive competences developing in adaptation to them.

From the historical overview it is possible to conclude that Western psychologists have occasionally penetrated the wall of their ethnocentrism to catch glimpses of alternative cognitive dimensions; this has been most noticeable in the last few years. From the empirical data presented, it is possible to conclude that in four different ecocultural systems, perceptual-cognitive skill development appears to be related to the ecological demands and cultural supports in each system. It is to non-Western psychologists that we must now turn for further evidence; if they can provide evidence of qualitatively different notions of cognitive competence, the argument presented here is strengthened.

If, in the end, the argument is supported, then we will know that our concept of intelligence is not a psychological universal; we will know that what we have supposed to be comparisons on a single dimension are in fact comparisons across dimensions; we will know that the notion of a universal intelligence must once and for all be dropped; and we will know that instruments designed to assess it (culture '-fair', '-free', or '-reduced') must be scrapped.

We will also know that much difficult cooperative work remains to be done if behavioral science is to comprehend the nature and variation of human cognitive competence.

REFERENCES

Berry, J. W. (1966) Temne and Eskimo perceptual skills. *Intern. J. Psychol.*, *1*, 207-229.

Berry, J. W. (1967) Independence and conformity in subsistence-level societies. *J. Pers. soc. Psychol.*, *7*, 415-418.

Berry, J. W. (1968) Ecology, perceptual development and the Müller-Lyer illusion. *Brit. J. Psychol.*, *59*, 205-210.

Berry, J. W. (1969a) On cross-cultural comparability. *Int. J. Psychol., 4,* 119-128.

Berry, J. W. (1969b) Ecology and socialization as factors in figural assimilation and the resolution of binocular rivalry. *Int. J. Psychol., 4,* 271-280.

Berry, J. W. (1971) Ecological and cultural factors in spatial perceptual development. *Canad. J. Beh. Sci., 3,* 324-336.

Berry, J. W. (n.d.) *Ecology, culture and perceptual development.* Monograph in preparation.

Biesheuvel, S. (1952) The study of African ability. Part 1. The intellectual potentialities of Africans. *Afr. Stud., 11,* 48-57.

Boas, F. (1911) *The mind of primitive man.* New York: Macmillan, 1911.

Burt, C. (1969) The concept of intelligence. *J. Assn. educ. Psychologists,* 16-38.

Ferguson, G. (1954) On learning and human ability. *Canad. J. Psychol., 8,* 95-112.

Goodenough, F. (1936) The measurement of mental functions in primitive groups. *Amer. Anthropologist, 38,* 1-11.

Goodnow, J. (1969) Cultural variations in cognitive skills. In D. Price-Williams (Ed.), *Cross-cultural studies.* London: Penguin.

Hsu, F. L. K. (1971) Psychological homeostasis and *Jen:* Conceptual tools for advancing psychological anthropology. *Amer. Anthropologist, 73,* 23-44.

Irvine, S. H. (1969) Factor analysis of African abilities and attainments. Constructs across cultures. *Psychol. Bull., 71,* 20-32.

Irvine, S. H. (1970) Affect and construct: A cross-cultural check on theories of intelligence. *J. soc. Psychol., 80,* 23-30.

Lévy-Bruhl, L. (1910) *Les fonctions mentales dans les sociétés inférieures.* (Page references are to the English version: *How natives think,* trans. L. A. Clare. London: George Allen and Unwin, 1926).

Nadel, S. F. (1937) A field experiment in racial psychology. *Brit. J. Psychol., 28,* 195-211.

Nadel, S. F. (1939) Application of intelligence tests in the anthropological field. In F. C. Bartlett et al. (Eds.), *The study of society.* London: Routledge & Kegan Paul.

Segall, M. H., Campbell, D. T. & Herskovits, H. J. (1966) *The influence of culture on visual perception.* Indianapolis: Bobbs-Merrill.

Sturtevant, W. C. (1964) Studies in ethnoscience. *Amer. Anthropologist, 66,* 99-131.

Vernon, P. E. (1969) *Intelligence and cultural environment.* London: Methuen.

Wober, M. (1969) Distinguishing centri-cultural from cross-cultural tests and research. *Percept. mot. Skills, 28,* 488.

Wundt, W. (1916) *Elements of folk psychology.* London: George Allen and Unwin.

PEGGY R. SANDAY   7
Carnegie-Mellon University, Pittsburgh

A model for the analysis of cultural determinants of between-groups variation in measured intelligence*

The purpose of this paper will be to present a model and a research design for the analysis of variation in measured intelligence between definable groups in a given country. Measured intelligence is defined in terms of the scores on tests designed to measure general mental abilities. A 'definable' group is any group of people who are socially separated from the mainstream culture because of real or perceived cultural differences. Such groups are usually labeled and are often bounded by observable characteristics such as race, ethnic affiliation, or social-class membership. Usually, though not always, such groups are in differing degrees isolated genetically from the mainstream unit because of endogamous marriage practices.

BACKGROUND

It is generally agreed that the determinants of intelligence are reducible to genetic and environmental components. According to the position taken by the U.S. National Academy of Sciences ('Racial studies . . .', 1967), it is fruitless to try to disentangle the relative roles of heredity and environment with present methods, since the results of such research would be unclear in meaning

* I am indebted to Lee Cronbach and S. C. Sanday for helpful comments on drafts of this paper. I am also indebted to Thomas Gregg who played a significant role in the development of this work and who commented extensively on the final draft.

and invite misuse. Even greater difficulties, according to the Academy's statement, are encountered when the goal is to assess the relative role of these factors in determining differences between populations.

Recently, the question of the relative role of heredity and environment in the determination of human intelligence has been reopened by Jensen and by the responses to his article (Jensen, 1969; Crow, 1969; Bodmer & Cavalli-Sforza, 1970; Brace, Gamble, & Bond, 1971). Jensen's article is devoted to a lengthy exposition of how the relative role of heredity and environment can be determined. His major conclusions are that heredity has a far greater role to play than environment, and that the reported mean differences in IQ of blacks and whites in the USA result from differences in gene pools. Jensen reaches his conclusions after careful consideration of the relative weights to be attached to heredity and environment in explaining the variance in a distribution of IQ scores. His conclusion that heredity has the most weight leads him to suggest that persons arising from a certain gene pool may be superior in some types of intellectual adaptation and not in others. However, a careful review of Jensen's major argument leads us to question both his conclusion and the implication that the difference between groups in certain types of intellectual attainment is genetic in origin.

Jensen bases his argument on the fact that heritability estimates for the white population (the only group we have estimates for) are quite high (0.80). In an analysis of the meaning of the concept of heritability Gregg and Sanday (1971) make it clear that heritability is not a measure of the absolute magnitude of the genetic contribution to a given trait (as Jensen leads us to believe) but a measure of the proportion of the variability in a trait attributable to variation in genetic factors. In a uniform environment the heritability estimate will be high. Correspondingly, in a population that is uniform genetically (i.e., is homozygous for the trait in question), the environmental estimate will be high. In neither case do we gain information on the magnitude of the genetic or environmental contribution. (For a similar analysis of heritability, see Caspari. 1968; see also Bodmer & Cavalli-Sforza, 1970).

Another approach, to be discussed in detail below in the section on the conceptual model, would be to make certain assumptions about the distribution of scores within any given group due to the genetic component alone, and to analyze mean differences in IQ between groups as possible effects of qualitative environmental differences. Recent discussion indicates the validity of concentrating on environmental differences. The geneticist Crow, for example, in his response to Jensen's argument referring to the reported differences between blacks and whites in the USA, says 'that the environmental factors may differ qualitatively in the two groups . . . (and) that being white or being black in our society changes one or more aspects of the environment so importantly as to account for the difference'. (Crow, 1969, p. 308). In distinguishing between 'culture difference' and 'culture deprivation', Cohen (1969) suggests that there may be children in the USA who are exposed to things and events qualitatively different from those usable in school. This can result, according to Cohen, in progressive decrements in pupils' information repertoires, which would account for some of the unexplained discrepancy between IQ and school achievement.

There is a growing body of evidence to support the existence of qualitative environmental differences is various American groups. Johnson and Sanday (1971) summarize some of this evidence on blacks and empirically establish a significant difference between blacks and whites in three urban poverty neighborhoods. These groups differ along several dimensions which anthropologists (Beals, 1967) have suggested as suitable boundary criteria for delimiting cultural systems. Other evidence (Tyler, 1965) comes from studies of orphanage children, mountain children, and from numerous studies of urban-rural differences.

Such groups have certain common characteristics. They are isolated in varng degrees from the American cultural mainstream of the white middle and upper classes, and their IQ scores are on the average lower and more uniform than those recorded for the mainstream group. The hereditarian would argue that genetic inferiority and selective migration explains the difference in means between rural, ethnic and urban majority groups. An alternative explanation is that these groups by virtue of their isolation are not exposed to the cultural elements related to the expression of mental ability. The hereditarian would argue that the homogeneity in measured intelligence in these groups (as indicated by a lower s.d.) is due to inbreeding. If the latter were the case then we might also expect a degree of homogeneity in other phenotypic characteristics, which, to our knowledge, does not exist. An alternative explanation is that these groups are exposed to an environment which is uniform in its lack of the relevant components which Cohen suggests are important in mental-test performance. An advantage of these alternative explanations is that they can be applied both to groups which may not represent different gene pools (such as orphanage children) and to groups which do (such as racial groups).

CONCEPTUAL MODEL

For the reasons discussed above, which are treated in somewhat more detail in Gregg and Sanday (1971), we assume that the distribution of intelligence due to the genetic component alone is the same for all groups of a population. The implications of this assumption are that the variation in measured general intelligence within groups is a function of genetic plus environmental components, while the variation in the means of general intelligence scores between groups is a function of environmental components alone.

Given any two groups where there is a reported mean difference in performance on tests measuring general intelligence (such as blacks and whites in the USA or upper- and lower-class groups), the problem is to see if these differences can be explained in part in terms of particular environmental variables and mechanisms. The salient dimensions of our model which interrelates these environmental variables and their effect on variation in general intelligence are as follows: the components of the mental system brought to bear by an individual in answering test questions, the components of the mental system test developers seek to measure, the cultural locus of the components being measured, and the process by which these components are diffused to individuals who are peripheral to or outside of the cultural locus.

Referring to the first two dimensions, we assume that there are a number of cognitive components which are part of the mental system and which are related to the expression of intelligence as measured by the IQ test. Davis (1948, pp. 63-65) has defined problem solving as a system of acts which are learned through cultural training and are interconnected with acts of genetic control and acts of the emotional system. Three types of acts – cultural, genetic, and emotional – comprise the mental system in operation. The cultural acts determine the goal of the total system's operation and direct the system toward solutions sanctioned by group consensus, whether the group be that of mathematicians or slum boys.

Referring to the third dimension, we infer from Davis' discussion that group differences occur in measured intelligence because individuals in the same society do not necessarily have at their command the same set of cultural acts or the same culture-based cognitive components. Such acts, or components, can develop within a single cultural group, and from this locus are relayed through the process of diffusion to other groups in the same society. The locus of the components which test developers seek to measure in tests of general intelligence resides, we assume, in the mainstream culture. (In the United States the locus, or point of origin, resides in the white middle and upper classes of the urban-suburban environment.)

The process of diffusion interrelates the first three dimensions. 'Diffusion', as the term is used by anthropologists, refers to the process by which material objects or patterns of learned behavior are relayed from a point of origin within a single society to any number of other societies. 'Diffusion' used in this sense is a crosscultural process. Here it refers to an intracultural process by which a behavior pattern is relayed from a point of origin within a society to other points in the same society.

The central hypothesis of the model can be stated as follows: Mean differences in test scores of groups within a given society are a function of the nature and degree of the group's contact with the mainstream culture. Degree of contact is a combined measure of psychological, social, and geographical distance from the mainstream cultural unit. The weights assigned to these dimensions will vary depending on the non-mainstream units being considered in the empirical test of the model. Nature of contact is a quantitative function of the affective interaction between members of the non-mainstream unit and the mainstream unit. Affective interaction can range from accepting to nonaccepting. The weights assigned to the distance dimensions may, conceivably, be dependent on the affective dimension.

The weights assigned to distance and nature of contact can be viewed as the parameters of the diffusion process (i.e., the rate of diffusion) for the groups studied in the empirical test of the model.

The empirical test of the diffusion model is currently underway using data drawn from an American urban public school system. As principal investigator in this project, I hope to interest colleagues in other countries in a crosscultural test of the model either through conducting similar projects in their home countries, or by providing data to the research team. The goal of the empirical analysis is to find the environmental conditions under which the cognitive components related to the expression of measured intelligence diffuse. These environmental conditions (the independent variables of the study) are defined in terms of variables measuring degree and nature of contact with the mainstream cultural unit. The research design employs historical data on the same individuals in order to hold the gene pool constant. Required as data are reasonably complete school records on a sample of individuals who have taken at least two IQ tests and who are members of at least two definable groups. In the empirical analysis the dependent variable is change in IQ, and the independent variables are indicators gleaned from school records which can be seen as signifying degree and nature of contact with the mainstream cultural unit.

RELATED RESEARCH

The consequences of varying degrees of contact with the majority culture can be seen in Gregg and Sanday's (1971) discussion of the effects of highly variable and of homogeneous environments on heritability estimates. These authors point out that heritability estimates will be much higher in a homogeneous environment, since not much of the variance will be accounted for by differences in the environment. Furthermore, in such a case, the total phenotypic variance will be smaller, since the proportion of the variance due to the environment is very low. It is interesting to note in this connection that the phenotypic variance of IQ in the black, rural, and orphanage populations is on the average much smaller than it is in the urban-suburban white population. The important factor in this discussion is the meaning of 'homogeneous environment'. By 'homogeneous', we refer specifically to a uniform degree of exposure to culturally determined cognitive components which are usable in school and which are related to performance on the IQ test.

In a study of Negro adolescents, Henderson (1967) showed that ghetto youth tend to perform very much alike on such measures of social performance as educational achievement, law-violating behavior, aspirations, and perceptions of life chances. Henderson found that the traditional explanatory variables of family structure and poverty level do not explain these results. Henderson stressed as an alternative explanation the uniformity of the ghetto environment resulting from the racial, physical, mental and social isolation imposed by the white subculture. This homogeneity is further intensified by the neighborhood public school system which in urban America affects blacks and whites differently (Johnson & Sanday, 1971). Urban schools in the white subcultural system provide the means for ever-expanding social contacts with the cultural mainstream as the student moves through the system. In the isolated urban black community, in contrast, the student is exposed to a homogeneous class and racial context and geared to a limited set of expectations. The debilitating effect of the ghetto school on black educational achievement is documented by the Coleman report (1966), which indicated that the racial composition of the school was an important factor accounting for the variance in black educational achievement. These points are underscored in numerous studies.

The nature of contact is another important variable in our

research framework. We are particularly interested in teacher's attitudes regarding children as an important variable influencing the child's performance. Many actual examples of the debilitating attitudes on the part of teachers have been vividly portrayed by Kozol (1967). One study (St. John, 1971) provides empirical support for a relationship of child-orientation or interpersonal competence in teachers to reading growth, improved conduct and attendance of black children. Considerations such as these led Johnson and Sanday (1971) to suggest that the documented failure of compensatory education (cf. Jensen 1969) can be traced to the predilection of the developers of such programs to assume cultural deficiency and inferiority, and the consequent internalization of these attitudes on the part of those who are supposedly being helped by the programs.

Another important body of research bearing on our problem is a series of longitudinal studies which have observed IQ change and constancy. A number of these studies are summarized by Tyler (1965, pp. 68-72) and by Kagan (1964). These studies show that IQ is not constant and that there can be a large variation in IQ over an individual's life cycle. In an examination of the correlates of change in mental ability, one study (Sontag *et al.*, 1958) found that sex and personality factors were related to reported increases and decreases. Other studies (see Tyler, 1965, pp. 70-71) have found the changes to be related to the educational level of a child's family and to school factors in general.

This research has several implications for mental-test development. First, if it can be demonstrated that traditional mental tests do, in fact, measure cognitive components which are differentially diffused, we will have a framework for testing the degree of culture bias of specific tests. Secondly, the results of such research can provide the test developer with additional insights into the cognitive components which are relatively culture-free and which are related to general intelligence. Finally, an approach oriented to a multidimensional cultural space lends support to the increasing use of tests designed for specific subcultural groups.

REFERENCES

Beals, A. R. (1967) *Culture in process.* New York: Holt, Rinehart and Winston.

Bodmer, W. F., & Cavalli-Sforza, L. L. (1970) Intelligence and race. *Sci. Amer., 223,* 19-29.

Brace, C. L., Gamble, G. R., & Bond, J. T. (Eds.) (1971) Race and intelligence. *Anthropological Studies,* No. 8.

Caspari, E. (1968) Genetic endowment and environment in the determination of human behavior: Biological viewpoint. *Amer. educ. Res. J., 5,* 43-55.

Cohen, R. (1969) Conceptual styles, culture conflict and non-verbal tests of intelligence. *Amer. Anthropologist, 71,* 828-856.

Coleman, J. S. et al. (1966) *Equality of educational opportunity.* Washington, D. C.: Govt Printing Off.

Crow, J. F. (1969) Genetic theories and influences: Comments on the value of diversity. *Harvard educ. Rev., 39,* 301-309.

Davis, A. (1948) *Social-class influences upon learning.* Cambridge: Harvard Univer. Press.

Gregg, T. G., & Sanday, P. R. (1971) Genetic and environmental components of differential intelligence. In Brace et al. (*op. cit.*).

Henderson, D. M. (1967) A study of the effects of family structure and poverty on Negro adolescents from the ghetto. Unpublished Ph.D. dissertation, Univer. of Pittsburgh.

Jensen, A. (1969) How much can we boost IQ and scholastic achievement? *Harvard educ. Rev., 39,* 1-123.

Johnson, N. J., & Sanday, P. R. (1971) Subcultural variations in an urban poor population. *Amer. Anthropologist, 73,* 128-143.

Kagan, J. (1964) American longitudinal research on psychological development. *Child Develpm., 35,* 1-32.

Kozol, J. (1967) *Death at an early age.* Boston: Houghton Mifflin.

Racial studies: Academy position on call for new research. (1967) *Science, 158,* 892-893.

St. John, N. (1971) Thirty-six teachers: Their characteristics, and outcomes for black and white pupils. *Amer. educ. Res. J., 8,* 635-648.

Sontag, L. W., & Baker, C. T. (1958) Personality, familial, and physical correlates of change in mental ability. *Monogr. Soc. Res. Child Develpm., 23,* No. 2.

Tyler, L. E. (1965) *The psychology of human differences.* (3rd ed.) New York: Appleton-Century-Crofts.

Note: *Sanday agreed with a comment that the indicators used to assess an individual's contact with a mainstream culture would have to be changed when a similar study is mounted in another region where social organization is different.* (Eds.)

LUTZ H. ECKENSBERGER 8
University of the Saar, Saarbrücken

The necessity of a theory for applied crosscultural research*

Often a psychological test originally constructed for cultural group A is applied to a cultural group B to select or classify individuals according to 'the same' ability. This procedure is crosscultural in nature, because the individual of Group B has to solve problems which were defined primarily with respect to individuals of Group A, and because the performance of the individual of Group B therefore is compared implicitly with the standardization Group A. Therefore, in this procedure which can be called 'implicit crosscultural research' the same problems of comparability are involved as in the case of 'explicit crosscultural research', where two or more cultural groups are directly compared.

There are problems of comparability with regard to the samples, the language and content of test items, the responses, and the testing situation as a whole. Such problems exist universally in psychological research, but in crosscultural psychology they are critical. From the point of view of 'cultural relativism', culture and thus the behavior of the members of a culture are interpretable only in the culture's own terms (the 'Malinowskian dilemma'; cf. Berry, 1969; Goldsmith, 1966). Hence, neither formally identical items, nor formally identical responses, nor formally identical situations can be compared, for then we would compare incomparables.

* Presentation of this paper was supported by the *Vereinigung der Freunde der Universität des Saarlandes e.V.*

The standard proposal to resolve this dilemma is to require the use of 'functionally equivalent' items, responses, and situations when a comparison is made. This procedure is psychometrically dubious, however, because the individuals investigated and the items used are different.

So far, the problem has seemed to be unsolvablẹ. However, it is my conviction that finding the basic solution is hindered by the fact that we usually are too willing to consider methodological issues connected with the application of crosscultural research without first reflecting on its real or basic subject matter. Therefore, I want to offer a definition of what the basic substantial issue of crosscultural research in psychology should be, and then derive the main theoretical and methodological consequences.

TOWARD A DEFINITION OF CROSSCULTURAL RESEARCH IN PSYCHOLOGY

If we accept the simple but clear scheme of Woodworth & Schlosberg which states that psychology deals with S-O-R relations, then in crosscultural research we deal with Sc-O-R relations, where the index 'c' refers to 'cultural conditions'. We can transpose this paradigm into the following working definition:

> Crosscultural research in psychology is the explicit, systematic comparison of psychological variables under different cultural conditions in order to specify the antecedents and processes that mediate the emergence of behavior differences.

Thus, the basic subject matter of crosscultural research should be to uncover 'if-then relations' (Barker, 1968), where the 'if-conditions' (i.e. independent variables) are the cultural conditions with which behavior (i.e. dependent variables) covaries. That means that the aim of crosscultural research should be to uncover that part of variance in behavior arising from different cultural environments.*

* This systematization consciously neglects the influence of the individual upon culture, because this is an aspect of the interaction between the

· Consequently, crosscultural psychology should be understood as complementing general and developmental psychology; it could support the experimental and quasiexperimental approaches of these disciplines by selecting key antecedent conditions for behavioral differences 'in nature', by maximizing the systematic variance of environmental conditions across cultures, and second by investigating behavioral consequences which do not occur in all cultural contexts (cf. LeVine, 1970; Sears, 1961).

(Kerlinger [1964, p. 283], in discussing the maximization of experimental variance, points to problems in psychology, where one can be interested in defining the effect on a dependent variable, resulting from a *minimal* variation of the independent variable. This approach generally seems to be a very fruitful, if not a necessary, complement to the maximization principle. In cross-cultural research this would lead to *intra*cultural variations of the cultural variable under study [cf. Frijda & Jahoda, 1966].)

CONSEQUENCES FOR RESEARCH STRATEGY

To transpose the definition into a general research strategy, thereby going beyond the suggestions of LeVine (1970) and Holtzman et al. (1969), three basic questions should be stated in the following sequence:

1. Which psychological variable (y) is influenced by (or covarying with) a specific cultural condition (x) in time?

2. Where is this cultural condition (x) presented and to what extent?

3. Which cultural conditions $(x_2 \ldots x_n)$ are still present there which could also influence the psychological variable (y) in question?

individual and his environment, which is the genuine concern of anthropology. This strong separation between psychology and anthropology as well as the definition of 'cultural conditions' as 'independent variables' is somewhat artificial − it is used, however, since it enables us to derive some basic methodological and theoretical implications for psychological research across cultures. These are not so easily recognized, if, from the beginning, the whole complex interaction between the individual and the environment is taken into consideration.

To give a meaningful answer to these questions, one must first frame a theory so that he can formulate hypotheses about the relationship between cultural antecedent conditions and psychological consequences. That is, one must formulate hypotheses about the 'systematic variance'. Second, a theory is necessary to preselect the samples with regard to specific hypotheses, to maximize the 'systematic variance'. Finally, because the experimenter cannot, save in a limited way, manipulate cultural conditions (normally cultural conditions are 'assigned variables'), assumptions with regard to variables which produce extraneous variance must be deduced from a theory.

With regard to research strategies, then, explicitly cultural conditions should be sought out in nature or should be 'simulated' by using the techniques of 'practice' or 'coaching'. These methods entail an endeavor to grasp 'culture-by-treatment interactions' by raising the testing experience of 'culturally deprived' groups through 'compensatory test presentations' (cf. the contributions of Biesheuvel, Dague, and others in this volume).

Developmental aspects should be taken in consideration. This can be done at best by combining the 'general model for the study of developmental problems' (Baltes, 1968; Schaie, 1965) with crosscultural comparison (Eckensberger, 1971).

It should be obvious that, from this point of view, in basic crosscultural research the intent should not be a generalization of a result over cultural groups; this would imply the underlying supposition that there are no differences. One should not seriously entertain the null hypothesis. Rather the interest should be to examine whether in general, and to what extent, cultural conditions influence psychological variables. This focuses on alternatives to the null hypothesis.

This point of view differs from that of other authors (cf. Campbell, 1961; Gutmann, 1967), but it seems to be defensible. In case data are not generalizable from one cultural group to another, one at worst requires 'culture-specific psychologies' (cf. Baltes & Goulet, 1970). With this, however, there is no clue as to why the data are not generalizable; i.e. it hinders the explication of the principles whereby different cultural conditions are related to different forms of behavior, and thereby it prevents the development of a general body of knowledge. The approach emphasized here seems to be more suggestive, because it cogently points to the kind of models of measurement, the kind of theory, and the kind of sampling procedure which can be productive in crosscultural research.

Models of measurement

A theory-oriented approach is advantageous, because the problem of functional equivalence becomes somewhat clearer. Items or tests can be said to be functionally equivalent when they refer to the same construct or latent variable.

But how can we ascertain that under different cultural conditions the same construct is covered? Obviously, the psychological variables investigated have to meet the criterion of unidimensionality. With regard to this, several models of measurement are in use (e.g. the coefficient of difficulty, cf. Irvine, 1969 inter alia; the coefficient of homogeneity, cf. Przeworski & Teune, 1966; and, of course, factor analysis, cf. Cattell, 1969). But all these models of measurement are based on classical testing theory. According to Sixtl (1967), they are 'circular' because, e.g., the difficulty of an item is defined by the number of subjects who pass it, whereas the ability of a subject is defined by the number of items he solves. Likewise, the decomposition of a data matrix by means of factor analysis is dependent on the sample investigated and the tests used. Thus, although adequate in relatively homogeneous groups, these methods based on classical testing theory seem not to be appropriate for crosscultural research. Instead of these methods, probabilistic models of test construction such as that of Rasch (1966) seem to be more productive. In this model, 'the comparison of any two subjects can be carried out in such a way that no other parameters are involved than those of the two subjects — neither the parameter of any other subject, nor any of the stimulus (item) parameters. Similarly, any two stimuli (items) can be compared independently of all other parameters than those of the two stimuli (items) . . . alone' (Rasch, 1966, pp. 104-105).

One can argue that it is not sufficient to determine the transcultural invariance of a research instrument – i.e. to demonstrate that all individuals belonging to different cultural groups 'get the same test'. Further, one might say, the validity (i.e. the meaning of the research instrument) has to be demonstrated. With that statement, it becomes evident that basic crosscultural research, as outlined here, is the necessary prerequisite for application of tests to compare or select and classify individuals. Basic crosscultural research is to be considered as part of the process of construct validation itself. The prediction of differences in the development of individual test scores in various cultural environments and the prediction of 'culture-by-treatment interactions' (where 'treatment' may be retest, practice, or coaching) validates the theory as well as the research instrument.

Hence, criterion-oriented approaches can be of no benefit in crosscultural research (cf. Gordon & Kikuchi, 1966).

Appropriate theories

No theory is independent of the operationalization of its variables. But the measurement of variables is dependent on the model of measurement used. Because psychological models of measurement usually are based on classical testing theory, most theories in psychology are dependent on special samples.

In basic crosscultural research we should seek the kind of theory that meets the following demands: It should be formulated independent of a special sample. It should explicitly contain assumptions about interactions between the individual and his environment. And it should be developmental in nature.

Theories meet these criteria in varying degrees. Factor-analytic theories of intelligence, for example, are not independent of their samples and, moreover, developmental aspects can be only included with difficulty (cf. the critique of Merz & Kalveram, 1965, and Fischer, 1968, according to the 'age-differentiation hypothesis').

Therefore, it seems to be much more convenient to refer, for instance, to a cognitive and developmental theory like Piaget's which meets all the criteria formulated above. While it has to be admitted that some methodological difficulties exist, on the whole the application of such a theory in crosscultural research seems to be very promising.

Appropriate sampling procedure

As mentioned earlier, the selection of samples should be hypothesis-oriented. Since the aim of crosscultural research is to determine the influence of 'cultural conditions' on behavior in time, the samples to be compared must not be representative of their corresponding 'cultural groups'; they need only represent the single 'cultural variable' in question in various degrees. It cannot be overemphasized, however, that this procedure demands an operationalization of the global concept of culture into single measurable dimensions.

'Purposive selection' instead of random sampling should be employed. One could even try to create cultural groups artificially (Eckensberger, 1971), assembling individuals from all over the world to represent the cultural condition in question in various degrees. Extraneous variance could thus be controlled as well as possible by adding it to erroneous variance.

The methodological and theoretical barriers to be overcome in crosscultural research are more general in nature than previously realized. The only advantage of crosscultural psychology seems to be that the basic assumptions and demands in theory construction, theory of measurement, sampling strategies, etc. are more easily realized than in 'homogeneous cultural groups', within which psychological problems are to be solved. Crosscultural research emphatically supports the development of new models of test construction and application of theories that stress process constructs (e.g. thinking, adaptability) more than structures (e.g. most of the intelligence factors), and the inclusion of experimental conditions into the validation process of tests. Carried to the extreme, the crosscultural strategy, combined with designs of developmental psychology and experimental manipulation of cultural conditions (coaching, practice, test sophistication), in itself is to be interpreted as a part of validating the instruments and theories of psychology. I.e., it is to be understood as a part of construct validation.

REFERENCES

Baltes, P. B. (1968) Longitudinal and cross-sectional sequences in the study of age and generation effects. *Human Develpm., 11,* 145-171.
Baltes, P. B., & Goulet, L. R. (1970) Status and issues of life-span developmental psychology. In L. R. Goulet & P. B. Baltes (Eds.), *Life-span developmental psychology: Research and theory.* New York: Academic Press. Pp. 3-21.
Barker, R.G. (1968) *Ecological psychology. Concepts and methods for studying the environment of human behavior.* Stanford: Stanford Univer. Press.
Berry, J. W. (1969) On cross-cultural comparability. *Intern. J. Psychol., 4,* 119-128.
Campbell, D. T. (1961) The mutual methodological relevance of anthropology and psychology. In F. L. K. Hsu (Ed.), *Psychological anthropology. Approaches to culture and personality.* Homewood, Ill.: Dorsey Press. Pp. 333-352.
Cattell, R. B. (1969) Comparing factor trait and state scores across ages and cultures. *J. Geront., 24,* 348-360.
Eckensberger, L. H. (1971) Methodological issues of cross-cultural research in developmental psychology. Paper read at the West Virginia conference on methodological issues in life-span developmental psychology, Morgantown, W.Va.
Fischer, G. H. (Ed.) (1968) *Psychologische Testtheorie.* Bern: Huber.
Frijda, N., & Jahoda, G. (1966) On the scope and methods of cross-cultural research. *Intern. J. Psychol., 1,* 109-127.
Goldsmith, W. (1966) *Comparative functionalism.* Berkeley: Univ. of California Press, 1966.
Gordon, L. V., & Kikuchi, A. (1966) American personality tests in cross-cultural research. A caution. *J. soc. Psychol., 69,* 179-183.
Gutmann, D. (1967) On cross-cultural studies as a naturalistic approach in psychology. *Hum. Develpm., 10,* 187-198.
Holtzman, W. H., Diaz-Guerrero, R., Swartz, J. D., & Tapia, L. L. (1969)

Cross-cultural longitudinal research on child development: Studies of American and Mexican school children. In J. P. Hill (Ed.), *Minnesota symposia on child psychology*. Vol. 2. Minneapolis: Univer. of Minnesota Press. Pp. 125-159.

Irvine, S. H. (1969) Factor analysis of African abilities and attainments: Constructs across cultures. *Psychol. Bull., 71*, 20-32.

Kerlinger, F. N. (1964) *Foundations of behavioral research: Educational and psychological inquiry*. New York: Holt, Rinehart, & Winston.

LeVine, R. A. (1970) Cross-cultural study in child psychology. In P. H. Mussen (Ed.), *Carmichael's manual of child psychology*. (3rd ed.) Vol. 2. New York: Wiley. Pp. 559-612.

Merz, F., & Kalveram, K. T. (1965) Kritik der Differenzierungshypothese der Intelligenz. *Arch. f.d. ges. Psychol., 117*, 287-295.

Przeworski, A., & Teune, H. (1966) Equivalence in cross-national research. *Pub. Opin. Q., 30*, 551-568.

Rasch, G. (1966) An individualistic approach to item analysis. In *Readings in mathematical social science*. Chicago: Science Research Associates. Pp. 89-108.

Schaie, K. W. (1965) A general model for the study of developmental problems. *Psychol. Bull., 64*, 92-107.

Sears, R. R. (1961) Transcultural variables and conceptual equivalence. In B. Kaplan (Ed.), *Studying personality cross-culturally*. New York: Harper. Pp. 445-455.

Sixtl, F. (1969) Faktoreninvarianz und Faktoreninterpretation. *Psychol. Beit., 10*, 99-111.

PART III

Testing procedure

Ortar and Kohan survey the problems of translating and adapting established tests so as to make them useful in a new setting. Şemin adds concrete details from her experience with Binet-type testing in Turkey. The papers agree that achieving validity in the new setting is far more crucial than adhering closely to the model of the original test. Revisions must go deeper than translation; whatever a sentence or picture is to communicate to S must be understood by him, and his response must be fully understood by the tester.

Cho identifies procedures to improve validity of large-scale testing. A brief summary of a symposium introduces the reader to two handbooks that give extensive recommendations on the organization and conduct of such testing programs, and to the IBP handbook which suggests tests to be employed to assess psychological functions in basic research. A recurrent theme in the conference, the acceptability of a test to the persons tested, is studied empirically in Akeju's paper.

Two final papers are empirical studies of test procedure. In that of Gitmez, manipulating the amount of knowledge Ss had about the difficulty of the items altered scores. One manipulation brought lower-class Ss to a level at least equal to that of children from better backgrounds. Cook and Molomo studied Botswana children who were strongly motivated for test taking; adding special incentives did not alter their performance.

9

GINA ORTAR
Hebrew University, Jerusalem

Some principles for adaptation of psychological tests

Most countries do not produce their own psychological tests and have to adapt instruments developed elsewhere. Change is needed to make the test suitable in circumstances different from those for which it was originally prepared. Modifications vary in kind and extent, and 'adaptation' may range from rewording of a few items to construction of a virtually new test based on the original model. The most frequent procedure, translation into a different language with changes in some items, is a specific point on the continuum.

It is obvious that the extent of modification required depends on the distance between the source culture and the culture for which the test is being adapted. However, there are no objective instruments (other than tests!) for measuring cultural distances, so that the components of a test requiring attention have to be dealt with directly. The components are the attributes to be measured, the criterion, the test 'language', subject background, and norms.

THE ATTRIBUTES TO BE MEASURED

Even a widely-known concept such as 'family', 'home', 'teacher', or 'exactness' is made up of elements (biological relationship, status in the family, role in society, tasks to be performed, etc.) which may be differently stressed in the two cultures. The same item, therefore, will not necessarily evoke similar responses in the two groups.

Similarity or even identity of concepts is often taken for granted, especially by an investigator embarking for the first time on a crosscultural study. He usually wishes to find out whether the trait he is working on 'is distributed in your country as it is in mine', and he writes to ask for the help of a 'graduate student or another reliable person who could translate the test or the questionnaire and perhaps also administer it'. The computation of results will then be 'done by himself at home'. And, 'of course, you see, I have not much time, the term is about to begin, so if you just could tell me the name of such a person and how to reach him, I would be very grateful'. As you can imagine, he is never really grateful for the explanation that tells him why his project failed to elicit support.

Two conditions have to be satisfied before the similarity of perception of a trait can be assumed:

> Each response of S and the configuration of responses should constitute a representative sample of S's characteristic behavior.

> The total range of behavior elicited in a proper sample of the population should correspond to that continuum of traits for which the instrument was originally constructed.

By way of illustration: When we present someone with the question 'What is the thing to do if you find an envelope in the street, that is sealed, addressed and has a new stamp? ', we are not particularly concerned with knowing his actual behavior in such a situation. Rather, we are measuring the construct 'comprehension'. A different, culturally more suitable question will serve if we are convinced that it is more representative of 'general comprehension' in the adapting society. 'Do you usually enter into conversation with fellow passengers on a bus?' or 'Do you like parties?' are meant, in the original instrument, to reveal tendency to establish contact with and to stimulate people. The 'establishing of contact' constitutes an element in the introversion-extraversion continuum, and the above questions are intended to differentiate in that area. In a culture where addressing a stranger on a bus is regarded as offensive or where participating in a party is against some ideological principles, however, the answers would relate rather to behavior connected with the aggression-submission continuum or would measure belief in a certain ideology. Similarly, an American questionnaire asks: 'When you begin an examination, do you feel pretty confident that you will do well? ' In the American culture, a student with a positive attitude is expected to answer affirmatively, but in Israel we found this item to have no discriminative value at all.

There is no rule of thumb that will prevent mistakes of this kind. Cultural differences (or their absence) must be investigated before it can be determined whether a given instrument promises to become a fair measure of the trait under consideration.

CHOOSING TESTS TO PREDICT CRITERIA

How to achieve validity in a predictive test cannot be adequately treated in this paper, since a multitude of theoretical and practical questions arise. The point to be stressed is this: the intent to predict similar behavior does not automatically call for use of a similar test. The adaptation (and elaboration) by Terman of the Binet-Simon Scale was again adapted (through translation and slight changes) for many European countries and it did indeed predict success in school. If there were a school system, however, that rewarded rote learning above all other achievements, the Stanford-Binet would be probably less valid than it is in schools that adopt 'Western' aims of schooling.

I would like to illustrate this point by an example from Israel. Several years ago, the need for a graded group intelligence test was acute and we decided to adapt the Lorge-Thorndike scales. After obtaining permission from the publishers, we proceeded first to work on the nonverbal parts of the test, where it seemed that only a translation of the instructions was needed. It was soon found that at the lower IQ level the test did not discriminate at all. An IQ of 100 was about the minimum needed for understanding the task itself. This was true in regard to the figural subtests as well as in Number Series. The actual Hebrew test therefore was made up of verbal subtests only; but this has not diminished its correlation with success in school.

A different example would be the 'Foreign Words Vocabulary'
test constructed for the entrance examination in the Department
of Psychology at the Hebrew University. A revived ancient language, Hebrew lacks many of the 'international' terms denoting
historical, scientific, artistic, and other concepts (mostly abstract). Because of their alien origin and linguistic structure, these
words are difficult for an Israeli to learn, yet they are indispensable for any reading that is not strictly literary and therefore
are usually included in a general dictionary of Hebrew. On the
strength of the well-known validity of high-level vocabulary tests
in *S*'s mother tongue for prediction of scholastic success, it was
reasoned that this quite abstract vocabulary was a good measure
of general level of information and should be a good predictor of
academic success. This assumption was, as a matter of fact, true,
the test predicting academic success better than a test of Hebrew
vocabulary did.

THE 'LANGUAGE' USED FOR IMPARTING THE TEST STIMULUS

A test conveys a certain message to *S* by means of one or more
media of communication. Some problems or instructions may be
expressed in several 'languages', while others are closely inter-
woven with a specific medium. Information about a certain shade
of color or a complex shape can, for instance, be transmitted
only by the shade or the shape itself, while the more common
colors or shapes can be precisely designated by a word. Concepts
like 'punishment' or 'culture' can be communicated only by
words, but relations such as 'near' or 'first' can also be imparted
by a drawing. 'Square' can be expressed also in a number.

Among accepted tests, an item might employ the written or
spoken word, number, picture, blot, relief, schematical drawing,
geometrical figure, small-scale model, object or an abstract sign.
As the *meaning* of an item is dependent not solely on its content
but also on its perception by *S*, and as the perception of different
'languages' of communication is liable to differ interculturally,
adequate *mediation* of a given problem may be as important as
the problem content.

The prevailing opinion is that visual stimuli, mainly drawings or pictures, are more 'crosscultural' than verbal communication. This assumption is usually, though seldom explicitly, based on an impression that verbal representation is always more 'abstract' and therefore communicates less well than a visual representation, especially if the test is to be adapted to a 'lower' culture. Not only is this assumption not supported by theory, it also has no corroboration in practice. There is no proof that the understanding of the noun 'tree', of a relation like 'bigger' or 'near' or of an adjective like 'pretty' or 'hot' demands a higher level of abstraction on the part of a normal person belonging to any culture than the perception of the same concept by means of its visual representation. I believe that the opposite is true, that the transfer of a configuration of symbols into concepts is a culturally determined process, dependent on previous training. The relatively low validity of most intercultural, crosscultural or international tests is probably caused by this difficulty.

As a principle, I should propose that for each culture the most common and most generally used medium is the best safeguard for transmitting a problem which is intended to measure abilities or behavior. Only if the medium is thoroughly familiar is it permissible to assume that S has expended his effort (and time) in response to the *content* of the test.

Since the use of words and numbers as a means of communication is universal, at least in the form of speech, it can be argued that this medium is more nearly crosscultural than any other. A reliable translation, being dependent on the existence of specific terms and usages in the adapting language, would serve as a protection against a gross cultural misinterpretation of meaning or problem. For instance, if somebody wished to use the Hebrew analogy of *olives : picking = grapes : . . .*, an attempt at translation would inform him whether the item is suitable. It would depend on the existence, in the adapting language, of specialized terms for the picking of different fruit.

This kind of a warning sign — the absence of a corresponding term — is not available when symbols other than language or numbers are used, so that 'translation' seems to be required.

PREVIOUS ACQUAINTANCE WITH TESTS

The general instructions, the examples and the directions for
subtests or for single items – including the extent of help which
might be given a subject who fails initially – are an important
part of the measuring instrument. Choosing instructions appropriate to a subject population may give the subject a better
understanding of the principles underlying the test may be
reached and make it unnecessary to change the test items.

Especially with illiterate *S*s who are not accustomed to answer
sudden and unconnected questions, even questions that touch on
everyday matters, a short introduction is necessary. Thus, a
woman who at first denies any knowledge of names of fishes (on
the Kent E-G-Y 'Emergency' questions) is perfectly ready to give
them if asked some preliminary questions in an informal tone
about her family's likes or dislikes of fish-dishes. The same
technique is usually efficient with children unaccustomed to
strangers. With this kind of change in the instructions, the Kent
E-G-Y questions were found (with little adaptation of content)
to be quite crosscultural.

A different approach, required where a test calls for a relatively new skill like reasoning with unfamiliar material, is the 'test-
coach-test' technique. It comprises three parts, the first and the
last of which are given in the usual manner of administering tests.
The results of the first part are not used for computing the final
score, since the aim of the first stage is to confront *S* with the
need of seeking a solution. The middle part is a training period
during which the examiner explains, with the help of specially
prepared items, the principles involved in the test. The third part
serves then as a proper measure of *S*'s ability to solve the relevant
kind of problems.

We have found the test-coach-test technique, though time-consuming, efficient for individual and especially clinical testing. We
are now about to standardize, as a part of a scale for measuring
intelligence in Grades 1-4, a subtest constructed for this technique. The test asks for completion of pictorial series, the principle of which is to be detected.

THE ADAPTATION OF NORMS

Strictly speaking, there is no *a priori* justification for applying the original norms, derived from population belonging to the source culture. Even if the differences in the perception of content and of the medium of communication were only slight, the distribution of scores might be different in the society for which the test is adapted.

The seemingly obvious solution – construction of new norms – is usually less simple in practice than in theory. Norms should be based on a representative sample of the population, but what about the countries where no adequate register of the population exists at all? Even for the population of school age, a representative sample is obtainable only if the schooling is compulsory and the law is truly enforced. Norms collected on a select school population are apt to set too high a figure as the 'average' performance.

In the developing countries, an interesting situation might prevail in connection with the influence of schooling on level of intelligence. The well-documented correlation between years of schooling and IQ might be much attenuated if the segment of population who have never been to school is included. According to my data, the mean IQ level of illiterates is higher than the IQ of persons having had only a few years of school, i.e. of persons who did have the opportunity to learn but left school early, probably owing to failure.

Whenever no adequate sampling is possible, the best substitute for general norms are separate norms for groups of specified educational background. This applies also to *S*s of preschool age, whose parents' education should be taken as a basis for classification into norm groups.

ADAPTING A SPECIFIC TEST

An example of adaptation during which diverse procedures have been used is the Israeli version of WISC.

No changes were made in three subtests: Block Design, Object

Assembly and Coding. The mean achievement on the first two was considerably lower than the USA means (1 s.d. or more), while the Coding means differed only very slightly. New norms had to be constructed.

With Digit Span there was a change of procedure. After a preliminary try-out which showed that the Israeli children get lower scores on Digit Span, it was decided to adopt the Stanford-Binet procedure, i.e. to allow three instead of only two trials, for a given number of digits.

Changes of content in other subtests were made. The most extreme modification occurred, of course, in Vocabulary, which had to be specially constructed. Most of the General Information items had also to be changed, owing to differences in usage or in cultural habits. Thus, a question about the finger *nail* was substituted for the thumb because in everyday Hebrew the thumb is just the 'big finger'. The item asking for the height of an average women was retained, though it is difficult in Israel, because comparatively few persons are aware of population statistics. On the other hand, some items, the question about hieroglyphics for instance, were much easier.

Among performance tests, many pictures had to be redrawn in order to make the persons (e.g. the policeman) or the objects (a window, a thermometer) recognizable. Norms for all the performance subtests had to be computed.

No norms for ages below 6 and above 14 could be computed owing to difficulties of sampling.

USING TEST RESULTS

We come finally, and briefly, to the interpretation of results. A given result is usually interpreted by the psychologist according to his knowledge of the population means and standard deviations, but what about the adapted test? The suggestions made by the test constructor for the original instrument should not, in general, be accepted as valid without supporting evidence. Even when the same parameters have been retained in the adapted scale, for example the WISC, it is by no means sure that the results should be understood as they are in the source culture.

Figure 1 shows the means of WISC subtests within groups of Israeli pupils classified by their Full Scale IQs. It is obvious that each level has its specific scatter of sceres which gets more pronounced as the IQ gest more extreme. Any individual results should therefore be first of all related to the specific background scatter of the appropriate IQ level.

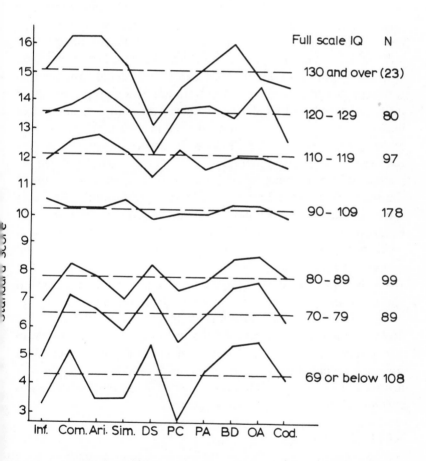

Figure 1. Mean subtest scores of groups selected according to WISC IQ

I would like to sum up my opinion on the best way to adapt a test for a culture which is not extremely different from the source culture. This is the most frequent occurrence, since if the culture is extremely different, there would probably be no demand for a test. I take a different view than Anastasi does in the following paragraph (1969, p. 242): 'Basically, cross-cultural tests endeavor to rule out one or more parameters along which cultures vary. A well-known example of such a parameter is language. If the cultural groups to be tested speak different languages the test should require no language . . .' According to my view, language is, along with numbers, the one parameter common to all cultures as a means of communication between human beings and certainly as a means and subject-matter at any level of schooling. It is therefore the verbal and arithmetic tests which are easiest to adapt. They can be translated. The translator, who should be well versed in both cultures and not merely in both languages, will be alerted whenever translation is impossible because the given concept does not exist in the adapting language, or whenever there is an obvious difference in the degree of familiarity with a given mental process. The comparatively simple remedy of constructing parallel items is then open. A specialist in the field can do this. In nonverbal tests, any cultural differences are comparatively well hidden, but the validity of the test might be disappointing. However, since in many situations a nonverbal or a performance test is necessary, the adapter should first analyze the instrument and separate the problem to be solved from the means of expression used for imparting the problem. If the means of expression is comparatively novel, S should first of all be given an ample opportunity to get acquainted with the symbols and only afterwards be required to solve the problem. In the absence of such a preparatory stage, any test is in reality a measure of behavior in a novel situation and not a measure of abstract thinking, special abilities, reasoning, or whatever else was the aim of the test in the source culture.

REFERENCES

Anastasi, Anne (1966) *Testing problems in perspective.* Washington, D.C.: Amer. Council on Educ.

NURIA CORTADA DE KOHAN
University of Buenos Aires

10

Test construction and standardization in different cultural settings

The purpose of this paper is to report difficulties and problems found in our attempts to translate and standardize in Argentina some verbal tests of general intelligence, aptitudes, and interests as well as personality inventories. Our experience relates to the clinical use and or the psychometric standardization in Buenos Aires of the following tests, among others: Pressey's Intermediate Classification Tests for Children, the Differential Aptitude Tests, the Kuder Preference Record, the Minnesota Multiphasic Personality Inventory, the Mooney Problem Checklist, the Strong Vocational Interest Blank, WAIS, and WISC. We will take into consideration observations and experiences gathered in constructing objective tests of achievement at the primary, secondary and university levels (Cortada de Kohan, 1964, 1969). An important part of this experience compares patients' responses to some psychometric tests in a New York mental hospital with Argentinian patients studied in a clinical setting in Buenos Aires.

In our judgment, the problems related with the sociocultural factors in the use and standardization of tests are mainly problems of language usage, timing, familiarity with types of tests, problems of administration, and attitudes towards mental measurement and selection of students (Cortada de Kohan, 1968a,b).

Language problems are a major handicap. The first difficulty is to secure a good translation of the items. In some instances this is a very difficult goal to reach. There is no general agreement on what is a good translation. Sometimes a word-by-word translation does not achieve the meaning of a statement and a freer translation adds nuances not intended by the author of the test. In spite of the dictum *'Traduttore, traditore'*, long texts can be fairly well translated from English into Spanish and vice versa. Spanish translations of English texts are approximatedly 15 per cent longer than the originals. This also happens with other languages such as Portuguese, Italian, French and German. This makes it quite difficult to translate opposites and synonym items, and items like those in the Miller Analogies Test where the language rhythm is important. In multiple-choice items the difficulty is at times insurmountable since it is necessary to translate a set of words (including distracters) that have rigidly specified interrelations. One cannot then resort to a paraphrase to translate the real meaning of the words.

Though some words have 'exact' translations the original and the translated equivalent may not be equally familiar. Sometimes the translator does not 'feel' the cultural implications associated with certain words. This difficulty shows up during item analysis, where some item has different levels of difficulty in the original and the translated form. For instance, words of Latin origin, commonly used in French, Italian and Spanish, are not so common in English where the preferred word is the Anglo-Saxon equivalent. Words written identically in the three languages nonetheless have different frequencies of usage. For instance *moral* in Spanish belongs to the first thousand while *moral* in English belongs to the third thousand and *moral* in French belongs to the second thousand. Even words with a very concrete meaning like *orange* and *pear* differ from more than two thousand places in frequency of use.

In spite of these differences linguists consider that any concept can be expressed in any language. But a particular concept may be easier to verbalize in one language than in another. A generalized style of thought in a particular culture may be detectable in lexical and syntactic forms, but such relations are subtle and very hard to establish (Locke & Booth, 1955).

The meaning of a sentence depends on three elements: the lexical meaning, that is, the categories that the words of the sentences designate; second, the structural meaning that depends upon relations among the words; third, the extralinguistic meaning that depends upon the inferences that can be drawn when the sentence is embedded in a certain context. There are many 'semantic' theories to explain verbal meaning. They range from primitive uncritical assumptions to highly elaborate applications of behavioral hypotheses. In some sense meaning could be defined in terms of a symbol and the symbolized object. The mediating processes that relate symbol to object are learned and influence one another. To explain the occurrence of one mediating process rather than another, motivation, perception, and personal experiences and expectations are important. Thus it becomes clear that meanings are actually dependent on a whole set of psychological factors belonging partly to the self and partly to different environments.

An added difficulty in translating verbal items, correctly with respect to exactness of meaning and level of difficulty, is that test authors rarely specify the reasons for including particular items, and even the item analysis is rarely reported. The usual report stops with a fairly general statement about indexes of validity and reliability for the whole test. Sometimes an item presents a double negative sentence. In Spanish this has to be translated by a positive sentence; a double negative cannot be used to express an affirmative.

In achievement testing it is important to use the terminology normal in the country where we apply the test. For instance, in the United States it is very common in set theory to talk about Venn diagrams, but in Argentina these are usually referred as Euler's diagrams. The same can be said about Pascal's triangle and Tartaglia's triangle, and so on.

Another handicap for test standardization is the use of proverbs and sayings. Even though there may be proverbs in both languages that have the same metaphoric meaning, their familiarity may not be at all the same in the two cultures.

The influence of cultural stereotypes is important for children, who cannot envision other cultural environments. Some years ago, using the 1937 Stanford-Binet, we found that to the statement: 'The judge said to the prisoner, "You are to be hanged, and I hope it will be a warning to you"' (Verbal Absurdities, XI), many children answered: 'Oh! This is silly!'. But when we inquired why they found it 'foolish' or 'silly' they said proudly: 'Of course it is foolish: no judge could give anybody the death punishment in Argentina, this would be against the law'. So, apparently they answered the item correctly, but not for the right reason!

Since the Wechsler scales have a large error variance, one wonders what is the use of translating it. Besides, all diagnostic and clinical interpretations associated with the patterning of subtests for different types of psychiatric patients necessarily lose their original meaning if the verbal tests have to be completely changed.

Verbal tests have been criticized as subject to cultural bias. No doubt the performance of an individual on a test is a combination of his ability and his experience. Groups that have been deprived of test-related experiences appear lower in the ability scale. Thus we are not being fair. Coffman (1963) insists in the importance of studying test items and language usage and adjusting time limits when trying to standardize a test for a different culture. Perhaps this is not enough; perhaps we should find new instruments dependent more on the real logical structures of thought than on language.

Margaret Mead (1965) has been thinking actively in the development of a systematic international coding of ideas similar to the archeological 'glyphs' or graphic signs, one for each idea, such as feminine, masculine, water, poison, danger, stop, walk, etc. In many countries hundreds of glyphs are used as street and traffic signs, but these frequently have ambivalent or contradictory meanings in different regions. Perhaps what we would need is a complete set of glyphs that constitute a system of visual signs with a frame of reference universally understood. In this system it would be necessary to avoid the symbols that are already charged with cultural references. For instance, the symbol + may be interpreted as the adding sign, as the Christian cross, as a reference to someone already dead, or as a road-crossing sign. As the world develops towards more and more international communication it seems that we all would profit by a second supplementary language which everybody could learn. This would not, of course, take the place of the mother language. Artificial languages are not subtle enough for the very complex goals of human communication, but perhaps they could be used properly for measuring some cognitive aptitudes and thought processes, devoid of emotional nuances.

Tests are more likely to be used to the advantage of the students when they are considered in the perspective of other relevant information about abilities and when it is known what they do and do not measure. One of the unfortunate consequences of verbal tests is that they put too much emphasis on superficial aspects of thought and too little on thinking processes, thus accentuating differences between social and cultural levels. Common, uniform examinations and tests for all students make less sense as teaching becomes more individualized. Dependence on verbal ability may not be so necessary if other perceptual and cognitive skills are stimulated by new teaching media. Considering all the handicaps and difficulties that pertain to the standardization of most verbal tests, this should not lead us to more frustrations. We believe that objective tests of achievement (multiple-choice type) should be constructed. Here the main goal of educators is to know *how much* a student knows of some matter and not how he learned it, how he got the information, etc. But of course, achievement tests should be specifically and critically constructed for each region, subject matter, socioeconomic and cultural level, etc.

In my judgment, verbal tests of general and specific abilities that focus on the success-failure dichotomy are difficult to standardize and risky to use crossculturally. They do not contribute to deeper understanding of the relation between overt performance and factors within the behavior itself. In this sense the writings of Duncker, Wertheimer, Binet, Bloom, and Piaget recognize the need for studying processes rather than products. The research conducted in this field by Rimoldi (in the USA and in Argentina; 1955, 1963, 1967) has developed an experimental methodology which permits operational definitions of behavior and precise quantification of the elements subjected to empirical verification. His technique goes much deeper into the core of the problem than does the mere counting of right and wrong answers. Rimoldi attempts to study the thinking processes used by the subject while solving a problem by analyzing the questions that he asks in order to reach a solution. The sequence of questions asked, called a *'tactic'*, is defined by number, type and order of questions asked. The main assumptions in this approach are: that people actively look for and combine information, that tactics are an index of the person's thinking process, that different tactics may maybe used by different persons, and that individual differences are more likely to be seen through the study of tactics than by the study of final answers alone. In each problem Rimoldi differentiates between formal properties or logical structure and 'language', so that each structure can be presented in several languages. He can thus define an 'ideal' or perfect tactic for each problem. This is important for cross-cultural research since the difficulty of an item is not referred to a sample of subjects; rather it is inherent in its logical structure, and known beforehand by the test author. We can consider this methodology devoid of cultural biases, if we assume that all mankind has the same logical scheme. The method can be used in different countries, with persons of different cultural levels, age, sex or socioeconomic background, scores have universal meaning.

Instruments such as these ought to be given emphasis, since they open new horizons in the field of measurement and individual differences.

REFERENCES

Coffman, W. E. (1963) Evidence of cultural factors in response of African students to items in an American test of scholastic aptitude. *20th yearbook, Nat. Coun. Measmt. Educ.* Pp. 27-37.

Cortada de Kohan, N. (1964) Construcción de un test de aptitud Verbal y Matemática 'Princeton'. *Arch. 4as Jornadas Uruguayas Psicol.* Montevideo: Univer. Uruguay Press. Pp. 33-43.

Cortada de Kohan, N. (1968a) Change of attitude towards statistics after objective testing. In K. H. Ingenkamp & T. Marsolek (Eds.), *Möglichkeiten und Grenzen der Testanwendung in der Schule.* Weinheim: Beltz. Pp. 853-859.

Cortada de Kohan, N. (1968b) *Manual para la construcción de tests objetivos de rendimiento.* Buenos Aires: Paidós.

Cortada de Kohan, N. (1969) Objective achievement testing: Need and difficulties for their use in Argentina. In J. A. Lauwerys & D. G. Scanlon (Eds.), *The world year book of education, 1969 (Examinations).* London: Evans. Pp. 198-202.

Locke, W. N. & Booth, A. D. (Eds.) (1955) *Machine translation of languages.* N.Y.: Wiley.

Mead, Margaret (1965) The future as the basis for establishing a shared culture. In G. Holton (Ed.), *Science and culture.* Boston: Houghton-Mifflin. Pp. 163-183.

Rimoldi, H. J. A. (1955) A technique for the study of problem solving. *Educ. psychol. Measmt., 15,* 450-461.

Rimoldi, H. J. A. (1963) A program for the study of thinking. *Bull. Intern. Assn Appl. Psychol., 12,* 22-50.

Rimoldi, H. J. A. (1967) Thinking and language. *Arch. gen. Psychiat., 17,* 568-576.

REFIA ŞEMIN

11

University of Istanbul

Why certain tasks from mental tests must be adapted whereas operational tasks need not

In order to clarify the matter of test adaptation, we propose to look at the tasks of the 1937 Stanford-Binet (SB) and the tasks of conservation of Piaget.

Let us consider first the SB. It is obvious that we cannot limit ourselves to translating tests for application in a culture other than the one for which they were constructed. It is necessary experimentally to determine the extent to which each task maintains its function in the new setting. For standardization purposes we have applied SB tasks to more than 1000 children of ages 5 to 18. We have come to realize that unless one alters some tasks the test will not perform the expected function. To set forth these changes and the underlying causes, we shall separate verbal from nonverbal tasks.

VERBAL TASKS

The vocabulary test was completely changed, as the Terman list contained many words that had no single Turkish word as counterpart. We prepared our own list and ordered the words on the basis of difficulty. Words such as 'dollar' and 'mile' were replaced by 'Turkish pound' and 'kilometer'.

The 'Problems of Fact' (L XIII) had to be changed. Terman has an Indian see a white boy riding a bicycle and say: 'The white boy is lazy; he walks sitting down.' This is not appropriate for

Istanbul children, perhaps because bicycles are too expensive to fall within their daily lives. In our version, '. . . the countryman sees a carriage going by itself and says, "Where are the horses? " '

In Verbal Absurdities (L IX) we had to replace Christopher Columbus and Spain, with Nasrettin Hoca (well-known in Turkey) and Istanbul.

Finding rhymes created a substantial difficulty, as Turkish is less rich in rhyming words than English. There are far fewer rhymes in our lullabies and children's songs than in the English ones. As for proverbs, it was quite easy to replace them with equivalent ones.

It is first of all necessary that the tasks be understood by the subjects. If the problem is posed in terms of elements that are unknown to subjects or foreign to their lives, no adequate response can be expected. If the Turkish language is poor in rhymes, how is the child to find the wanted rhyme? If the child does not know bicycles well, how is he to imagine the picture called up by the test?

NONVERBAL TASKS

Happily, the majority of the SB nonverbal tasks do serve with Turkish children. But items using pictures need to be adapted as much as the verbal ones. For example, Picture Vocabulary shows a telephone and a cowboy hat; we replaced them with the more commonplace sewing machine and sailboat. In the Patience Pictures (M III-6) the pig has been replaced by a sheep because Turks rarely use pork.

One Picture Absurdity item presents a countryman and his wife seated in the rain outside their house. In the SB picture, some Turkish children found the bonnet of the wife odd (as women of that age wear scarves in Turkey), and others found bizarre the feet of the rocking chair (rarely used in Turkey). These children could not grasp the scene when the elements in it were unknown to them. Our first thought was to present two peasant women, one knitting and the other smoking a narghile. But that did not work.

Children in Istanbul were not sufficiently familiar with peasant costume. Of 50 7 years olds, only 42 per cent responded correctly; and only 46 per cent at age 6. We turned, then, to the most commonplace forms of chairs and costumes. To the seated woman we gave a book to read and to the man a cigarette to smoke, in order to give an impression of relaxation. Then the majority of 7 year olds grasped the absurdity.

Another example is the man who holds his saw in a way improper for cutting wood. We do not cut wood in this manner and the costume of our workers differs from that in the SB. Changing the costume was not sufficient. The whole arrangement had to be revised to make it familiar: one piece of wood was placed against another, and an axe replaced the saw. In homes, an axe is used for cutting; the saw is employed only in workshops.

Other changes: The weighing machine (Absurdity, M VII) was changed to a Turkish form. Indians (unfamiliar) were replaced by bandits (Absurdity, L X). In Response to Pictures (L III-6) the postoffice was replaced by a market, the Dutch house was replaced by a Turkish house, and the river scene was revised to show a familiar boat and costume.

Whether a test employs words or pictures, any sign not universally known ought to be modified to use symbols relevant to the culture where the test is to be used. Consider the rocking-chair picture. The universal feature of a chair is that one can sit on it. But in certain countries it is used for rocking and then the feet are rounded; this is a sociocultural variation superimposed on the essential function. It is matters like this that we have tried to take into account.

The more a test uses symbols known to the majority of people, the more likely it is to be used everywhere. From this point of view, the conservation tasks of Piaget can be applied in various cultures without alteration. His tasks are physical experiments using plasticine, water, and so on. The SB, to be sure, includes items such as bead chain, maze, and concept of number which can be applied in our culture as well as the original, but other items − even nonverbal items − involve cultural elements. The conservation tasks, however, contain no sociocultural element.

SOCIAL-CLASS DIFFERENCES

We examined at greater length the nature of socioeconomic factors. Since Binet and Simon it has been recognized that the IQs of children from well-to-do families (A) average higher than those of the less well-to-do (B). Burt rightly reasoned that the poorer child's body is weakened, his capacity to learn impaired, and his experience with the world restricted. What is most important is the cultural atmosphere of the home. The poor parents do not stimulate the child to enrich his knowledge, so that he does not possess the mental images of objects that the tests expect. Let us take into consideration first the items where groups were equal: Memory for Sentences (L XI) and Repeating Digits Backward (M XII). There was also equality of performance on finding differences (M VI) and on Orientation (M A. A.). Only on Problems of Fact (L XIII) was Group B superior (53 per cent succeeding in Group A, 88 per cent in B). Group A was superior on the great majority of items, the largest differences being identified in Table 1. One sees differences particularly in absurdities, comprehension, and comparison tasks.

Table 1.   *Stanford-Binet items where children of higher SES do much better than others*

Task	Form, level	Percentage of success	
		High SES	Lower SES
Repeating digits	M S. A.	97	69
Similarities	L XI	88	36
Repeating thought	L S. A. II	77	42
Picture absurdities	L X	75	54
Verbal absurdities	L VIII	72	44
Verbal absurdities	M VIII	72	40
Verbal absurdities	L IX	36	16
Similarities and differences	M IX	32	12

There is some reduction in the difference between SES groups as children grow older (Table 2).

Table 2.   *Items where the superiority of high-SES children disappears with age*

Task	Form, level	Percentage of success		
		High SES	Lower SES	Differ-ence
Bead chain	L VI	64	32	32
	M XI	85	73	12
	L XIII	91	82	9
Paper cutting	L IX	40	20	20
	L XIII	72	56	16
	M A. A.	93	88	5
	L S. A. III	31	28	3
Opposite analogies	M VI	46	32	14
	M VIII	72	64	8
	M A. A.	98	96	2

The effect of schooling in causing socioeconomic effects to disappear is seen also in results with Piagetian tasks. A doctoral thesis of Belma Özbaydar on 500 children aged 4 to 11 indicates that the stages of thought are reached in the same order and at the same age as in Geneva — conservation of matter at 8 years, of weight at 9, and of volume at 11-12. Conservation of weight and volume seemed to be unrelated to social class. Only at age 8 was there a significant difference ($P < .01$) between a high-status and a low-status group.

This fact seems very important, as it gives us the key to solve the problem of children from less favorable settings. Since schooling causes the handicap imposed by family conditions to disappear, one should introduce socially regulated care at an early age, creating preschools where one can supply the experience the family does not.

One final remark must be made. For all the usefulness of tests in investigating the education of the retarded and the maladjusted, and for educational guidance, one still faces the question, 'Exactly what is it that the tests measure? '

SAM CHO

American Institutes for Research and
West African Examinations Council

12

Procedure for group test administration in developing countries*

Whereas in industrialized, test-sophisticated nations procedures for test administration have been conceived and implemented more or less to perfection, the situation is different in developing nations. The findings and observations described in this paper are based on direct experience gained in administering aptitude tests developed in West Africa by psychologists from the American Institutes for Research (AIR), and tried out in other countries by AIR staff and host-country counterparts.

Most of these tests were administered to examinees with primary- or middle-school education in experimental testing programs in which the examinees encountered multiple choice-type tests for the first time. In many developing countries, primary- and middle-school leavers make up the bulk of the technical, vocational, and semiskilled manpower pool. It is necessary to develop or adapt tests that can be used to sample ability of examinees who are not experienced in test taking. The methodology of test adaptation for use in developing nations was described by Biesheuvel (1952) and Schwarz (1961). The procedures to be followed in test administration in developing countries are for the most part not unique, however.

* The series of projects upon which this paper is based was planned and supervised by Paul A. Schwarz, who provided the author with suggestions and guidance during the writing of earlier versions of the manuscript. James G. Snider read the manuscript during the later stages of completion and made valuable suggestions.

FORMAT

Schwarz (1962) described test- and answer-sheet formats best suited for uneducated or primary-school subjects in Africa. The test- and answer-sheet should be stripped to essentials. For without test-experienced candidates, a simple integrated format requiring the examinees to mark the answer immediately beneath the correct alternative should be used. This integrated format was found to be satisfactory in Brazil, Korea, and Thailand for selecting trainees for various technical, vocational, or semi-skilled jobs. Integrated format was also found to be superior to separation of test booklet and answer-sheet in testing American third graders (Aleyideino, 1968).

The ability of examinees to follow instructions varies with educational level and with prior experience in test taking. For example, in Brazil, Korea, Thailand, and Anglophone West African countries, examinees at the upper-secondary level can cope with printed standardized test instructions in almost the exact form used in the United States of America. Elaborate instructions with visual aids, found necessary for the primary-school population in West Africa and elsewhere, led to restlessness, boredom, and inattention in the upper-secondary-school, according to Hill (1968).

In many countries the official language is the second language, not employed as the medium of instruction in the early primary grades. Thus, in testing primary-school-level examinees, it is necessary to translate the instructions into local tribal language. In a mixed group, a language common to all members (Pidgin in Anglophone West Africa) should be used. It should be noted that American usage of English is somewhat different from that of many Anglophone countries and hence American tests should be edited for local use.

A study was conducted on seventh-grade students by AIR's Thailand team to compare printed vs. spoken instructions, and integrated vs. separate answer sheets (Hill, 1968). The relative effectiveness of spoken or printed instructions depended on the type of test administered, the spoken instructions having a slight overall advantage. It was also found that integrated format yielded higher scores than the format which separated question and answer. The latter finding was confirmed in a Nigerian study in which a Verbal Analogies test was administered to a group of eighth graders (Akeju, 1971).

SECURITY

There is inadequate emphasis on test security in most measurement courses offered by universities. In most developing countries in which the outcome of a single examination may determine one's career for life, security precautions should be most carefully observed.

Precautions must be taken during item construction, printing, proofreading, storage, shipping, testing, scoring, and disposal. It is advisable to set aside a restricted area for the staff who are directly involved with handling test materials. Tests should be printed by bonded security printing firms, and all the plates, negatives, and rejected copies should be disposed or kept in secure storage. If possible, the printer should number the tests serially and package them in 50's or 100's; the packets should be sealed. If the seal is found to be broken, it may be assumed that the test papers have been leaked. If security has been broken an alternate form of the test has to be given.

It has been found useful to distribute booklets containing sample test items. Besides serving as a guide to the examinees the booklet can inform responsible administrators, shop foremen, general managers, the military commander, police chief, school principal, etc. about the testing program. The booklet can inform any observers who cannot be kept out of the testing room not to photograph test papers, not to stare at the examinees' papers, not to assist the examinees, not to take the test papers, and not to talk to examinees, proctors, or the test administrator.

PRELIMINARY ARRANGEMENTS

For many reasons it is desirable to have host-country nationals make preliminary arrangements and conduct test sessions. If there are no trained host-country nationals to administer tests, they must first be trained as thoroughly as time permits. The method and level of training should be tailored to suit local needs as there is considerable variability in prerequisite skills of the trainees within the nations as well as between various countries. In general the training should cover technical aspects of test research and development, security, and test-administration.

Whether testing is to be done at the administrative center of the testing organization or in the field, it may be necessary to obtain clearances from a government ministry (in most cases the Ministry of Education), military organization, or managing director of a firm. The responsible test administrator should arrange for suitable agencies to dispatch an official communication to state or provincial offices, local school authorities, local military commander, etc. indicating that testing is to take place and that the testing team should be provided with necessary logistic support (e.g., safe passage for the personnel and testing material). One must follow up to ensure that such communications have been dispatched. A copy of such an official communication should be taken to the field site.

The communication addressed to the authorities at the peripheral testing site should indicate the date, time, and scene of testing as well as the number of examinees to be tested, the number of proctors to be provided locally, and the physical and environmental support needed. In most cases it is necessary to have the local authority confirm in writing that this support will be provided. The confirmation letter should be taken to the field site. In some cases, confirmation may be made by telephone or telegram.

Provisions should be made to inform the examinees to report for testing. Notification may be made by local authorities or by testing center. The notification should indicate, if applicable, the following items of information: eligibility, purpose of test, brief description of tests with sample questions and answers, procedures for registration, date, time and place of examination, registration card and other identity papers to bring, method of payment, issuance of results, and a brief explanation of test scores.

An advance-man should arrive at the field site to see that local arrangements are satisfactory. He should ensure that the examinees will be available for testing, provide a briefing session to the local authorities, and if necessary, train the local proctors. He should also ensure that minimum standards for testing are met.

Testing should be conducted indoors if at all possible since inclement weather may (and often does) disrupt testing sessions. The proctors should be instructed to control whispering and talking among the examinees. The recess periods for the adjacent classes or the workers' rest periods may be a source of distraction. Control of such extraneous noises should be the duty of the school administrator, shop manager, or the like. An alternate procedure is to arrange the examinees' rest periods to coincide with recess periods of adjacent classes or workers' rest periods. The examinees should be provided with adequate work space. The minimum work space required may be a lecture-room chair with a small deskarm on which the answer sheet may be filled out. If there are no chairs, a clip-board or the like may be substituted. It is necessary to provide sufficient separation between examinees to prevent copying. Adequate illumination should be provided. Well placed 'hurricane lamps' are preferable to the candles if a session has to be conducted at night. If at all possible, testing sessions should be conducted during the daylight hours.

TESTING SESSION

The testing session should be directed by a test administrator who is thoroughly trained with respect to the examiner's manual, instructions, supervision of the proctors, time limits, security, and coordination with local administrators.

It may be necessary in some cases to check a registration card with the bearer's identity. This can be done before candidates enter the testing room. Candidates should be told to use the toilet before they enter the examination room. If the session is unduly long, rest periods should be provided.

After the examinees are seated, they should be counted, and warned not to make any marks on test papers and answer sheets to be distributed. Then test papers, answer sheets, and pencils are distributed. Each proctor is responsible for distributing and collecting test materials in his assigned area. The examinees are then instructed to provide identification data (e.g., center name/code, school, grade, factory, age, etc.). The proctors should verify information filled in.

The main testing then begins. The procedure for administering each test should be specified in the examiner's manual. The manual should also provide information required for scoring and interpreting tests as well as instructions for test security, time limits, setting up visual aids, demonstration and practice trials, and proctoring.

During the test session the test administrator instructs his proctors to monitor and control examinees' performance as specified by the test publisher. For example, if a battery of tests is to be administered the proctors should ensure that the examinees are working on the correct test, and if tests are timed, the proctors should ensure that the examinees do not attempt to complete preceding tests or proceed to a later test.

After the testing session, all test materials should be accounted for. If test booklets are to be re-used, a page count must be made before examinees leave the room.

REFERENCES

Akeju, S. A. (1971) Recording aptitude test responses on separate answer sheets in Nigeria. Lagos: West African Examinations Council, TEDRO Research Report.
Aleyideino, S. C. (1968) Effects of response method and item type on the working time scores and grade equivalent scores of high and low achieving third graders. Unpublished doctoral dissertation, Univer. of Iowa.
Biesheuvel, S. (1952) The study of African ability. *Afr. Stud., 11,* 18-22.
Hill, A. H. (1968) Research and development of aptitude testing: Thailand country report. Pittsburgh: Amer. Inst. for Res.
Jones, D. H., & Cho, S. (1968) The project in Korea: country report. Pittsburgh: Amer. Inst. for Res.
Schwarz, P. A. (1961) Aptitude tests for use in the developing nations. Pittsburgh: Amer. Inst. for Res.
Schwarz, P. A. (1963) Adapting tests to the cultural setting. *Educ. psychol. Measmt., 13,* 673-686.

Three handbooks on crosscultural testing

One session of the conference provided a review or preview, plus discussion, of three handbooks designed to serve testers. Biesheuvel discussed the 1969 handbook produced for the International Biological Program (IBP), Johnson a handbook soon to be published on the basis of experience in Malawi and other countries, and Cieutat a handbook prepared by Schwartz, Krug, and others from the staff of the American Institutes for Research, also soon to be published.

Biesheuvel, S. (Ed.) (1969) *Methods for the measurement of psychological performances*. (I.B.P. Handbook No. 10). Oxford: Blackwell.
Johnson, R. T. (1971) *Conducting large-scale examinations: A handbook*. Limbe, Malawi: the author (P.O. Box 5759).
Schwartz, P.A. & Krug, R.E. (1972) *Ability tests and cultural factors: A handbook of principles and techniques*. New York: Praeger (in preparation).

IBP sponsors a research program on human adaptability, including studies of nutrition, human genetics, etc. The projects need psychological tests for use as control variables or as dependent variables. It is hoped that data from projects around the world will be comparable, and therefore a committee was asked to identify certain tests for this purpose. The IBP handboek (Biesheuvel, 1969) outlines procedural suggestions, precautions, and conditions under which tests can be used crossculturally, addressing itself to investigators not experienced in psychological work. Recommendations regarding sampling, and on reporting of information on habitat, procedures, and results, etc. are made. To provide supplementary data on acculturation, a Modernity scale adapted from Smith and Inkeles is included. The first area of testing, psychophysiology, is especially important to IBP. The working group suggested collecting EEG data for interpretation with respect to brain damage, arousal, and neural maturity; finger plethysmograms, interpretable with respect to temperamental lability and affective tension; PGR measures, again interpreted from the viewpoints of temperament and arousal; and cardiotachometric measures.

The psychomotor category could often be studied by observation in a natural or slightly contrived setting, but laboratory procedures to study the following were also put into a standard form and recommended: hand grip, finger dexterity, throwing skill, handedness, balancing, and two-hand coordination.

Perception, having to do with awareness of the environment, is clearly important in biosocial research. Primary-process measures suggested were of visual acuity, auditory acuity, color vision, and tactile discrimination. At a higher level, data on adaptive integration, particularly intersensory transfer and degree of interpenetration of sensory modalities, were desired. Tests recommended are Birch's Intersensory Modality test, Embedded Figures, Rod-and-Frame, and Geometric Illusions. For more highly developed perceptual functions, the form-perception tests of NIPR and Ord's Observation test (after Kim's game), and Elithorn's Perceptual Maze were recommended. Tests of time perception could not be recommended as the procedures are not standardized to an adequate degree.

Agreement on tests for higher mental processes was not easily obtained. The handbook stresses precautions needed in interpretation. To test general ability or general adaptability the group compromised on Progressive Matrices, with procedural suggestions derived from Irvine's experience. Ord's Design Construction (after Kohs) was second choice. Alternates recommended: Porteus Mazes, Shipley Abstraction, NIPR Form Series, Elithorn's Perceptual Maze. No specific tests with verbal content were recommended because of the requirement that tests fit the local setting. For mechanical-technical, clerical, and vocational aptitudes, the GAB of NIPR and the battery developed by the American Institutes of Research were suggested.

The last-named set of tests was at the center of the work on which the AIR handbook (Schwartz & Krug, 1971) is based. Cieutat described to the conference the history of AIR work in foreign nations since 1950. The first step was the development of a battery of tests in Nigeria which was then evaluated, refined, and extended as it was applied in other countries. The so-called ID Battery of 21 tests has been used and validated in Brazil, Korea, Thailand, Iran, Micronesia, and various African nations.

The handbook is to a large degree concerned with the movement from test development to test application, emphasizing the building of institutions to administer tests and install testing programs, and the development of programs for use in decision making. The working titles of the nine chapters of the handbook are as follows: The importance of 'cultural' factors in testing; testing reform as an investment; the abilities to be measured; the design of suitable tests; the design of effective testing procedures; The ID aptitude tests; development of operational testing programs; the feasibility of a centralized institution for testing; organization and operating procedures.

The handbook described by Johnson seeks to fill in the multitude of details that make the difference between success and failure in a large-scale program where examinees are competing for place and utmost fairness and accuracy are desired. In a developing country there may be 20,000 applications for 100 places in a new college. Traditional selection methods break down, and even where they can be carried out, they are often unjust. Objective testing, combined with traditional sources of data, has been shown to greatly increase the proportion of superior achievers admitted.

The handbook is based, not on experience where tests are well established but on experience in developing countries of the Pacific and in Western and Southern Africa, where special requirements have to be met. This kind of knowledge is not generally available except by word-of-mouth; the handbook systematizes recommendations for making a testing program work.

The chapters cover the following matters: publicity, registration, item preparation, pretesting, editing, reproduction, distribution of tests and administration, scoring, data processing and reporting, overall security, and costs. Specific models of item-analysis technique, a register for stores of testing materials, and instructions to item writers, for example, are provided.

L.J.C.

P.J.D.D.

Note: *Biesheuvel pointed to the value of systematic testing by citing the remark of an Army colonel in an African nation who described how he handled a flood of 20,000 would-be soldiers. First, he said, we send home all the tall ones and all the short ones; that reduced the problem of outfitting the men. Then we look at them and send home all those who look bloody silly. That makes the group small enough to test.*

A controversy developed around the decision of IBP not to recommend a reading comprehension test, which Ortar thought provided important data on verbal development. It was Biesheuvel's view that for IBP purposes such a test could not be rendered standard enough when revised in various languages; but Ortar pointed to the success of the International Study of Educational Achievement in making comparable reading tests. Turgut was uncertain whether a general reading measure is of great value even in scholastic prediction. Reading content drawn from a specific school subject seemed in his Turkish work to predict success in that subject, but a general reading test was a less useful predictor than vocabulary. (Eds.)

S. S. A. AKEJU   14
West African Examinations Council

Attitude to multiple-choice tests in West Africa*

Examinations have both social and educational importance in Anglophone West Africa, where entry into various aspects of life depends directly or indirectly on one's success in examinations. These important examinations are usually provided by the West African Examinations Council (WAEC). The WAEC was created by statute in 1953 (i) to review and consider annually, the examinations to be held in West Africa for the purpose of furthering the public interest in West Africa, and (ii) to conduct such examinations as the council may think appropriate to the purposes of this Act and to award certificates and diplomas on the results on the examinations so conducted.

Since the early 1960's, the Council has been faced with the need to improve testing techniques and to cope with an ever-increasing numbers of candidates. One effort to improve techniques and to cope with large numbers of candidates resulted in the introduction of structured response (multiple-choice) questions to supplement essay-type questions in some examinations which WAEC develops.

Objective testing was first introduced in 1966 at the West African School Certificate Examination (WASCE) level. This was done only after preliminary investigations had established the usefulness of the technique and ascertained that it was 'at least as valid, if not more so, than the essay tests' (Laryea & Cieutat,

* Suggestions of B. Axtell, Sam Cho, A.I. Fiks, and J.G. Snider are acknowledged.

1968). This occurred despite doubts by students and teachers who were used to essay testing and who were suspicious of what they described as 'an American importation'. The WASCE itself is perhaps the single most important examination in West Africa. The results are a measure of an individual's success or failure at the end of secondary-school education; they usually determine who will obtain jobs; and they identify those likely to be accepted for further education.

The multiple-choice technique has now been used for five years; it is conceivable that the technique has affected many aspects of education such as teaching methods and study habits, and that the educational community has altered its unfavorable attitude. This study was planned to ascertain the present attitude of members of the community regarding the technique. It was expected that the finding would provide feedback to the Test Development Office of WAEC concerning its test-building efforts. A study of attitudes regarding multiple-choice tests was considered worthwhile, for its implications with regard to the continued use of the technique by WAEC and the future of mental testing in West Africa.

The specific purposes of the study were to develop an attitude questionnaire, to determine the proportion of the population expressing a favorable attitude to the multiple-choice technique, and to determine the relation of this attitude to sex and academic standing.

METHOD

Questionnaire development

Since no measure satisfying the specific requirements of the study was available, a Likert-type attitude questionnaire was developed for measuring attitude toward objective testing. The first-year degree and postgraduate diploma students in educational psychology at the University of Lagos were invited to make statements about objective testing.

About 100 statements were collected; 40 remained after the

editing. Officials of WAEC known to have favorable attitudes to multiple-choice tests were invited to comment on the 40 statements in terms of their relevance and asked to judge the polarity (favorable or unfavorable) of the items. Their comments were used to place the items into positive and negative categories and as evidence of face validity. The items were pretested on a group consisting of young graduates undergoing a summer course in Tests and Measurement at WAEC, together with certain senior staff of WAEC. Their responses were scored and the 19 items with the highest point-biserial coefficients were retained in the questionnaire (Table 1).

Table 1. Items retained in the questionnaire

Multiple-choice (objective) tests

---

1. should be used only in lower classes
2. ensure a coverage of all aspects of the syllabus
3. are very dependable
4. should be encouraged
5. are easy to mark
6. should be abandoned completely
7. quicken the release of examination results
8. should be used only along with essay-type test
9. should be used for testing mathematics
10. should be enforced throughout our schools
11. should be used right from primary one
12. should be used in promotion exercises
13. constitute an excellent technique of testing
14. should be used as a basis for awarding certificates
15. provide the best method to test a large group of students
16. are suitable for testing languages
17. are strongly recommended
18. must be used only sparingly
19. do encourage creative thinking

Pilot study

The 19-item questionnaire was administered to 225 students (138 males, 87 females) of Adeyemi College of Education at

Ondo, Nigeria to establish reliability and homogeneity. The responses 'strongly agree', 'agree', 'undecided', 'disagree', and 'strongly disagree' were assigned 5, 4, 3, 2, and 1 points, respectively, for favorable statements, and 1, 2, 3, 4, and 5 for unfavorable statements. An omitted response was scored as undecided.

The alpha reliability coefficient was 0.81. The item-questionnaire correlations, ranging from 0.20 to 0.74, were taken as high enough to indicate that 'the questionnaire consisted of stimuli of the same general class, the responses to which were assumed to have covaried because they were mediated by the same hypothetical variable' (Green, 1954, p. 335).*

Table 2 gives the percentage of the sample falling at each of five score levels, with higher scores indicating more favorable attitudes towards objective testing. A consistent response of 'undecided' would produce a score of 57. The majority of the pilot sample expressed favorable attitudes.

Table 2. Percentage of each sex falling in each score category (pilot study)

Score	Males (N = 138)	Females (N = 87)	Total (N = 225)
85 – 95	2.12	1.14	1.75
74 – 84	29.08	17.25	24.56
63 – 73	35.46	32.33	34.65
52 – 62	22.70	36.78	28.07
41 – 51	8.51	11.50	9.65

The most favorable attitude score attainable is 95; the lowest is 19.

Main study

For the main study, subjects were selected on sex and academic advancement, in a 2x2 factorial design. Two levels of academic

* Note: *Perhaps it is better only to say that an adequately large sample of the class of items has been drawn. The coefficients reported do not give evidence on the factorial complexity or causation of these attitudes.* (Eds.)

advancement – end of secondary school and second-year of university – were considered. Accordingly, 80 girls and 80 boys were randomly selected from the two top classes of five randomly selected Lagos secondary schools (two boys' schools, two girls' schools and one coeducational school). 80 men and 80 women were selected from among the education students of Lagos University. The study was limited to the Lagos urban area.

The attitude questionnaire was administered to the 320 *S*s and scores were subjected to two-way analysis of variance (mixed model) using the interaction sum of squares as the error term for sex and academic advancement. The mean and standard deviation of the item-scale correlations for each subsample were also computed.

RESULTS AND DISCUSSION

70.4 per cent of the total group were favorable, scoring 63 or above on the attitude scale. The percentage was 77.7 for secondary-school boys, 85.0 for secondary-school girls, 67.5 for university men, and 51.2 for university women.

Means and standard deviations are presented in Table 3. There was a significant effect for academic achievement and a significant interaction of sex with advancement (Table 4).

Table 3. Means and standard deviations of scores of subjects classified by educational level and sex

	N	Mean	s.d.
University level			
Males	80	66.8	11.77
Females	80	63.0	9.66
Secondary level			
Males	80	69.3	9.64
Females	80	70.2	8.33

Table 4. Analysis of variance for the classification variables

Source	df	MS	F
Sex	1	172.58	0.38
Academic advancement	1	1896.38	22.62*
Interaction	1	453.63	5.41*
Within cell	316	83.62	
Total	319		

*$P < .05$

The evidence did not support the presence of a sex effect on attitude at either level of academic advancement. In the present sample, the attitudes of male and female students were not dissimilar. This is contrary to findings of a sex difference in attitude (Berk, Rose, & Stewart, 1970). Students in secondary school reacted more favorably to objective testing than did university students. This effect is especially marked among females.

The university students, by virtue of their longer years at school, could be assumed to be more familiar with and more knowledgeable about objective testing. The finding that they expressed a less favorable attitude suggests that the measured variable may have a cognitive dimension. One wonders whether attitude to objective testing in West Africa becomes increasingly unfavorable as the educational level of Ss rises. Are university teachers and other intellectuals, for example, more opposed to objective tests than their students? An alternative explanation for the less favorable attitude expressed by the academically advanced Ss is that they, having experienced traditional tests for so long, are more conditioned to them and consequently less receptive than secondary-school students to the new multiple-choice technique.

A higher proportion in the main sample was favorable than in the pilot sample. This apparently resulted from the inclusion of secondary-school students, who were generally more favorable.

The present study did not provide conclusive evidence relating to the causation of attitudes. It is concluded that attitude to multiple-choice (objective) tests was generally favorable at the time of study, and that the more highly educated persons tended to be less favorably disposed towards objective testing than the less educated.

REFERENCES

Berk, L. E., Marion, H. R. & Steward, D. (1970) Attitudes of English and American children toward their school experience. *J. educ. Psychol., 61*, 33-40.

Green, B. F. (1954) Attitude measurement. In G. Lindzey (Ed.), *Handbook of social psychology.* Vol. 1: Theory and method (1st ed.) Reading, Mass.: Addison-Wesley. Pp. 335-369.

Laryea, E. B. & Cieutat, V. J. (1968) Comparative validity of objective and essay tests at the G.C.E. Ordinary level. Yaba, Nigeria: Tedro. Unpublished report.

Haçettepe University, Ankara

Instructions as determinants of performance: the effect of information about the task*

INSTRUCTIONS AS 'INFORMATION'

Bruner (1964), Bourne (1968) and others view the performing organism as operating actively on the information supplied by the environment; this action depends upon the techniques and strategies of the individual rather than upon his ability alone. Ludvigson and Caul (1967) claim that '. . . the response is like the response to instructions alone', and not to the problem itself. Motivation theorists such as J.W. Atkinson suggest that instructions help Ss to organize their efforts, and affect different individuals to various degrees.

In accordance with these new views, decision theorists suggest that individuals do not always perform a task according to the rational requirements of an objective situation as defined by the experimenter; rather, they make decisions in accordance with the stimulus environment. In many problem-solving experiments and in mental testing in particular, standard instructions are thought to control the behavior of all individuals equally. It is usually forgotten that each individual selects certain features of the stimuli which appear relevant to his action. It might, therefore, be agreed that it is the emphasis of instructions on certain aspects of the experiment and the ambiguity of communication that

---

* This study is part of a thesis presented to Nottingham University, England, in fulfilment of the requirement for the degree of Doctor of Philosophy.

make some individuals, but not others, catch the experimenter's intentions.

It may be assumed that goal setting elicits search behavior which will determine the amount of effort extended. A rational problem solver should allocate effort so as to maximize his expected success, weighting each goal appropriately. It may further be assumed that the rate of approach to the task varies according to the attributes of the goal object for the individual.

Stedry (1960) finds that results in problem solving vary with the perceived difficulty of the problem; those who see the problem as difficult do better than those who regard the problem as easy. Charnes & Stedry (1964) postulate that problems perceived as more difficult will receive more effort than those perceived as easy.

Since personal pacing and perception of stimuli are subject to external influence and particularly to incitement, the performances of individuals may be affected differently, depending on the type of external influence. One may, then, assume that some variations in performance are caused by variations in the way individuals identify the task to be performed. The response one makes would then not be the result solely of his wired-in-ability, but rather would in part result from his interpretation of the task.

Studies of level of aspiration as well as those of decision-making rely mainly on the fact that a person's behavior will be strongly related to his past experience and his consequent expectations. The study of environmental and conceptual complexity, which are presumed to interact, may provide information about the cognitive structure of the organism. It is argued that stimulus-poor environments contain too little information to warrant complex processing, whereas complex environments contain too much information to be processed.

It is the contention of this study that instructions to S determine his attitude to the task. That is to say, performance is determined not only by the content of the task, but also by S's interpretation of the task, by his perception of outcomes, and by his experience of incentives and risks involved in making decisions.

EXPERIMENT I: PROCEDURE

*S*s were 13-14-year-old schoolchildren. On the basis of a socio-economic questionnaire which obtained information concerning the father's occupation, number of books in the home, rooms per person, holiday travel abroad, and selected home properties, two groups were identified: The Extended Experience (EE) group came from 'intellectually stimulating homes', and the Restricted Experience (RE) group came from 'intellectually less-stimulating homes'.

The *S*s of each SES level were randomly assigned into three experimental groups. In Condition A, *S* was asked only to indicate the correct answer. There were 36 EE and 29 RE *S*s in this condition. In Condition B, *S* was to give the answer he thought correct and to indicate his confidence on a 5-point scale. 37 EE and 18 RE *S*s were in this condition. In Condition C, *S* was given objective information about how difficult each problem was, and was also required to indicate his confidence in his answer. There were 34 EE and 25 RE *S*s in this condition.

The task was a set of 31 multiple-choice problems, similar to usual mental-test items. Among these, 18 were selected as 'object items' to form stimulus sets. On the basis of the objective 'standardization' data, .6 problems (solved by 20-35 per cent) were selected as 'difficult', 6 (solved by 45-60 per cent) as 'moderate', and 6 (solved by 70-85 per cent) as 'easy'.

The problems were given to 15-20 *S*s at a time. There was no time limit, but *S*s were told to hand in their papers as soon as they finished.

EXPERIMENT I: RESULTS

Mean percentages correct were 59, 58, and 62 for conditions A, B, and C, respectively. The difference between the three experimental groups is far from significant. This appears to be the case at all levels of difficulty.

Table 1. *Percentage of correct responses in groups with different*
experience under three conditions

Stimulus set	Experience of Ss	Percentage correct		
		Condition A (uninformed)	Condition B (uninformed)	Condition C (informed)
Difficult	EE	34	37	34
	RE	33	30	44
Moderate	EE	73	69	72
	RE	68	57	71
Easy	EE	87	86	88
	RE	83	82	92
All problems	EE	61	60	61
	RE	57	53	63

Table 1 shows proportions correct in the EE and RE groups as a function of experimental conditions for each stimulus set. Changes as a function of conditions arise mainly among RE Ss. The performance of EE Ss does not vary much with experimental conditions.

Mann-Whitney U tests reveal that, considering all problems, the EE Ss are significantly higher than RE Ss in Condition B ($P < .05$). In Condition A there is a nonsignificant advantage for EE Ss and there is a nonsignificant advantage for RE Ss in Condition C. According to a Kruskal-Wallis test based on one-way analysis of variance, the EE Ss performed equally well in all three conditions, whereas the performances of RE Ss fluctuated significantly from one condition to another ($P < .10$).

The RE Ss performed best in Condition C where they were supplied with information, and worst in Condition B where they were not given information, but were required to make confidence judgments. By a Mann-Whitney U test the difference between Conditions A and B for RE Ss had a probability level $P < .20$; for A and C, $P < .20$; and for B and C, $P < .01$ (all two-tailed). An analysis of variance indicates that the difference between the conditions and the interaction between backgrounds and experimental conditions were significant ($P < .05$ for both). Under Condition C the RE group seem to have performed better than the EE group on the hard and easy problems, but not on the intermediate problems. The respective differences have probabilities of 0.14, 0.42, and 0.78 of having arisen by chance. Condition B is considered 'uninformed' and Condition C 'informed'. The EE group performed better than the RE group when uninformed, but the latter performed better than the former when informed. Information improved the performance of RE Ss significantly ($P < .05$, Mann-Whitney U test), whereas there is a nonsignificant decline in performance for EE Ss with the presence of information. An analysis of variance reveals that the difference between the informed and uninformed groups on various stimulus sets is highly significant ($P < .01$) and that a significant interaction ($P < .05$) may be attributed to the backgrounds of the Ss.

In their confidence ratings the EE Ss were more accurate than the RE Ss under the 'uninformed' Condition (B) whereas the situation was reversed under the 'informed' Condition (C). The accuracy of the EE Ss in Condition B was most superior with the difficult problems, and the least difference was seen with the intermediate problems. The superior accuracy of the RE Ss in Condition C followed a similar pattern. Very strong linear trends are exhibited by both SES groups under all conditions. This is more apparent in the EE group ($F = 113.5$, $df = 1,180$) than in the RE group ($F = 82.9$, $df = 1,85$) under Condition B; whereas it is more apparent in the RE group ($F = 62.3$, $df = 1,73$) than in the EE group ($F = 34.9$, $df = 1,99$) under Condition C.

DISCUSSION AND A FURTHER EXPERIMENT

There are considerable differences between the two groups. The RE Ss improved when supplied with information, both relative to performance in other conditions and to the performance of the EE Ss. The improvement is far greater than appears in the statistical comparisons. Their performances were much hampered when they were required to make confidence judgments, but they recovered significantly when making confidence judgments after receiving information about the task. Even so, performance may have been somewhat hampered in Condition C, which employed confidence rating. It seemed likely that the improvement in the performances of RE Ss would have been even greater under Condition C had they not been asked to make a confidence rating. To test the effect of information only, without confidence ratings, another experiment was carried out.

Experiment II was carried out with the same Ss who had already served in Condition C, the informed group. The task was a set of 31 problems (Set 2), parallel to Set 1. Instructions were essentially the same as those given in Condition C, except for the directions calling for ratings of confidence.

EXPERIMENT II: RESULTS

The EE and RE groups averaged 52 per cent and 59 per cent respectively. The difference is significant ($P < .05$, one-tailed Mann-Whitney U test). For the stimulus sets separately, the relations were similar but the differences were not significant.

Spearman rank correlations between the performance in Condition C and in Experiment 2 were as follows: for the total group (EE and RE Ss combined) 0.72, for the EE group 0.81, and for the RE group 0.59. This suggests that whereas the performances of the EE Ss did not change much, those of the RE Ss underwent a considerable change when not asked to make confidence judgments.

DISCUSSION

It is fairly well established that so-called working-class children perform poorly in solving conceptual problems. Some explain this in terms of environmental handicaps whereas others attribute it to genetic factors.

When the usual testing condition was employed, such performance differences between the two groups of different background were observed in this study too. But the finding was almost reversed when Ss were supplied with some information about the difficulty of the task to be performed. The information presumably helped RE *S*s to 'identify' the task and to set their goals. This may have helped them to allocate their efforts realistically, that is, in accordance with the type of problem. It would appear that some children might be unable to assess the difficulty of tasks, and their failure on some problems might be caused by this. Another interesting feature of the results is that, in the case of Condition C, the superiority of the RE group over the EE group was even greater in the case of difficult problems. This result is in contrast with some evidence (Harvey et al., 1961; Sieber & Lanzetta, 1964; Scott, 1965) that lower-class children perform better on easy tasks which may be described as 'concrete', whereas middle-class children become more effective as the items become more 'abstract'.

The main findings of this study reject the commonly held belief that, for all practical purposes, instructions to *S*s provide an adequate control of motivational and mental set. The ability of an individual to solve problems is not free from the situational demands, nor from his perception of the costs and rewards of his action.

This leads to an assertion that a performance in a certain situation may not be a *sample* performance of an individual, for what we are dealing with is not his wired-in ability, but rather his reaction to a situation which is not at all stable. It is meaningless to talk of a wired-in ability when performance varies up and down, depending on the conditions and type of task.

In addition, the provocative conclusion can be suggested that the general orientations and cultural backgrounds of respondents account for more variability in choice behavior than the more traditional ability and personality traits. Further, the interaction between cultural background and experimental setting seems to vary considerably, which prevents one from making clear-cut generalizations about the nature of the interaction.

REFERENCES

Bourne, L. E. (1968) Concept attainment. In T. Dixon & D. Horton (Eds.), *Verbal behavior and general behavior theory.* Englewood Cliffs, N.J.: Prentice-Hall. Pp. 230-253.

Bruner, J.S. (1964) The course of cognitive growth. *Amer. Psychologist, 19*, 1-15.

Charnes, A., & Stedry, A.C. (1964) Exploratory models in the theory of budgetary control. In W.W. Cooper, H.J. Leavitt, & M.W. Shelly (Eds.), *New perspectives in organization research.* New York: Wiley.

Gitmez, A. S. (1969) Problem solving as choice behaviour. Unpublished doctoral thesis, Nottingham Univer.

Harvey, O. J., Hunt, D. E., & Schroder, H. H. (1961) *Conceptual systems and personality development.* New York: Wiley.

Ludvigson, H. W., & Caul, W. F. (1967) Spatial generalization as a function of variation in a non-spatial attribute, instructions, and individual strategies. *Amer. J. Psychol., 80*, 186-195.

Scott, R. (1965) Social-class correlates of selected cognitive functions. *Psychol. Rep., 17*, 63-68.

Sieber, J., & Lanzetta, J. (1964) Conflict and conceptual structure as determinants of decision-making behavior. *J. Pers., 32*, 622-641.

Stedry, A. C. (1960) *Budget control and cost behavior.* Englewood Cliffs, N. J.: Prentice-Hall.

Stedry, A. C., & Kay, E. (1966) The effects of goal difficulty on performance: a field experiment. *Behav. Sci., 11*, 459-470.

PAUL F. COOK and MATLAPENG RAY MOLOMO   16
Regional Testing Resource and Training Center, Gaborone

Effects of incentives on the test-taking behavior of Botswana primary-school children*

One factor affecting test validity is what a particular culture values. The relationship between incentives and values is a close one in that a person will work for an incentive if he values it. A prodigious amount of research is currently progressing in American classrooms under such labels as behavior modification, precision teaching, and behaviorally engineered environments. Incentives are systematically applied in an attempt to improve classroom learning of both typical students and those in special education (Jung & Lipa, 1970). It has been demonstrated quite conclusively that incentives can influence learning.

If incentives can influence the learning of children, can they also influence test performance by inducing greater effort? It was the purpose of this study to determine the effects of certain incentives on the performance of Botswana primary-school children on a verbal ability test and a speed test requiring simple repetitive performance. For this paper it was decided to identify some of the implications of the findings for other developing nations in meeting manpower requirements or in applying standardized tests crossculturally.

* The study was conducted by staff members of the Regional Testing Resource and Training Center which is the result of an agreement among Malawi, Botswana, Lesotho and Swaziland; it is supported by the U.S. Agency for International Development. The work is carried out under contract by the American Institutes for Research. The opinions expressed herein do not necessarily reflect the position or policy of USAID or AIR, but are those of the authors.

Another question is: Are children motivated to do well on tests in all cultures? If not, then conceivably scores on ability or achievement tests could be raised if examinees could be rewarded for applying themselves on the tests. In industrial societies such as the USA, most middle-class school children and university students are not only testwise, but they are usually motivated to succeed in test situations. The exception to this may be with what are termed 'culturally deprived' students who likely gain their self-respect through satisfactory relations with classmates outside of school rather than in school achievement. Reviewing the literature, Cronbach (1970, p. 61) concluded that where children are motivated to perform well on tests through a desire to maintain self-respect and the respect of other, test scores are not readily altered by simple incentives such as prizes, pep talks, and monetary payments for increases in scores. It is not clear whether incentives affect speed and power tests in the same way. In one study with black mine workers in South Africa (van der Walt, 1952) subjects performed faster on a Two-Hand Coordination Test under simple incentive conditions, but they made more mistakes than persons not offered incentives.

METHOD

Subjects

The Ss of this study came from Gaborone, the 6-year-old capital city of Botswana. Since the primary school Ss are attending has a 7-year course, all of them must have begun their primary schooling outside Gaborone, before the town was established. They started schooling in rural villages, and the sample therefore provides a relatively good cross-section of both rural and urban Botswana backgrounds.

The schools in the study were the Bontleng, Lesedi, and Camp primary schools. The pupils of Bontleng suffer some amount of deprivation although the school could be classified as semiurban. Lesidi is situated within the city and its people are somewhat better off than in Bontleng. Camp School is situated about

2 miles out, and the parents are similar in social class to those of Lesedi. There were, in all, 168 Ss, 84 males and 84 females with ages ranging from 11 to 15.

Incentives

Incentives expected to have strong influence on the Botswana children, as well as ones powerful in Western cultures, were used. Two kinds of competition were utilized, tribal pride and boy-vs.-girl. No tribal member would like to know that members of other tribes have achieved more than he or his tribal group. Similarly, a Botswana man will not allow a woman to do better than he. Consequently, women do not exert themselves very much in competition against men. A third incentive was knowledge of results. This incentive is used universally and has proven to be very effective: it is the main incentive in programmed-learning devices, for example. Our Ss were promised that they would find out how well they did on the tests immediately after they took them. A fourth incentive was material incentives. Ss were promised a Rand note ($ 1.41 US) if they performed at a specific high criterion level, and their choice among packages of candy, sweets, nuts and potato chips if they performed at a lower criterion level. The fifth incentive, vicarious reinforcement, was introduced by bringing a child who had excelled in a previous testing and praising him lavishly. After this was done, Ss were asked if they thought any of their group could do as well. Lastly, as punishment is often used by teachers to motivate children, it was decided to use an aversive consequence for poor performance. The Ss were told that anyone who failed to reach a specified level of performance would have his name placed on the blackboard for all to see. (This threat was not carried out.)

Instruments

Two tests were chosen from the ID Series (Schwartz, 1961) for use in the study. The ID Tests are aptitude tests specifically designed for use in Africa.

The first test is called Verbal Analogies Lower. It is a verbal reasoning test for people with 6 to 8 years of formal education. A representative question is: *Mark one of the five alternative words that best completes the following analogy. Air and bird, water and . . .* The examinee must choose among *fish, man, cow, monkey,* and *pig.* The test is used to predict success in school or in a job requiring formal studies. It is a 30-minute power test; most examinees complete it. It contains 8 sample problems, 6 practice problems, and 40 test problems. The Kuder-Richardson reliability is 0.87 for 374 boys and 0.86 for 58 girls. Secondary-school entrance-test scores correlated 0.45 with scores on the Verbal Analogies Lower Test of 58 boys in their last year of primary school.

The Marking Test is a test of speed in a simple repetitive task. It is intended for the selection of operatives and other semiskilled personnel. This task instruction is: *Mark a letter X inside each box. Do as many as you can in the allotted time.* There are 300 boxes to be marked during the test. The total time to administer the test is 15 minutes, including time for practice items. Test-retest reliability for the Marking Test for 44 girls at the end of primary school was 0.87. There are no data on validity.

Procedure

All *S*s were tested in the same room, a Standard VII classroom at Lesedi School, by the same examiner. *S*s were randomly assigned to groups for testing. Seven separate groups of 24 *S*s (12 male and 12 female) were administered the two tests, the Marking Test being followed by Verbal Analogies Lower. Testing took place in the afternoons of three consecutive days. The control group, the first group to be tested, was tested under standard conditions. Each of the following groups was tested under an experimental incentive condition.

The following is an example of the incentive instructions which were read to the *S*s between the practice questions and the actual test.

Who is better at thinking — boys or girls? *(Wait for response.)* Some think the boys are better and some the girls. Who is really the best? *(Wait for response.)* We are now going to give you a test in thinking to find out who is better, boys or girls. Up at the front of the room we have a chart, can you see it? *(Wait for response.)* After you have taken the test we will put your marks on the chart. If you are a boy your mark will go under boys and if you are a girl your mark will go under girls. The group who has the highest average mark will win. Do you understand? *(Wait for response.)* Remember, how your group does will depend on how well you do. Alright, you may begin.

HYPOTHESES AND RESULTS

The following null hypotheses apply to both tests:
There is no significant difference between the control group and any experimental treatment group.
There is no significant difference between males and females within treatment.
There is no significant interaction between treatment and sex.

Table 1. Means of treatment groups, by sex

Group	Verbal analogies test			Marking test		
	Male	Female	Total	Male	Female	Total
Control	14.25	17.25	15.75	210.00	226.58	213.83
Knowledge-of-results	16.25	14.00	15.13	182.58	173.17	177.88
Sex competition	18.92	11.83	15.38	222.08	206.83	214.46
Tribal competition	12.00	11.83	11.91	197.50	216.50	207.00
Aversive consequence	18.75	14.91	16.83	247.17	216.25	231.71
Vicarious reinforcement	16.91	12.25	14.58	225.50	237.83	231.67
Material incentives	15.42	15.85	15.63	246.83	223.25	240.04

Separate analyses of variance were performed on the scores for the two tests. Table 1 presents the several means, and Table 2 summarizes the analysis of variance for the Verbal Analogies Test. There was no significant difference.

Table 2. Summary of analysis of variance for Verbal Analogies Test

Source of variation	SS	df	MS	F
Sex	182.29	1	182.29	2.71
Treatment	339.48	6	56.60	.85
Sex x treatment	423.16	6	70.50	1.05
Within cell	10305.92	154	66.92	
Total	11250.85	167		

Table 3 summarizes the analysis of variance for the Marking Test. On this test there was a significant difference between experimental groups. A comparison of groups two at a time showed that the significant differences reflect the inferior performance of the knowledge-of-results group vs. the material-incentive group, $t = 4.50; P < .001$; vs. the aversive-consequence group, $t = 3.45, P < .01$; and vs. the vicarious reinforcement group, $t = 4.03, P < .01$. For knowledge of results vs. control, $t = 2.60, P < .05$. The pooled experimental group did not differ significantly from the control group.

Table 3. Summary of analysis of variance for Marking Test

Source of variation	SS	df	MS	F
Sex	130.00	1	130.00	.05
Treatment	62610.00	6	10435.00	4.03*
Sex x treatment	15621.00	6	2604.00	1.01
Within cell	398573.00	154	2588.00	
Total	476934.00	167		

* $P < .01$

There was no significant difference between males and females within treatments, nor was there a significant interaction between treatment and sex.

DISCUSSION

The results for the Verbal test resemble those of studies donè elsewhere: incentives administered in the test situation did not significantly alter test scores. On the speed test, knowledge of results had an adverse effect.

One other incentive that came close to a significant influence on Marking Test performance was material incentives ($P < .10$). This incentive tended to increase test scores. It is possible that other incentives would have increased test scores if the Ss had been less motivated by the testing situation, but indications were that the Botswana children thought the tests were important and that they should do their best on them. For example, when tickets for testing were passed out some children did not receive one, as there were more girls than boys in the schools and the design called for equal numbers of boys and girls. Several children who did not receive a ticket asked for one repeatedly and it had to be explained carefully that the testing had no bearing on their Primary-School-Leaving Examination or their selection into secondary school. Of the children who were given an examination ticket, fewer than 10 failed to come for the tests, even though many of them had to walk about a mile to school where the tests were being given, at a time after their normal school hours. It is also possible that more powerful incentives could have an influence on test scores.

REFERENCES

Cronbach, L. J. (1970) *Essentials of psychological testing.* (3rd ed.). New York: Harper and Row.

Jung, S. M. & Lipe, D. (1970) *Study of the use of incentives in education and the feasibility of field experiments in school systems: A literature review.* Palo Alto: Amer. Inst. for Res.

Schwartz, P. A. (1961) *Aptitude tests for use in developing nations.* Pittsburgh: Amer. Inst. for Res.

van der Walt, N. (1952) The influence of incentives on the performance of African native mine-workers on a psychomotor test. Unpublished masters thesis, Univer. Pretoria.

PART IV

Testing devices

Although each paper in this section gives extensive information on a test or group of tests, the papers also contain considerable amount of substantive interest. Reuning describes both older and more recent tests developed for South African use. The paper gains added interest from Reuning's close observation of the Bushmen.

Work in the Pacific was originally introduced into the conference program as a set of four papers by Bennett, Kearney, Ord, and St. George. In the end, Kearney's paper was not available and Bennett and St. George did not attend the conference; Ord and McElwain therefore presented the program of work. This volume contains the formal papers of Ord, St. George, and Bennett, together with more informal comments by McElwain. The data cover work in Fiji, New Guinea, and among Maoris and aborigines, using tests which arose out of a single program of studies.

Georgas and Georgas describe a battery assembled for use in Greece, and examine relations of scores to sex, age, SES, and school marks. Kagıtçıbası explores the usefulness of the 'dominoes' test as a measure of scholastic aptitude, reporting Turkish data, and Abul-Hubb reports preliminary data on application of Matrices in Iraq.

McDaniel introduces a set of filmed tests of complex information processing. Rimland describes attempts to develop new tests that would be little dependent on schooling but related to success in practical work. Pauker proposes to score a child's preference among pictured activities as a means of judging the extent to which he shares the outlook of the mainstream culture. Wickert reports an empirical trial of the method of self-assessment as a possible replacement for ability tests.

National Institute for Personnel Research, Johannesburg

Psychological studies of Kalahari Bushmen

This work was begun in 1958, on a suggestion by Biesheuvel, at a time when crosscultural psychological research had hardly been heard of (Reuning, 1959). In planning our expeditions, we had to ask ourselves how the psychological study of Bushmen, who were assumed to be dying out, could be justified. In the materialistic world with its numerous burning problems, Bushmen are not regarded as significant and would not rank high on a list of research priorities. Yet it seems to us that the importance of the Bushmen as a unique part of mankind is great and that we can learn much from them. It is urgent to recognize this, for their and our benefit — if it is not already too late.

The Bushmen of the Kalahari have been studied extensively by other scientists, especially anthropologists, linguists, and geneticists (Tobias, 1959, 1964, 1970). Prior to our efforts they had been almost totally neglected by psychologists, although there are good reasons why psychologists should take a keen interest in the Bushmen and similar peoples (Reuning & Wortley, 1972).

At the beginning of our work with Bushmen, we were not so much concerned with *why* we should study them, but *how* we could do it. Porteus (1937) travelled 4000 km in 1934 through the Kalahari in order to obtain six test scores from each of 26 Bushmen. This was the first time ever that a psychologist tried to test Bushmen, and it was no mean achievement. Reading Porteus' report, one realizes that the most likely reasons for the lack of experimental psychological work in this field are the methodological and practical difficulties involved.

Field work is tough under the best of circumstances, even with modern equipment. A survey of how we spent our days on five Kalahari expeditions shows that only about half of the time of an expedition could be considered productive testing time; 3/8 of the time was needed for travelling, camping, packing, repairs and shopping, and 1/8 was spent with local officials and with searching for subjects. Table 1 shows what could be obtained once the Bushmen were found and good rapport was established: on the average about six test scores from each of 100 subjects during a field trip lasting about five weeks. The situation improves a little as one gains experience, but there seems to be a limit to the output per tester per day, depending to some extent on the type (individual or group) and length of the tests used, but not on the ·number of testers in the field. This is inherent in testing hunter-gatherers like the Bushmen, who live in small bands widely dispersed over large areas.

Table 1. Number of subjects tested and number of results obtained on five Kalahari expeditions

	1958	1959	1962	1963	1966	Total
Testing days	20	17	15	16	$20\frac{1}{2}$	$88\frac{1}{2}$
Testers	2	3	4	3	7	17
Total tester-days	40	$66\frac{1}{2}$	47	48	117	$318\frac{1}{2}$
Test results	478	786	400	547	962	3173
Subjects tested	137	154	60	71	90	512
Average number of tests per subject	3.5	5.1	6.7	7.7	10.7	6.2
Test results per tester-day	11.95	11.82	8.5	11.4	8.22	9.97

Since there is this limit to the number of test responses one can collect, it is important to ensure that the responses one does obtain in fact answer the questions posed. It makes no sense to set a problem simply because it is of vital interest to you, the investigator, if it does not normally exist in the world of your respondents or is put to them in an incomprehensible form. Take the example of the maze test, which is generally regarded as universally applicable. In the Central Kalahari there is *never* a situation in which you have to ask yourself: 'Should I turn left here? Will I get stuck in a blind alley if I turn right? ' A motorist may get stuck in the sand, but the ordinary Kalahari dweller can go straight as far as he wants. There is no barrier or wall of any kind for him. One just *cannot* expect a Bushman to see the thin lines on a tester's maze as impregnable barriers. Furthermore, how can one who does not speak the subject's language fluently make clear to him such arbitrary rules as 'Don't cross the lines with your pencil', 'Don't enter a "blind alley" ', 'Do not retrace your way', etc.? If one tries, he must not be too surprised if the results indicate, e.g. that the average mental age of the adult Bushman is, say, 7½ years (Porteus, 1937). This is probably still better than the conclusion a Bushman would draw should he put the average European to the test by, say, leaving him alone in the Kalahari for three days; he would not get a response at all.

If one genuinely wishes to communicate with a stranger, it is best to discuss matters which are familiar to him. In the same way, if one hopes to elicit a response from test-unsophisticated subjects it is desirable to include at least some elements in the test which are familiar to the subjects. For Bushmen, that rules out almost all the tests which psychologists have ever produced, the socalled 'culture-free' tests being no exception. It was perhaps fortunate that our frantic search for relevant titles through more than 50 volumes of *Psychological Abstracts* prior to our first expedition yielded not one report which could have served as a precedent for psychological experiments with Bushmen. (Porteus' early work did not come to our attention at this time.) Thus we had to think for ourselves.

Among the 8 instruments which we took on our first expedition (Reuning, 1959), only is well known, the Ishihara Charts for detecting color blindness. Another one which many readers may know, but which did not work too well, was the series of geometric illusions of Herskovits et al. (1956). A recognition test, a scanning and sorting task, and the Cube Construction subtest of the NIPR's General Adaptability Test Battery could only be applied to a few subjects, because the conditions of testing were too unfavorable. Three tests, however, were very successful from the beginning: a sand-drawing task, a symmetry-completion test, and a sequence-continuation test, Object Relations (Zilian, 1956, 1957).

Sand Drawing was designed to provide information on a specific question. We know (although some anthropologists still doubt it) that most of the fine rock paintings and engravings in Southern Africa, comparable to the best art in the world, were produced by Bushmen, before they became extinct in those areas. Today's Bushmen do not paint, and we were interested to learn whether this is due to lack of opportunity or lack of ability. Our equipment consists of a flat, black tray, covered with a thin layer of sand. A camera, mounted above the centre of the tray, enables one to photograph the finger drawings in a constant scale, for later evaluation. The task is demonstrated by the tester who draws a side view of a petrol can and then asks the examinee to draw a large plastic bottle, propped up as a model; thereafter, drawings of a springbok and a man are requested. This is all done very informally, is well understood by all Bushmen, and is ideally suited as an opening of the testing program, which sets the examinees at ease.

Pattern Completion – its group-test version is called Symmetry Completion – originates from a rather novel idea of a former colleague (Hector, 1959; Reuning & Wittmann, 1963). It appeared to be remarkably 'culture fair'; some of its items have puzzled university professors and yet have been solved correctly by many of the Bushmen. Each item, on a separate page of a booklet, presents a configuration of three bars, two colored or gray ones and one black one. A cut-out black bar must be added to make the whole pattern symmetric. There are two parts of the test, one involving bilateral (or 'mirror') symmetry, the other rotational symmetry. The number of patterns completed correctly is scored.

In the Object Relations test (and its group version, Object Series), sequences of round or square, black or white objects, similar to pieces in the game of checkers, are placed on a ring-shaped test field. The tester begins by putting a certain number of pieces in certain locations. S is to derive a rule or principle governing the sequence and to extend the pattern until the ring is closed. The score is the number of pieces correctly selected and placed.

On the basis of experience gained during the early expeditions, other tests were selected and new ones developed. As an alternative to the introductory Sand Drawing, an experiment on Size Constancy was designed (Winter, 1964). The simple equipment comprises 11 disks of masonite varying in diameter from 15 cm. to 25 cm., and a standard disk of 20 cm. diameter which is mounted on a pole one meter high. S has to compare the disks, held up one by one in a random order at distances of 3 m. and 12 m., with the standard disk which is seen at a distance of 6 m. S has to say or signal whether the particular disk held up is larger or smaller than the standard. The disks are shown twice at each of the two observation distances, and from each set of 22 judgments a long-distance threshold and a short-distance threshold are determined. A small difference between the two threshold values is taken as a measure of size constancy, a zero difference indicating perfect size constancy.

Noteworthy among the later tests are: Tests of Hearing and Visual Acuity (Humphriss & Wortley, 1971); a battery of six skill tests, involving sensori-motor activities like picking up nuts and threading them over a vertical rod by means of tweezers, 'chopsticks' and the like, balancing and ring throwing (de Wet, 1967); a 'solid' version of the Mazes (Winter, 1964); a Continuous Beadstringing test, done in an uninterrupted session of one hour and reflecting temperamental characteristics of work behavior, such as accuracy and speed of work, increase or decrease in output with time, and variability; plus further pencil-and-paper tests. (For details, and full results, see Reuning & Wortley, 1972).

The latter are administered by means of a poster demonstration with enlarged replicas of the practice items. Fret Repetition involves the copying of simple designs within a double row of dots, by joining the relevant dots with more or less straight lines. Fret Continuation is similar, but requires the continuation of more complex designs. The former was designed as a kind of 'programed instruction' to give illiterate Ss practice in the use of a pencil before they were subjected to the actual Fret Continu-

Table 2. Variability of cultural groups on Pattern Completion, Tapping Fast, and Beadstringing

Test and Group	N	Mean	s.d.	Variability (s.d. as per cent of mean)	
Pattern Completion:					
Forest workers, Knysna	80	37.35	7.29	19.5	
Illiterate black mine recruits	32	35.49	6.41	18.1	
Illiterate black mine recruits	33	38.42	8.03	20.9	
Literate black mine recruits	14	40.50	4.37	10.8	
Bushmen, 1959	108	30.53	6.49	21.3	
					Mean taps per 10 seconds
Tapping Fast :					
Bantu mine workers					
(30″ trials) 2nd trial	251	139.47	25.96	18.6	46.5
White female factory operatives (30″ trials)					
1st trial	33	157.55	28.70	18.2	52.5
2nd trial	33	173.36	24.96	14.4	57.8
Bushmen, 1959 (10″ trials)					
1st trial	69	58.91	11.42	19.4	58.9
2nd trial	69	60.62	9.21	15.2	60.6
Bushmen, 1963 (30″ trial)	43	154.56	25.61	16.6	51.5
		Beads/ hour			
Continuous Beadstringing :					
White students, College of Education, 1963	58	1300	225	17.3	
Bushmen, Motokwe, 1962	41	768	163	21.2	
Bushmen, Sunnyside, 1963	22	615	103	16.7	
Bushmen, ≠ Xade,* 1963a	12	433	112	25.9	
Bushmen, ≠ Xade, 1963b	12	539	170	31.6	

* The Bushman name for a dried-out pan in the central Kalahari, 22°25′ South, 23°14′ East. The name is encoded phonetically to show that the initial sound is a 'click'.

ation test. Both these tasks require attention to detail, accuracy, and some manipulative skill in drawing the pencil lines. Whereas the Bushmen found the copying of the Fret designs difficult, they did fairly well in a task which we had expected to be similar and at least equally difficult, Squares Detection. (This, and the Fret tests are modifications of test ideas by Hector, 1960, 1964). Apparently random arrangements of dots are given on each of the test pages, next to a model square, four dots connected by lines. *S* has to find groups of four dots which form corners of a square of the same size as the model, and to connect the relevant dots by straight lines. We were surprised at how quickly many of the Bushmen learned to find the squares and complete them, although it is likely that none of them had ever seen a square in the Kalahari.

SOME RESULTS

The first observation we made, soon confirmed by the analysis of actual scores, was that there were large variations between individuals on practically all our tests. Some Bushmen were only able to give correct answers to a few of the easier items, while others were able to answer most of the items correctly. Variances among Bushmen were as large as or larger than those found in other groups (cf. Table 2). This was an unexpected finding, particularly in view of the fact that the environmental conditions of the Bushmen we studied appeared to be much less heterogeneous than those of most other populations. Furthermore, there is also the possibility of a restricted gene pool for the small and thin Bushman populations. Both these considerations lead one to expect less variability in performance. Our enquiries into the *S*s' backgrounds did not yield much evidence of the factors usually held responsible for performance differences. Formal education was nonexistent throughout. Contacts with other cultural groups, Bantu and white, appeared to have essentially specific effects, e.g. enhancing the richness of the *content* of free drawings, and speed of work. Correlations of tests with age and sex were negligible. It is an open question whether the moderate correlations between performance on some tests and amount of culture contact indicate an effect of the latter, or whether those Bushmen who are more alert and able *seek* more culture contact and venture further afield. The fact that male sex always correlated with the extent of culture contact, especially contact with white people, points in this direction.

At this stage the question may be asked: Could the wide range of test scores among the Bushmen be due to the crudeness of our instruments and procedures? In other words, how reliable are our tests? Clearly, the assumptions made in modern test theories, at least for the more refined reliability estimates, are inappropriate in this context, mainly because much rapid learning takes place during the tests. Thus we assessed reliability from intercorrelations between items or parts of the tests. Reliability values ranged from 0.63 (for an early version of Squares Detection) to 0.97 (for speed of bead-stringing) and averaged 0.80 for 25 tests which could be divided into separately scorable parts. This seems high when one considers the unfavorable conditions under which we inevitably had to test (wind, sand being blown over test materials, children crying or playing and shouting nearby, flies stinging, etc.). It confirms the finding of large individual differences, since high reliability can only occur if the measurements are good or if the differences are so great that even crude instruments can measure them. The latter is more likely in our case.

In perceptual tests of vision and hearing, the Bushmen were equal or superior to other groups (such as South African whites and Bantu). For example, age deterioration of hearing sets in later and is less pronounced than in Europeans. In the size-constancy experiment, the Bushmen's judgments showed a smaller 'range of uncertainty' than those of Bantu and whites; and they came closer to perfect size constancy. Since size constancy plays a role in distance estimation, one is tempted to attribute the Bushman's high size constancy to the effect of hunting practice. But the women never hunt and their daily activities do not demand distance estimation, yet their size constancy is about the same as that of the men.

Scores on perceptual and cognitive performance tests, as well as quality ratings of artistic products (drawings, clay models, etc.) are substantially intercorrelated in each of the Bushman groups. Because of variation in numbers of cases — we could not get all the Bushmen to do all the tests — factor analyses of these intercorrelations are not possible. However, cautious cluster analysis indicates that besides a strong general factor some specific factors may be operative, notably perceptual and motor speed, analytic ability, formal-conceptual thinking and accuracy. The correlations between performance scores on the one hand and artistic preferences and measures of brain activity (derived from EEG recordings, Nelson, 1968; van Wyk, 1964) on the other, suggest that personality traits, for example freedom from tension and receptiveness to new stimuli, exert an influence on performances.

The validity of the tests applied to the Bushmen is as yet an open question. By Hofstätter's (1966) definition of 'intelligence' as the 'ability to discover redundancy' (i.e., inherent order), most of these tests could be regarded as 'intelligence tests'. They seemed to have this face validity to the *S*s themselves, because the Bushmen accepted as a matter of fact that the 'clever ones' would do well in them. The kind of individual the Bushmen recommended to us, e.g. as a guide when we needed one or as one whose opinion in important matters must be obtained, tended to have above average scores on our tests. The Bushmen's concept of 'practical intelligence' does not appear to differ essentially from ours.

This encourages one to conclude that diagnostic psychology has a wider applicability than has been indicated by recent crosscultural psychological research carried out elsewhere. Practical problems like selecting those who would respond to training can be solved even with groups who are living under the most extreme environmental conditions.

REFERENCES

de Wet, D. R. (1967) Simple skill tests applied to Africans. *Psychol. Afr.*, *11*, 189-205.

Hector, H. (1959) A coloured version of the Pattern Completion test. *J. Nat. Inst. Personnel Res.*, *7*, 204-205.

Hector, H. (1960) Results from a simple gestalt continuation test applied to illiterate black mine workers. *J. Nat. Inst. Personnel Res.*, *8*, 145-147.

Hector, H. (1964) The 'form' detection test. *Amer. J. Psychol.*, *77*, 135-136.

Herskovits, M. J., et al. (1956) *Materials for a cross-cultural study of perception.* Evanston: Program of African Studies, Northwestern Univer.

Hofstätter, P. R. (1966) Zum Begriff der Intelligenz. *Psychol. Rundschau*, *17*, 229-248.

Humphriss, D., & Wortley, W. L. (1971) Two studies of visual acuity. *Psychol. Afr.*, *14*, 1-19.

Nelson, G. K. (1968) Adaptability and brain function. *So. Afr. J. Sci.*, *64*, 177-182.

Porteus, S. D. (1937) *Primitive intelligence and environment.* New York: Macmillan.

Reuning, H. (1959) Psychologische Versuche mit Buschleuten der Kalahari. *Umschau*, *59*, 520-523.

Reuning, H., & Wittmann, G. (1963) Relative difficulty of two kinds of symmetry in the PATCO Test. *Psychol. Afr.*, *10*, 89-107.

Reuning, H., & Wortley, W. L. (1972) Psychological studies of the Bushmen. *Psychol. Afr. Monogr. Suppl.*, (in preparation).

Tobias, P. V. (1959) The Nuffield-Witwatersrand University research expeditions to Kalahari Bushmen, 1958-1959. *Nature*, *183*, 1011-1013.

Tobias, P.V. (1964) Bushman hunter-gatherers: A study in human ecology. In D.H.S. Davis (Ed.), *Ecological studies in Southern Africa*, The Hague: Junk. Pp. 67-68.

Tobias, P. V. (1970) Human biological research in the Anatomy Department, University of the Witwatersrand, 1959-1969. *The Leech, 40, No. 2, 23-32.*

van Wyk, I. (1964) Electroencephalography in the Kalahari. *Psygram*, *6*, No. 1, 17-22.

Winter, W. L. (1964) Recent findings from the application of psychological tests to Bushmen. *Psygram*, *6*, 42-55.

Winter, W. L. (1967) Size constancy, relative size estimation and background: A cross-cultural study. *Psychol. Afr.*, *12*, 42-58.

Zilian, E. (1956) Über einen sprachfreien Intelligenztest. *Bericht üb. d. 20 Kongress d. deutschen Gesellsch. f. Psychol.* Göttingen: Hogrefe. Pp. 198-200.

Zilian, E. (1957) *Der kognitive Objekt-Relationen-Test*, Berlin-Charlottenburg: author (Duplicated).

Note: *The finding in the Kalahari is consistent with an emerging generalization that peoples who live by hunting and gathering average well above Westernized groups on spatial and perceptual tests. Such evidence is available for Eskimos, Northern Canadian Indians, and Australian aborigines also. This supports the argument that ecological demands are important in the development of abilities, according to Berry (see pp. 77-88).* (Eds.)

I. G. ORD

University of Waikato

18

Assessing cognitive capacities of nonliterate New Guinea adults and children

New Guinea (we include Papua) was one of the first places where systematic studies were initiated regarding cognitive functioning of nonliterate, non-European peoples. As early as 1898 A.C. Haddon directed the now-famous 'Cambridge Anthropological Expedition to the Torres Strait Islanders' (Haddon, 1901). Psychomotor and sensory capacities rather than the higher mental processes were investigated. Among the investigators were psychologists destined to fame, such as W.H.R. Rivers, C.S. Myers, and William McDougall.

No serious attempt was made to apply measures of higher cognitive processes in New Guinea prior to 1957. McElwain and Griffiths (1957) conducted a brief field survey to investigate the feasibility of using tests to reduce serious training wastage among recruits to the Pacific Islands Regiment (PIR). They considered that performance tests could be adapted for such a purpose, but that because of the difficulties encountered in widespread recruiting in remote areas and because of problems of communicating, such tests would probably need to be administered individually through interpreters, and to be essentially nonverbal. I was then assigned the task of developing a battery of such tests.

I have just completed a detailed account (Ord, 1971) of the peculiar problems confronted, the development of tests, and the major findings and outcomes of testing nonliterates in the New Guinea setting, also comparing the tests so developed with tests developed for similar purposes in other parts of the world. I wish here to highlight aspects presumably of interest to those similarly placed in other countries.

POPULATION CHARACTERISTICS AND TESTING CON-
STRAINTS

At the time of the main PIR Test development (1957-1959), literate Papuans and New Guineans were at a premium. For Army purposes, by far the majority of recruits had to be drawn from nonliterate and relatively uneducated villagers. It was assumed that an illiterate villager with better-than-average intelligence could cope with the basic military training – conducted mostly in the *lingua franca*, Melanesian pidgin.

New Guinea has an incredible ethnic diversity. Mountains, jungles, swamps, and seas have ensured the relative isolation of a tribe once it is established in a pocket. New Guinea, particularly along its coasts, must have acted as the main land route for migratory waves of peoples from Southeast Asia towards more remote island chains of the Southwest Pacific. People can be readily recognized as coming from particular areas by their distinct physiques, facial structure, and skin coloring, as well as by speech, adornment, and behavior. There are no fewer than 625 mutually unintelligible languages.

Traditionally, intertribal communications have been rather restricted. The immediate out-groupers have been treated with extreme suspicion and open hostility, entrenching tendencies towards social encapsulation and interethnic conflict.

Nevertheless, the environmental controls of the region as a whole have resulted in fairly universal behavioral characteristics. The livelihood is primarily one of sedentary subsistence agriculture, supplemented in coastal areas by fishing and in inland areas by some sporadic hunting and foraging.

A quest for so-called 'culture-free' tests is futile, but it was hoped that a sufficient array of tests could be found or devised to sample cognitive capacities generally for all such groups, without obviously placing any ethnic group at a serious disadvantage.

The immediate task was approached empirically, without close regard for theoretical constructs of abilities other than to assume it was unlikely that there would, in fact, be marked differences between the ethnic groups concerned. While a particular test type might favor an ethnic group slightly due to local cultural influences, it was considered that the effects of these would probably even out over an array of tests. If not, so long as recruiting was conducted at field locations centered within each group and applied only to members of that group, and so long as recruiting was continued for a group until the intended number of persons from that group had met the standard, there would be no grounds for saying that tests were unfair.

It was assumed that if tests could be devised which differentiated quick learners from slow learners among recently trained soldiers of PIR, and which could be understood by nonliterate villagers from the remotest parts, discriminating sufficiently among them, we would have an instrument for universal practical use in New Guinea. Such an instrument would have good prospects for use among other nonliterate peoples.

The approach of the General Adaptability Battery of NIPR, administered to groups by mime and the use of cinema, with abundant apparatus, and with proctors to set up materials and score performances, was most attractive. It was a matter of some political importance to recruit representatively from widespread, diverse ethnic groups and it proved not to be immediately practical to use G.A.B. The physical barriers to transportation of materials from one site to another by mobile vans or to attract isolated groups to major centers were too great.

In arriving at the ultimate battery which came to be known as the PIR Test, the following criteria were stringently applied.

1. Any test whose requirements seemed not to be readily understood by all Ss after simple explanation and practice, using an interpreter − who had himself performed the task and shown understanding of the requirements − was to be discarded.

2. A selected test would have to be capable of simple demonstration by the manipulation of concrete material with the barest instructions. Evidence that S had understood would have to be immediately apparent in his manipulations during initial practice.

3. The manipulative skills required to perform any test item would have to be uncomplicated and not to place

anyone at an obvious disadvantage. Item difficulty would have to depend on increasing perceptual and conceptual complexity rather than on demands for manual dexterity.
4. Cultural content of the material should be minimal or such that familiarity would be fairly irrelevant to the correct solution. This was the most difficult criterion to fulfil and to test.
5. Information concerning the correct performance of any of the items should be very difficult to divulge to other prospective Ss. This would be particularly important where persons of the same kinship group would be virtually queueing up for testing. It did not seem to matter much if the subtest requirements were discussed, provided that particular items would not be readily remembered and divulged. In fact, some discussion was probably advantageous, in that rapport and instruction would thereby be facilitated.

Table 1 lists the test types initially tried in 1957. At that stage, all tests save Cube Imitation, Bead Threading, Passalong, Form Assembly, and Observation were found wanting. The requirements of most tests, particularly Binet items and those from group nonverbal tests, proved too hard to communicate to unsophisticated Ss. Total failure was frequent on tests requiring either the interpretation of pictures or symbols or the use of pencil.

Because of consistently favorable reports of the use of such tests as Porteus Maze, Draw-A-Man and Kohs Blocks among nonliterate peoples elsewhere, it came as a surprise when these tests were not universally understood or did not discriminate usefully in New Guinea. Although many Ss could understand the Kohs Blocks, too many did not perceive how two-dimensional designs were abstracted from three-dimensional materials. They thought that the designs represented both the tops and sides of the blocks. When ultimately the third dimension was removed by using tiles of limited depth (along with other modifications), this proved to be in fact the best test-type so far tried (Design Construction Test, Ord, 1968a).

Test behavior of these nonliterate peoples generally did not

Table 1. Test item types tried in 1957, preparatory to development of the New Guinea Performance Scales

Plan of Search (SB L XIII).
Pictorial Likenesses and Differences (SB L VI).
Mutilated Pictures (SB L VI).
Picture Absurdities (SB L VII, first 3 only).
Copying a Diamond (SB L VII).
Paper Cutting (SB L XIII).
Memory for Designs (SB L IX).
Picture Vocabulary Test (SB L II). Enticknap Version.
Bead Threading (Modification of SB L XIII).*
Object Assembly. Profile and Manikin subtests only, Wechsler-Bellevue.
Goodenough's Draw-a-Man (simplified scoring).
Porteus Maze.
Picture Arrangement. Time-sequence item from ACER J2**
Squares Completion.*** Items from ACER J2.
Army Test GB. (Easier items from Stephenson's GVK series. Not unlike Raven Matrices.)
Modified Cube Imitation.*
Alexander's Passalong (modified).*
Space-Form Assembly. Adaptation of ACER J2.*
Observation (Kim's game).*
Modified Kohs Blocks. Reduced to tiles, later became the Design Construction
:test.*

* Tests found acceptable in this version.
** Refers to ACER Junior Non-Verbal test 1, second version.
*** Patterns of squares are completed by drawing in crosses, not unlike Hector's (1960) Gestalt Continuation Test.

deviate unduly from patterns typical of literate Europeans. If anything, there was more cooperation and interest and less inattention and carelessness. Excessive willingness to please or overcompliance had to be guarded against. Irrelevant gestures and expressions were thought to be cues. There was much less concern for speed at the expense of correctness of performance. Among children, lack of care and caution seemed to relate directly to amount of schooling. Testees became so engrossed in the tasks that care was needed in terminating tests so as not to discourage or even to offend them.

THE TESTS AND THEIR USES

The PIR Test, first standardized in 1957, was revised substantially in 1959 and again in 1961. These revisions added items, and changed the scoring systems to achieve greater discrimination at low- and medium-levels of difficulty. In 1963 a revised form of the Form Assembly Test was introduced. (On the several variations of the PIR Test, see Ord, 1968b.)

Locally designed group intelligence and attainment tests being lacking, the initial form of the test was used in the selection of pupils for scholarships to attend the main Australian secondary schools, during the period 1957-1959. It was possible to check the test's validity against past and subsequent school success and against teachers' ratings for intelligence and with other group intelligence tests. The tests gave useful predictions of school success, as work by van den Hout in West Irian confirmed. It was found that the tests could be used as low as age 8 and still discriminate. No significant differences were found between male and female performance.

It seemed that tests of this type, if modified to lower difficulty levels, would apply yet at still lower ages. This subsequently proved to be the case with the Pacific Infants Performance Scale, applied to children of ages 5-1/2 to 7 (Ord & Schofield, 1969, 1970). In this, only the best three tests were retained: Cube Imitation, Bead Threading, and Design Construction. This was quite a fair predictor of school success in the first two years of school in a crosssection of New Guinea schools. It is now used extensively as a screening device at school entry, wherever aspirants far exceed available places.

The PIR tests and the Design Construction test have been integrated under the title of the New Guinea Performance Scales. The Design Construction test by itself is used extensively in selection of semiskilled workers and trainees in New Guinea where circumstances have called for a quick, easily administered instrument. Its reliability equals that of the remaining tests combined, and its validity as a predictor is only slightly less. The International Biological Program handbook (see p. 141) has recently recommended the Design Construction test for measuring

higher mental processes in human adaptability projects.
A brief description of the subtests of the New Guinea Performance Scale may be given.

Cube Imitation. (5 min.) An adaptation of Cattell's version of Knox's original test. Finer discrimination than
Cattell's for quality of performance; near-correct reproductions gain part credits. Ideal buffer test.

Bead Threading. (10 min.) Of the Binet type, considerably extended. Scored mainly for accuracy.

Passalong. (15 min.) Alexander's test with materials in
plastic and of larger dimensions. Item 9 has been deleted.
Altered time limits. Less emphasis on speed. Simplified
scoring, with corrections for number of moves.

Form Assembly. (8-10 min.) *Multiple Form.* An individual, concrete adaptation of an ACER paper-and-pencil
test, with some rearrangement of item order and pro-
vision of new items. *Single Form.* Templates placed over a
square on the single form board provide the basis for each
item.

Observation. (5-10 min.) Objects of varied materials, sizes,
shapes and colors are observed and memorized, then
recognized amid newly added material. Scored mainly for
accuracy.

Design Constructions. (10-15 min.) Flat plastic tiles are
used to make red-and-white designs as in the Kohs Blocks.
Some new items. Other modifications consist of displaying
designs and materials of equal size, providing plastic trays
in which to make the design, simplified scoring with less
emphasis on time and with partial credits.

The PIR battery was used in the period 1957 to 1966 to select
no fewer than 2,000 recruits. The test since has been phased out
in favor of group tests as more educated aspirants are forthcoming. In an analysis of PIR results on all potential recruits re-
senting themselves for testing in 1959-1967, there were no significant district and regional performance differences (Ord, 1971).
This refuted common assertions that Highlanders are more intelligent than lowlanders, New Guinea Islanders are more intelligent
than Papuans, and so on. It also gave us some cause for satisfaction

regarding the universal cultural relevance of the test across the many groups concerned. (One therefore cannot as a general rule interpret district comparisons as comparisons of ethnic or tribal groups. Sometimes a district is heterogeneous. Hence it is not established that there are no tribal differences on these tests.)

A somewhat unusual study (Kearney, 1966a) of 140 nonliterate Orokaiva males demonstrated a distinct positive relationship between cash crop productivity and the New Guinea Performance Scale.

The Queensland test — the battery in modified form and without the Observation test, which did not lend itself readily to mine — was used in studies of Australian aborigines (McElwain, 1966; Kearney, 1966a, b; McElwain, Kearney & Ord, 1967). 538 Australian aboriginal children and adults of low and medium contact with Western culture are compared with 328 Australian children and adults of European origins. The tests were valid predictors of school success. Norms were compiled.

EVALUATION OF THE TESTS

The split-half reliability of an early version of the PIR test was 0.81 for a recruit sample of 100 and 0.79 for a sample of 100 'primary final' pupils. Later test revisions enhanced these figures; KR20 reliabilities around 0.92 were obtained for Kearney's aboriginal samples.

Reliable criteria are not readily available, nor is the procedure of correlating new tests with tests of established validity possible, since the established tests do not apply to nonliterates. Testing Ss with sufficient schooling to permit the use of other tests, for instance, gives some indication of the validity among nonliterate Ss of the same origins.

The accumulation of evidence from an array of small samples using whatever criteria are available tends to build up a consistent picture of the test's validity for predicting adaptation of nonliterates to school, military, and industrial training (Table 2).

The reliabilities and validities compare favorably with those for various other tests among nonliterate and semiliterate populations, and do not fall far short of figures obtained for the performance scales of Wechsler, Arthur, Leiter, and the like for literate populations.

For groups of heterogeneous ability, within age bands, the New Guinea Performance Scales predict educability with r about 0.60. For assessing practical intelligent adaptive behavior among adult males, r is about 0.70 (See Table 2). The Pacific Infants Performance Scale, a somewhat truncated version of the adult scales, surprisingly enough correlates about 0.65 with teacher's estimate of general school performance in the first two years of schooling.

The tests were designed pragmatically and according to no particular theoretical constructs. The limited studies so far regarding factor content (see Ord, 1971), have revealed only a general factor and no more than two group factors: a broad spatial/perceptual factor and a memory factor. The general factor could well be compounded of something akin to Alexander's $g + F$ factors, claimed by him to be present in about equal proportions in his performance tests, in contrast with the $g + v$ present in so many measures of verbal ability. We suspect that in studies of nonliterates with large batteries the factor content of the New Guinea tests would break down into more specific factors, much in the way Grant & Schepers (1969) suggest.

The evidence indicates that both the New Guinea Performance Scales together and the Design Construction Test by itself are adequately valid for their main purpose, that is of screening out large proportions of nonliterate applicants who are unlikely to adapt adequately to training for moderately skilled work. The fact that the training wastage for PIR was cut from 12 to 3 per cent in the first three years of test use is a cogent argument. Their use for selection or for general assessment of mental ability of nonliterates, particularly where comparisons are made among individuals within their own subcultural groups, appears likely to prove similarly valid.

With the full battery, gross group differences in performance from one nonliterate culture to another are unlikely; if they do occur, they are unlikely to be very meaningful *per se*. It is not

Table 2. *Summary of validity studies**

Criterion	Sample	N	Statistic	Result**	Comments
Achievement					
Aggregate exam results English and Maths (in standard scores)	Scholarship aspirants	102	r	0.42	
Queensland Public Scholarship exam 1958	Scholarship students in Australia	14	ρ	0.49 $P<.05$	Group somewhat homogeneous in ability
Queensland Junior Exam 1958	as above	18	ρ	0.40 $P<.05$	as above
Place in class (exam results)	Various aboriginal groups	Range 11-29; 27 samples	ρ	Range 0.23 – 0.74; $P<.05$ in 18 of the samples	Modified PIR battery
Estimated intelligence					
Pooled ratings by European officers	Men serving PIR	93	C	0.57	Ratings for 6 manifestations of intelligent behavior averaged

* In some studies the PIR battery was modified, most often by dropping Observation and adding Design Construction.
** $P< .01$ unless otherwise indicated

Table 2. Summary of validity studies (continued)

Criterion	Sample	N	Statistic	Result	Comments
Ratings by New Guinean NCO's	as above	52	C	0.58	One overall rating
Upper and lower quartiles (concealed teacher judment)	New Guinea pupils with age range 14 to 17	30	Fisher's 2 x 2 contingency test		One overall rating
Teacher's rank order	Teacher trainees	7	ρ	0.94	
Teachers' rank order within schools	Various groups of scholarship aspirants	Range 5-16; 7 samples	ρ	Average, 0.61; $P < .01$ for 3 samples	
Teachers' rank order within schools	Children entering primary school in environs of Port Moresby	9 classes, average size 31	r	Average, 0.66	Estimate made at end of first school year. PIPS given at beginning of year.
Measured intelligence Design Construction Test (slightly modified)	Australian aboriginal schoolchildren and adults	Range 37-241; 6 groups	r	0.86 to 0.91	

Table 2. Summary of validity studies (continued)

Criterion	Sample	N	Statistic	Result	Comments
Campbell Picture Intelligence Test	Scholarship students	22	ρ	0.82	
Pacific Reasoning Series Test. Group test	Accepted recruits, sufficiently literate to take a group test	186	r	0.57	
Hector's Gestalt Continuation	Illiterate Orokaiva adult males	140	r	0.68	
Snijders-Oomen Non-Verbal Test	European children at School for deaf	107	r	0.74	
WISC and Binet	Aboriginal group, Queensland	37	r	0.82	
Colored Progessive Matrices	Aboriginal school children, Queensland	241	r	0.79	

difficult to imagine how such findings could be turned to some political advantage or put to misuse. On the other hand, insofar as the subtests can be shown to measure different things, different patterns of performance crossculturally on various subtests do seem likely. They could open fruitful areas of research if they can throw light on the factors and processes operating to cause such differences.

REFERENCES

Grant, G. V. & Schepers, J. M. (1969) An exploratory factor analysis of five new cognitive tests for African mineworkers. *Psychol. afr., 12,* 181-192.

Haddon, A. C. (Ed.) (1901-35) *Reports of the Cambridge Anthropological Expedition to Torres Straits.* Cambridge: Cambridge Univer. Press. 6 vols.

Hector, H. (1960) Results from a simple Gestalt continuation test applied to illiterate black mineworkers. *J. Nat. Inst. Personnel Res., 8,* 145-147.

Kearney, G. E. (1966a) Cognitive capacity among the Orokaiva. *New Guinea Res. Bull., No. 13,* 1-24.

Kearney, G. E. (1966b) *Some aspects of the general cognitive ability of various groups of aboriginal Australians as assessed by the Queensland Test.* Brisbane: Univer. of Queensland Press.

McElwain, D. W. (1966) The cognitive abilities of aborigines. Paper presented to 2nd Conference of Austral. Inst. of Aboriginal Studies, Sydney.

McElwain, D. W. & Griffiths, D. McG. (1957) Report on the possibility of using psychological procedures as an aid to recruiting in the Pacific Islands Regiment. Unpublished report for H.Q. Northern Comd, Victoria Barracks, Brisbane.

McElwain, D. W., Kearney, G. E. & Ord, I. G. (1967) *The Queensland Test of Cognitive Abilities* (2nd ed.). Melbourne: Austral. Coun. Educ. Res.

Ord, I. G. (1968a) *The Pacific Design Construction Test and Manual.* Melbourne, Austral. Coun. Educ. Res.

Ord, I. G. (1968a) The PIR test and derivatives. *Austral. Psychologist, 2,* 137-146.

Ord, I. G. (1971) *Mental tests for pre-literates.* London: Ginn.

Ord, I. G. & Schofield, J. (1969) An infant performance scale. A prospective test for use at school entry. *New Guinea Psychologist, 1,* 18-20.

Ord, I. G. & Schofield, J. (1970) *Pacific Infants Performance Scale and Manual.* Brisbane: Jacaranda.

ROSS ST. GEORGE
University of Waikato

19

Tests of general cognitive ability for use with Maori and European children of New Zealand

While New Zealand ranked in economic terms is a highly develop-ed state, the level of sophistication with respect to the availabili-ty of suitably normed mental tests is low. The Otis tests have recently been restandardized by the New Zealand Council for Educational Research. A few other group tests have been de-veloped. The major individual mental tests are used on the basis of Australian norms, where available, or on the basis of British norms, American norms, or guesswork.

While little has been published in the more accessible inter-national journals, it would be erroneous to assume that no studies with mental tests have been undertaken. Many unpublished papers and theses report on a variety of mental tests over a range of New Zealand Polynesians (Maoris) and New Zealand Europeans, in terms of age, sex, locality and socioeconomic factors. A review by St. George (1970) concluded that Maoris do not perform as well as Europeans on such tests as the Otis, WAIS, WISC, PMA, Lorge-Thorndike, and Raven's Matrices.

Most studies readily acknowledge the depressing effect of cultural and linguistic factors on the performance of Maoris on tests designed for use within a 'European' frame of reference. This acknowledgement upholds the politically and educationally acceptable proposition of equality in general mental capacity. To suggest otherwise, or even to suggest that 'specific' abilities may vary between populations, has not been politically acceptable. The author, however, views Vernon's (1969) model of the organi-zation of intellectual ability as appropriate and heuristic. This model allows for a common 'central' factor without demanding common lower-order 'specific' factors between populations of varying cultural and linguistic histories.

One dramatic consequence of the lack of adequate tests has been waste of talent among the Maoris (see Watson, 1967). Kenworthy, Martindale, and Sadaraka (1968) reported statistics showing that in 1966 85 per cent of the Maoris left school without any kind of educational certificate (compared with 48 per cent of the non-Maoris). Among the school leavers, one per cent of non-Maoris intended to study at a university, compared with 10 per cent among non-Maoris. When this is considered along with the comparative youth of the Maori population (60 per cent under age 21), its rapid growth rate, and the increasingly large numbers of Pacific Island peoples in New Zealand, there is no room for complacency. New Zealand has not averted the danger of creating a 'brown-skinned Polynesian proletariat'.

Testing is an integral part of New Zealand's educational process. Through tests such as the Otis, pupils are screened and streamed both in their primary- and secondary-school careers. The dependence of various psychological services on individual mental tests that are equally unsuitable for New Zealand's multicultural context has likewise limited the identification and educational acceleration of the talented among New Zealand's non-Europeans.

Under a grant from the Nuffield Foundation a program of mental-test development has been initiated. The broad aim is to investigate, develop, and produce a series of instruments more suitable for the assessment of mental abilities within New Zealand and its South Pacific territories. The program rests heavily on the extensive work of Ord (see above) in New Guinea, and McElwain and Kearney in Australia (McElwain, Kearney, & Ord, 1967; Kearney, 1966). From the work of these researchers, the IBP handbook of Biesheuvel et al., and the summary of Vernon, guidelines for more appropriate mental tests became apparent.

Materials employed must in all cases be clear and unambiguous, and as far as possible, materials and cues extraneous to the task at hand should be eliminated. Adequate practice must be incorporated into the tests, so that *S*s fully comprehend the nature of the item type. The tests should be non-cyclic in nature, in that items of any one type are grouped and administered together before the introduction of a new item type. Where possible, tests should be administered by mime, as opposed to verbal instruction in English, vernacular, or dialect. Speed should not be a major component.

It is desirable to have comparative reference group norms to aid in decision-making where individuals are moving across cultural divisions (e.g., an indigene seeking employment in a distinctly 'European' context). The accept-reject decision may best be made by comparing the score with scores in the target group aspired to. (This departs from the common procedure of comparing a particular *S*s performance against that of a norm group similar to *S* in origin.)

THE QUEENSLAND TEST OF COGNITIVE ABILITIES

Developed from Ord's PIR test, the QT is an individual test of general cognitive capacity. It consists of five test types — Knox Cubes, Bead Sequencing, Passalong, Form Assembly, and Pattern Matching (a tile version of Kohs Blocks, as in Ord's Design Construction, p. 189).

The total test consists of 60 items scored right-wrong. The test is essentially unspeeded. Mime has been the medium of administration in the Australian studies. Comprehensive details are presented in the handbook (McElwain & Kearney, 1970; see also Ritchie & St. George, 1971).

A departure from the Australian procedures has been the use of limited verbal instructions and verbal reinforcers in New Zealand. Instruction is not given on the solution of particular tasks at hand. The repertoire is dominated by the instruction 'watch carefully what I do and you do the same', during practice for each item type. Reinforcers such as 'good' or 'fine' are used. All other conventions indicated in the manual are maintained. The reason for the departure is that not speaking (in English) to a child — even a Maori child — contravenes the expectation that you will speak. Not communicating when one can speak and is expected to would, it is believed, be somewhat strained and detrimental to testing. In practice, once the nature of *S*'s role has been clarified, little verbal interaction is required to maintain the performance of Maori and European children.

RESULTS

Schools were selected for the QT project with a view to maximizing comparability of Maori and European samples. Selected whole classes were tested to facilitate more detailed study. The remainder of the sample was derived randomly from the class levels Standard 4 and Form II within the selected schools. Class-for-class, Maori children tend to be older than Europeans of the same level. This may necessitate selective sampling to obtain normal age distributions before calculating test norms. The results of the preliminary analysis on 406 children, 176 Maori (89 male and 87 female) and 230 European (122 male, 108 female), are available.

Table 1. Raw-score statistics on the Queensland Test for
          Maori and European children

Age range	Group	N	Mean	s.d.
10-6 to 10-11	M	16	38.88	4.88
	E	40	42.40	5.29
11-0 to 11-5	M	35	40.43	5.17
	E	56	38.96	5.16
11-6 to 11-11	M	30	40.07	4.76
	E	30	40.23	5.70
12-0 to 12-5	M	25	36.56	8.90
	E	17	45.50	6.60
12-6 to 12-11	M	14	44.36	4.55
	E	32	43.63	5.23
13-0 to 13-5	M	32	44.22	4.30
	E	37	46.57	5.41
13-6 to 13-11	M	24	42.50	6.24
	E	18	43.61	5.77

An unpublished study by Zimmerman (1971) reports on the use of the QT with a group of Maori and European detainees, of age about 18. The Maori sample (N = 29) achieved a mean raw score of 42.1, compared to 43.2 for the European sample (N = 14).

Table 2. *Correlations of QT, PRST, and Otis with other measures for five classes*

Class	N	Otis	PRST	Class tests, mathematics	Teachers' rankings	
					General ability	Achievement
Correlation for QT						
1	31	.48	—	.32	.12	.23
2	34	.05	.17	.03	−.14	−.04
3	22	.14	.53	.39	.50	.45
4	38	—	.48	—	.57	.54
5	17	—	−.11	—	.45	.50
Correlations for PRST						
2	34	.47	—	.54	.46	.54
3	22	.13	—	.53	.34	.25
4	38	—	—	—	.78	.74
5	17	—	—	—	.53	.47
Correlations for Otis						
1	31	—	—	.42	.51	.69
2	34	—	—	.61	.68	.76
3	22	—	—	.41	.39	.31

Further information on samples:

Class 1: Mean age ca. 10.   Includes 10 Maoris. Class level, Standard 3.
Class 2: Mean age ca. 11.   Includes 6 Maoris.   Standard 4.
Class 3: Mean age ca. 11½. Includes 8 Maoris.   Standard 4.
Class 4: Mean age ca. 11.   Includes 13 Maoris.   Standard 4.
Class 5: Mean age ca. 11½. Includes 4 Maoris.   Standard 4.

A one-year follow-up of an urban class ($N = 31$) provides a test-retest r of 0.46. (The Otis test with the same sample gave an r of 0.77.) Various correlations for the initial testing appear in Table 2 (Class 1 data). On the second testing, the Otis and PRST correlated 0.17 and 0.55 with the QT.

Four complete classes from urban schools were tested. The correlations of QT with class performance and teacher assessment are presented in Table 2 (Classes 2-5).

PRST

The Pacific Reasoning Series Test (Ord, 1968) was given with a 30-minute time limit instead of the customary 45 minutes. The means were 26.48 for Europeans ($N = 65$) and 25.59 for Maoris ($N = 22$; both groups 11 years old). Correlations are given for four classes in Table 2.

DISCUSSION

Correlations are also reported for the Otis test in three classes. The Otis correlations with school performance tend to be higher than those for PRST, and tend to exceed the correlations for QT. This may reflect on the character of the criteria. If QT is loaded on *g* (Kearney, 1966) and the Otis on *v : ed,* the differences in correlation are to be expected. The employment of QT scores involves a different framework than that maintained by the 'level of functioning' view which has pervaded educational selection and guidance in New Zealand.

With the questioning of the validity of the predictive criteria above there is possibly a need to consider 'rates of learning' and performances on tests such as the QT, rather than criteria heavily loaded with the sorts of *v : ed* activities reflected in the Otis. To break into the circular and self-fulfilling reasoning behind the 'level of functioning' arguments, validation of these mental tests as predictors of the potential to learn is a necessary extension of current research.

REFERENCES

Kearney, G.E. (1966) *Some aspects of the general cognitive ability of various groups of aboriginal Australians as assessed by the Queensland Test.* Brisbane: Univer. of Queensland Press.

Kenworthy, L.M., Martindale, T.B.& Sadaraka, S.M. (1968). Some aspects of the Hunn report: A measure of progress. Victoria, N.Z.: Univer. of Wellington.

McElwain, D.W.& Kearney, G.E. (1970) *Queensland Test Handbook.* Melbourne: Austral. Coun. Educ. Res.

McElwain, D.W. & Kearny,, G.E.& Ord, I.G. (1967) *The Queensland Test of Cognitive Abilities* (2d. ed.). Melbourne: Austral. Coun. Educ. Res.

Ord, I. G. (1968) *Pacific Reasoning Series Test.* Melbourne: Austral. Coun. Educ. Res.

Ritchie, J. & St. George, R. (1971) *Cross-cultural ability testing: Report of a research workshop.* Hamilton: Univer. of Waikato.

St. George, R. (1970) *Cognitive ability assessment in New Zealand: A cross-cultural perspective.* Paper presented to ANZAAS, Port Moresby.

Vernon, P. E. (1969) *Intelligence and cultural environment.* London: Methuen.

Watson, J. E. (1967) *Horizons of unknown power: Some issues in Maori schooling.* Wellington: N.Z. Coun. Educ. Res.

Zimmerman, M. L. (1971) An assessment of the cognitive ability and the attitude to rehabilitation of European and Maori trainees at a Borstal institution. Unpublished bachelor's thesis, Univer. of Waikato.

MICK BENNETT   20
University of the South Pacific, Suva

Patterns of reasoning test responses in the South Pacific

Constraints and pressures operate in Fiji to which psychometric methods must conform. The population of approximately half a million is divided between those of Indian descent and those of Melanesian descent. The former (marginally the numerical majority) are in Fiji largely as a result of an indentured labor policy of the British administration at the end of the 19th Century. The Indians tend to live in or near urban areas, and have no guaranteed land rights; the constitution and party structure of the newly independent Dominion tends to relegate them, to a continuing 'opposition' role in Government. These factors together with the normal exigencies of rural education predominating in Fijian areas – few inspections, small schools, poor facilities, multiple-class teaching, etc. – have made the Indian population more successful in gaining entry into secondary education. The Secondary Schools Entrance Examination consist of attainment tests in English, Mathematics and General Knowledge. Sixty per cent or more of Indian applicants pass, and generally fewer than 40 per cent of Fijians pass.

One proposal to solve this problem of unequal educational performance, dear to the hearts of many educational administrators with few funds, has been to locate a test which minimizes the achievement differential yet still predicts educational success, given improved conditions.

TEST DEVELOPMENT

A balance has to be struck between the desire to minimize group differences and the desire for predictive validity. 'Best' predictors such as verbal tests are unacceptable politically, and performance tests are impracticable because of the numbers to be tested. The compromise solution is usually to adapt a 'Shipley-type' reasoning test. Our test was based on the Pacific Reasoning Series Test (Ord, 1968).

In the initial stages of adapting this test (originally developed for a higher educational level), an attempt was made to write into the test 6 sets of items requiring very similar manipulations of data, but with the data in different sets taking the form of numbers, letters, or symbols (Bennett, 1971). For example, two sets would be

4883   3884;   6119   9116;   7441   ......

EAAN   NAAE; SFFC   CFFS; NUUL   ......

At all stages of test development four representative subgroups were used: Indian, Urban and Rural; and Fijian, Urban and Rural.

The symbol items were more difficult than the number and letter items even when the solution seemed to require appreciation of the same positioning cues.

These findings are similar to those of Vernon (1966) in Tanzania, where he used Classification, Number Series, and Matrix items. He reported that 'the order of difficulty of the items in the first and third tests was quite different to that expected. Many items which would be quite easy for an English child turned out difficult here and vice-versa. In contrast, arithmetical relationships are perceived in much the same way in different cultural groups, so that the order of difficulty in the Number Series test was much as expected.'

For certain symbolic (figural) items which apparently had similar difficulty levels in the four experimental subgroups, tetrachoric r indicated acceptable item validity in three subgroups but negative item validity in the Fijian urban group. A number of such items were discarded, as were other items showing large discrepancies between subgroups.

ADMINISTRATION

The restricted item type and narrowness of response required (simple series continuation) made it possible for the administrative procedure to inculcate an appropriate imitative set. The front page carries a minimum of written instruction: 'This is a test to see how well you can think. Listen to the person giving the test and you will be told what to do.' Three examples and 8 practice items give experience of various types of series continuation items. The examples and practice items are also represented on wall charts hanging at the front of the classroom. There is minimal need to understand spoken English since every response required is amplified by the use of the wall charts. The respondent is to imitate the test-answering activity demonstrated with the wall charts.

Thus, with the practice item

        TO   T;   DO   D;   NO   ......

the tester points to each of the letters on the wall chart as he slowly says,

        'T   O,   T'   − pause, pointing at wall chart −
        'D   O,   D'   − pause, pointing at wall chart −
        'N   O,'   − pause, 'What comes next?' −
        wait for class to respond − 'Yes, N'.

The *N* is then written on the wall chart which has a strip of blackboard paint corresponding to the place on the test paper where the examinee is required to write the answer.

This administrative procedure seemed acceptable. There was no obvious bimodality or heavy skewing of the lower end of the distribution with 'nonstarters', which would have suggested failure to understand.

Before the test was widely used, two other precautions were taken. The instructions were phrased within the appropriate structural level of the Tate Oral Syllabus, the English teaching method predominating in Fiji. Also, copies of the front page of the test, showing the examples and practice items, were sent to all children who were to take the test.

RESULTS AND INTERPRETATION

Table 1 presents statistics for two parallel versions of the test given to some 1,600 children after 6, 7, or 8 years of education (Bennett, 1970).

Table 1. Statistics for reasoning test scores

	Grade 6		Grade 7		Grade 8	
	Form A	Form B	Form A	Form B	Form A	Form B
N	266	260	284	278	253	237
Mean	17.4	17.5	20.4	19.3	24.4	24.1
s.d.	8.3	8.6	7.7	8.8	7.1	6.9
KR20 reliability	0.92	0.93	0.91	0.93	0.90	0.89
Average of item-total correlations	0.66	0.67	0.64	0.70	0.64	0.65

As these data seemed encouraging, the parallel tests were administered to 13,000 children in two education areas at the same three scholastic levels in July, 1970, as an adjunct to the attainment tests used for secondary selection. Two further versions were applied in June and July, 1971, to 9,000 children in the remaining educational administrative areas.

Analysis of variance indicates the expected urban-rural difference, with race differences (in favor of Fijians) tapering off as the educational level advances (Table 2).

The race differences are not regarded as of great importance since they are in part due to deliberate item choice. The tapering-off of this difference in Grades 7 and 8 is doubtless due in some measure to the practice of creaming off Fijian children at this level to attend 'elite' boarding schools; these were not included in the samples tested.

Sex differences do not emerge in either racial group, although such differences are often reported in other cultures. Nor, in Fiji, do sex differences emerge in primary and middle levels of school achievement.

Some inferences can be drawn from the item-total correlations in the subgroups. The mean biserial correlations are consistently

Table 2. *Significance levels from analysis of variance at three educational levels*

	Grade 6 $N = 533$	Grade 7 $N = 566$	Grade 8 $N = 486$
1. Race	***	**	n.s.
2. Habitat	***	**	**
3. Sex	n.s.	n.s.	n.s.
1 x 2	*	n.s.	n.s.
1 x 3	n.s.	n.s.	n.s.
2 x 3	n.s.	n.s.	*
1 x 2 x 3	n.s.	n.s.	n.s.

$*P < .01$; $**P < .02$; $***P < .01$

higher in the rural groups, and, at Class 8, differences between the subgroups in this index are more often significant than are differences in test means.

If the item-total correlations reflect stability of test response, and this in turn relates to the stability of the environment, then it would seem that the more homogeneous the experience of the examinee the easier it is to elicit stable test responses. Test-development problems in these situations are very often seen as being a function of population heterogeneity. The likelihood of this is demonstrated when one studies the behavior on the test of homogeneous groups within the heterogeneous population.

It should be made clear that 'homogeneity' refers to the kinds of experiences common in, say, a rural village community, rather than the type of homogeneity resulting from selection that Irvine (1969) refers to when he suggests that 'an apparently stable factor pattern emerges . . . except where populations within these broad groups are relatively homogeneous'. This may result in 'the disintegration of the general factor,. . . and more variance . . . associated with item types.'

It is too early to assess the predictive value of the test. Initial results indicate that, although the internal validity of the test is highest with rural groups, perhaps because of the non-invariant nature of the abilities tested (McFie, 1961), predictive validity is highest with urban groups. Whether this is a consequence of factorial differentiation of the predictor or criterion cannot yet be assessed.

REFERENCES

Bennett, M. J. (1970) Reasoning test response in urban and rural Fijian and Indian groups in Fiji. *Austral. Psychologist, 5,* 260-266.

Bennett, M. J. (1971) Some problems of general ability testing in Fiji. In Ritchie, J. E. & St. George, R., *Cross Cultural Ability Testing: Report of a Research Workshop.* Maori Research Series, No. 1, Hamilton. University of Waikato.

Irvine, S. H. (1969) Factor analysis of African abilities and attainments: Constructs across cultures. *Psychol. Bull., 71,* 20-32.

Ord, I. G. (1968) *Pacific Reasoning Series Test.* Melbourne: Austral. Coun. Educ. Res.

Vernon, P. E. (1966) Selection to secondary schools in Tanzania. Report to Ministry of Education, Dar-es-Salaam. (mimeographed.)

Remarks on testing in the Pacific*

These remarks about crosscultural testing arise not only from our own work from the Pacific region but also from some other papers at this meeting.

Ord, to develop the individually-administered PIR Test, tried a very large number of item-types empirically, so as to learn which could separate soldiers known to be bright from those known to be dull in the training situation. Only a few were efficient under the extreme conditions applying in New Guinea. Ord rejected, for instance, the Progressive Matrices and the Porteus Maze.

When Kearney and I decided to extend the testing program to Australian aborigines (where testing conditions are often even more difficult), we began by looking at the PIR Test (along with Design Construction) as it had been developed. We asked 'what features do the subtests of the PIR have in common, and how are these different from other tests generally? ' We thought it probable that if we intensified these features the test might become more efficient with our *S*s.

Ord's successful performance tests did employ oral instructions, given through interpreters. We found that by relying on mime we could eliminate speech of tester and respondent from the testing proper, and so run less risk of faulty communication. Speech is used only as support: 'Good', or 'Keep trying'.

Secondly, the material was nonrepresentational. No objects or

* This paper is a summary of informal remarks made by the author in discussion.

pictures of objects having common use or names were included. (The recent NIPR tests reported here by Grant and Blake use the same principle.)

Thirdly, the 'goal to be reached' was made as overt as possible. The target to be reached is before S throughout his attempt at solution. This important feature explains in part the repeated finding that Alexander's Passalong Test (which has this feature, and is included in the PIR and Queensland Tests) is efficient in diverse cultural groups.

Where the task involved the assemblage of parts, as in assembling beads to make a chain, or pieces to make a pattern, templates were used. The template reduces the difficulty of the items for Ss who do not have facility in applying number systems.

An S who fails an item is shown (nonverbally) the correct solution. This brings a practice effect into the test itself. It increases the probability that S will learn, from the item he has failed, an appropriate tactic for solving a later item.

Both the New Guinea version of PIR and the Queensland Test (McElwain, Kearney, & Ord, 1970) have the overall feature that the tester takes some physical material, manipulates it to match a presented goal or target, gives S a similar set of material, and invites him to imitate. The 'set to imitate' is easily induced; it appears to be a universal feature of human social behavior. The tasks become progressively more difficult, and require more complex cognitive mediation.

Psychological testing requires some communication between tester and subject. The tester sufflies S the formulation of the task or problem, and S supplies the tester his response. This communication channel has to be wide. The Queensland Test is described as a 'test of general cognitive capacity for use under conditions of reduced communication'. Communication is always reduced in crosscultural testing.

Ortar has stressed that complex thinking is verbally mediated and that complex thinking ought therefore to be tested only by verbal tests. I disagree with this conclusion. The fact that presentation and response are nonverbal does not imply that the mediation process of S is nonverbal. This is precisely the point of the theory – developed by Vygotsky (1962) and Luria (1961) – that language is used to 'control' ideational processes, even when these are expressed overtly in a nonverbal format.

The Whorfian hypothesis (Whorf, 1956) suggests that different languages have different facilities for encoding (and thus manipulating) particular kinds of material. If this is so, the format of the presentation of the problem may be critical. Let me illustrate with Beadthreading where reproduction of a sequence is required. The usual form of this test, as in the Binet test itself, requires a sequence of shapes. If *S*'s language does not have words for these shapes then he is seriously handicapped; the test score is a reflection of the language and not of *S*. Suppose instead that the elements are distinguishable by color as in Reuning's Kalahari studies. In Fiji and in Melanesia generally no verbal distinction is made between green and blue. One has to search for material where a verbal-perceptual barrier does not intervene to lower *S*'s apparent ability to handle cognitive operations. And it is these operations we are interested in, whether we are making group comparisons or selecting or counseling within a group.

Kohan and Rimoldi stress that psychologists concerned with cognition should look more closely at the thinking process itself, particularly as it relates to test performance. With this I entirely agree. But to do so is very difficult. An obvious thing to do is to ask *S* how he solved the problem, but often he cannot give an answer. This should not surprise us. A child of five years can speak his native language perfectly, showing complete mastery of its deep-structural grammar or rules yet being quite incapable of formalizing these rules. If we wish to find out how *S*s 'think' we must ourselves become clever enough to make explicit the rules they are implicitly following. An example of such analysis is Ord's modification of the Kohs Test, replacing the blocks with flat tiles. Some naive but not unintelligent *S*s have great difficulty is seeing how a vertical block surface can be placed in a horizontal orientation. Ord puts all the stimulus material horizontally. *S*'s task is still to make up the required patterns. The Kohs test in the original or WAIS form does not function under extreme conditions. *S*s known to be bright cannot solve the problems with blocks but can with tiles. The revised format is

more valid, in that bright and dull Ss can be discriminated more
sharply from each other.

The mean performance also rises. It seems generally to be the
case that, where a test is applied to exotic Ss, the format of a test
which is most 'valid' *for those subjects* is also the one where their
score is best. Many (perhaps most) reports of differences between
groups in mean test performance are of little value because a test
valid in the one group is not necessarily valid in another.

Another example of a 'tactic fully available to one group and
less so to another' appears with bead threading. In the Binet form
of this task the assemblages to be reproduced are center-symmetric. An S who detects this symmetry halves the difficulty of
the item. European Ss appear to be sensitive to this property.
They make errors which are themselves center-symmetric. But
Australian aborigines err by nonsymmetric omissions or substi-
tutions. When the chains to be reproduced are nonsymmetric, the
differences in the group means is much reduced without, as far as
can be seen, a drop in validity for either group.

May I turn to the relevance of these ideas to the formulation
of a strategy for a testing program?

In this meeting, I feel, insufficient distinction has been made
among various kinds of crosscultural testing. The constraints on
such testing range very widely, from Reuning's work in the
Kalahari where competitive selection is irrelevant to Bennett's
work where the selection issue is paramount.

Cronbach clarifies the issues of the selection paradigm as
applied to persons from different groups, but his paper does not
generalize the conceptualization. His stress on the necessity for
using regression techniques instead of correlation techniques cannot be overemphasized. We ought to abandon the notion of a
single critical score for selection. We ought to have at least two
tests, one a 'best predictor' for the first group and the other a 'best
predictor' for some or all of the second. One would apply both tests
to all candidates. An efficient strategy is to use a disjunctive
combination of the tests for selection, and a conjunctive combination for rejection. The relative proportion of the total sample
allowed to be 'selected by one but not both tests' may be optimized
for a given situation. Under Western conditions this proportion will

probably be small. Where the cultural differences (and test differences) between the groups are large, this proportion will also be large.

We very much need an explicative model which contains the differences between groups in terms of differentiated cognitive capacities, the differences between tests inasmuch as they are measures of these capacities, and the relation of these capacities to the rate of learning of various skills. Van der Flier has outlined some of the features of such a model.

Let me conclude with some indications as to where in a developing country 'basic psychological assessment' may be useful, and where selection as such is not the primary objective. In this last few months we have been trying out the Queensland Test in Fiji as an aid in planning mental-hospital treatment. The hospital intake is very heterogeneous in culture and language yet means must be found to determine, for instance, whether occupational therapy should be continued or dropped. Likewise in a corrective institution for delinquent male adolescents, again with a heterogeneous intake, decisions have to be made as to whether a given child will benefit from the available formal schooling.

I have little patience with arguments about 'culture fair' testing. The central issue is how best we can, if at all, assist developing countries to use the psychometric techniques that have been found useful elsewhere.

REFERENCES

Luria, A. R. (1961) *The role of speech in the regulation of normal and abnormal behaviour.* New York: Pergamon.
McElwain, D. W., Kearney, G. E. & Ord, I. G. (1970) *The Queensland Test: A test of general cognitive ability for use under conditions of reduced communication.* Melbourne: Australian Council for Educational Research.
Vygotsky, L. S. (1962) *Thought and language.* Cambridge: M.I.T. Press.
Whorf, B. L. (1956) *Language, thought and reality.* Cambridge: M.I.T. Press.

JAMES G. GEORGAS and CATHERINE GEORGAS
The Athenian Institute of Anthropos

A children's intelligence test for Greece

Psychometric properties, intracultural effects, crosscultural comparisons

There has been a growing awareness in Greece of the need to measure intelligence to aid in the evaluation of learning difficulties, behavioral and emotional problems, and neurological impairment. In the past, Greek psychologists attempted to meet the increasing demand for assessment of intelligence by employing tests standardized in other cultures such as the Binet Scale, the Wechsler Scale, or Progressive Matrices. IQ scores were derived from foreign norms or the psychologist intuitively estimated the level of intellectual functioning. Since such practices can result in invalid assessments which could have grave consequences on the lives of individuals, Greek psychologists have begun to recognize the need for Greek norms. Up to now, most normative studies have been directed toward specific or local groups such as Army inductees or a particular school.

The purpose of this project was to construct a children's intelligence scale for the general population. This paper focuses on the Athenian standardization studies conducted in other areas of Greece cannot be discussed here.

The scale consists of 4 subtests. A Vocabulary Scale was constructed by selecting 500 Greek words randomly from a Greek dictionary. These words were given to over 700 children, aged 6 through 19. Per cent passing each word at each age level was plotted; words which did not discriminate between age levels were rejected. Approximately 100 words were selected which discriminated according to the above criterion and which spanned the age range 6-18. Two parallel scales of approximately 45 items each were employed in the standardization. The other subtests are the Beery Visual-Motor Integration Test (VMI, paper-and-pencil, reproduction of geometric forms, the Good-enough-Harris Drawing test (Draw-a-Man and Draw-a-Woman), and the Progressive Matrices under a rule that terminated testing after 6 successive failed items.

These scales were given to 227 Athenian Children, of ages 6 through 12. 52 boys and 52 girls from each of these 7 age levels were assigned to socioeconomic classes according to a questionnaire filled out by the parents. SES was determined on the basis of occupation of the head of household, household income, amount of formal education of head of household, and neighborhood. These criteria have been previously used to devise a SES scale for Athens. The frequencies of children per SES level were predetermined to reflect the distribution of families in metropolitan Athens. The children were drawn from 16 schools, public and private, throughout metropolitan Athens, which at that time had a population of approximately two million inhabitants. The children were tested individually by research assistants from the Athenian Institute of Anthropos, who were specially trained by the author for this project. The average grade of each child at the end of the academic year, taken from the school records, was used as a measure of academic achievement.

KR20 reliabilities were computed separately for each age and sex. The reliabilities for Vocabulary range from 0.73 at age 6 to 0.88 at age 12, increasing with age. The Drawing scale reliabilities range from 0.85 at age 6 to 0.95 at age 12. Most of these coefficients are in the 0.90's. The VMI reliabilities range from 0.66 at age 6 to 0.80 at age 10, after which they decrease. This may be due in part of the low ceiling of the test. Matrices reliabilities range from 0.60 at age 6 to 0.98 at age 12.

On the basis of what is known about the construct 'intelligence' since Binet's landmark work, it would be expected that the percentage of children passing each item should increase with age. For each item per cent age passing was plotted against age. As indicated above, the vocabulary items were originally selected in this manner; curves for the normative sample supported the findings from the pilot study. Item analysis of VMI, Drawing and PM indicated satisfactory relationships between

Table 1. Correlations of tests with marks and SES
         (mean over age groups)

Test	Correlation with marks		Correlation with SES	
	Boys	Girls	Boys	Girls
Voc A	.59	.56	.43	.46
Voc B	.60	.57	.41	.48
DAM	.38	.44	.47	.24
DAW	.35	.44	.44	.24
VMI	.37	.44	.35	.20
Matrices	.35	.39	.46	.42

percentage passing and chronological age, although the Greek data are not identical with American or British findings.

Concurrent validity was measured by correlating each scale with the child's marks at the end of the academic year, separately for each age and sex. The correlations were averaged across age, using Fisher's z (Table 1). Vocabulary correlated highest with academic achievement. At lower ages, correlations were in the .40's and .50's and at higher ages reached into the .70's. These findings suggest that the Vocabulary scales are adequate predictors of school achievement, and are consistent with the expectation that a measure of verbal ability would correlate higher with school achievement than would nonverbal measures. The DAM, DAW and VMI correlations are quite similar. PM correlated least with school achievement.

Culture-free tests of intelligence, or at least culture-fair tests, have been a recurrent topic in intelligence testing, and much of the research has involved the Goodenough test and Matrices. It is therefore important to explore the relationship of SES to test performance here. Correlations between test scores and SES were computed separately for each age and sex, and then averaged across ages (Table 1). The relatively strong relation of vocabulary to SES was expected, but the equally strong relationship of the Goodenough-Harris and Raven tests was not. The lower correlations for males on DAM, DAW, and VWI were puzzling; this led us to explore further the relationship of sex to SES. School marks were correlated with SES, for each age and sex. The correlations, averaged across age, were 0.45 for females and 0.35 for males. The correlation was higher for females at ages 6, 7, and 8, but no consistent sex difference was found at ages 9-12.

One expects a significant correlation between SES and marks. It was surprising that girls' marks should be more tied to SES, particularly at the lower ages. One possible explanation is that at lower ages, where the evaluation of academic performance is less precise, teachers tend to be influenced by the girl's SES, while they are more sensitive to the boy's performance level.

Results from a study with Athenian adults, employing three verbal scales adapted from WAIS, appear to be relevant here. On each of the verbal scales, scores of females correlated higher with educational level than those of males, and the mean scores of males on the tests were higher than those of females. Traditionally the female in the Greek culture has been in less contact with the events outside her family life. She is expected to concern herself with the family, with raising children and with matters of the home. The male has had more contact with the outside world. We interpret the higher correlation with educational level for females as indicating that her sources of information about the outside world are constrained and dependent upon knowledge acquired from authority such as the school, the church, or male authority figures. Since her familial role excludes her from transactions with the non-familial world, she tends to passively accept what she has learned without questioning or investigating further.

For each scale in the present study, means of sex groups at each age were compared (Table 2). On Vocabulary A, males were consistently higher than females; on Vocabulary B, differences are similar but not significant at the lower ages. This sex difference is consistent with that found for Greek adults on the Wechsler Verbal scale. In most studies with children in the USA, girls tend to score higher than boys on verbal scales. On DAM, there is no sex difference. In the 1963 standardization, Harris found that American girls scored higher than boys, but a 1963-1965 study conducted by the USPHS on a national sample found no sex difference. Sex differences favoring girls have been found in Canada, Japan, Argentina, and among Eskimos. Sex differences favoring boys have been found in India. Sex differences were absent in a South African Bantu sample, in Turkey,

Table 2. *Smoothed means for each test, by age and sex*

	Voc A		Voc B		DAM		DAW		VMI		Matrices	
Age	Boys	Girls	Boys	Girls	Boys	Girls	Boys	Girls	Boys	Girls	Boys	Girls
6	14.38	13.05	14.11	13.91	18.08	18.65	17.56	19.59	12.34	11.72	9.40	10.04
7	16.51	14.98	16.74	16.47	21.36	22.31	20.67	23.73	13.11	12.56	9.98	10.78
8	20.22	18.22	21.15	20.68	25.68	27.10	25.18	29.50	14.35	13.97	11.15	12.07
9	24.45	21.56	26.41	25.13	30.55	31.21	29.67	33.80	15.60	15.09	14.31	14.30
10	27.89	25.08	29.96	28.83	34.89	34.21	34.25	36.82	16.78	16.01	18.55	16.73
11	30.93	27.67	33.33	31.19	38.29	37.86	36.95	39.91	17.50	16.34	23.52	19.13
12	32.56	29.10	35.01	32.53	39.83	40.79	37.21	42.76	17.71	16.37	26.05	20.18

and in Syria. On DAW, girls do better at each age. This is the only test on which girls consistently score higher than boys. Harris found, in both the 1963 and 1963-1965 samples, that females scored higher than males, which is consistent with our findings. Harris suggests that girls tend to identify with the female role more readily than do boys, and hence are more perceptive of details of the female figure. In Harris' view, Western cultural values emphasize the male role, producing less differentiation between the sexes in perceiving details of the male figure. This interpretation would apply to Greece, and likely to many non-Western cultures which emphasize the male, and the woman is openly acknowledged as of lesser importance.

On VMI boys tend to score higher than girls, especially at ages 10-12. In Beery's American standardization, girls were slightly superior up to the age of 8, after which age boys began to pull ahead. On PM no sex difference was found at the lower ages. As with VMI, there is a trend at ages 10-12 for boys to score higher than girls. Numerous studies in the United States have shown that during the early school years boys begin to show a marked superiority on spatial ability. This is consistent with the results in Greece with VMI and PM.

Means for the Greek sample on the Drawing and VMI tests were compared with those of the American standardization samples. Harris presents data for the original 1963 standardization and a 1963-1965 nationwide sample; the results differed slightly. The means of Greek boys and girls on DAM and DAW at each age are closer to those of the 1963 standardization, but on DAW the American boys and girls score a bit higher. Compared to the

1963-1965 standardization group, Greek children outperformed Americans at age 8 and above, on both DAM and DAW. On VMI there is no difference between Greek and American means for either sex at age 6 or 7. Beginning with age 8, means of American boys and girls are higher than thoss of the Greek children, the difference increasing with age.

A valid comparison on Matrices cannot be made because Raven's data are not in a form comparable to ours. This study does not allow us to explain differences in mean scores between the Greek, American and British samples, but it does make it clear that the norms developed in one culture cannot be applied directly to other cultures.

One source of the mean-score differences between cultures is the different SES distributions in Greece, the USA, and England. In Greece, the distribution of SES is skewed, while in the United States and Britain, it is more nearly normal. For example, the proportion of families within of upper-middle SES is higher in the USA than in Athens. Therefore, differences in mean score between these two cultures could be largely a function of the weighting of the several social classes, rather than evidence of real differences in intellectual ability.

Another source of the mean differences could be the items. The items of VMI, DAM/DAW, and PM were selected within the American or British culture. That is, the final sets of items was selected from a larger universe of items because they discriminated in the U.S. or Britain between children according to certain psychometric criteria. It is thus possible that some of the items favor the American or British sample, and this may contribute to the differences between Greek and other samples.

In conclusion, the above discussion emphasizes the necessity for each culture to devise its own relevant and valid measures of intellectual functioning, and notes some of the problems inherent in comparing intellectual functioning from culture to culture.

Note: *Ahumada reports that Mexican DAM norms match American norms at age 6 but later fall behind; indeed, the mean raw score reaches a peak around age 12 and then declines. Ahumada's data also show a DAM difference favoring males.* (Eds.)

CIĞDEM KAGITÇIBAŞI 23
Middle East Technical University, Ankara

Application of the D 48 test in Turkey*

The D 48 or 'Dominoes' Test of general intellectual ability is well known and widely used in Europe. It has only recently been introduced to the USA by Gough and Domino (1963). In Turkey it is known very little.

In this study an attempt has been made to apply this test to a group of sixth- and seventh-grade children in Turkey. A basic aim was to determine the extent to which the D 48 may be used effectively in Turkey. There is a great need in Turkey for tests of this sort for screening purposes.

CHARACTER OF THE TEST

The D 48 Test is essentially a nonverbal test of *g*, the general factor in intelligence. It consists of 44 problems (plus 4 examples) regarding relationships among sets of dominoes. These relationships, based on analogies and progressions, vary from problem to problem and involve such principles as simple addition, identity, identity with reversal, double progression, subtraction, subtraction with progression, etc.

Items progress in difficulty, the problems having a wide range of difficulty. The mean scores of groups that have been tested vary from 12 to 31 raw score points (Table 3). The testing time is

* I am indebted to Miss Ayhan Aksu and to Miss Ulku Baysal for their assistance.

25 minutes. It is possible, however, to use the D 48 without a time restriction (Ferracuti & Rizzo, 1959).

The D 48 has a number of attractive features. First of all, it is highly saturated with *g*, its loading on *g* being even higher than that of Progressive Matrices. It is free of the spatial factor which is a problem with the Matrices.

Secondly, the D 48 has high potentiality as an instrument for crosscultural application and comparison. The game of dominoes is known in most literate societies, thus in crosscultural use there is not an important problem of unequal familiarity with the testing stimuli. The usual tendency in crosscultural testing is to search for stimuli that are novel to all cultures. Another logical approach would be to search for stimuli that are equally known to all cultures, to equate experience. Under this second principle, the D 48 seems to be a potential candidate for wide crosscultural application. Research with the D 48 has shown, further, that *S*s who know how to play the game of dominoes do not score any better than *S*s who do not know how to play the game. This is as would be expected, for the principle used in the game of dominoes is not utilized in the D 48.

The D 48 is entirely nonverbal, except for the short and simple instructions. This feature extends its use to nonliterate people. *S*s of lower intelligence can understand the test as well as Matrices.

In the D 48 chance is almost completely eliminated. Finally, it is easy to administer in a short time and to score, and it can be used as an individual test or as a group test, without modification.

Spearman long ago showed that tests which require the eduction of correlates have the greatest *g* saturation. The principle involved may be represented diagrammatically as follows:

$$\frac{A \qquad B}{C}$$

S is asked to discover the existing relationship between A and B, and to apply this relationship to C so as to find a fourth element, D, which will be related to C as B is related to A. Later work showed, further, that tests with the greatest saturation of *g* contain nonverbal perceptual material.

Progressive Matrices was constructed by Penrose and Raven in

1938, utilizing the above principles. This test proved to have the greatest saturation in *g* at that time, and was adopted by the British army. As mentioned before, however, the Matrices had the disadvantage of containing certain poorly defined group factors, in particular a visual perception factor.

In 1943 Anstey and Illing (as reported by Gough & Domino, 1963) first developed the domino item as a parallel to Progressive Matrices. The same principles were used as in the Matrices, but to avoid the nuisance loading of the spatial factor, homogeneous material, consisting solely of domino patterns was used. In a factorial comparison made by Vernon (1950) the following factor loadings were obtained:

	g	*k*	*v*	*n*
Progressive Matrices	.79	.15	.00	--
D 48 Test	.87	.00	.00	.05

Various versions of the test were developed by Anstey and are currently used in England. A French adaptation was made by Binois in the late 1940s (reported by Pasquasy & Doutrepont, 1956). This version, published under the name 'D 48' in France and Italy, was introduced to the States in 1962 by the Consulting Psychologists Press. This version had been used in the present study.

PLAN OF THIS STUDY

The desirable features of the D 48 led us to think that the test would have great potential for use in crosscultural settings and in particular for application in Turkey. Few tests of intellectual aptitude have been adapted for use in Turkey. There are Turkish adaptations of the Stanford-Binet, Army Alpha, WAIS, etc., but these are not widely known and applied. Among the possible reasons for their limited application might be the facts that they contain verbal material and that their administration and scoring require much training, time, and money. The D 48 avoids these difficulties.

The simple instructions for the test were translated by the writer. The D 48 Test was administered to 100 sixth- and seventh-grade students in a coeducational secondary school* in Bursa**, Turkey, in the fall of 1967. The modal ages in the two grades are 11 and 12, respectively. The 25-minute time limit was observed. The complete school achievement records of these students over the subsequent three years were then obtained, and statistical analyses were performed on the basis of these academic achievement data.

RESULTS AND INTERPRETATION

The percentage of students answering each item correctly and the rank order for each item were examined. The progression of difficulty follows the order of the items, with some exceptions. For example, Item 9 occupies rank 23 in difficulty, and Item 33 has rank 24, for sixth graders; they occupy the ranks 21 and 25, respectively, for seventh graders.

The rank-order correlation between these ranks and similar ranks obtained from American pupils (Grades 5 and 6 pooled. Gough & Domino, 1963) was very high (0.94 for sixth-grade and 0.95 for seventh grade). This result shows that the relative difficulty level of the 44 test items is rather constant for different age groups, even when tested in different languages in different countries.

Table 1, most of which is taken from Gough and Domino (1963), gives mean scores on the D 48 for a number of samples. Data from Cusin (1959) show higher scores for engineering and science graduates than for those in jurisprudence, letters and philosophy. Gough and Domino (1963) report that this progression was taken by Cusin as evidence for the validity of the D 48.

---

* In Turkey primary education starts at the age of six and lasts for five years. The secondary school that follows has a three-year program, leading to the *lycée* (high school, three years), which in its turn leads to the university.

** Bursa is a city of about 250,000 in western Turkey, near Istanbul.

This conclusion might be considered doubtful; however, these data may point to a potential significance of the test, mainly, sensitivity to (or indication of) scientific aptitude or, mathematical reasoning. More research is needed to clarify this point. If this is found to be the case, the test would be able to serve a special purpose in the search for scientific talent – an important service especially for underdeveloped countries where there is an urgent need for it.

D 48 scores increase with age and educational level for both sexes. This is direct evidence for the validity of the test. The Turkish data also show higher scores in the older group. This difference of 5.49 points is greater than would be expected from a one-year age difference. It is difficult to explain this finding. It could be due to some unknown characteristics of the groups, especially of the sixth graders, or to situational factors to be mentioned below.

Related to the above is a consideration of the comparison of scores in different countries. Means for our sixth and seventh graders are 12.08 and 17.57, respectively. These averages are somewhat lower than those for similar age groups in Europe and the USA (Table 1). The Turkish standard deviations are very similar to those of the other groups. The lower means may be due at least partially to the fact that our subjects had absolutely no test sophistication; this was the first time they were taking a test of this sort. The test was given on the first day of school in order to divide both sixth and seventh grades into homogeneous class sections. The sixth graders took the test on their first day in a new secondary school, having come from primary schools where they did not have any experience with tests. The fact that they were in an entirely new environment might have increased their insecurity and thus have affected their scores adversely.

The predictive validity of the D 48 was assessed from records of academic achievement during the three years following the test administration. Only academic subjects were included in the grade-point average (GPA). The subjects included in the GPA were the following: Turkish language, social studies (history, geography and civics), mathematics, science (biology in Grade 6; biology and physics in Grade 7; biology, physics and chemistry in

228   *Cığdem Kagıtçıbaşı*

Table 1. Statistics for the D 48 Test on various samples

Samples	N	M	s.d.
Italy (Cusin, 1959)			
a) Graduates in engineering	160	32.46	4.67
b) Graduates in science	28	30.71	5.10
c) Graduates in economics and commerce	47	30.04	4.79
d) Graduates in jurisprudence, letters, and philosophy	28	27.96	5.98
Italy (Ferracuti & Rizzo, 1959)			
a) University students, male	100	26.70	5.60
b) University students, female	100	24.80	6.20
France (Maury, 1954)			
a) Primary-school graduates			
1. Males	307	14.25	6.06
2. Females	246	13.15	6.82
b) Students, *quatrième classe* (ninth)			
1. Males	144	22.87	5.40
2. Females	191	23.73	6.94
c) Students, *deuxième classe* (eleventh grade)			
1. Males	60	27.70	4.68
d) Students, *baccalaureat* (twelfth grade)			
1. Males	73	30.70	5.04
2. Females	118	27.82	5.12
France (Pasquasy & Doutrepont, 1956)			
a) Young men, ages 20-25	522	19.78	8.61
b) Engineers and military officers, males	118	30.34	5.11
Belgium and Switzerland (Pasquasy & Doutrepont, 1956)			
a) Students, both sexes, ages 10:6 to 11:5	34	20.00	5.75
b) Students, both sexes, ages 11:6 to 12:5	127	19.07	6.34
c) Students, both sexes, ages 12:6 to 13:5	199	19.33	6.45
d) Students, both sexes, ages 13:6 to 14:5	253	19.93	6.62
e) Students, both sexes, ages 14:6 to 15:5	181	20.21	7.14
f) Students, both sexes, ages 15:6 to 16:5	125	22.84	7.05
g) Students, both sexes, ages 16:6 and over	87	25.57	6.72
France (Vautrin, 1954)			
a) Students, both sexes, ages 11 to 13	78	20.76	5.36

Table 1. Statistics for the D 48 Test on various samples (continued)

Samples	N	M	s.d.
U.S.A. (Gough & Domino, 1963)			
a) Fifth-grade students, both sexes	34	18.68	5.38
b) Sixth-grade students, both sexes	52	20.02	5.86
Turkey (Present study)			
a) Sixth-grade students, both sexes, age about 11	38	12.08	7.04
b) Seventh-grade students, both sexes, age about 12	54	17.57	5.94

Table 2. Correlations of the D 48 with grades (6th-grade students, N = 50)

	1st Year	2nd Year	3rd Year
Turkish language	.52	.47	.54
Social studies	.56	.42	.45
Mathematics	.70	.62	.46
Science	.58	.50	.59
Foreign language	.32	.28	.30
GPA	*.62*	*.57*	*.58*

Table 3. Correlations of the D 48 with grades (7th-grade students, N = 50)

	1st Year	2nd Year	3rd Year
Turkish language	.38	.29	—
Social studies	.34	.31	—
Mathematics	.36	.15	—
Science	.28	.29	—
Foreign language	.39	.18	—
GPA	*.50*	*.40*	*.31**

* A conservative value, as 8 students who failed or dropped out were not included. Since their test scores and grades were low, their inclusion would have increased the correlations.

Grade 8) and foreign language (English). The academic records covered the above for the sixth graders. For the seventh graders, two years' records covered the above. In the third year, they were in *lycée*. As the lycée subjects are numerous, for the third-year record only the academic CPA was used.

Tables 2 and 3 present the correlations of the D 48 scores with the various grades. The first year's values are higher than those reported by Gough and Domino (1963) and still higher than those observed by them for any of the four parts of the Stanford Achievement Test* (Gough and Domino do not provide any data for subsequent years). Thus, it seems that the D 48 is a good predictor of scholastic performance at the secondary-school level in Turkey. It is important to note that the D 48 test shows high predictive validity not only for a short time but rather consistently predicts academic achievement for as long a period as three years. This prediction is at an even higher level for our sixth graders than for our seventh graders – a result in agreement with most of the similar prediction data found in the literature.

In conclusion it may be said that D 48 Test of general ability shows high potentiality for effective use in Turkey as a predictor of school success. In this capacity, it may be used by schools, government and other agencies which provide scholarships to promising students as an efficient tool of screening. It can thus be considered a useful device for manpower planning in developing countries. It is efficient and useful in such large-scale application. In another capacity, it seems to be a potentially promising test for crosscultural comparative research on intelligence and general abilities. In both capacities its strength seems to lie in its inherent characteristics, namely, its high saturation with g, its easy administration and scoring, its nonverbal nature and cross-cultural relevance.

REFERENCES

Cusin, S. G. (1959) Contributo alla taratura italiana del D 48. *Boll. Psicol. Soc. appl.*, No. 31-36, 259-261.

* For fifth graders Gough and Domino give the following correlations of GPA: with D 48: 0.58; with Stanford Achievement Test (SAT)-Arithmetic: 0.42; with SAT-Language: 0.52; with SAT-Reading: 0.51; and with SAT-Spelling: 0.26. For sixth graders the corresponding correlations of GPA are the following: with D 48: 0.45; with SAT-Arithmetic Comprehension: 0.25; with SAT-Arithmetic Reasoning: 0.37; and with SAT-Total Score: 0.35.

Ferracuti, F. & Rizzo, G. B. (1959) Studio sul test D-48 applicato ad una populazione italiana di livello scolastico superiore. *Boll. Psicol. Soc. appl.*, No. 31-36, 77-83.

Gough, H. G. & Domino, G. (1963) The D 48 Test as a measure of general ability among grade school children. *J. consult. Psychol.*, 27, No. 4, 344-349.

Pasquasy, R. & Doutrepont, G. (1956) Le test des dominos (D 48). *Bull. Orient. scol. profess.*, 5, 20-34.

Vautrin, H. (1954) Etude du D 48. *Bull. Inst. nat. Orient. prof.*, 10, 158-164.

Vernon, P. E. (1950) *The structure of human abilities.* London: Methuen.

DHIA ABUL-HUBB
University of Baghdad

24

Application of Progressive Matrices in Iraq

Iraq, as a newly developing country, has witnessed a modern trend of using test and measurement activities. The University of Baghdad and the Ministry of Education have established centers for educational and psychological research. In the departments of psychology and education of both the University of Baghdad and Al-Mustanziriya University, Baghdad, some evaluation and measurement courses are given to students preparing to give psychological services.

One of the newly introduced tests is the Raven Progressive Matrices, which is also being used in the EAR. The statistical calculations for the standardization have not so far been undertaken. The present paper can reflect only tentative findings. No final findings about its usefulness as a culture-free test for Middle Eastern countries have been reached.

The Ss are 1389 citizens from different walks of life and occupational groups. Both sexes are represented; the age range is limited to 18 to 35. Secondary-school and college students were more interested in taking this test, while illiterate and less able members of the society did not cooperate easily, hence the results might be biased in some age groups. Urban Ss are prominent in the sample, although some rural areas were included.

The test was individually administered by qualified students of the universities already mentioned.

In his Guide to the Standard Progressive Matrices, Raven did not mention the number of Ss in each of his age groups. He has given only the percentile points calculated from scores of 3665

soldiers and 2192 civilians of ages 20 to 65. For comparison of
the Iraqi data with Raven's, which deal only with 5-year periods,
we have pooled adjacent age groups to form intervals corresponding to Raven's.

RESULTS

Table 1 presents percentile points for Raven's sample and ours. It
must be noted that the Iraqi subjects were not as well qualified
to face this kind of test situation, even though they did adjust
themselves easily after they were informed about the way the
test works. The time factor was undoubtedly significant.

Table 1. Percentile points of the Iraqi sample compared to those of Raven(Total N = 1389)

Percen- tile	Age 14 - 17		Age 18 - 22		Age 23 - 27		Age 28 - 31		Age 32 - 35	
	Raven	Iraq $N=204$	Raven	Iraq $N=547$	Raven	Iraq $N=331$	Raven	Iraq $N=242$	Raven	Iraq $N=65$
95	53	52	55	56	55	56	54	56	53	56
90	52	52	54	52	54	52	53	52	51	56
75	48	44	49	49	49	48	47	48	45	48
50	44	40	44	44	44	44	42	46	40	44
25	38	28	40	37	37	36	34	40	30	36
10	28	16	28	28	28	24	25	28	—	20
5	23	12	24	23	23	20	19	24	—	16

Total N = 1389

At age 14-17 the lower half of the Iraqi sample does less well
than the lower half of Raven's. There is little or no difference
between the samples at ages 18-27. In the oldest group, all the
percentile points of the Iraqi sample are higher than in Raven's.

Table 2. Skewness indices for Iraqi samples

Age	sk_s	O_{sk}	T	P
14 - 17	−1.5	1.3	−1.1	n.s
18 - 22	−9.4	5.3	−1.8	< .05
23 - 27	−3.8	.8	− .48	n.s.
28 - 31	− .5	.8	− .6	n.s.
32 - 35	− .32	2.28	− .14	n.s.

This might be ascribed to the greater experience of the individuals tested or to the rejection of the test by some adults who do not want to disclose their inadequacy. There are a number of very low scores in the 32-35 age group, however.

Table 2 shows the results of calculations of the percentile coefficient of skewness and the standard error of skewness. (No such calculation could be made for Raven's data). The tails of the distribution extend toward the lower end of the scale, hence the skewness is negative; but the skewness is not marked, only the largest sample (18-22) showing a significant departure from normality.

REFERENCES

Abul-Hubb, D. (1970) Raven's Standard Progressive Matrices, Arabic version (Mimeographed).

Raven, J. C. (1960) *Guide to the Standard Progressive Matrices.* London: H. K. Lewis.

ERNEST McDANIEL   25
Purdue University, West Lafayette

The Purdue motion-picture tests of visual perception*

This paper describes the rationale and development of a series of motion-picture tests of perceptual abilities of young children. These tests meet the criteria for instruments appropriate for crosscultural research set forth by Dr. Reuning (p. 171): The test situation and task must be understandable to the testee without verbal explanation; when confronted with a test item, the testee must know without further instruction what he is expected to do; the subject's response must be nonverbal.

These tests are designed to measure four abilities which are components of more complex perceptual processes:

Form perception	The ability to perceive visual patterns
Visual memory span	The ability to perceive and remember multiple stimuli
Spatial orientation	The ability to perceive and appreciate the arrangements of objects in space
Serial integration	The ability to accumulate visual stimuli over a period of time and organize them into meaningful patterns

Much experimental and theoretical work has been accomplished

* These tests were developed with the support of a grant from the Bureau of Education for the Handicapped, U.S. Office of Education, N.C. Kephart has served as continuing consultant for the project and Mrs. Carla Coffman has been the full-time research assistant.

in each of these four areas. Zusne (1970) lists 2500 studies of form perception.

Motion-picture film permits the realistic representation of objects in three-dimensional space. It also permits well controlled sequencing of visual information over a time period. This information must be accumulated and organized if an individual is to make sense of his visual world. Kephart (1971) discusses the relationship between such visual tasks and the demands of the real world and, particularly, school learning.

The film tests described here are mostly patterned on earlier work accomplished by Gibson (1947). Gibson and his colleagues developed a series of filmed tests measuring distance and motion perception, and other abilities related to the performance of aircraft crews. Seibert and Snow (1964) used a number of Gibson films together with tests of their own to study visual perception, cognition and memory. These and subsequent studies (Seibert, Reid & Snow, 1967) identified a cluster of factors which seem to account for performance on a variety of perceptual and cognitive tasks. Clinical experience with children exhibiting learning disabilities suggests additional visual tasks potentially useful in diagnostic work with children (Strauss & Kephart, 1955).

THE TESTS

Ten tests were developed which, unlike paper-and-pencil tests, incorporate móvement, cues from three-dimensional space, and the integration of stimuli occurring through time. Stimulus material is projected on a screen and the child indicates his response by marking the appropriate design in an answer booklet. Each of the 10 tests may be described briefly.

A film demonstrating these tasks was shown at the conference. The actual tests are on 'super-eight' film.

> *Spatial Orientation of Objects* (16 items). On the screen red, yellow, and blue pegs move into new positions on a board. The child must choose the correct ending position from among three pictures in his answer book.

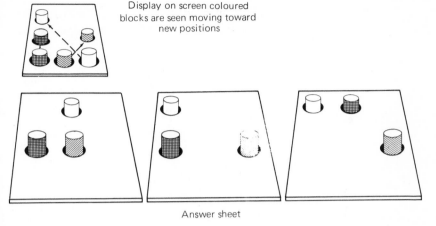

Display on screen coloured
blocks are seen moving toward
new positions

Answer sheet

Figure 1. Spatial orientation of objects

Form Identification (18 items). A geometric design appears briefly on the screen. The child must identify the design from among four alternative figures in his answer book.

Moving Slot (16 items). A design moves upward behind an open slot so that only a portion of the design is seen at any given time. The child identifies the design from a group of four.

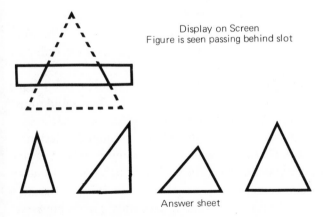

Display on Screen
Figure is seen passing behind slot

Answer sheet

Figure 2. Moving Slot

Figural Memory Span (18 items). From two to five free form designs are displayed briefly in an arbitrary sequence. The child must select the correct sequence on the printed page.

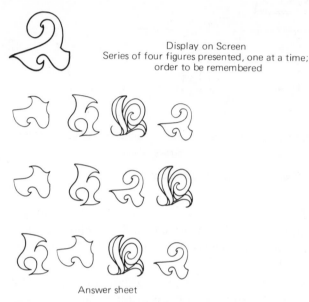

Display on Screen
Series of four figures presented, one at a time;
order to be remembered

Answer sheet

Figure 3. Figural Memory Span

Temporal Memory Span I (18 items). Common objects appear successively on the screen; for example, a hammer, block, shoe, and spoon. The child must number objects on his answer book to indicate their order of appearance.

Pathfinder (18 items). A white dot moves on a dark background tracing an irregular path. The child must identify the correct path from among four alternatives.

Embedded Figures (18 items). A geometric design is exposed briefly on the screen. The design is hidden in one of four designs on the answer sheet; the child is to mark that design.

Successive Figures (18 items). Separate lines appear on the screen one at a time. The child must correctly iden-

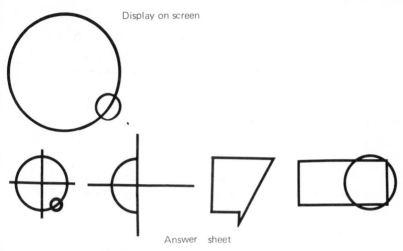

Figure 4. Embedded Figures

tify the figure which would be formed by organizing the separate elements.

Temporal Memory Span II (18 items). A series of free-form designs appear on the screen, one at a time. The child must identify the correct order of appearance from among three alternative displays.

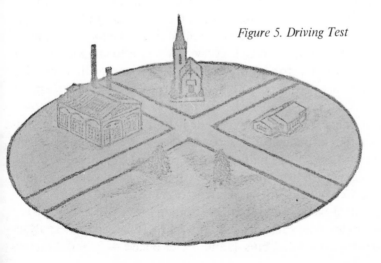

Figure 5. Driving Test

Figure 5. Driving Test

Driving Test (12 items). A toy truck moves through the intersection of a model village. The child must trace the path of the truck on a drawing of the village rotated 90° from the original observation point.

The design presupposes that the 10 tests measure four perceptual abilities.

Form perception	Form Identification
	Embedded Figures
Visual memory span	Figural Memory Span
Spatial orientation	Spatial Orientation of Objects
	Driving Test
Serial integration	Moving Slot
	Temporal Memory Span I
	Pathfinder
	Successive Figures
	Temporal Memory Span II

FACTOR ANALYSIS

The first question of general theoretical interest refers to the relations exhibited by tests purporting to measure some underlying factor or ability. 140 children took the tests in Grades 1, 2, 4, 6, and 8. Factor analysis yielded very nearly a unifactor solution. Factor I, on which every test had a loading of 0.66 or higher, accounted for 56 per cent of the variance. The tests with the high loadings represented all four of the basic perceptual processes thought to underlie the battery. The pooling of Ss over a wide range undoubtedly tended to produce a strong, undifferentiated first factor. A second factor accounted for 9 per cent of the variance; it was represented in four tests: Pathfinder (0.52), Driving Test (0.48), Moving Slot (0.44), Figural Memory Span (0.40). Two of these are serial integration tests.

The data were reanalyzed by forming groups spanning two or three grades. One such analysis appears in Table 1. Other analyses for grades 1 plus 2, 2 plus 4, and 4 plus 6 gave 4, 2, and 2 factors respectively. There was no consistent pattern. Tests which had been designed to measure similar abilities did not fall into the same factor in these analyses.

Two tests – Embedded Figures and Successive Figures – seem almost always to show a larger number of significant correlations with other tests in the battery, and appear on Factor I in every

Table 1. *Factor loadings in 10 perceptual tests for pupils in Grades 6 and 8 (N = 59)*

	I	II	III	IV
Spatial Orientation of Objects			.67	
Form Identification		.77		
Moving Slot				.72
Figural Memory Span			.60	
Temporary Memory Span I		.63		.48
Pathfinder			.84	
Embedded Figures	.73			
Successive Figures	.85			
Temporal Memory Span II	.37			.70
Driving Test	.39	.64		

analysis. The ability to hold firmly a visual gestalt despite distracting elements and the ability to construct such gestalts from pieces may be fairly fundamental abilities.

We have limited evidence indicating some correlation of these testw with reading ability. We anticipate that the tests may be useful in studies of the deaf, the brain damaged, and the aged. There is some scattered crosscultural work on visual perception (see Segall, Campbell, & Herskovits, 1966; LeVine, 1970; and certain papers in Al-Issa & Dennis, 1970). In general crosscultural studies have dealt with perceptions of geometric illusions, pictorial depth, color perception, binocular rivalry, and various studies involving social perception. It would seem that, as LeVine suggests, the most valuable studies in this area would be crosscultural studies of perceptual development involving longitudinal collection of data during the childhood years when perceptual development is exhibiting maximum growth. Such data should provide insight regarding the mediating effects of environmental factors on the development of perceptual abilities.

REFERENCES

Al-Issa, I. & Dennis, W. (1970) *Cross-cultural studies of behavior.* New York: Holt, Rinehart & Winston.

Gibson, J. J. (Ed.) (1947) *Motion picture testing and research.* Army Air Forces aviation psychology program, report No. 7. Washington: U.S. Government Printing Office.

Kephart, N. C. (1971) The relationship of measured perceptual abilities to school achievement. Paper presented at the meeting of the Amer. Educ. Res. Assn., New York.

LeVine, R. A. (1970) Cross-cultural study in child psychology. In P. H. Mussen (Ed.), *Carmichael's manual of child psychology* (3rd ed.). New York: Wiley. Pp. 559-612.

Segall, M. H., Campbell, D. T. & Herskovits, M. J. (1966) *The influence of culture on visual perception.* Indianapolis: Bobbs-Merrill.

Seibert, W. F. & Snow, R. E. (1965) Studies in cine-psychometry I: Preliminary factor analysis of visual cognition and memory. Final Report, OE Grant 7-12-0280-184.

Seibert, W. F., Reid, J. C. & Snow, R. E. (1967) Studies in cine-psychometry II: Continued factoring of audio and visual cognition and memory. Final Report, OE Grant 7-24-0280-257.

Strauss, A. A. & Kephart, N. C. (1955) *Psychopathology of the brain injured child.* New York: Grune and Stratton.

Zusne, L. (1970). *Visual perception of form.* New York: Academic Press.

BERNARD RIMLAND

Naval Personnel and Training Research Laboratory, San Diego

A search for tests of practical intelligence

For the past several years our laboratory has been engaged in an extensive research effort intended to devise and evaluate tests suitable for use with personnel who score markedly below average on existing aptitude tests. If we are sufficiently skillful, and sufficiently lucky, we will produce tests which will find useful nonacademic aptitudes in men classed as 'failures' by conventional tests.

THEORY

One approach which has been used in a variety of settings in the past as a means of penetrating this problem has been the use of 'culture-free' or 'culture-fair tests.' While we have experimented with tests of this sort, it has not been the primary focus of our attention. For one thing, most research on culture-fair tests has shown that these tests do not permit low aptitude individuals, such as minority-group members, to score any higher relative to the general population than they do on more typical intelligence tests. Another reason for not concentrating on culture-fair tests may be seen in the Raven Matrices, which is to all appearances a nonverbal culture-free test, yet is also one of the best available measures of g.

Our approach was suggested by four findings which are firmly established in psychometrics yet which are quite paradoxical.

The usual types of intelligence test do a very good job of what they are supposed to do, mainly, to measure scholastic aptitude. Typical mental tests do not predict job performance at all well, in civilian life or on the military services. Ghiselli's *Validity of occupational aptitude tests* (1966) documents the large drop in test validity found when one moves from predicting training or school performance to the prediction of actual field or on-job performance. Numerous studies of the mentally retarded, in both the U.S. and England, show that their job performance after they leave school does not differ markedly from that of their classmates of 10 or 20 years earlier.

The grades one achieves in school are very rarely predictive of later on-the-job performance. This finding too has been very often reported in both the civilian and military literature.

The types of tests that predict grade average are not the types which predict on-job performance. Vocabulary, reasoning, and similar measures are by far the best for predicting school grades. In both civilian life and in the military tests of perceptual or clerical speed are the best predictors of job performance (though even *their* level of prediction of job performance is not very high).

Taken together, these four facts suggest that job performance may involve a rather different type of intelligence than the abstract or academic type of intelligence measured by most present intelligence tests. For some years I have been puzzled by these findings and have tried to understand and characterize this practical type of intelligence.* Undoubtedly, the variety of sub-types of practical intelligence accounts for the fact that each person does best on particular jobs. It seems that the most important cognitive characteristic of on-job performance – the key difference between people who do very well on jobs and those who do less poorly – may be in what I will call 'with-it-ness' or 'here and now' intelligence.

Let me give some examples. Some of the greatest thinkers in human history, people whose abstract powers of reasoning are unsurpassed, appear to have had rather low levels of 'with-it-ness'

---

*Intelligence factors called 'practical' by others (e.g., Vernon) do not seem to me to be adequate.

or 'here and now' intelligence. There are many stories of Einstein walking around in the Princeton snow with his overcoat unbuttoned, perhaps with one shoe untied, thinking such deep thoughts that he had little time to devote to the 'here and now'. Another example might be Sir Isaac Newton, a man of extraordinary powers of concentration, about whom is told the following story: Once, while entertaining a houseful of guests, Newton left for his wine cellar to replenish the wine. When he did not return after a lengthy absence, the guests went down to the cellar to try to find him, thinking that perhaps he had stumbled in the dark and injured himself. They found him sitting by a dusty barrelhead scribbling mathematical formulae in the dust atop the barrels. He had become engrossed with an abstract problem while on the errand. A third and more recent example might be J. Robert Oppenheimer, whose biography was recently published. Oppenheimer was so deeply involved in the intricacies of physics that he had not become aware of the stock market crash of 1929 until Lawrence mentioned it to him the following May. A recent magazine article mentions that when the library of the Union Theological Seminary burned in New York several years ago a certain Hebrew scholar had to be physically removed from the burning building, so engrossed was he in the ancient manuscripts he was studying. In another article, Tigran Petrosian, the chess champion, was reported to say, 'It's funny, even when I'm skiing I'm thinking about chess.'

On the other hand, we have people whose abstract intelligence must be quite low, as is evidenced by the fact that they have failed the Armed Forces Qualification Test yet who have managed to conduct themselves very well in the everyday world. Some famous professional athletes have reportedly failed military classification tests, yet they are obviously well able to carry on nonabstract business in the daily world. I am reminded of a good friend of mine who had an unusually high IQ and earned good grades, but was a poor baseball player in high school. He reports that frequently he would find himself in the outfield during a school baseball game with people shouting at him from some distance away. He would then look down and find that the ball had rolled to a stop at his feet. He would pick it up and look around and try to figure out what he ought to do with it. Needless to say, his 'with-it-ness' or 'here and now' intelligence is very much open to question.

I am not contending that the two types of intelligence described above are necessarily uncorrelated, even though my examples were of men high in one and low in the other. In actuality, they are probably positively correlated, as are most types of cognitive ability. But there is more reason to expect to find persons high in one but low on the other of these abilities than is true with most other abilities. The two types represent a 'trade-off' situation — if you are a pitcher studying the batter, a waiter taking an order, or a pilot landing on a carrier, you had better not be daydreaming or otherwise attending to intra-cerebral stimuli. You cannot do both. Human attention is surprisingly unidirectional and indivisible.

That is enough on the theoretical underpinnings of our work. Those especially interested in the relationships between intelligence, memory, and attention as related to abstractive ability may wish to see my book *Infantile autism,* especially Chapters 5 and 13. Arthur Jensen's recent article 'How much can we increase IQ and educability? ' makes use of very similar concepts in the discussion of Type-1 and Type-2 intelligence. Type-2 intelligence is similar to the abstract intelligence I describe here and in the *Autism* book, while Jensen's Type-1 intelligence seems to be identical to what I call high-fidelity low-bandwidth functioning.

It is intimately involved in the stimulus-tied practical intelligence described here.

CURRENT RESEARCH

Our research consists primarily of testing large numbers of recruits with a variety of operational and experimental tests, following the students through school to determine the validity of the tests against academic criteria, and finally following them to see how they perform in the fleet.

The research is being conducted in several phases. The first phase started in 1967, and consisted of testing approximately

10,000 recruits entering the Navy at the San Diego Naval Training Center. About 1000 of them had been admitted into the Navy as part of a special program. Their scores on an intelligence test ranged between the 10th and 30th percentiles. In addition to the standard Navy operational tests, the sample was given several experimental tests, including the Hand Skills Test, Digit Span, and a repeat of the AFQT taken earlier. Hand Skills requires the man to make as many tally marks as he can in a number of small squares on the answer sheet. There are several separately timed intervals; as attention and motivation flags, scores decrease. Digit Span was patterned after the similarly named test in the Wechsler and Stanford-Binet. It was tried because of the studies done by Arthur Jensen on minority-group children. Digit Span is one of the few tests that showed very little mean difference between whites and blacks yet which correlate with school performance.

We have now completed the administration of five 'phases' of experimental tests, each phase trying four or five novel tests on about 10,000 recruits. Many of the tests are adaptations of well-known tests: mazes, matrices, dominoes, following directions, digit-symbol substitution, mechanical comprehension, etc. A more novel test uses simple problems such as a choosing a route on a map, with the verbal question posed by an audiotape recording. Another is of the series-completion form, but uses the familiar symbols for suits in playing cards to set up the patterns. In addition to the cognitive tests there are several motivational questionnaires asking about job interests and experience, self-image, attitude toward the Navy, and other attitudes.

FINDINGS TO DATE

Since we are primarily interested in predicting job performance, we are forced to wait until the men tested have been well settled into Navy jobs before collecting criterion information. We have completed the analysis of data for only the first two phases; we are collecting and analyzing criterion data for the more recently tested samples.

So far only a few generalizations can be made:

The traditional aptitude tests (verbal, reasoning, etc.) are *far* better than any of the new tests at predicting *school* and *training* achievement, even for the low aptitude men. None of the newer tests so far analyzed is as good as predicting job performance as we had hoped.

Although the validities of the new tests are not high, some of these tests do show promise for specific jobs and are being studied further.

Meanwhile, we are continuing our search for measures of practical intelligence. Perhaps one of the many tests for which the data have not yet been analyzed will provide us with the clues we seek.

JEROME D. PAUKER   27
University of Missouri, Columbia

A culture-assimilation measure and its relationship to intellectual performance*

Black children above age 4 usually score lower on tests of intelligence than do white middle-class children (Boger & Ambron, 1969). Data have been marshaled to support both genetic and environmental explanations of this difference. Two of the views among those on the environmental side are 1. that deprivation of a variety of sorts (e.g., poor nutrition, limited range of stimulation, stimulation overload, absence of a parent) reduces the ability of the child to capitalize on innate capacities or on real potentiality for development, the effect being cumulative with age; and 2. that the content of traditional tests, being based on the white culture, is not representative of black learning situations and black language, and so does not provide an appropriate sampling of black intellectual performance

If these two views are sound, then one would expect intelligence test scores of blacks to be positively related to SES. High-SES blacks should have, on the average, higher IQs than those of lower SES, and blacks in the Northern USA should have, on the average, higher IQs than those in the South. Although studies have shown this generally to be true, the fact that the average IQ of blacks still does not reach the level of the average IQ of whites has left the question open.

*This research project received partial support from General Research Support Grant Fr 5387 NIH. The following psychology technicians of the Psychometric Laboratory of the University of Missouri Medical Center contributed generously in administering and scoring tests: Sue Bowie, Sue Cook, Mary Daugherty, Judy Goldberg, Glenda Hood, Ellen Horowitz, and Carol Wood.

One of the problems seems to be that measures of SES usually do not take into account the extent of acculturation. A black living in a middle-level neighborhood and having a middle-level income is not necessarily similar in interests, attitudes, and motivations to middle SES whites. There will be differences among blacks in their histories of deprivation and of contact with the middle-class culture. Deutsch et al. (1967; Whiteman & Deutsch, 1968) have developed a 'Deprivation Index' which they have found to be associated with variations in learning and intelligence test scores. However, this measure is made up of several environmental indices, and does not indicate the extent to which a child has been actually influenced by them. What is needed is some measure of the *extent* to which a child has assimilated the middle-class culture.

This paper describes an attempt to develop a psychometric indicator of cultural difference. Such indicator could find use as a moderating or correction factor in the interpretation of intelligence test scores of persons who come from cultural backgrounds different from the background of those on whom the intelligence test was developed and standardized.

I shall review briefly the development of an objective, non-verbal test of personality for children, the Missouri Children's Picture Series (MCPS), some comparisons of MCPS scores of black and white schoolchildren in the USA, some comparisons of European samples with the American norm group, and some efforts to develop on MCPS scale based on cultural differences. We also examine relations of MCPS to Wechsler scores.

MCPS was developed (Sines, Pauker & Sines, 1963; Pauker, 1970) to provide a psychometric personality assessment which would be non-verbal, be easily administered and scored, require a simple mode of response, hold the interest of children, and provide a reasonably large number of responses.

MCPS consists of 238 cards, each one with a numbered picture on it. (Each card shows an activity such as playing in a group, or fighting). The child is asked simply to sort the cards into two piles, those which look like fun to him and those which do not. The test can be given individually or to a roomful of children, using one set of cards for each child. Instructions can be given in one or two minutes, and the test is usually completed in 20 or 30 minutes.

The norm sample consists of 3,877 schoolchildren, mostly white, tested in several school systems in the USA. There are at least 100 children of each sex at each year interval from age 5 through 16. There is a separate conversion table for each sex-age combination.

The eight MCPS scales have names which describe the basis on which they were developed. The Conformity scale consists of items which were sorted by most of the norm group into the same pile. The Masculinity-Femininity scale is made up of items to which boys and girls in the norm group responded differently. The Maturity scale has items to which younger and older children responded differently.

A behavioral checklist (Sines, Pauker, Sines, & Owen, 1969) was filled out by the mothers of a large number of clinic children. Five groups of children, each group scoring high on one of the checklist behavorial factors, were identified. Five corresponding MCPS scales were developed, consisting of items which differentiated a criterion group from a subsample of the norm group matched to it for age and sex. These MCPS scales are named Aggression, Inhibition, Hyperactivity, Sleep Disturbance, and Somatization. The eight scores, in standard score form, can be plotted as a profile.

In 1969 we attempted to develop an additional scale based on differences in response between low and middle SES children. Several hundred children were given MCPS in a number of schools in a large city. Included were children of low and middle SES, boys and girls, 7-8 year olds and 10-11 year olds, and blacks and whites. We searched for MCPS items which would separate the low- and middle-SES children, regardless of what other descriptive category they fit. It did not work out that way, however, because the low- and middle-SES black children do not respond very differently, although low- and middle-SES whites differed. At least part of the reason for the lack of differentation within the blacks may have been our crude indicator of SES, which was based on the income level of the community from which each school drew its pupils. Many of the 'middle level' black children

were from families relatively new to the middle level neighborhoods, and many were from families in which a middle-income
level was reached through the *combined* salaries from parents
who were both working at jobs which paid very modest wages.

In 1967 and 1968, schoolchildren were given MCPS in England, Belgium, and Holland.* In each of these countries, approximately 60 children were tested, including 8-year-old boys, 8-year
old girls, 11-year-old boys, and 11-year old girls. The responses in
each country to individual items and scores on each scale were
compared with those for the corresponding age-sex group in the
USA. The British children were the most similar to the American
children, followed by the Belgian and Dutch children in that
order. Differences between the American and European samples
were greater at age 11 than at age 8.

In looking at MCPS item differences between the responses of
the white and black American children, it was noticed that these
differences overlapped with MCPS differences found between the
USA norm group and the European children, and that both black
and European children differed from te norm group in the same
direction. This finding suggested the idea of developing an MCPS
'Dominant White American Culture Scale.' (hereafter, Culture
scale). This in turn led to consideration about the possible
relationship of such a scale to intelligence test scores. Effects of a
culture on intellectual performance and on responses to intelligence test items should vary with amount of acculturation.

The Culture scale was developed by selecting MCPS items to
which the black and white boys, all SES combined, responded
differently ($P < .01$ in each age group). There were 96 black and
134 white boys in the 7-8 year group, and 80 black and 145 white
boys in the 11-12-year group. Boys only were used to develop the
Culture scale because the next step was to compare Culture scores
with intelligence test scores in a pilot study, and it was decided to

---

*Data in England collected by A. Cashdan and his students, and in
Belgium by M.–P. Arnould. In Holland arrangements for data collection
were made by T.J.C. Berk, and data were collected by B. van der Werf and
the writer. Comparisons of the samples are being prepared for publication.

use boys alone at this stage in order to keep things as un-complicated as possible.

The Wechsler scale (WISC) and MCPS were administered to a number of black and white boys in a suburban school. The school is in a middle-income, previously all-white neighborhood into which blacks are moving at a rapid rate. The sample consist-ed of 65 boys distributed as follows: 18 black boys of ages 7-8, 24 black boys of ages 9-10, and 23 white boys of ages 9-10. Product-moment correlations between the MCPS Culture scale raw scores and the WISC Verbal and Performance IQs were calculated separately, by age within race. There were, then, six correlations.

The only large correlation was 0.78, between the CPS Culture scale and WISC Verbal IQ for 7-8-year-old black boys ($P<.01$). No correlation was found for the older black boys nor for white boys: the correlations for these groups ranged from 0.02 to 0.27. Among younger black children in a racially mixed and changing middle-class neighborhood, those with higher Verbal scores are more like the middle-class white children in their choice of culture-related MCPS pictures. This finding takes on added signi-ficance when it is recalled that the verbal part of the WISC is the best predictor of achievement in middle-class, white schools. These results, however, are based on a small sample, and conclu-sions are tentative at most. The study needs to be replicated on larger and more diverse samples.

REFERENCES

Boger, R. P. & Ambron S. R. (1969). Subpopulation profiling of the psychoeducational dimensions of disadvantaged preschool children. In Grotberg, E. (Ed.) *Critical issues in research related to disadvantaged children.* Princeton: Educational Testing Service.

Deutsch, M. *et al.* (1967) *The disadvantaged child.* New York: Basic Books.

Pauker, Jerome D. (1970) The use of age, sex, response communality, and behavioral descriptive categories in the development of an objective, non-verbal test of personality for children. Paper, Midwestern Psychological Association.

Sines, J. O., Pauker, J. D. & Sines, L. K. (1963) *The Missouri Children's Picture Series.* Columbia, Mo.: the authors.

Sines, J. O., Pauker, J.'D., Sines, L. K & Owen, D. R. (1969) The identification of clinically relevant dimensions of children's behavior. *J. Consult. clin. Psychol., 33,* 728-734.

Whiteman, M. & Deutsch, M. (1968) Social disadvantage as related to intellective and language development. In M. Deutsch, I. Katz & A. R. Jensen (Eds.), *Social class, race, and psychological development.* New York: Holt, Rinehart and Winston. Pp. 86-114.

Note: *In discussion the point was made that Pauker's scale, like the Strong Interest Blank, is purely empirical. It was urged that efforts be made to explain, in terms of scale content or correlates, what its psychological nature is. While Pauker acknowledged the usefulness of such work, he anticipates that his own efforts will move more in the direction of practical application.*

The keying by contrasting two groups (e.g. high and low SES) is perhaps disadvantageous when several cultures are considered. It would be possible to build eight keys, one consisting of responses given by (say) high SES white boys, and others for low SES black girls, etc. These would make available the same information as the conventional 'contrast' key, but would also allow comparison of a subject with a great number of cultures or subcultures. (Eds.)

FREDERIC R. WICKERT   28
Michigan State University, East Lansing

Self-perceived abilities and on-the-job performance of culturally disadvantaged workers

As Holtzman (1971) states, 'One of the great success stories of modern psychology is the development of objective tests for measuring human abilities that are important to society.' He goes on to say, however: 'By the late 1950's, it became generally apparent that the large-scale normative use of objective tests for rewarding selected individuals among many in competition has serious social consequences of debatable value.' It has been a real shock for psychologists to accept the downgrading of a technique that seemed on the surface to be so logical and fair.

In non-Western cultures, of course, tests imported from Western culture have not been particularly at home. In Surinam it is considered impolite to pose direct questions of the sort a test asks. In the Middle East, a Standard Oil Company subsidiary found the population to be tested organizing itself to combat the test. Each man sitting in the first administration agreed to do nothing but memorize five test items during the time he was supposed to be tested. Each man, after the testing, was systematically debriefed by an inner council of ringleaders. The whole test was in effect reconstructed by the community and the right answers figured out; each job applicant from then on was furnished with the right answers. Other resistances to tests could be documented. The point is that although many instances of the more or less successful application of Western-style ability testing could be cited, there are also plentiful examples of resistance.

MEASURED SELF-PERCEIVED ABILITIES

One possibility in the difficult personnel-selection situation that is emerging is to adopt procedures that make sense to examinees. One such procedure is to ask each applicant in a systematic way to state what he thinks he can do, what he thinks his abilities and limitations in a work situation are. Such self-estimates may be called self-perceived abilities (SPA) or self-perceived competence.

Korman (1971), among others, has conducted a good deal of research in SPA, and has also summarized the literature. Among other things, Korman (p. 46) cites 10 pieces of evidence that individuals will perform in a manner consistent with their self-conceptions. This is contrary to employer fears of applicant dishonesty.

Three types of SPA emerge, he says: generalized self competence (the persistent opinion one has of oneself over many situations; situational (everyone has a situation or two in which he sees himself as better or worse than his typical behavior); and socially-influenced confidence. This paper deals with all three of these. There is evidence that the performance of blacks in the USA is a function of their self-perceived competence. Hence it is especially appropriate to try the technique with disadvantaged applicants for employment.

In developing an SPA measure for the present study advantage was taken of task analyses of factory work described in the *Dictionary of occupational titles,* and the work of Fleishman, E. J. McCormick, and others. A list of 10 common skills used on factory jobs was derived. A scale was provided so that each *S* could indicate his degree of SPA for each of the 10 items.

DATA COLLECTION

An opportunity arose to administer the SPA measure to all persons hired to do assembly-line work in a large American automobile factory. Most of those hired could be considered culturally disadvantaged although fewer than 25 per cent were black or of Mexican or Puerto Rican ancestry.

The typical individual was under 20 years old, unmarried, a highschool graduate, uncertain of his educational and vocational future, and new to the automobile-factory environment. Also, he appeared to expect concerned, intelligent, and fair supervision, cooperative coworkers, average or clean working conditions, interesting work, to get some satisfaction from the job, and to be moved about somewhat but not too often.

Up to perhaps five years ago, the company had used a 7-hour battery of selection tests for this level of worker, but for many reasons had discontinued all employment testing. This company, along with most other companies with an 'affirmative action program' to hire culturally disadvantaged workers had, however, encountered severe problems of absenteeism, tardiness, and turnover, although the delicately-balanced assembly line requires precise numbers of each type of worker to be on hand. Companies trying to carry on manufacturing in developing countries face similar difficulties.

The company had been imaginatively studying the causes of absenteeism and tardiness. Among many other approaches, chronically absent employees were brought together in groups which discussed absenteeism. They did not perceive themselves as being chronic absentees and saw little wrong in their being absent; they were, however, to a surprising extent concerned about the company's problem. Foremen also presented their views, sometimes in separate meetings and sometimes with the chronic absentees. Questionnaire items were developed from these discussions. The SPA items were administered as part of the questionnaire. The occasional applicant whose reading skills were minimal was helped with the questionnaire.

Actual hiring and questionnaire administration began in late August 1970 but was interrupted by a strike in September. Work and hiring resumed by mid-December. A total of 171 new workers were hired during the August-September period, 144 men and 27 women. Another 48 men and no women were hired in December and January, at which time hiring again stopped as no more new workers were needed. Actual turnover was worked out on all 171 cases, but it turned out to make most sense in this chaotic situation to analyze intensively the questionnaire data of

90 assembly-line workers (hired in both employment waves) who were still on the job in March 1971.

A second wave of questionnaires were given to all the new workers still on the job in March 1971. This second administration included not only SPA but a wide range of on-the-job experience items, as well as questions from the first questionnaire which it made sense to ask once again, as responses might have changed with work experience.

FACTOR ANALYSIS

Factor analyses of the SPA items by themselves were carried out for the first administration (N = 123) and the 6-month follow-up (N = 90). Four factors emerged from each analysis. The four factors in the first administration accounted for 72 per cent of the variance and in the second for 83 per cent. The factors were not very similar from one administration to the next, nor was it clear how to interpret the factors.

When SPA items were factored with many additional questions, they always stood out as highly related to each other and belonging within the same factor. For the 6 SPA items considered most important after several months on the job, the alpha reliability was 0.65. Individual SPA items also had loadings on other factors that more often than not made some sense, as we shall see.

A special follow-up form of SPA asked S to tell how much

SPA Items	Percentage
Spotting small mistakes	81.9
Doing jobs that require coordination of both hands and feet	78.4
Reacting quickly when you see a dangerous situation	74.7
Remembering the names of people you meet	55.4
Using your fingers to work with small things, like repairing a watch	54.2
Using words to communicate to others	48.1
Checking written material for mistakes	44.5
Thinking through a difficult problem	38.0
Reading a map	27.7
Solving arithmetic problems quickly	25.4

each of his skills helped in doing the job he now had. The following shows the percentage of 83 Ss on whom data were available who considered each ability as helping on his present job.

From the above list, one can see what the SPA items used in this study actually were. The percentages give an idea of the Ss' collective notions of the skills involved in the kind of work they were doing. There were wide differences in the degree to which each of the abilities was endorsed.

EXTERNAL CORRELATES OF SPA

Among all the responses at the time of employment, the only one significantly correlated with SPA was an item that asked, 'How much confidence do you have in your ability to do the job here at X factory? 1. A great deal of confidence. 2. I am fairly confident. 3. I have little confidence.' High SPA, then, was probably a part of an applicant's self-confidence with respect to the job. No significant correlations appeared with biographical items including those asking about previous automobile-factory experience, skilled-trades experience, age of first full-time job, etc.

It was possible to check SPA with a number of external measures among the 90 Ss still on the job in March 1971.

A 15-item job involvement (JI) scale (Lodahl and Kejner, about 1965) has been much used in recent job-satisfaction research in the USA. The correlations of these JI items and SPA items did not exceed the chance level. SPA is evidently not particularly associated with job involvement or job satisfaction.

Intercorrelations of 8 typical job needs (secure job, good pay, etc) and 12 SPA items (including two items added to the basic 10 in the March, 1971 readministration) showed relations well above what would have been expected by chance. One of the needs, 'Develop myself by learning new skills', was particularly highly related to high SPA; 10 of the 12 intercorrelations between this need and the 12 SPA items were significant.

Correlations between the 12 SPA items and self-ratings of 16 varied performances after several months on the job showed only

17 of 192 significant at the 0.05 level, not many more than would have occurred by chance. However, high self-ranking on job performance showed 6 of the 12 correlations with SPA items significant. Four of 12 correlations with a self-rating of how fast one thinks one works (as compared with others) were significant. Those thinking they work fast had higher SPA.

The only 'hard' criterion measure available when this report was prepared was turnover. Of 165 employees on whom data were available, 90 were still on the job as of March 1971 while 75 had left. The only items associated with staying on the job were having relatives in the company, expecting that the job would require a great deal of skill, and having confidence in ability to do the job. SPA items showed no direct relationship with turnover. However, in view of the significant correlation of turnover and job confidence — which, it will be recalled, is also correlated with SPA — SPA might predict turnover in future research.

REFERENCES

Holtzman, W. H. (1971) The changing world of mental measurement and its social significance. *Amer. Psychologist, 26,* 546-553.
Korman, A. K. (1971) *Industrial and organizational psychology.* Englewood Cliffs, N. J.: Prentice-Hall.

PART V

Educational intervention and educational influence

Feuerstein describes his procedure for training children and adults in reasoning such as tests require. The performance on transfer tasks after training is considered to be a superior indication of 'learning potential.'

Lambert reports on the success of an instructional program in which children from English-speaking homes are given their entire elementary schooling in French.

Smith draws on experience with classroom observation to critize the conventional view of performance as a reflection of ability, and reinterprets performance in terms of role-playing and other social phenomena. Belbin and Belbin report on a training program for immigrants which promotes their conceptual skill and circumvents the tendency to memorize rules and perform in a stereotyped fashion. Failure rates among bus drivers are reduced by the method.

Rural and urban groups are contrasted in a preliminary report on Kyöstiö's longitudinal study in Finland, and Thrane gives preliminary data on the effect of additional schooling on test performance, from a Norwegian longitudinal study.

REUVEN FEUERSTEIN
Hadassah Wizo Canada Research Institute and
Youth Aliyah Child Guidance Clinic, Jerusalem

29

Cognitive assessment of the socioculturally deprived child and adolescent*

The assessment of the cognitive functioning of the culturally different and the socially disadvantaged child and adolescent poses difficult problems for the practitioner and the theoretician. Individuals belonging to disadvantaged subgroups almost always average lower on tests, even when the tests are culture-free, culture-fair, or developmental. It is now accepted that the attempts made to render the psychometric instruments more sensitive to true cognitive capacities have failed, either because differences between the populations were found on the modified instruments or because the instruments had low predictive value.

Our incapacity to properly assess cognitive potentialities supports and in certain cases even generates a pessimistic attitude toward the possibility that the disadvantaged can attain a higher

* This paper is part of an extensive study on the Learning Potential Assessment Device applied to culturally deprived children and adolescents within a variety of settings, youth villages, and day centers. It is being conducted with the generous support of the Ford Foundation granted to the Hadassah Wizo Canada Institute, through the Israel Foundations Trustees, Tel Aviv.

Our thanks are expressed to the staff of the Institute, especially to Mrs. H. Schachter-Bloomfield from whose study we have borrowed liberally; Mrs. L. Kyram, Mrs. D. Katz, who are involved in the clinical aspects of the work; Mr. H. Shalom and Dr. Y. Schlesinger who are directly involved in the experimental phase of the work; Mr. H. Hoffman, Co-Director of the Research Institute, for his invaluable contribution in the analysis of the data; and to Ruth Zenger and Gloria Geller for the help in putting this paper together.

level of sociocultural integration. The resulting negative stereotype causes the pessimistic outlook to become a fact by determining the *amount, nature,* and *quality* of educational investment. Further, it affects negatively the theoretical understanding of the nature of intelligence and the dynamics of its development. That the attempted modifications have failed, and that findings based on culture-fair tests do not alter the low expectations held for these populations, is clearly illustrated by Jensen's conclusions. He finds that socioculturally different individuals tend to be almost as good on certain tests characterized by a low level of elaborative process as their Occidental, middle-class peers (Jensen, 1969, p. 112). His conclusion — which seems not only fallacious but dangerous — is that the nature of the differences between populations is not only quantitative, but also qualitative. Level I ability, which according to Jensen is characteristic of the disadvantaged population, can easily be perceived as typical of subhuman species whereas Level II is characteristic of homo sapiens. Thus the striving of Jensen toward a more equitable way to assess the deprived individual has turned into a pessimistic, passive-acceptant attitude toward the phenomenon of human incompetence.

How should this failure of the psychometric approach be explained? It is the contention of the author that the failure to create appropriate methods to assess the deprived individual is determined by the static goal of psychometric theory. This goal confines the search to the most stable characteristics of the individual and totally neglects — one may say, actively rejects — any evidence which may point to the modifiability of the organism under scrutiny. An inventory of existent manifest, easily elicited behavior patterns is established, and the static inventory is used as a point of departure for predicting the future development of the individual. The presentation of the task is kept as standardized as possible in order to insure not only comparability but also to eliminate any factors which may modify the stable patterns of the individual. This calls for a rather rigid relationship between examiner and examinee which does not take into consideration the cognitive and motivational characteristics of the deprived child, who responds adequately only in a more flexible personal relationship. The interpretation of results stresses 'all or none' criteria, with analysis of product more than process.

Our dynamic approach represents an attempt to measure the capacity of the individual to change under a set of specified conditions. Instead of using spontaneous responses, we employ a test-learning-test situation to measure the capacity to use recently acquired principles, skills, strategies, and attitudes. Figure 1 illustrates the model upon which such a Learning Potential Analysis Device (LPAD) can be constructed. The center represents a

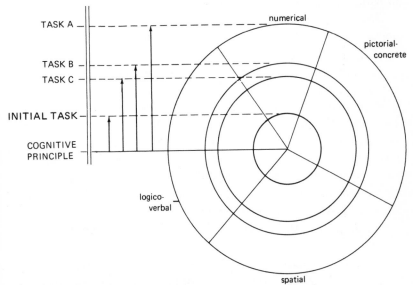

Figure 1. A model of the Learning Potential Analysis Device

principle taught to the examinee, together with a series of meta-learning skills required to grasp the principle and gain insight into strategies required. The concentric circles represent situational variations that become progressively more remote from the initial task. As suggested by Rey and by Vigotsky, the modifiability of the individual is then measured by his capacity to use the learning experience for the solution of new problems.

Modifiability can be measured by the centrifugal distance to which the person can carry the learned principle, and by his extension of it over various modalities: logicoverbal, figural-abstract, numerical, and pictorial-concrete. The model can also be extended into a third dimension representing a variety of logical operations.

One can also consider the nature of modifiability. Problem content stays familiar while operations vary. This relieves the examinee of constantly familiarizing himself with new objects prior to setting to work. The constancy of the analogy operation over the variations enables us to perceive the capacity of the individual to detach the operation from one context and apply it to situations progressively more distant from the initial one. A great variety of useful instruments can be constructed on the basis of such a model.

The construction of such an instrument cannot by itself overcome all the difficulties. The whole of conventional testing procedure has to be changed to deal with the culturally deprived. The culturally deprived child does not have an intrinsic motivation towards the task presented in the test. This makes his results much more dependent upon his relationship with the examiner than is the case for the middle-class child. He will become motivated towards the task to the extent that the examiner himself shows sincere interest in the nature and quality of his work. A relationship that provides for constant feedback is of utmost importance.

This is even more so because of the poverty of strategies the culturally deprived child has. A dynamic assessment turns the examiner-examinee relationship into a teacher-student relationship. The great difficulty is the standardization of the interactive process, and the measurement of the investment required in order to reach the desired result. At this point, the method requires a great amount of insight, innovation, and creative capacities on the part of the examiner.

The interpretation of the results also to be changed. Following Jastak, we stress the high point in performance as an indicator of the person's true capacity, rather than an overall index which ignores the high point.

This clinical method has been used by the author with culturally different and socially deprived adolescents, and accepted

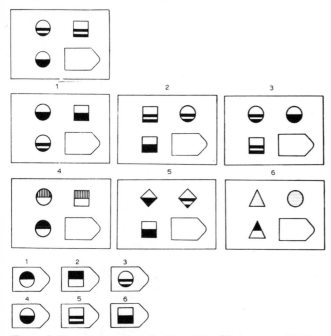

Figure 2. Exercise based on Problem B 8 of Progressive Matrices

by the Youth Aliyah educational system.* Children examined by us in Morocco with this method have been included in a follow-up study which brought clinical evidence for the validity of this approach. In the last few years more experimentally controlled studies have been conducted in the Hadassah Wizo Canada Research Institute.

* Youth Aliyah is a Jewish nongovernmental organization which took over the responsibility for the bringing of children and adolescents from all over the world to Israel, and providing them with total care. Since 1933 Youth Aliyah has dealt with almost 120,000 adolescents, some rescued from concentration camps and countries in which they were a persecuted minority. Youth Aliyah children represent a high-risk segment of the population and it is on this background that one has to consider the achievements of Youth Aliyah. The children were dealt with in kibbutzim and youth villages, by means of three major educational pillars: active participation in the peer-group, personal contribution to one's own community through work, and academic achievements.

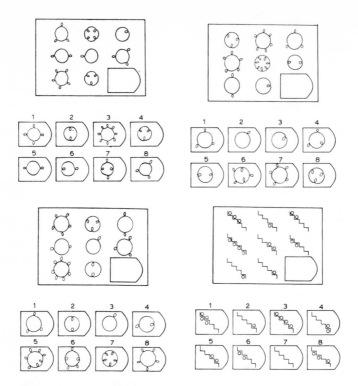

Figure 3. An advanced set of LPAD matrix tasks **

A CLINICAL STUDY

Tasks
We have submitted two groups of children of ages 11 to 14 (grades 5 to 7) to 4 tests based on the model.

The first test (see fig. 2 and fig. 3) is Coloured Progressive Matrices along with the LPAD variations of tasks B8 to B12 (published by Hadassah Wizo Canada, 1970, for research purposes). On the basis of his extensive data on tasks B8 and B12, Raven (1965, p. 25) claims that these tasks represent a level of cognitive functioning which is inaccessible to the child of IQ 70-80 even if training is instituted.

** Figures 2 and 3 from Raven, 1965, reprinted by permission of the Raven Estate.

The second test, conceived by Rey, is Organization of Dots. A figured pattern must be located in an amorphous cloud of points, as in the last row of Figure 4 below. The third test is the plateau of Rey, and the fourth the difficult Stencil Design Test of Arthur. Space does not permit description of these tasks.

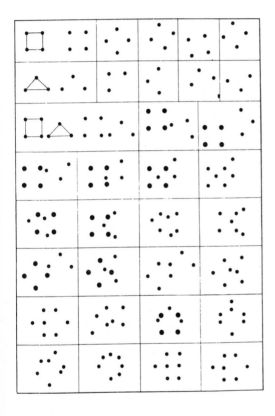

Figure 4. Training sheet for organization of dots

All 4 tests require representational, internalized, abstract thinking, and hence require a considerable amount of perceptional, organizational, and operational behavior on the part of the examinee. This level is considered by many authors as rather inaccessible to the low-functioning, culturally and socially disadvantaged individual.

Procedure

This battery was applied to children diagnosed as retarded, with IQs ranging from 55 to 70, who were placed in a school for the EMR. Their ages ranged from 11-14½ years. The overwhelming majority of these children belong to a disadvantaged socioethnic group. A second group was composed of 55 children referred to the Youth Aliyah Child Guidance Clinic for acceptance into programs for the culturally deprived. This very heterogeneous group is functioning very poorly both in school achievement, many of them being functional illiterates, and on psychometric tests. As a group, however, they were considered to have a higher level of functioning than the EMR group.

The training given the examinees embraces two basic interventional strategies. One implies an attempt to induce skills, learning styles, and attitudes considered prerequisite to appropriate problem-solving behavior. This includes such elements as inducing the need for precision both in input and output, planning, comparing, and inducing the need for logical evidence, all these by shaping the communication patterns between the examiner and the examinee. The second category involves the teaching of content directly related to the problem at hand. The child is taught orientation in space (right, left, up, down, horizontal, and vertical), and he is made aware of certain categories of relationships, with or without verbal labeling. In certain cases these contents are transmitted via exposure to the action of a model without use of verbal behavior. In Matrices, the first category of intervention employs a series of inferential questions aiming at the induction of precision, formulation of relationships, search for evidence for a given response or statement, justification of choices; and finally, press for anticipatory and internalized behavior (instead of trial and error). In Organization of Dots, as can be seen from the training sheet (Fig. 4), the task requires repeated rediscovery of the stimulus figures in new situations. In a testing session a positive score is allowed only for a response which did not require any intervention save for orienting the child's perception, request for focusing, or for motor planning. Whenever direct intervention is made, no credit is assigned. The child is given feedback regarding response and in certain instances, attempts are made to produce insight in the child as to the nature of strategies which have led to success or to failure.

Results

In what follows, we present the results obtained by the EMR and Clinic groups on each test. The EMR group has an N of 36 and the Clinic group an N of 55.

The mean for the Raven Matrix (max. 36) is 28.4 for EMR (s.d., 4.6); for the clinical group 27.8 (s.d., 4.1). There is no significant difference. According to various sources, the average for retarded children is usually around 18-22, the norm for age 8 or 9. On the LPAD variations of B8-B12 (max. 35), the EMR average 29.6 (s.d. 4.8), and the Clinic group average 29.7 (s.d., 3.3); again, no significant difference. In these two tests many of our cases almost reached the ceiling, this being the direct result of the investment prior to and during the test. One has to keep in mind that the LPAD tasks are at a high level of difficulty.

Organization of Dots (max. 40) shows a slight difference between the two populations; the EMR group mean of 35.3 (s.d. 4.3) is significantly lower than the Clinic group mean 37.4 (s.d. 2.7).

There is a considerable difference between the groups in the Plateau test; for EMR the mean is 10.2 trials (s.d. 7.2) vs. only 6.48 (s.d. 4.6) for the Clinic ($P < .05$). There is a similar difference for number of errors. This changes when the task requires anticipatory internalized behavior. The difference observed on the sample Plateau I disappears when children are given a more complex plateau task (e.g., with 2 fixed knobs out of 9); the number of trials (and of errors) does not differ significantly between groups.

Stencil Design shows no difference between the groups; the mean is 10.9 for EMR (s.d. 4.2) vs. 10.4 for the Clinic group (s.d. 2.9). The results obtained by these groups on the Stencil Design Test are high considering the severity of the criteria and the way in which the problem has to be solved.

We find, then, that children previously defined and treated as mentally retarded reach, in the LPAD, levels of functioning once considered inaccessible to them. After training, they perform in many ways comparable to their peers. Even among children classed as mentally retarded, representational, internalized, and abstract thinking can be achieved. Individual differences were reflected not so much in the level of achievement of the individual (although these were apparent) as in the amount of investment and the nature of strategies required to reach a given level of modification.

The EMR group was retested two months after the pretest, during a school holiday period. The results show a clear tendency toward further improvement which in certain cases is statistically significant.

Children examined by means of the LPAD are placed in a variety of settings: children's villages for the culturally deprived, *kibbutzim,* and other institutions. After a period of preparation lasting one or two years, the great majority of these adolescents can be integrated among normal children, even though they may still manifest gaps in subject matter achievement.

A CONTROLLED STUDY

Another study used a group form of the test-learning-test technique. Cases were adolescents with IQs 70-90, and ages 12-15 ($N = 956$; N with complete data used for final analysis, 551).

To explore the differential effectiveness of specific learning procedures, cases were randomly assigned to 7 treatment groups and 1 control group. The test consisted of one mental operation, analogies, presented in 2 modalities: logico-verbal and figural. The treatments consisted of metalearning – verbal or figural or both – and/or direct training for analogies – verbal or figural or both. All the treatment groups including the control, have gained significantly from pre- to post-test, with significant differences between treated and control groups.

The most effective treatments were those which introduced both metalearning and training strategies via figural modalities.

The next best procedure was the combination of verbal meta-learning and training. The group modality allows us to apply LPAD as a screening device to larger numbers of children, and enables us to gather more comparable data through standardized procedures. Its results cannot, however, be considered a true measure of modifiability. This is so because of the limitation inherent in the group test as compared with a more intimate interactional process.

An interactional examiner-examinee process has proved to be very important, both for enhancing the functioning of the deprived individual for isolating the areas of deficiency. Thus, the individual technique allows the examiner a measure of the elaborative modifiability of the individual, above and beyond his deficiencies on the input or the output level. Such a distinction is of utmost importance in pointing to the locus of the deficiency and its meaning, and in guiding remedial work.

REFERENCES

Jensen, A. (1969) How much can we boost IQ and scholastic achievement? *Harvard Educ. Rev. 39,* 1-123.
Raven, J. C. (1965) *Guide to using the Coloured Progressive Matrices.* London: H. K. Lewis.

W.E. LAMBERT
McGill University, Montreal

30

Consequences of attending elementary school in a second language

This paper reports on a longitudinal study of two groups of English-Canadian children (a pilot class and a follow-up class) who underwent schooling exclusively in French in Kindergarten and Grade 1, and mainly in French in Grades 2-5, except for two half-hour daily periods of Language Arts in English. This report focuses on the working hypotheses that guided the evaluation and on the assessment of the program's impact on cognitive development. This experiment has universal relevance since it touches on an educational matter faced by minority groups in all countries and by most citizens in developing nations.

The parents of the children were concerned about the ineffectiveness of current methods of teaching foreign languages, and were impressed with recent accomplishments in teaching science and mathematics in the early elementary grades. They also realized that, as residents of a bicultural and bilingual society, they and their children are part of a much larger experiment in democratic coexistence that requires people of different cultures and languages to develop mutual understanding and respect. An essential first step for them was learning the other group's language thoroughly.

This program may well serve as a model because the overall scheme (referred to as a home-school language switch) is simple enough to be tried out in other bicultural or multicultural communities and, perhaps of more importance, in essentially unicultural settings where a serious desire exists to develop second-language proficiency. Rather than estimating how many years of schooling should be provided in order to develop an undefined level of ability in a foreign language, we propose to ask how one goes about developing complete bilingual balance in the home and school languages (see Lambert & Tucker, 1971).

We have compared the linguistic, cognitive, and attitudinal development of the pilot and follow-up groups with that of control children, carefully matched on nonverbal IQ and social-class background, who followed normal English-Canadian and French-Canadian academic programs. The experimental and English-control classes were comparable as to parental attitudes toward French people and culture and in motivation to learn French. If given the opportunity, the large majority of the control parents would have placed their children in experimental classes.

RESULTS

How well do the experimental children progress in the home language? The overall answer is that they are doing just as well as the controls, showing no symptoms of retardation or negative transfer. On tests of English word knowledge, discrimination, and language usage, the experimental pilot class falls above the 80th percentile on national norms, as do the controls. Their reading ability in English, their listening comprehension, and their knowledge of concepts in English (Peabody Picture Vocabulary) are all at the same level as those of the English controls.

Their progress in English expressive skills appears good. When asked to retell or invent short stories in English they do so with as much comprehension as the controls and with at least as good a command of rhythm, intonation, enunciation, and overall expression. Their spontaneous productions are as long and complex and their vocabulary as rich and diverse.

Their facility at decoding and utilizing descriptive English speech produced by children or adults is also at the same level as that of the controls, and their word associations in English show as much maturity and appropriateness. Since they were at the same time reliably *faster* in making associations in English than the controls, their speed of processing English may be advanced over that of the controls.

How well do the experimental children progress in French? Compared with children from French-speaking homes who follow a normal all-French program of study, they fare extremely well. Their French listening comprehension score was comparable to that of the controls from Grade 2 on, and their knowledge of complex French concepts, measured with a French version of the Peabody Picture Vocabulary Test, is remarkably advanced. In fact, in Grade 4 they score as well as the French controls. From Grade 1 on, they have developed control like a native's over the smaller units of French. When they are asked to retell and invent short French stories, the linguists who rate their oral proficiency find their rhythm, intonation, and overall expression in French noticeably inferior to those of the French controls, even at Grade 4. They have much better overall expression, enunciation, rhythm, and intonation when inventing stories of their own than when simply retelling stories; this suggests that they are particularly motivated and clever when permitted to express their own flow of ideas with their own choice of expressions. Their productions in French are as long and complex as those of the controls, and show a similar comprehension and diversity of vocabulary. They make more errors in their French productions, especially errors of gender and contraction, but after Grade 2, they do not make more mistakes in syntax. Their free associations in French are as rapid, mature, and appropriate as those of the controls. They show as much aptitude as the controls in decoding spontaneous descriptions given by French adults or by children. By Grade 4, however, they are no longer as able as native speakers to decode the descriptions given by other children even though they are still as proficient as the controls when decoding adult descriptions. Amazing as the progress is when one considers their concurrent competence in English, there is room for improvement in expressive skills in French, assuming that it is desirable to speak like a native. Imaginative changes could be introduced into the program so as to maintain the high level attained in the more passive skills while increasing expressive capacities. For one thing, physical education, music and arts (which lend themselves naturally to social communication) could be taught in French. The teachers, being new at this type of program, have perhaps overlooked the need to compensate for the lack of occasions outside school for improving skill in French expression. We believe now the attention can be directed to the content and fluency of the child's speech without sacrificing appropriate form, structure, and style. Interaction with French children (up to now practically nonexistent) would also prove decoding abilities.

How well do the children perform in subject matter such as mathematics? They perform at the same high level as the controls (both groups scoring beyond the 80th percentile of the norms) in both computation and problem solving. One can be confident that these children have been able as the French control groups to grasp, assimilate, and utilize mathematical principles through French, and that they are able to transfer this knowledge acquired exclusively through French to English, when tested on arithmetic in English. The teachers in the experimental program are not better trained in mathematics than those in the control classes nor in more time devoted to mathematics. The texts are French versions of those used in the English control classes.

What effect does this bilingual program have on measured intelligence? There is no sign at the end of Grade 4 of any intellectual deficit or retardation attributable to the bilingual experience, judging from yearly retesting with Progressive Matrices and the Lorge-Thorndike test. On a standard measure of creativity there is evidence that the experimental children are also at the same level, and slightly advanced in generating imaginative and unusual uses for everyday objects. This mental alertness is consonant with their generally faster rate of free association in English, noted earlier.

What effect does the program switch have on the children's selfconcepts and their attitudes towards French people? In Grades 2 and 3 their attitudes were much more fair and charitable than those of the English and French controls. They were less ethnocentric and less biased in favor of their own ethnic group. They had healthy views of themselves as being particularly friendly, nice, tall, and big, but not extreme in smartness or goodness. The data suggest that suspicion and distrust between groups may be effectively reduced by means of this particular academic experience.

In the Spring 1970 testing, however, we found both the Grade-4 and Grade-3 groups similar to the English controls in their attitudes: neutral or slightly favorable toward European French, more hostile toward French-Canadians, and clearly favorable to their own group. We are not certain what caused this shift. (The French-Canadian demands for separatism were intense at this time. The few French-Canadians they meet at school happen to be of lower SES and are academically poorer. Perhaps they just want to be like others in their peer group as they grow older, not wanting to appear too French.)

There is no evidence that their self-concepts are confused in any way. The experimental children at all grade levels describe themselves as being very good, happy, strong, friendly, etc., relative to the control children's self-ratings.

DISCUSSION

Although the procedure seems remarkably effective in this Canadian setting, permitting us to challenge various claims made about the harmful effects of early bilingual education, still the scheme is not proposed as a universal solution for those nations planning programs of bilingual education. Instead a more general guiding principle is offered: in any social system where there is a serious, widespread desire or need for a bilingual or multilingual citizenry, then priority for early schooling should be given to the language or languages least likely to be developed otherwise, or most likely to be neglected. In the bilingual case, this will often call for the establishment of two elementary school streams: one conducted in language A and one in language B, with teachers who are monolingual or who function as if they were. If A were the more prestigious language, then native speakers of A would start their schooling in B, and after functional bilingualism is attained, use both languages for their schooling. Depending on the sociocultural setting, various options are open to the linguistic minority: prekindergarten or very early schooling, with half a day in B, and half in A; concentration on B until reading and writing skills are certified, with switching delayed; or a completely bilingual program based in two monolingually organized streams, etc. Rather than teaching languages A and B as languages, emphasis in all cases would be shifted from a linguistic focus to using the languages as vehicles for academic content.

The Province of Quebec provides a convenient example. Here the French-Canadians — a national minority group but a clear majority in the Province — have a fairly powerful political movement underway based on French as the 'working language' and a desire to separate politically from the rest of Canada. For English-speaking Canadians who see the value and importance of having two national languages, the home-school language switch as described here is an appropriate policy since French for them would otherwise be bypassed except in typical (hence ineffectual) second-language training programs. French-Canadian have reason to fear a loss of their language, faced as they are with the universal importance of English and the relatively low status attached to minority languages in North America. French-Canadians also may denigrate their dialect of French, since it is at variance with that version given such high status in France. The home-school switch would worry them, as it would any North American minority, because they believe that English would easily swamp out French. Moreover, their home language is not standard enough, making training in 'school' French a requisite. In such circumstances, a valuable alternative would be to start a prekindergarten program at age 4 with half a day in French and half a day in English, taught by two different teachers presenting themselves as monolinguals, this to continue through kindergarten. Starting at Grade 1, two separate academic offerings could be instituted, one fully French and the other fully English, with options for the student to move from one to the other for one or several courses until the two languages are brought to equivalent high levels. Such a program could, of course, integrate French- and English-Canadian children who so far have remained essentially strangers to one another because of separate schools based on religion and language.

In the Canadian setting, however, political decisions could have important counteracting consequences. For instance, a widespread movement for unilingualism and separatism could postpone thorough mastery of English beyond the receptive early years. Then all the advantages of being bilingual could pass from the minority group to the powerful English speaking majority whose children now have the opportunity to become fully proficient in French *and* English.

REFERENCES

Lambert, W. E. & Tucker, G. R. (1971) *The bilingual education of children.* Rowley, Mass.: Newbury House.

LOUIS M. SMITH
Washington University and Cemrel, Inc.

31

Continuities in observational field methods and mental testing*

THE NATURE OF PARTICIPANT OBSERVATION

Our approach

During the last few years, several colleagues, graduate students, and I have been using a methodological approach which we have called by several names: participant observation, naturalistic observation, and observational field work.

The approach seems closer to anthropological methods than to psychological methods.

Our procedures have been simple. We have asked such questions as: 'How does a middle-class teacher cope with a group of lower-class children? ' (Smith & Geoffrey, 1968). 'What happens when one starts a new elementary school, with a novel building, a novel curriculum, and a novel organizational structure? ' (Smith & Keith, 1971). 'What happens when a 21st Century educational technology, computer-assisted instruction, is instituted into poverty-stricken rural highlands? ' (Smith & Pohland, 1971).

Our procedure has simply been to be around, observe care-

* The research reported herein was supported in part by CEMREL. Inc. a private nonprofit corporation supported in part as a regional educational laboratory by funds from the United States Office of Education, Department of Health, Education and Welfare. The opinions expressed here do not necessarily reflect the position of policy of the Office of Education, and no official endorsement by the Office of Education should be inferred.

fully, and take careful notes. Typically, the records have been of three kinds: *in situ* field notes, summary observations and interpretations, and documents. The field notes are composed of careful behavioral descriptions — who said or did what to whom in what situation and sequence — and interpretive asides — bracketed notes to ourselves that reflect momentary insights, intuitions, or hunches about the more general meaning of the events we are recording. The summary observations are longer interpretative accounts of what had happened and what we thought about what had happened, usually recorded onto tape as we drove to and from the setting under study. The documents included further memorabilia of the setting: pupil notes, papers, and tests; teachers' lesson plans; minutes of faculty meetings; and administrative bulletins.

With these extensive data we tried to reach two goals: first, the development of a narrative in lay language — the full story of what had happened; second, as an abstraction from this, a set of concepts, hypotheses, and miniature theories which would account for the data and which would be useful in thinking about similar problems elsewhere.

Standard field methods? *

Initially we described our procedures as in the tradition of 'standard participant observation', but. more recently we have come to believe that there is no such reality as standard participant observation or standard field-work procedures. Our position now is that the particular intent of the researcher and the particular circumstances determine the specific procedures to be utilized. To a considerable degree, such intents also determine the form and content of the published account of the research.

As indicated in Table 1, inspection of observational field studies suggests at least five dimensions along which their research styles vary. We have labeled these as descriptive narrative

---

* These materials are elaborated in more detail in Smith & Pohland (1971).

generation of theory, verification of theory, quantification of data, and involvement as participant. For illustrative purposes we compare and contrast our efforts with those of field workers from anthropological, sociological, and social psychological traditions: Glaser and Strauss's (1967) general analysis, the study of a medical school by Becker and his colleagues (1961), the study of a group predicting the end of the world (Festinger *et al.*, 1956), Blau's (1955) study of two government agencies, and Wolcott's (1967) study of an Indian village and school.

Table 1. Variations in field work

Dimension of field work	Emphasis see in each exemplar		
	Low	Moderate	High
Descriptive narrative	2		1 3 4 5 6
Generation of theory	4 5	3	1 2 6
Verification of theory	1 5	2 3	4
Quantification of theory	1 4 5	2	3 6
Involvement as participant	1 2 6	3	4 5

Exemplars of varying field-work traditions

1. Smith & Pohland, *Computer-assisted instruction*
2. Glaser & Strauss, *Grounded theory*
3. Becker et al., *Boys in white*
4. Festinger et al., *When prophecy fails*
5. Wolcott, *Kwakuitl village and school*
6. Blau, *Dynamics of bureaucracy*

Only Glaser and Strauss deemphasize the narrative, the clear 'full story' of the program, group, organization, or culture under study. The generation of theory — that is, the invention of concepts, hypotheses, and models — is what differentiates the research styles. Festinger et al. come to the field with an intensively developed theory; traditional educational anthropology is less interested in theory generation. In contrast we, and Glaser and Strauss, strongly accent such efforts. We minimize the verification of theory, while Festinger et al. see that as their principal target.* Wolcott's atheoretical position minimizes both verification and generation of theory. Quantification is minimized by Wolcott and Festinger and by us. Glaser and Strauss are more moderate. Becker and Blau quantify in different ways; the former quantifies field notes while the latter quantifies interactional data (see Smits & Brock, 1970). Field workers vary in the degree to which they are active participants in the group rather than participating observers.** Festinger's group were 'believing members' of the group; Wolcott taught school in the Blackfish village; and Becker has sometimes joined a contending side at a time of conflict in the group observed. Glaser and Strauss, and we ourselves, remain more in the observer role.*** A simple conclusion follows: It seems imperative that field workers describe carefully the methods used in each study and that codification of procedures continue.

IMPLICATIONS OF MENTAL TESTING FOR OBSERVATIONAL FIELD METHODS

Valid data

In our study of computer-assisted instruction we observed teachers, pupils, machines, and a variety of lessons. We talked with

---

*Our personal preference is to move toward verification in settings where careful controls can be instituted, careful measures developed for significant concepts, and large-enough samples of subjects obtained. The concept of 'teacher awareness' (Smith & Geoffrey, 1968), has received such attention in Smith and Kleine (1969).

** The original use of 'participant observation' was to contrast it with methodologies such as interviewing and the questionnaire. More recently, as investigators have studied groups in which they have direct standing or responsibilities as members, new distinctions have been made. Junker (1960) and Gold (1969) distinguish among complete participation, participation as observer, observing as participant, and observing only.

*** Even here variants exist. Geoffrey and I played 'inside-outside' roles, a division of labor where he was an 'insider', a complete participant, and I an 'outsider', an observer only.

teachers and pupils informally about their problems, plans, activities, and reactions. We talked informally with the members of multiple organizations: school principals and supervisors, telephone repairmen, computer experts, and so forth. In most instances we got along very well. We were interested strangers from outside the authority structure; we knew what was going on, who would listen, and who would empathize. We believe that we obtained a valid picture of the computer-assisted-instruction program.

In pursuing the logic of the validity of such data, we found considerable help and some questions in the technical test-development literature, e.g., the APA Standards (1966), and the Campbell-Fiske paper (1959) on convergent and discriminant validation. They stress that data on personality traits should be collected by measuring a number of traits with a number of methods. For instance, one might be interested in variables such as ascendency, hostility, and activity level. One might measure these through methods such as objective personality tests, projective devices, and sociometric nominations. Campbell and Fiske argue that the pattern of intercorrelations indicates reliabilities, validities, and method or instrument factors. Test data on personality traits contain large components of method variance. Only when one obtains several kinds of measures of each dimension can he locate these method errors. Some variables converge, showing high correlations; others diverge; such data are relevant to an expanded conception of construct validity. Our reasoning about participant-observation technique has a fundamental similarity to that of Campbell and Fiske.

We have expanded their scheme into a multimethod, multivariable, multiperson, multisituation matrix. Table 2 indicates that our methods in the CAI study included observation, informal interviewing, and collection of documents. We were concerned with classroom group variables and organizational variables, as well as with personality characteristics. Besides the teachers, pupils, and CAI curriculum which were our focal interests, we cบserved other teachers, principals, and individuals in diverse positions in multiple organizations. Finally, the situations in which we found ourselves were multiple. Within the classrooms,

various areas of the curriculum were being taught. We arrived
unannounced as well as announced. We were in different schools
and in several organizations. While we have not glorified our
procedures with the term 'construct validity', we think our
approach captures the best of that point of view. When we say in
the vernacular 'that's the way it was' we have few doubts about
our description and analysis.

*Table 2. Validity of participant observation: a multimethod, multiperson,
multisituation, and multivariable matrix*

1. Methods
   1.1 Observation
   1.2 Informal interviews
   1.3 Documents, lesson materials, computer printouts, etc.

2. Persons
   2.1 Pupils
   2.2 Cooperating teachers
   2.3 Principals
   2.4 Other teachers
   2.5 Multiple incumbents of multiple positions in multiple organizations

3. Situations
   3.1 Pupils at terminals
   3.2 Classroom teaching: announced and unannounced visits
   3.3 Multiple parts of the curriculum – in addition to arithmetic
   3.4 Multiple schools
   3.5 Multiple organizations
   3.6 Multiple parts of the country

4. Variables
   4.1 Individual: schemas, traits, motives
   4.2 Group: classroom interaction, activity, sentiments
   4.3 Organizational: schools, universities, Research and Development,
       Title III (1965 ESEA)

The most helpful model for us has been Polya's (1954) *Patterns
of plausible inference.* As he discusses verification of consequences, successive verification of several consequences, verifi-

cation of improbable consequences, and so forth we find ourselves saying, 'That's the way we are working our data.'

IMPLICATIONS OF OBSERVATIONAL FIELD METHODS FOR MENTAL TESTING: SOCIAL COGNITION IN THE CLASSROOM

The implications of observational field methods for mental testing are less clear than the reciprocal propositions. Mental testing has a longer, more codified history than field methods; applications seem simpler in going from the sophisticated to the unsophisticated. However, our tentative thinking suggests major reservations about much of mental testing as it contributes to a psychological theory of teaching. We have been particularly concerned with that domain which Guilford (1967) called 'behavioral' content in his structure of the intellect or which Thorndike labeled 'social intelligence'.

Teacher awareness

The most important implication of field methods for mental testing lies in the generation of new concepts. As I observed in one class, I noted that the teacher seemed to know a good bit about the children, their backgrounds, and their covert activities in and out of the classroom. For example, he made oblique references to a boy-girl dating relationship underlying classroom chatter and conversation and the need to change seating arrangements. We labeled this phenomenon 'teacher awareness', and began to inquire into its antecedents and consequences. We hypothesized that intellectual characteristics such as cognitive differentiation (measured by Witkin's Embedded Figure Test) and cognitive complexity (measured by an adaptation of Kelly's Role Concept Repertory Test) would correlate with teacher awareness (measured by congruency between teacher ratings and pupil sociometric nominations). In turn, we felt that pupil esteem for the teacher (measured with a questionnaire) would be a consequence of teacher awareness. In one study of 69 teachers significant correlations were found between cognitive differentiation and teacher awareness, and between teacher awareness and pupil esteem for the teacher (Smith & Kleine, 1969).

The status of the concept 'teacher awareness', proved a problem. Is it a 'trait', a 'characteristic', or an 'ability' of the teacher? Is it susceptible to usual mental-measurement procedures? Or, is 'teacher awareness' conceived more appropriately as a kind of 'interaction', 'relationship', or 'social role'? Perhaps the more powerful conceptualization is the latter. My hunch is that the mental-testing movement – with its concern for abilities, traits, and characteristics – has been so powerful that it has tended to foreclose the kind of thinking necessary for understanding in this area of educational psychology (cf. Tyler, 1959).

The child: abilities, traits, interactions, roles .

There are similar difficult and puzzling problems regarding the child. In general as pupils have been tested, measured, or assessed the results have typically been taken to make inferences about the personality structure, abilities, or dispositions of the individual. In some fundamental sense, the testing movement tends to commit one to psychological trait theory rather than to, say, psychological interaction theory or psychological role theory. Again, in our slum classroom, some of the children appeared to play different roles in the classroom; e.g., the court jester was a child who carried on and 'got away with' a teasing, humorous relationship with the teacher. Another child was 'on contract', characterized by a tacit agreement that 'if you don't bother me I won't bother you.' A significant part of classroom life involved this kind of phenomenon. I am not arguing that certain personality dispositions and abilities of the teacher and the children were not involved. Mental testing has an underlying implicit stance that makes it very difficult to handle phenomena such as these, though our field data suggest that they are important.

Teaching social cognition to pupils

My final illustration combines several threads of the prior discussion. Several colleagues and graduate students at Washington University have been devising curricular and instructional materials and theory which attempt to develop 'abilities to think critically' in social studies.* We have been studying the process with observational methods. The lessons involve value dilemmas: individualism vs. conformity for example. Classroom activities include reading, discussions of issues and role playing. The learning outcomes include careful defining of terms, perceiving values as continuous phenomena rather than as all-or-none principles, and using reasons and data in arguments and discourse.

Seif identified a 'teacher perplexity stance' as one element in teaching the new curriculum. The teacher 'played a role' of ignorance, provoking the pupils to define terms, to present data and reasons, and to view values as continua. Is it legitimate to speak of 'teacher perplexity stance' as an ability susceptible to measurement? And what is the most appropriate way to conceptualize this 'stance' as an element in the teacher's cognitive structure as she thinks through her lessons, makes plans for the day, and considers her objectives? Are these phenomena susceptible to mental measurement?

What have usually been conceptualized as abilities and traits of teachers and pupils may have limited utility in a psychological theory of teaching. Insofar as mental testing has contributed implicitly to that heoretical stance, it too may need to be reconsidered.

REFERENCES

Becker, H. S. et al. (1961) *Boys in white.* Chicago: Univer. of Chicago Press.
Blau, P. M. (1955) *The dynamics of bureaucracy.* Chicago: Univer. of Chicago Press.
Campbell, D. T. & Fiske, D. W. (1959) Convergent and discriminant validation by the multitrait-multimethod matrix. *Psychol. Bull., 56,* 81-105.

* The social studies materials are being prepared by Berlak and Tomlinson. Observational studies of the new curriculum are being made by Applegate, Solomon and Seif.

Festinger, L., Riecken, H. & Schachter, S. (1964). *When prophecy fails.*
New York: Harper Torchbook.

Gold, R. L. (1969) Roles in sociological field observations. In G. J. McCall
& J. L. Simmons (Eds.), *Issues in participant observation: A text and
reader.* Reading, Mass.: Addison-Wesley.

Glaser, B. G. & Strauss, A. L. (1967) *The discovery of grounded theory:
strategies for qualitative research.* Chicago: Aldine.

Guilford, J. P. (1967) *The nature of human intelligence.* New York: Mc-
Graw-Hill.

Junker, B. H. (1960) *Field work: An introduction to the social sciences.*
Chicago: Univer. of Chicago Press.

Polya, G. (1954) *Patterns of plausible inference.* Princeton: Princeton Univer. Press.

Smith, L. M. & Brock, J. A. M. (1970) '*Go, bug, go!* ' *Methodological issues
in classroom observational research.* Occasional Paper Series, No. 5. St.
Ann, Mo.: CEMREL.

Smith, L. M. & Geoffrey, W. (1968) *The complexities of an urban classroom.*
New York: Holt, Rinehart & Winston.

Smith, L. M. & Keith, P. M. (1971) *Anatomy of educational innovation.*
New York: Wiley.

Smith, L. M. & Kleine, P. F. (1969) Teacher awareness: social cognition in
the classroom. *School Rev., 77,* 245-256.

Smith, L. M. & Pohland, P. A. (1971) Education, technology and the rural
highlands. In D. Sjogren (Ed.), *AERA Evaluation Monograph Series,
No. 8.* Chicago: Rand McNally.

Standards for educational and psychological tests and manuals, Washington,
D. C.: Amer. Psychol. Assn. 1966.

Tyler, Leona. (1959) Toward a workable psychology of individuality. *Amer.
Psychologist, 14,* 75-81.

Wolcott, H. (1967) *A Kwakuitl village and school.* New York: Holt, Rinehart & Winston.

Note: *Leboyer remarked that Smith suggested a greater separation of
observational work from testing than occurs in reality. Industrial psychologists, for example, base criteria of success based on observation of performance and apply to them precisely the same concepts of reliability and
observer agreement that they apply to tests. Insofar as there is a contrast, it
is between observational studies of a purely descriptive or exploratory
nature and those such as Festinger's that work from a theoretically elaborated hypothesis. Studies of the later type resemble in style the work with
quantitative methods.* (Eds.)

EUNICE BELBIN and R. MEREDITH BELBIN   32
Industrial Training Research Unit, Cambridge, England

The abilities and problems of immigrants in learning to drive busses

Each year about 400 bus conductors in London apply for training to become bus drivers, but fewer than half of those accepted for training succeed in gaining their licensce. The pass rate is inversely related to age. Trainees born in the United Kingdom have the highest pass rate, and immigrants from underdeveloped countries have very low pass rates; Irish immigrants fall in between. A battery of aptitude tests proved less useful as a predictor of pass rate than the combination of age and country of origin.

An experimental program was designed to give preparatory training on a special track before the trainer took a bus out on the road. The tuition replaced part of the conventional program but did not add to the overall training time. The exercises comprised gear-changing, steering a course between two columns of cones, maneuvering a bus past stationary objects into simulated bus stops, reversing, and other component activities of bus control.

The likelihood that a United Kingdom trainee would receive a license improved as a result of this experimental training. The Irish benefited to a lesser degree. Immigrants from underdeveloped countries did not improve at all, and even fell slightly below their normal expectation of passing. Whereas performance on the track exercises had some predictive value for the ultimate success in the examination of UK trainees, it had none for immigrants from underdeveloped countries.

The immigrants are reasonably adept at acquiring the psychomotor skill needed in driving a bus. They also succeed in learning the road signs that are incorporated in the Highway Code. But they are poor in making decisions, and have difficulty in reading and interpreting road situations. Part of their difficulty in training arises because they see learning as memorizing 'correct' procedure. Some instructors respond to this expectation by living up to the role of an authority figure, which further reinforces the view of the trainees that obedience to the instructor is the key to passing the test.

Style of instruction may therefore become very important. In a pilot study, the instructor was interviewed regarding his approach to teaching. Some instructors described their approaches in terms which suggested that they adapted their teaching to the individual (a trainee-oriented style), while others encouraged their trainees to follow a model which they themselves set (an instructor-oriented style). Instructor statements were classified with respect to these styles by an independent person who had no knowlegde of the success of the instructors. The results indicated superiority of the trainee-oriented teachers. Trainee-oriented teaching seems to develop the trainee rather than attempt to mold him.

One way to develop decision-taking is to present trainees with plenty of problems that call for decisions. A new section was consequently introduced into the training program directed towards the learning of road strategy of roadmanship. The extension of the training program – in content rather than in time – involves four components.

Static position exercise. This exercise consists of a large board containing an aerial view of a road network. Vehicles are in various colours indicating their type, and contain insignia showing whether they are moving or stationary, and numbers so that they can be identified. In the first task, trainees have to decide whether certain numbered vehicles are in the correct position or not, and in the second task, what is the nature of the hazard of which the driver of a numbered vehicle has to beware. Once the trainees have committed themselves, the instructor discusses results.

Road-sense exercise. Some items in the exercise are presented as cards. One side presents a right and a wrong situation and the trainee has to decide which is which. The other side presents the answer, usually in pictorial rather than verbal form.

Film exercise. A 20-minute film presents a view of the road from the driver's seat, while the driver negotiates a series of situations. Sound cues, especially those related to gear changing and braking, play an important part in discriminating between right and wrong in the sequence of discrete problems.

Route-planning exercise. Trainees are presented with a sequence of still photographs on which a choice of bus positions is given for planning a route from one location to another in a traffic complex. After making their choice and marking it on a test paper, trainees examine the backs of the photographs, which now supply information on other traffic, and so allow the traffic flow to be more clearly assessed. Trainees can write in a revised route in their test paper. The results are then discussed.

To evaluate the effectiveness of the new methods, the errors the examiners recorded for immigrants and nonimmigrants were compared. Comparison was possible both before and after the introduction of the new exercises.

The results showed that all groups of trainees improved in aspects of driving related to road sense, the largest improvement being registered by the immigrants. Further trials under more carefully controlled field conditions are now being run.

DISCUSSION

The experience of the Industrial Training Research Unit in training on the buses and in other field experiments has brought out the need to distinguish between different forms of learning. These differences significantly affect the nature and underlying principles of the training methods to be applied.

Psychomotor learning is one of the most important components of driving skill. The decline in this type of ability is reflected in the extremely sharp drop in the passing rate with increase in age.

Of almost equal importance to bus driving is conceptual skill, which tends to be spoken of as 'road sense'. The essence of this skill is interpretation, comprising ability to see gestalts where signals are constantly changing and to establish which items in a highly complex field demand priority of attention.

A third ability is putting into practice previously learned procedures, akin to the benefits commonly attributed to experience. It is easier for the driver to perform better on a route with which he is already familiar, for here the ability to move the bus into a series of correct positions has already been learned and is subject only to the minor modifications that arise from contingencies. Individual differences are of less account where this type of experience has an important bearing on performance. The fourth type of ability is memorizing, important because the examiner has to be satisfied that the examinee is conversant with all road signs and with all sections of the highway code.

Immigrant trainees tend to memorize conscientiously, in spite of language and literacy barriers (although few fail in these ground). An inclination to memorize is also shown in unquestioning acceptance by immigrants of everything their instructors say, and by their tendency to repeat things they do not fully understand.

This has little payoff. What can be learned by memorizing does not count for a great deal. Even the amount that can be learned by procedural experience is limited. Since the examiner is at liberty to take the examinee along any route of his choosing, the instructors too continuously vary their routes, so that few familiar situations repeat themselves. Whereas an increasing number of hours at the wheel correlates with passing among most groups of trainees − older, UK-born, Irish, and so on − the relationship is not borne out among immigrant drivers.

In summary, it appears that a low capacity to engage in conceptual learning lies at the root of the immigrant's problems in training as a bus driver. Our hypothesis is that conceptual learning, with its emphasis on transfer effects, has little place in the cultures from which most immigrants come. Their behavior in training is set towards repetition of fixed response patterns (which are socially rewarded in cultures less advanced industrially and educationally. If this is the Achilles heel of the immigrant trainee, his suitability as a potential driver may be related to one particular aspect of his trainability – his willingness to employ conceptualization during learning.

Work to establish the relationship between progress on the conceptual learning tasks and performance on the driving examination test is now under way.

O.K. KYÖSTIÖ

University of Oulu

Divergence among school beginners caused by different cultural influences

Preliminary report

The differences between the Southern and Northern parts of Finland (and of Norway and Sweden too) are great, considering the climate, ecological, and economic factors as well as cultural influences in general. In what ways do these differences express themselves among school beginners and how can they be measured reliably? What conclusions can be drawn from the results?

To clarify the problem six districts were drawn from different parts of the country: two from the extreme North, above the Arctic Circle; two from a more southerly province of Northern Finland; and two from Southern Finland. All children who entered the public school for the first time in autumn 1970 were included in this research. They numbered over 700.

Some hypotheses connected with the problems were formulated and data collected to verify them. Because there are still very few standardized tests in Finland the first task was to develop measures. This work had begun some years earlier. Raven's Progressive Matrices was used to indicate reasoning ability and the KTK Performance Test (a Finnish nonverbal test) more versatile intellectual performance. There was also an attempt to measure children's skill and knowledge in reading, writing and arithmetic. Finnish children enter the school at seven. Many of them have therefore learned some reading, writing, and arithmetic before starting school. Tests to measure these abilities do not exist in Finland and any that are introduced therefore have to. be developed on the basis of some foreign patterns. Some smaller studies were carried out and a larger pilot investigation started in 1969. The materials for the main part of the research were gathered in autumn 1970. Apart from tests, other kinds of materials were obtained, e.g., background information on children, districts, parents and teachers. In addition to these, all the children were medically examined.

The research is planned to cover the development of these groups during the whole of the compulsory schooling (ages 7-16). The test results were put onto punched cards when the first achievement tests were carried out in late spring 1971.

Because of technical difficulties, the materials of the investigation had not been treated by computer when this report was prepared. Calculations are presently available only for the following measures.

Tests given when children entered the school for the first time in autumn 1970. Progressive Matrices; KTK Performance Test (two subtests), reading test for school beginners; arithmetic test for school beginners.

Tests given in the spring of 1971, at the end of the school year. Reading test; writing test; math test; test of perceptual speed; test of verbal reasoning.

The results for the autumn testing are shown in Table 1, and the results of the spring testing in Table 2.

One may compare the results of different areas to see whether there are any systematic trends between culturally different groups. On Matrices, the rural areas (Hyrynsalmi and Pelkosenniemi) stand at the bottom; the difference between them and the other groups is statistically significant. The test results from urban centers in Northern Finland are, however, quite comparable to those in the South. The difference between rural and urban results in the South is also significant; this needs further investigation. It seems that Matrices works well in Finland. The means are comparable with Raven's medians in the remote areas, and elsewhere are significantly higher. But Raven himself states that his norms may be too low. Raven's norms for England (for one city only) are 20 years old. The KTK-test results show the same tendency, namely a lower level in the remote areas. The

Table 1. Means and standard deviations at beginning of first year

	Elimäki Rural, South N = 144*		Lohja Urban, South N = 175 – 176**		Hyrynsalmi Rural, North N = 115 – 119		Raahe Urban, North N = 141 – 142		Pelkosenniemi Rural, Arctic N = 45 – 47		Kemijärvi Urban, Arctic N = 135	
	Mean	s.d.	Mean	s.d.	Mean	s.d.	Mean	s.d.	Mean	s.d.	Mean	s.d.
Reading	63.6	28.9	53.8	26.6	51.8	23.0	53.0	27.4	50.6	28.8	60.1	26.6
Arithmetic	38.3	12.2	38.0	12.0	32.1	10.6	36.3	11.3	36.8	11.2	39.9	10.2
KTK (performance test)	14.5	5.9	7.8	6.5	8.1	3.1	9.6	3.5	7.9	4.3	9.3	4.3
Raven	18.7	3.4	17.4	4.5	14.5	3.4	18.1	4.5	16.0	4.4	18.2	3.6

* Except for KTK where N = 14
** Except for KTK where N = 47

Table 2. Means and standard deviations at end of first year

	Elimäki Rural, South N = 133 – 135		Lohja Urban, South N = 188 – 198		Hyrynsalmi Rural, North N = 112 – 113		Raahe Urban, North N = 139 – 142		Pelkosenniemi Rural, Arctic N = 44		Kemijärvi Urban, Arctic N = 130	
	Mean	s.d.	Mean	s.d.	Mean	s.d.	Mean	s.d.	Mean	s.d.	Mean	s.d.
Writing	17.1	6.5	16.7	6.6	13.9	6.6	14.3	6.6	15.4	6.4	17.4	6.5
Reading	23.4	10.1	23.8	8.2	21.1	8.4	23.5	9.2	21.8	7.9	26.0	8.6
New math	13.9	7.8	13.9	6.8	10.0	7.0	14.6	7.7	14.7	7.9	22.9	7.7
Perceptual speed	17.8	5.8	17.2	6.2	15.3	6.0	17.1	6.5	14.4	5.3	21.1	6.2
Verbal reasoning	14.0	7.0	14.9	6.4	12.6	6.0	13.7	5.8	11.2	5.8	16.3	5.1

number of Ss in the South is too small to allow comparison.

The initial test results in reading and arithmetic are in accord with the ability results; school beginners in the remote areas are in general less able in these skills than their contemporaries in the other districts. (The differences are not always very significant.) It is difficult to explain these differences at this stage of the investigation. The background variables will give valuable information in this respect.

Table 2 indicates the results of the spring testing, after the children had been in school about 9 months. On ability tests in perceptual speed and verbal reasoning (whose reliability is satisfactory), the children in the remote areas again stood at the bottom. The high level of the Arctic urban center (Kemijärvi) is of interest. In the main groups, school achievement was in accord with the mental-ability scores. There were, however, some small divergences which probably show the influence of school instruction. Judging by the initial test in reading, the Arctic rural district (Pelkosenniemi) derived most benefit from the teaching. The leading position of the Arctic town (Kemijärvi) is remarkable. The results are not quite comparable since the new math curriculum was not introduced everywhere. The standardization of this test was also limited.

Mass media and social welfare are rapidly expanding their influence in the remote areas. These reduce differences between remote districts and urban centers. Increased mobility from the countryside to the cities causes changes whose characteristics are difficult to predict. It is hoped that this longitudinal study will be able to describe and explain the changes.

Norwegian Research Council for Science and Humanities,
and Institute of Applied Social Research

Adolescent changes in ability in relation to schooling

Preliminary report

In the ABC longitudinal study of adolescents from a Southeastern region of Norway, 6 group tests were given in Grade 7, around age 14, to all pupils leaving the obligatory primary school; in Grades 8-10 to subsets who continued in school; and at age 19 to the boys classified for military training. The tests are addition (1), substraction (2), surface development (3), figure matrices (4), arithmetic problems (5), and synonyms (6). These are paired in later analyses: 1 with 2, 3 with 4, 5 with 6.

Each test was put onto a normalized scale that has mean 50 and s.d. 20 in the original difference scores for numerical, figural,

Table 1. Change in score from age 14 to age 19

Years at school	N	Mean change in score				
		Numerical (1, 2)	Figural (3, 4)	Verbal (5, 6)	Reasoning (3 − 6)	Spread
13	142	23	23	38	30	17
12	723	17	20	33	26	11
11	328	19	19	29	24	8
10	395	14	17	24	21	5
9	409	11	15	20	18	4
8	498	7	12	16	14	3
7	482	2	8	12	10	4
All Ss	2977	12	16	24	20	7

Grade 8 retest sample:

7	380	0	7	5	6	1

and verbal tests, as well as for tests 3-6 together. The intraindividual range of scores on tests 3-6 was also determined at each testing. The last column of Table 1 gives the mean change in spread for each subsample. The last line of Table 1 refers to a sample of boys retested at the beginning of Grade 8. Whereas there was, on the average, no change in the well-practiced calculation skills, the conventional tests of intelligence (3-6) showed gains on the order of 1/4 s.d. This may be interpreted as primarily a short-range benefit from practice; it was largest for relatively unfamiliar test types.

Upon retest after 4-6 years, the group as a whole improved on the reasoning tests by 20 points (1 s.d.). The gain was largest on verbal tests, but gain on the figural tests was also considerable. The numerical tests showed the smallest changes. The variation over tests is reflected in the measure of intraindividual spread, which increased by 7 points.

Consider now the effects associated with schooling. For each additional year of schooling, mean reasoning scores increased by 3 or 4 points. Those with no further schooling improved about 10 points, but the change was much greater (30 points) for those who stayed in school the whole time.

There is a striking discrepancy between tests in this respect, as can be seen in the small mean for change in spread up to 10 years of schooling, beyond which it increases rapidly. While the verbal score shows a rather regular increase of some 4 points per year, there appear to be diminishing returns for the figural tests.

Performance of those without additional schooling improved on all types of tests: but very little in calculation, and most for arithmetic problem solving and word comprehension. The maximum differentiating effect of schooling, judged from the range of uncorrected difference scores, would appear to be around 3/4 s.d. for the figural tests, 1 s.d. for elementary calculations, and up to 1 1/2 s.d. for conventional verbal tests.

Evidently formal schooling was a powerful but not the only differentiating factor in the development of the cognitive functions examined.

Note: *Recent work in psychometrics shows that analysis of change scores is an incomplete procedure, and sometimes misleading. In Thrane's study, more would presumably be learned by estimating the regression of the retests on the initial true scores. (See Cronbach & Furby, referred to on p. 423).* (Eds.)

PART VI

Correlates and determinants of test performance

While the papers in this section are unusually diverse, virtually all are concerned with explanations of mental development and particularly with the role of home environment and language. Leboyer looks at occupational mobility in France, relating it to tested ability. Papers by Harrold-Stroebe and by Ataman and Epir examine classifying processes of schoolchildren in Malaysia and Turkey. Harrold-Stroebe examines particularly the influence of the language of the home and the language of instruction, to check on an hypothesis advanced by Bruner and his associates.

Mittler analyzes language performance of twins and finds larger heritability indices for tests that have no auditory-vocal component; social-class differences are also lower on these than on auditory tests. Poortinga reports a failure to confirm the hypothesis that Africans develop their auditory capacities to a greater degree than their visual ones (compared to Europeans).

Bakare and Uçman apply the Draw-a-Man test to Nigerian and Turkish samples, noting a strong social-class effect.

Silvey reports on educational correlates of test performance in Uganda.

CLAUDE LÉVY-LEBOYER   35
University of Paris V

Intergenerational mobility as a function of social origin and mental test results

Human behavior is subject to change, and the factors that determine the conditions of change are a function of the starting point, that is, of the level attained before the forces of change go to work. At least that is what we find in such diverse phenomena as the course of learning, the gradient for sensations, changes of attitude, and even the successive states of individual aspirations. Is the same to be found when we turn from a well-localized psychological phenomenon to the global type of development represented in socioeconomic indices?

Some indication is given by the facts to be reported here, drawn from a study of the comparative status of father and son, i.e., of intergenerational mobility. The general idea of this research is this: Some persons have a status equal to their fathers', as with sons of workers who are themselves workers, or sons of physicians who enter a comparable profession. Others attain a higher status, for example, the worker's son who becomes a technician or engineer. Still others decline in status. Lacking psychological studies of this, we know little of the factors that condition the progress or fall of the son from the SES of his father. It would seem evident that aptitudes should play an important role in this. But what form does the influence take? May one expect the sons who surpass the level of their fathers to be among the most talented? And would such a relation hold all along the social scale, regardless of the father's level?

To construct a hypothetical model we may consider two well-established relationships which, in this context, seem hard to reconcile. Mental-test scores are related to the occupational level one reaches (de Montmollin, 1958; Ministry of the Army, 1963). That has been explained by the facts that throughout schooling successive selections advance the best endowed, and also, that school experience increases success on the tests. Hence, among those coming from similar social backgrounds, the more mobile are expected to be the most talented ones. Secondly, social origin appears clearly to be a determinant of success on tests, as a consequence of cultural and material advantages of all kinds (see esp. Girard et al., 1950).

Among persons who have all reached the same educational and vocational level, then, the advantage should have been working in favor of the 'nonmobile'; these should be intellectually superior to the 'mobiles' because the 'nonmobiles' would have started at a higher level. One could compare within the social and occupational level reached, or within the social level of origin; one might expect the mobile to appear to be the least gifted, among those in their final status, or the most gifted, among their category of origin.

PROCEDURE

To test these hypotheses, we have organized information on 1,945 young men questioned at the time of entry into military service. The sample was restricted to those of urban origin so as not to confound movement to the city with upward mobility, their causes surely being different. To increase the representation of mobile *S*s we questioned an extra number among the men asking for deferment in order to complete their educational programs. The sample, then, is not to be considered representative of the generation. But it is a homogeneous group: the age range is 18 to 23 (19 being the mean); the educational levels are distributed normally, from persons with no diploma to students of the *Grandes Ecoles* and the universities. Comparison with the census of 1962 verifies that the distribution of fathers' occupations is essentially that of the population, save, of course, for underrepresentation of farming occupations.

All *S*s filled out an anonymous questionnaire specifying their origin, education, occupational status, and future aspirations, as well as their attitudes on various aspects of occupational life. The questionnaire was filled out under very good conditions. Among 2000 *S*s questioned, only 55 records (fewer than 3 per cent) were too incomplete to be used. In evaluating social mobility it was not possible to impose a rigorous scale; it would be unrealistic to look on professional status as a simple continuous variable. Each *S* was placed in one of six categories; upward mobility (strong, evident, slight – hereafter called Mobile 1, 2, or 3); in same status as father; or downward mobile (markedly, or slightly). In the sample, 27 percent were upward mobile, 58 per cent unchanged in status, and 15 per cent downward mobile.

All *S*s took an Army general classification test containing two subtests measuring *g*, two verbal subtests, and two tests of educational achievement. Scores are reported on a 20-point scale (standardized to have a mean of 10, on a larger sample than ours). Because of the conditions we imposed in selecting *S*s, the mean for our sample is 14.6, but the scores range from 3 to 20 and the s.d. is 3.4.

RESULTS

We find relations of mental ability with education and initial social status similar to those of other studies. The mean score increases with educational level from 8.3 for those with no diploma to 18.9 for those with the most education. Likewise with social origin: an increase from 13.0 for sons of manual workers to 18.5 for sons of the elite.

The relation between scores and mobility is more complex. Among the 109 *S*s in category Mobile 1, not one scored below 10, and 89 per cent scored 18, 19 or 20. The corresponding percentages were 42, 38, and 23, respectively, for Mobile 2, Mobile 3, and the remaining *S*s. It appears that success on tests is a virtually obligatory requirement for marked upward mobility. But it is not a sufficient condition. An appreciable number of highly able *S*s starting from social levels well below the highest did not make use of their ability to rise in status.

When, to check the first hypothesis, we group the *S*s according to educational level reached, we find rather weak relations of degree of mobility to score. Various explanations can be suggested. While the categories applied to schooling are relatively broad, at high levels the test scores show little variation. Also, there are certainly cases of downward mobility that came not from failure in school but from causes having nothing to do with level of aptitude.

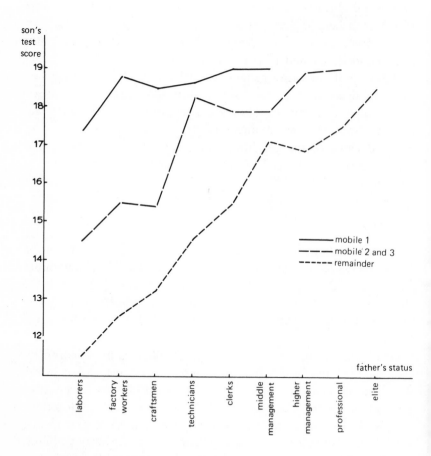

Figure 1. Mean test scores of young men as a function of father's occupation and son's mobility

When, on the other hand, we group Ss by social origin, there is a marked difference between mobiles and nonmobiles of the same origin.

The relation varies, depending upon the occupational level reached, as Figure 1 shows clearly. On the horizontal axis appears the father's status, and on the vertical axis the son's test score. There are curves for the Mobile-1 group, for Mobile 2 and 3 combined, and for the remainder. Six score points separate the mean for workers' sons in Mobile 3 and the mean for workers' sons who are nonmobile. But only two points separate the Mobile-3 mean from the mean of nonmobiles when both come from middle-management families.

To sum op: the mobile Ss are not outclassed on tests by the group they join, but they surpass markedly the tests of others in the group of their origin. These differences take on more importance because they reverse, to some extent, inequalities of cultural advantage. Many of less advantaged overtake and even pass the more advantaged. It appears that, to move upward from his original level, the boy needs to possess greater intellectual powers than it takes merely to hold at the level of one's father. It is as if there were a psychological barrier to surmount, and possession of above-average ability markedly increases one's chances of surmounting it.

How is this to be explained? Perhaps aptitudes play an instrumental role, so that the better one is endowed the more he has the resources to triumph over social viscosity. This could be elaborated into a theory that considers a complex chain of variables, which further studies would have to verify. One could suppose that the highly able persons arising in the lower end of the social scale do better in school than others of their class. Because this is comparatively rare in the group, that success could develop selfconfidence, promote higher occupational goals, and stimulate motivation to succeed.

There have been many statements in this conference about the importance of attitudes as a determinant of academic and professional performance, and as a consequence of cultural and ecological forces. The same remark applies here, as Ss' motivation to raise themselves socially appears linked to their concepts of themselves, of their aptitudes, and of their chances of success. On this point I could draw considerable evidence from the questionnaire. I cite only the observation that Ss from different mobility groups gave different answers, when questioned about what would facilitate their success in life. Among mobiles, about half put first their aptitudes or school success, and only one-fifth of the others did this. That is no more than an indication, but it could explain why, in the dynamics of change, success promotes success when it takes the form of *relative* success and is seen as that by the group around one.

REFERENCES

Girard, A. et al. (1950) *Le niveau intellectuel des enfants d'âge scolaire.* Paris; Presses Universitaires de France.

de Montmollin, M. (1958) Etude sur le niveau intellectuel des recrues du contingent. *Population, 13,* 259-269.

Ministry of the Army. (1963) *Le contingent vu par les psychotechniciens militaires.* Paris.

M. S. HARROLD-STROEBE
University of Bristol

Cognitive development of children from selected ethnic, educational and language backgrounds in Malaysia*

The work that I am going to report was carried out in Malaysia to examine influences on cognitive development A number of previous studies in cultural milieu outside Western Europe examine the way in which culture may shape development. Such studies have looked at variables other than age which could affect the course of growth. This has been the particular interest of investigators under the direction of J. S. Bruner at Harvard, who consider that the child's ways of achieving and using knowledge receive an important impetus from the surrounding culture.

The aspect of development with which this team of research workers has been concerned, and with which the Malaysian study specifically deals, is the change in cognitive structure that occurs between the ages of about 5 and 7 in a Western child. In Bruner's framework this is the transition from the 'ikonic' to the 'symbolic' mode of representation. At the 'ikonic' stage the child represents the world to himself by an image or spatial scheme, and deals with information in terms of perceptual appearances, one aspect at a time. The features of this type of representation would seem to indicate little use of stored information by the child. In contrast, at the 'symbolic' level, the child is able to deal with sets of invariant features, taking several at a time into some structured relationship; he is able also to represent by using common attributes superordinate to the particular items.

* Support for this research was provided by a grant from the Nuffield Foundation and the Social Science Research Council (UK).

In some of the previous studies, development of representation was studied with particular regard to its manifestation in categorization. This we have done in Malaysia. Olver and Hornsby (in Bruner et al., 1966) examined the way in which the techniques of representation that come into force as children grow are reflected in the changing ways children have of grouping things in their world. They hypothesized that one should be able to infer the mode of representation from responses on a task involving classification. When asked to group objects they see as alike in some respect, children functioning at different levels of representation were expected to emphasize features of the environment consistent with that mode.

At the 'ikonic' level one would expect grouping according to perceptual likeness, whereas at the 'symbolic' level there would be less dependence on immediate sensory cues. The findings of Olver and Hornsby (in Bruner et al., 1966) were consistent with this. When they gave 'equivalence' tasks, the younger children (6 year olds) tended to classify according to perceptible features, such as color, shape, or a detail of the objects; e.g., 'They are both pointed'. On the other hand, an older child would say that the items were the same on the basis of some common use to which they could all be put (e.g., 'They are the same because I can wear them all') or on the basis of the linguistic classifiability of the items (e.g., 'They are all tools'). This shift from perceptual categorization to use of the more abstract 'functional' and 'nominal' categories, as they are termed, would seem to reflect the change from an ikonic to a symbolic mode of functioning, and to be consistent with the features of each stage.

The crosscultural work carried out within the theoretical framework outlined above has revealed a number of factors other than age which are important in development to symbolic representation. Maccoby and Modiano (in Bruner et al., 1966) found greater use of functional attributes and 'abstraction' in an urban area in Mexico than in a rural sample. Reich (in Bruner et al., 1966) found a similar course of growth among white American and Eskimo children in Anchorage, although the Eskimos achieved symbolic representation later than the white children.

This was attributed by the investigators to differential exposure to an urban environment, rather than to a difference in culture. The study most important as background to the present investigation is that of Greenfield, Reich, and Olver (in Bruner et al., 1966) on the Wolof tribe of Senegal. Urban and rural schoolchildren were tested, and also a sample of unschooled rural children. All the schoolchildren moved away from an initial reliance on color, the bush children moving mainly towards form and the city children towards form and function. The unschooled rural children continued to rely on color as a basis for their groupings. Schooling was understood from this to be the 'single most powerful factor . . . in the stimulation of abstraction' (p. 351). However, the Greenfield study could not include an urban unschooled sample, as only in rural areas was it possible to find unschooled children; without this group it would not seem possible to generalize about the influence of schooling. One cannot assume that an urban unschooled sample would show a pattern similar to that of the rural unschooled group. It may be that school experience is more important for development to a symbolic level in a rural setting, where facilities in the home and the village are considerably less conducive to abstraction than in the town. In the rural area the school acts as a compensation. In the urban area alternative experiences may make the school less significant. Another part of this work in Senegal is also important here; Greenfield manipulated the language in which the tests were conducted. The oldest children, who had command of two languages, were less prone to respond at the symbolic level when tested in their native language (Wolof) than when tested in the language of their education (French).

Bruner and his associates believe that the difference between the city child and the rural child derives from 'differential exposure to problem solving and communication in situations that are not supported by context – as is the case with, for example, most reading and writing, the use of monetary exchange, and schooling' (Greenfield, in Bruner et al., 1966, p. 315). The evidence for this comes largely from the differences in schooling mentioned above. Language is judged to be important in these situations insofar as it is a means of communicating information

and experience, when this transmission refers to events that do
not give direct perceptual support. Thus the children in the
Greenfield study were understood to respond more 'symbolically'
in the language of their education because that language is more
often used than the native language when information about
remote experience is transmitted; this is particularly the case
with written language. This interpretation is based on comparison
of only one language used as a school medium with one which is
not. Greenfield et al. conclude, however, that 'any written language used out of a concrete context should produce these same
cognitive results'. They reject an alternative interpretation regarding the possible linguistic relativity of the two languages. Greenfield et al. claimed that although the Wolof language is very
restricted (in comparison with French) in the number of color
words it contains, the native-language speakers have a far greater
tendency to group objects in terms of color likeness than
speakers of French do.

Our study in Malaysia is a sequel to that in Senegal. It was
intended to examine the following matters which arise from the
previous findings and their interpretation. First, does schooling
universally produce effects consistent with Bruner and Greenfield's view that context-free experience is the most important
aid to development? Could the differences they found between
schooled and unschooled samples be attributed instead to the
fact that the school presents varied experiences, which are of
value when the environment does not offer diverse knowledge for
the child to assimilate? This question stems from a more general
concern to learn more precisely what experience is important to
transmit to the child to help him shift from ikonic to symbolic
functioning. Second, will Malaysian data provide evidence that
language is important because of its use in school (that is, as the
means whereby the context-free school experience is transmitted
to the child)? Are differences between the language of instruction and the vernacular language, such as those Greenfield reported, found with other languages? From these two points, can
one conclude that context-free experience is the crucial factor in
development?

The importance of school could not be measured by a comparison of schooled and unschooled groups since in this type of investigation – even if unschooled children are available – the latter might be less familiar with the testing procedures and materials. In Malaysia it was possible to test children within the same urban area, coming from a variety of language and cultural backgrounds, who receive schooling in different languages. In Malaysia there are three main ethnic groups; Malays (roughly 50 per cent of the population), Chinese (38 per cent) and Indians (12 per cent). At the time of the research primary education was available in four language media; Malay, Chinese (mandarin) English, and the most widely spoken of the Indian languages, Tamil. Common syllabi and standard timetables were used in all four media. In Malaysia primary schooling is free and compulsory, and the medium is chosen by the family. Not surprisingly, one tends to find each ethnic group attending the school of its own language almost exclusively, though a fair proportion of Chinese and Malay children, and a few Indians, attend the English-medium schools.

In this study children were selected from two cultural milieus, Chinese and Malay. All were from an urban area. One sample of Chinese attended Chinese schools, and a sample of Malays came from Malay schools. Further Chinese and Malay children were selected from English-medium schools. The language of testing was varied; at the English medium 9- and 12-year old children were randomly assigned to testing either in their vernacular language or in English. At the Chinese schools testing was in Hokkien, and at the Malay medium it was in Malay.

The sample consisted of first, third, and sixth grade children (ages 7, 9, and 12).* Generally, in the town of the investigation, the children at the English-medium schools were of higher SES than those attending the other schools. The former were drawn from a fairly wide range of 'white-collar' occupations; the Chinese- and Malay-medium samples, although comparable with each other, were had a lower SES. Groups of first grade boys at

---

* English-medium samples consist of boys and girls. There were no sex differences in development to symbolism. Chinese- and Malay-medium samples consisted of boys only.

English-medium schools from middle- and working-class backgrounds were included in the sample to examine the importance
of social class. Results are therefore presented separately for
7-year-old English-medium children.

For Greenfield's results and interpretation to be substantiated,
children tested in the medium of instruction would have to give
more symbolic responses than those tested in languages which
were not used in instruction. At the English-medium school, for
example, Chinese and Malay children tested in English would give
more symbolic responses than those tested in Hokkien or Malay.
If the nature of the vernacular language is of primary importance,
regardless of the medium of instruction, however, one would
expect ethnic groups to differ in the same way when tested in the
vernacular languages, no matter what the school medium. If more
general cultural factors were important, one would expect the
ethnic-group differences to appear no matter what their language
of schooling and testing.

Two equivalence tasks were adapted from those of Olver and
Hornsby (in Bruner et al., 1966). One was a picture task and one
a word task. In each, the child was required to give reasons for
the equivalence of a number of common objects. The content of
the reasons for grouping was analyzed. (Bruner's associates also
used a 'syntactic' analysis; this has not been made to date on the
Malaysian results.) The responses from the Malaysian children fall
almost entirely into the functional categories. Few of the
children were unable to respond, and none gave the sort of
perceptual, nominal, and 'affective' responses found in Boston.
The results presented here employ a combined score from the
two tasks as a measure of equivalence judgment. For each child
responses were scored; not all could be assigned to the three main
categories.

With increasing age perceptual responses decreased; functional
and also nominal responses increased from age 7 to 12 (Table 1);
here and in later tables, significance tests are based on Kendall's S
coefficient, using a two-tailed test. The result is that expected if
there is a developmental trend from ikonic to symbolic representation. Chinese- and Malay-medium schoolchildren were
slower than English-medium children to attain symbolic

Table 1. Mean number of responses of each type as a function of age and medium of instruction

Type of response	English-medium boys and girls			Chinese- and Malay-medium boys			
	Age 9 (*N* = 90)	Age 12 (*N*= 90)	*P*	Age 7 (*N*= 30)	Age 9 (*N*= 30)	Age 12 (*N*= 30)	*P*
Perceptual	1.89	0.77	.001	4.80	3.60	0.73	.001
Nominal	3.13	3.71	n.s.	1.03	2.23	3.20	n.s.
Functional	3.91	5.24	.01	2.66	2.86	5.83	.01
Other	1.07	.28		1.51	1.31	.24	

Table 2. Mean number of responses of each type as a function of ethnic origin and medium of instruction (7 years old)

Type of response	English-medium boys			Chinese-medium boys	Malay-medium boys	
	origin Chinese (*N*=15)	origin Malay (*N*=15)	*P*	(*N*=15)	(*N*=15)	*P*
Perceptual	1.40	3.07	.05	4.40	5.20	n.s.
Nominal	2.53	1.66	n.s.	1.13	0.93	n.s.
Functional	5.53	3.73	n.s.	3.66	1.66	.05
Other	.54	1.54		.81	2.21	

Table 3. Mean number of responses of each type as a function of ethnic origin and medium of instruction (9 years old and 12 years old)

Type of response	English-medium boys and girls			Chinese-medium boys	Malay-medium boys	
	Chinese (*N*= 90)	Malay (*N*= 90)	*P*	(*N*= 30)	(*N*= 30)	*P*
Perceptual	1.44	1.21	n.s.	2.33	2.00	n.s.
Nominal	2.98	3.85	.05	1.53	3.90	.001
Functional	4.94	4.21	.05	5.46	3.23	.01
Other	.64	.73		.68	.87	

Table 4. Mean number of responses of each type within the English-medium group as a function of language of instruction and ethnic origin
(9 years old and 12 years old, both sexes)

Type of response	Chinese children			Malay children		
	Tested in English (*N*= 60)	Tested in Hokkien (*N*= 30)	*P*	Tested in English (*N*= 60)	Tested in Malay (*N*= 30)	*P*
Perceptual	1.48	1.37	n.s.	1.11	1.40	n.s.
Nominal	3.21	2.53	n.s.	4.15	3.76	n.s.
Functional	4.66	5.50	n.s.	3.76	5.10	.05
Other	.65	.60		.98	.26	

functioning: at age 9 they were considerably more dependent on perceptual bases for grouping, though by age 12 their results were like those from the English-medium. It is likely that this difference reflects social class. 7-year-old English-medium working-class boys gave more perceptual responses, and fewer nominal and functional responses than the middle class.*

Data comparing Chinese and Malay boys in their first year of schooling are presented in Table 2. Both groups of Malay children responded more at the perceptual level than the Chinese (the difference being significant for English-medium boys). From Table 3 it can be seen that this was no longer the case at ages 9 and 12. Consistently, Chinese responded with more functional attributes than Malays (Tables 2, 3, 4). The difference occurred whether the language of testing was the first language or English, and regardless of medium of schooling. For neither Chinese nor Malays was there a significant increase in symbolic performance when the school language was used in testing. Children at English-medium schools performed as 'symbolically' in their own first languages as in English (Table 4).

* The working-class samples had fewer than 10 cases, and these results do not reach the .05 level of significance. The importance of social class in development towards symbolism is also indicated in Ataman's paper (p. 329).

These results do not seem to support an explanation in terms of 'context-free' experience. A more salient factor appears to be the amount of 'enrichment' in the child's environmen. The finding that Chinese and Malay children do not classify items more symbolically in the language of their education implies that the importance of language does not come from its transmission of knowledge in the school. Schooling may enrich environmental experience and so aid development in this urban setting, but only when there is a need to compensate for other lacks. For example, there are considerable differences in cultural background of the two ethnic groups (despite their similar SES), which may contribute to the ethnic difference in symbolic functioning. Although all the children come from an urban area, the Malays have strong ties with rural communities and retain many features of a rural way of life (Wilson, 1967). The Chinese have a much longer tradition of urban life. Possibly, then, differential exposure to an urban environment is the key factor here. Like the Eskimos in Reich's study, the Malay children initially gave fewer symbolic responses than the Chinese (although the groups were equal after two years of education). Perhaps this is because their homes do not emphasize urban values and patterns as the Chinese do.

Another cultural contrast is the outlook on the upbringing and education of children. Hunter (1966), in discussing the differences in value and achievement patterns, states, 'Chinese . . . come from a society where education is esteemed and where the pressure of competition has been inordinately strong . . . Habits of frugality, hard work, and unquestioned parental control drive the Chinese pupil to the limits of his ability. Nationals with whom the Chinese compete take a far more easy going view.' It seems likely, then, that the home environments of the Chinese and Malay pupils are quite dissimilar in ways which could be expected to cause differences in cognitive development. Support for an 'enriched environment' point of view comes also from the SES differences: children coming from lower social classes (who could be expected to have less variety of experience) performed less well. Cynthia Deutsch (1968) testifies that this is generally the case for the working-class child: 'There is less stress on . . . teaching him the more subtle differentiations between stimuli . . .

The slum child has, in his stimulus field, both less redundancy and less education of his attention to the relevant properties of stimuli. As a result, he could be expected to come to school with poorer discrimination performance than his middle class counterpart.'

The importance of a general milieu effect rather than an effect specifically of 'context-free' experience is also implied by the Chinese-Malay differences in style of symbolic functioning. Chinese children gave more functional responses and the Malays more nominal responses, no matter what the medium of instruction or the language of testing. This would seem to reflect cultural emphases. The suggestion is that the Chinese child, because of the nature of his society with its pressures, is encouraged to think in terms of the use which items in his environment can be put. The Malay child would not have the same encouragement towards making the functions of items explicit. Possibly the reason the Malay child is later in developing 'symbolism' is that in the home no emphasis is put on labeling objects by their functions, which are implicit in the nominal classifications. The present study would seem to support the view that use of functional categories promotes earlier emergence of symbolism' The Harvard investigators all regard nominal classification as being the most sophisticated and the last type to develop, as 'It is totally dependent on symbolic representation and transformation' (Greenfield et al., *op. cit.*) The Malay child, therefore, has to rely longer on perceptual attributes in order to classify because he lacks the additional information offered by defining objects in terms of uses, which would act as a preliminary to thinking about invariant, superordinate features of objects, and would develop discrimination and act as the precursor of a more concise mode of representation.

Apparently the child receives an important impetus towards symbolic representation from his environment, but this does not require that the experience be 'context-free'. The particular features of the environment that promote development of symbolic thinking seem to be, first, the variety and diversity of the stimuli present in his environment, and, second, the teaching the child receives to construe the properties of items in his world, informally in the home or (if that does not occur) later in the school. Although this interpretation is subject to further analysis of data from Malaysia, and will be examined in further work in England, evidence from a variety of cultures (for example, Davey, 1968; de Lacey, 1970; Serpell, 1969) seems to be consistent with this view.

REFERENCES

Bruner, J. S., Olver, R. R. & Greenfield, P. M. (1966) *Studies in cognitive growth.* New York: Wiley.

Davey, A. G. (1968) The Tristan da Cunhan children's concepts of equivalence. *Brit. J. educ. Psychol., 38*, 162-170.

de Lacey, P. R. (1970) A crosscultural study of classificatory ability in Australia. *J. cross-cult. Psychol., 1*, 293-304.

Deutsch, C. (1968) Environment and perception. In M. Deutsch, I. Katz & A. R. Jensen (Eds.), *Social class, race, and psychological development.* New York: Holt, Rinehart & Winston. Pp. 58-85.

Hunter, G. (1966) *South-east Asia: Race, culture, and nation.* London: Oxford Univer. Press.

Serpell, R. (1969) The influence of language, education, and culture on attentional preference between colour and form. *Intern. J. Psychol., 4*, 183-194.

Wilson, P. (1969) *A Malay village and Malaysia.* New Haven: Hraf Press.

Note: *H. Philp provided a written comment on a study similar to Harrold-Stroebe's done in Papua-New Guinea by Kelly and Huntsman of Macquarrie University. Some 250 children on four language areas were matched with similar children who had never attended school, and given tasks in the Piaget-Bruner tradition. It appears that the unschooled children develop ability to form concepts more rapidly than the schoolchildren, up to about the sixth year of schooling. In classification tasks the nature of the vernacular language has an important influence; if a language is rich in names useful in classifying, children from that group do better. Giving task instructions in English rather than the native language draws more abstract performance from schooled children. Once the effect of schooling is partialed out, contact with Western culture seems not to account for differences among villages in task performance. Harrold-Stroebe noted that the nature of the vernacular language did not appear to be important in Greenfield's data from Senegal; in her Malaysian data, the fact that Malays performed similarly in either language of testing also casts doubt on the importance of the vernacular. Contact with Western culture appeared to be important in de Lacey's data on aborigines.* (Eds.)

IŞIK ATAMAN and SHIRLEY EPIR   37
Haçettepe University, Ankara

Age, socioeconomic status and classificatory behavior among Turkish children

The process of classifying dissimilar objects as the same or equal is accepted as an important aspect of cognitive activity. Most tests of mental abilities from the Binet to those most recently published have items involving classification. Ability to classify is assumed to change with time much as general cognitive development does. As learning is expected to influence the ability to classify cultural differences should be expected. While the process of classifying is universal, the categories and principles governing class formation are the products of societies (Bruner et al., 1956).

Descriptive studies of classificatory behavior in widely diverse societies appear in the literature and some cultural differences are found. (Annett, 1959; Bruner, 1966; Davey, 1968; Price-Williams, 1962; Sigel, 1964). These studies, using object-sorting tasks, have noted that the attributes prefered as a basis for placement of objects into groups, the age at which a preference predominates, and the principles used in group formation vary with the society.

The purpose of this study was to describe classificatory behavior in a Turkish sample, using a similar procedure. The data should provide a basis for further developmental studies in Turkey and information pertinent to test development.

METHOD

Subjects

To study developmental trends and the influence of social background in urban Turkey, 120 children (60 of each sex) at four
age levels were selected from primary and secondary schools
located in three sections of Ankara representing high, middle,
and low SES. *S*s were in the first, fourth, seventh and tenth
grades; the mean ages of the respective groups were 7, 10, 13.1,
and 16 years. Since the criterion for selection was birthdate
within a specified range, age was not associated with sex or SES.
To control somewhat for intelligence, normal class placement
was also a criterion for selection. SES was judged from location
of school and father's education. The high-SES group were living
in a high-rent area of the city; their fathers were university
graduates. The middle-SES *S*s were living in a moderate-rent area;
their fathers were graduates of the *lycée*. The low-SES *S*s were
living in a squatters' housing area, and their fathers had primary-
school education or less. Children who met these criteria were
selected randomly from the class list by the experimenters.

Procedure

An object-sorting task modeled upon several appearing in the
literature (Halstead, 1940; Annett, 1959; Bruner et al., 1966)
was used to obtain samples of classificatory behavior. 29 objects
were chosen – for example, a red plastic saw and a red plastic
letter *D*. Each object had in common with one or more of the
other objects a perceptual attribute (color, form, etc.), a use or
activity (they move, carry things, etc.) and a class name (vehicles,
animals, etc.). A pilot study established that all items were easily
recognizable, and capable of being named by Turkish children of
age 7.

The administration customary for an object-sorting task was
used. Restrictions on responses were minimal. The instructions
placed no limitations on the number of groups, the number of
times an object could be used, the number of objects in any

group, or the basis for grouping. *S*s were seen individually. The task required about 15 minutes; it was terminated when the subject indicated that he had finished. Responses were written down *verbatim*. One examiner tested all *S*s*.

Scoring

For each *S*, attention was paid to the number of groups formed, the mean number of objects per group, and *S*'s explanations for the groups formed.

A system of analysis adapted from Olver and Hornsby (Bruner et al., 1966) was used to place each explanation in one of five broad categories:

1. *No principle.* *S* failed to specify the organizing principle for group membership. E.g., gave no response, named objects or enumerated activities or structural aspects, etc., or merely said 'They go together'.

2. *Relational.* Membership depended upon the relationship of objects to each other. These relationships were expressed in sentence form, as in 'The soldier rides the horse'.

3. *Perceptual.* Group membership was organized around a perceptual attribute such as color, structure, or other immediately observable feature of the objects.

4. *Functional.* Membership was organized around a use or activity, as in 'They are used for repair'.

5. *Nominal.* Group membership was based on nominal characteristics. *S* explained his grouping on the basis of a class name such as 'animals' or 'toys'.

Subclassification of the responses was attempted but this decreased considerably the reliability of the scoring system. Therefore, subclassifications were not used. Where *S* gave more than one basis for a grouping the response was placed in a sixth category, 'Combination'. These rare responses were ignored in the quantitative tabulation.

* We thank Miss Fersun Hamami for assistance.

RESULTS

Table 1. Number of groups formed by age and SES

Age	Low SES		Middle SES		High SES		All Ss	
	Mean	s.d.	Mean	s.d.	Mean	s.d.	Mean	s.d.
7	5.4	4.0	7.0	2.8	10.3	6.2	7.9	5.0
10	6.4	4.1	10.7	3.5	11.5	3.5	9.5	4.3
13	9.2	3.2	11.5	2.9	10.0	1.8	10.2	2.8
16	9.6	2.7	8.5	2.0	11.6	3.0	9.9	2.8
All Ss	7.6	3.8	9.4	3.3	10.8	4.0		

Table 2. Number of objects per group by age and SES

Age	Low SES		Middle SES		High SES		All Ss	
	Mean	s.d.	Mean	s.d.	Mean	s.d.	Mean	s.d.
7	2.65	1.16	2.30	0.48	2.38	0.50	2.45	0.77
10	3.44	1.88	2.61	0.40	3.12	1.32	2.29	1.77
13	3.11	1.08	2.98	1.17	3.19	0.16	2.33	1.60
16	4.41	0.92	3.26	0.69	3.85	1.17	2.90	1.87
All Ss	3.40	1.42	2.77	0.81	3.13	1.07		

The data were analyzed to determine the effects of age, SES, and sex on number of groups formed and mean group size (Tables 1 and 2). There was a significant effect for SES ($P < .01$, by three-way analysis of variance). Low-SES Ss formed significantly fewer groups than middle- and high-SES Ss and middle-SES Ss formed significantly fewer groups than high-SES Ss ($P < .05$). Age differences approached significance ($P < .10$). The main effect for sex was not significant nor was any interaction. On mean group size there were significant age effects ($P < .01$) and SES effects ($P < .05$). 7 year olds made significantly smaller groups than others, and 16 year olds made significantly larger groups ($P < .05$). The difference between ages 10 and 13 was not significant. Middle-SES Ss differed significantly from both low- and high-SES Ss ($P < .05$), but a significant difference did not occur between low and high SES.

Table 3. Percentage of responses in each category, by age

Age	No principle	Relational	Perceptual	Functional	Nominal
7	22.84	9.91	43.10	11.20	12.93
10	7.63	8.01	26.74	11.81	45.80
13	4.94	11.18	4.27	10.85	68.75
16	0.35	5.39	3.59	3.59	87.05

Table 4. Percentage of responses in each category, by SES

SES	No principle	Relational	Perceptual	Functional	Nominal
High	3.58	8.13	21.05	9.09	59.13
Middle	6.97	14.47	16.89	9.65	52.01
Lower	16.84	1.74	14.73	9.12	57.54

Table 5. Percentage of responses in each category, by sex

Sex	No principle	Relational	Perceptual	Functional	Nominal
Boys	8.88	6.39	21.13	10.83	52.75
Girls	7.64	11.11	14.47	7.64	59.25

When reasons given for grouping objects were classified, inter-judge agreement was 92.2 per cent.* Frequency counts for each category were made by age, SES, and sex, and χ^2 tests were computed. Tables 3, 4, and 5 give the percentages of responses in each category.

Effects of age, SES, and sex were significant ($P < .001$). With increasing age, responses classified as 'Nominal' increased and responses classified as 'No principle' and as 'Perceptual' decreased.

* We thank Miss Ruvide Bayraktar for serving as a judge for scoring.

'Relational' and 'Functional' responses were less affected by age, except that at age 16 their use decreased sharply.

Social-class differences were greatest in the categories 'No principle', 'Relational', and 'Perceptual'. Children of lower SES gave more responses which lacked an organizing principle, and fewer responses on a relational or perceptual basis. 'Relational' grouping occurred with greatest frequency for middle SES, while 'Perceptual' responses were most frequent among high SES Ss. However, χ^2 computed at each age level indicated less association between SES and type of reason in older groups: at age 7, $\chi^2 = 67.39, P < .01$; at 10, $\chi^2 = 33.06, P < .01$; at 13, $\chi^2 = 29.84, P < .01$; at 16, $\chi^2 = 2.91$ (df = 8 in each instance). Figures 1 to 4 show how the similarity of responses given by Ss of differing SES increases with age.

Sex differences were greatest in the use of perceptual attributes, such grouping being most common among boys. Girls tended to use more relational and nominal explanations and fewer functional ones than boys.

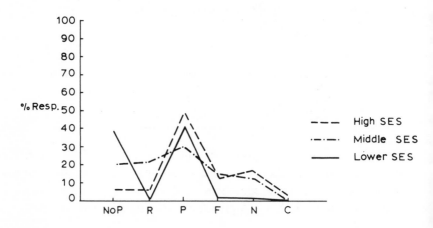

Figure 1. Percentage of responses falling in each category for 7 year olds

Figure 2. Percentage of responses falling in each categories for 10 year olds

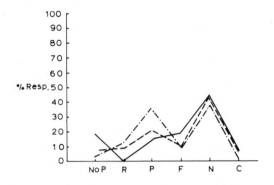

Figure 3. Percentage of responses fauung in each category for 13 year olds

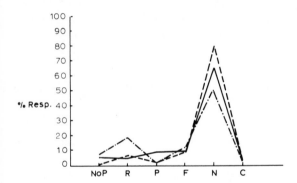

Figure 4. Percentage of responses falling in each category for 16 year olds

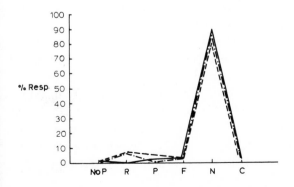

DISCUSSION

Age trends of classificatory behavior among Turkish children resemble those found elsewhere. Older children tend to form groups of larger size, as noted by others (Annett, 1959; Bruner et al., 1966; Davey, 1968; Sigel, 1953). Among 7-year-old Turkish children, 44 per cent made only groups of size 2. The increase in group size at later ages was accompanied by a change in the basis for grouping. Older Ss relied less on the immediately observable qualities of objects and formed more conceptual groups. Details of objects were used as a basis for grouping only among 7 year olds. Nominal groupings varied and improved in quality with age. Broader, more exhaustive groupings, such as dividing objects into living and nonliving, occurred most frequently at age 16 and not at all at 7. There was a similar trend in the use of qualified class names such as 'carpenter's tools', 'land vehicles', 'large animals'. Such qualified class names appeared only after age 10 and with greatest frequency among 16 year olds. This trend in responses reflects an increasing ability to make what Piaget (Inhelder & Piaget, 1959) refers to as hierarchial classification; that is, to recognize subclasses within broad groups and to combine sub-classes into larger groups.

Some differences between this sample of Turkish children and children in other societies were noted. Studies of American and English children have noted affective responses ('I like them') and responses of self-reference ('I use them') among the re-sponses of 7 year olds. Such responses did not occur among Turkish subjects. Groupings on the basis of function appear less often among Turkish children then among Ss from American and other societies. Olver and Hornsby (Bruner et al., 1966) found that at age 8 as many as 45 per cent of the responses could be classified as functional. Among Turkish Ss, this type of grouping never exceeded 11 per cent at any age.

One might expect differences among children from different socioeconomic backgrounds. These differences, in part, appear related to verbal abilities and/or responsiveness. Children of low SES formed fewer groups. More of their responses were simple enumerations ('This is a ball; this is a doll'.) and fiat-type explanations ('They just go together.'). They tended also to do more misleading, such as calling a group of letters and numbers, 'letters'; and they tended to use more general labels. Finally, it was only low-SES children who formed conventional groups but gave no reply when asked to explain the basis of their grouping.

The decline in SES differences with age may reflect education or the fact that a large percentage of low-SES children leave school after five years. Further research should investigate the relationship of verbal skills and responsiveness to ability to classify.

In summary, an attempt was made to investigate the important features of classificatory behavior in Turkey. Age and SES of Ss appear to have important effects. Sex differences were small.

REFERENCES

Annett, M. (1959) The classification of four common class concepts by children and adults. *Brit. educ. psychol. 29*, 223-36.

Bruner, J. S., Goodnow, J. & Austin, G. (1956) *A study of thinking*. New York: Wiley.

Bruner, J. S., Olver, R. R. & Greenfield, P. R. (1966) *Studies in cognitive growth*. New York: Wiley.

Davey, A. G. (1968) The Tristan da Cunhan child's concepts of equivalence. *Brit. J. educ. Psychol., 38*, 162-170.

Halstead, W. C. (1940) Preliminary analysis of grouping behavior in patients with cerebral injury by the method of equivalent and non-equivalent stimuli. *Amer. J. Psychiat., 96*, 1263-1291.

Inhelder, B. & Piaget, J. (1958) *The growth of logical thinking from childhood to adolescence*. New York: Basic Books.

Price-Williams, D. R. (1962) Abstract and concrete modes of classification in a primitive society. *Brit. J. educ. Psychol., 32*, 50-61.

Sigel, I. (1953) Developmental trends in the abstraction ability of children. *Child Develpm., 24*, 131-143.

Sigel, I. (1964) The attainment of concepts, in Hoffman, M.L. & Hoffman, L. W. (Eds.), *Review of child development*. I. New York: Russell Sage Foundation.

P. MITTLER
University of Manchester

38

Genetic and environmental influences on language abilities

There has recently been a marked revival of interest in genetic and environmental influences on human development. The 'nature-nurture' controversies of the 1930's were unproductive, partly because the questions being asked were too general, and partly because the techniques used were insensitive. While both genetic and environmental variables contribute to development, it is unrealistic to assign a precise numerical value to the contribution of either source of variance. Furthermore, there is a continuing and complex interaction between them.

Renewed interest in these questions is reflected in the appearance of a large number of twin studies (Vandenberg, 1968; Mittler, 1971). Recent studies are less concerned with global constructs such as 'intelligence' or 'personality' than with specific cognitive skills and abilities. Twin studies using the standard tests of intelligence such as the Stanford-Binet have in fact yielded remarkably consistent results, suggesting that a substantial portion of the variance is probably genetic in origin. But a more detailed analysis of specific cognitive skills may show that the genetic component is stronger for some cognitive processes than for others.

Similarly, 'environment' is too global a construct. Most studies have limited themselves to estimating effects of SES. We need to move towards a finer-grain analysis of specific environmental variables, since some environmental influences may exert a more powerful influence on specific cognitive skills than others.

The present study represents an attempt to assess genetic and environmental influences on language abilities. The work is based on the Illinois Test of Psycholinguistic Abilities (experimental edition) which consists of 9 subtests each purporting to assess a different aspect of language skill (McCarthy and Kirk, 1961). The test is based on Osgood's (1957) language model which distinguished between *levels* (i.e. representational cr. automatic-sequential), *channels* (auditory vocal or visual-motor) and *processes* (decoding, association, and encoding).

The Ss were 200 twins and 100 singleton controls. All the children were tested within four weeks of their fourth birthdays. The twins were recruited from public-health registers, and were unselected except by age and parental cooperation. The singleton controls came from state nursery schools in onw town. Middle-class children are overrepresented among both groups, at the expense not of working-class children from Social Classes IV and V but of the large intermediate group from Social Class III. Twins were seem in the same proportion as they occur in the population; about 30 per cent monozygotic (MZ) and 70 per cent were dizygotic (DZ). DZ twins were evenly divided between same-sex and opposite-sex pairs.

COMPARISONS BETWEEN TWINS AND SINGLETONS

A number of previous studies have shown that twins are late in beginning to speak, and continue to show language immaturity at least until they enter school. The language delay commonly shown by young twins may be due in part to the unique social environment in which they live. Writers such as Luria (1959) have described the 'closed communication system' inhabited by twins. Many of them develop a private language in their early years, and tend to isolate themselves from the language experiences normally provided by the mother.

On the other hand, a biological type of explanation could also be advanced. Twins are subject to a number of reproductive complications of a kind which render them 'at risk' for the development of handicapping conditions. They are of low weight and gestational age, and one in six of all twin pregnancies in

Britain ends in the death of one or both twins (Dunn, 1965). Moreover, they tend to be slightly retarded in physical development throughout childhood, and perhaps up to 18 years. In the present study the twins were retarded, at age 48 months, by about 6 months of language development compared to normal controls (Mittler, 1970). The scores of the normal controls were indistinguishable from those of the American standardizatior population.

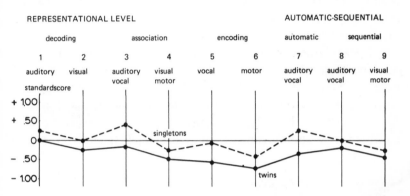

Figure 1. Profile comparison of all twins and all singletons on ITPA subtests (in standard scores)

Next, we can consider the subtest profile, converted to standard scores (Figure 1). The graph shows an overall similarity in the general profile of the two groups. The twins do not show any specific pattern of linguistic organization. Their performance can best be described as an overall immaturity compared to the controls and also to the USA standardization sample, corresponding to 2/3 s.d.

Identical twins, considered as individuals rather than as pairs, did not differ significantly from fraternals. Both types were equally retarded.

We can now go on to examine the language scores as a function of biological and social variables. This was done by a series of discriminant-function and multiple-regression analyses.

Biological factors were only minimally associated with language scores at 4 years. This applied to difficulties in pregnancy and delivery, and to a lesser extent to low birth weight and gestational age. Twins with low birth weight certainly tended to have power language scores at 4, but the association was not at all powerful.

Much more obvious was the association between language development and certain environmental variables, particularly family size and social class. Language scores of both twins and singletons were strongly affected by SES. Of particular interest is the finding that middle-class twins showed relatively much more language retardation, compared to middle-class controls, than was found in the case of working-class twins. Comparisons of twins and singletons *within* social classes showed a language retardation corresponding to 9 months of language development for Social Classes I and II, 4 months for III, and an insignificant 2 months for IV and V Table 1). Why middle-class twins should be

Table 1.   Mean 'language age' (in months) by social class.

	Twins	Singletons
Social class I + II	44	53
Social class III	44	48
Social class IV + V	39	41

at a particular disadvantage is not clear. Perhaps being a twin cuts the child off from the 'linguistically facilitating environment' conventionally associated with the middle-class home.

COMPARISONS BETWEEN IDENTICAL AND FRATERNAL TWIN PAIRS

We can use the data to carry out a classical twin-study analysis by comparing within-pair correlations for MZ and DZ pairs. The rationale of this method is that the strength of the genetic contribution to the variance of a test score can be roughly estimated by the extent to which identical pairs resemble each other more than fraternal pairs. The method rests on some difficult assumptions, but has been shown to be useful and reliable, and to agree with other more independent methods of genetic analysis. (See Mittler, 1971, for a review of twin studies in psychology).

In the present study the intrapair correlation on ITPA total raw score for 28 MZ pairs was 0.90, while that for 64 DZ pairs was 0.68 (Mittler, 1969). The difference between identical and fraternal correlations varied widely over the 9 subtests (Table 2), suggesting that the relative contribution of genetic and environmental factors was by no means uniform over all psycholinguistic

Table 2. *Interclass correlations for MZ (N = 28) and DZ (N = 64) twins on ITPA showing Falconer's heritability index (h^2)*

	MZ	DZ	h^2	Rank
REPRESENTATIONAL LEVEL				
Decoding				
1. Auditory	0.52	0.72	−40.0	9
2. Visual	0.74	0.24	100.0	2
Association				
3. Auditory	0.81	0.68	26.0	6
4. Visual motor	0.78	0.15	126.0	1
Encoding				
5. Vocal	0.63	0.43	40.0	5
6. Motor	0.66	0.35	62.0	3
AUTOMATIC-SEQUENTIAL				
Automatic				
7. Auditory vocal	0.82	0.55	54.0	4
Sequential				
8. Auditory vocal	0.56	0.49	14.0	7
9. Visual motor	0.46	0.49	−6.0	8
TOTAL	0.90	0.68	44.0	

skills and abilities. A statistic resting on 28 cases must be regarded with caution, especially as the correlation is sensitive to fluctuations in s.d.

Several methods of quantifying the extent of the genetic contribution to a characteristic have been developed. The one adopted here is that of Falconer (1960), which doubles the differences between the MZ and DZ correlations: $h^2 = 2 (r_{MZ} - r_{DZ})$. When ITPA subtests are ranked in order of this index, it is at once apparent that tests sampling the visual motor channel carry a larger genetic component than tests on the auditory-vocal channel. For example, none of the first three tests (visual-motor association, visual decoding, motor encoding) requires the child to speak. The auditory-vocal tests mostly carry the lowest genetic loadings, and can therefore be regarded as more affected by environmental variables.

The provisional suggestion arising from these findings – that the genetic component is stronger for tests on the visualmotor channel, and that auditory-vocal tests are more strongly affected by environmental factors – can now be examined with fresh data.

THE INFLUENCE OF SOCIAL CLASS ON THE SINGLETON CONTROLS

We can now look more closely at the singleton controls, and examine the influence of environmental variables on language abilities. There is already a considerable literature on the effects of SES on language development (including Lawton, 1968). Unfortunately, many of the studies may have been unable to control for intelligence, so that it is not clear whether the association is one between SES and language or between SES and intelligence. The distinction is not an easy one to make operationally, on account of the substantial verbal element in most tests of general intelligence. However, there is a good deal of evidence to support the suggestion that working-class children are at a considerable disadvantage in the use of language for classification and conceptualization. Even where basic vocabulary and general fluency appear to be adequate, these children do not use language so effectively either as a means of communication or as a mediational tool (Brandis & Henderson, 1970). Nevertheless, Houston (1970) has recently questioned the whole hypothesis from a linguistic point of view.

There have been surprisingly few studies of ITPA performance as a function of SES. The authors of the test reported a correlation of 0.21 of ITPA total score with SES at the age of about 8 years (McCarthy & Olson, 1964). However, they did not carry out systematic profile comparisons.

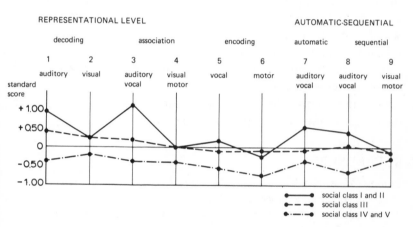

Figure 2. Mean ITPA standard scores by social class

The results of our own analysis of SES differences is shown in Figure 2 (Mittler & Ward, 1970). The graph compares profiles for three SES groupings (I + II; III; IV + V). Once again, the superiority of middle-class children is apparent. Moreover, it is particularly marked for tests in the auditory-vocal channel (e.g. auditory-vocal association, auditory-vocal automatic) and comparatively smaller for tests in the visual-motor channel. These findings confirm the suggestion of the twin study that the visual-motor channel carries a substantial genetic component. We now find evidence from a group of singleton children of the same age that environmental influences − as indexed by SES − seem to affect tests on the auditory-vocal channel to a somewhat greater extent than tests on the visual-motor channel. Social class is, of course, a crude and limited index of environmental influences. One of the most important tasks for the These will need to include techniques to analyse the ongoing interaction between mother and child, the nature of the language stimulus normally provided both by her and by other members of the family. Instead of construing environment in a global and undifferentiated way, we need to adopt a multidimensional approach in order to identify and isolate at least some of the numerous processes involved. When this has been done, we shall be in a better position to plan social and educational programs which are based on a thorough analysis not only of the child's relative strengths and weaknesses in language and intelligence, but also of the precise nature of the environmental forces which are influencing his total development. future lies in the development of more detailed and specific measures of 'environmental influences' (Rutter & Mittler, 1971).

REFERENCES

Brandis, W. & Henderson, D. (1970) *Social class, language and communication.* London: Routledge and Kegan Paul.

Dunn, P. (1965) Some perinatal observations on twins. *Develpm. Med. Child Neurol., 7,* 121-134.

Falconer, D. S. (1960) *Introduction to quantitative genetics.* S. H. (1970) A re-examination of some assumptions about the language of the disadvantaged child. *Child Develpm., 41,* 947-963.

Lawton, D. (1968) *Social class, language and education.* London: Routledge and Kegan Paul.

Luria, A. R. & Yudovitch, F. Ia. (1959) *Speech and the development of mental processes in the child.* London: Staples.

McCarthy, J. J. & Kirk, S. A. (1961) *The Illinois Test of Psycholinguistic Abilities* (Experimental ed.) Urbana, Ill., Univer. of Ill. Press.

McCarthy, J. J. & Olson, J. L. (1964) *Validity studies on the Illinois Test of Psycholinguistic Abilities.* Milwaukee: Univer. of Wisconsin.

Mittler, P. (1969) Genetic aspects of psycholinguistic abilities. *J. Child Psychol. Psychiat., 10,* 165-176.

Mittler, P. (1970) Biological and social aspects of language in twins. *Develpm. Med. Child Neurol., 12,* 741-757.

Mittler, P. (1971) *The study of twins.* London: Penguin Education, 1971.

Mittler, P. & Ward, J. (1970) The use of the Illinois Test of Psycholinguistic Abilities with English four year old children: a normative and factorial study. *Brit. J. educ. Psychol., 40.* 43-53.

Osgood, C. E. (1957) A behavioristic analysis. In Osgood, C. E. (Ed.), *Contemporary approaches to cognition.* Cambridge, Mass.: Harvard University. Press.

Rutter, M. & Mittler, P. (1971) Environmental influences on language development. In M. Rutter & A. Martin (Eds.), *The child with retarded speech.* London: Spastics Society and Heinemann (in press).

Vandenberg, S. G. (Ed.) (1968) *Progress in human behavior genetics.* Baltimore: John Hopkins Univer. Press.

YPE POORTINGA

National Institute for Personnel Research, Johannesburg
and Free University of Amsterdam

39

A comparison of African and European students in simple auditory and visual tasks

Psychologists working in Africa have apparently been more impressed with the auditory than the visual capabilities of Africans. It has, for example, been observed that Africans show good musical abilities (Oliver, 1932) and that they have a quick grasp of languages (Biesheuvel, 1943, p. 56). It has also been reported that Africans generally perform poorly on tests involving spatial relations (Verhaegen & Laroche, 1958; Hudson, 1967). In view of the technological development of Africa and the importance of visual media in Western society, especially for diffusion of knowldge, such observations can have substantial practical implications.

The present study examines basis sensory and perceptual performance. The hypothesis was formulated that Africans will, relative to Europeans, acquire a higher score on auditory tests than on visual tests. Experiments were carried out with 80 South African students, 40 of them of Bantu-speaking ethnic origin and 40 of Caucasian descent. There were 20 males and 20 females in each group. The two groups were widely different in cultural background.

During various stages of the project, attention was paid to the comparability of the tests for the two groups. Stimuli with little cognitive content were selected, and training was given to familiarize *S*s with the stimuli and the test situation. In addition, certain analyses were carried out on the test results to check whether they met certain conditions which can be expected to hold for comparable measurements (Poortinga, 1971).

The hypothesis entails a comparison between the two groups of subjects, but only the *relative* level of performance on auditory and visual tests is to be compared. Formally, we may write two alternatives:

H_0 : M(Aud. Afr.) − M(Vis. Afr.) = M(Aud. Eur.) − M(Vis. Eur.)
H_1 : M(Aud. Afr.) − M(Vis. Afr.) > M(Aud. Eur.) − M(Vis. Eur.)

Biasing cultural factors common to an auditory and a visual test (such as the type of response required, cultural aspects of the instruction, etc.) do not affect the outcome of a test of such a hypothesis. The hypothesis can be tested by means of an analysis of variance in which the type of test (i.e., auditory vs. visual) and the culture of the sample are taken as factors. H_0 must be rejected if there is a significant interaction between these two factors. Significant effects on the main factors do not bear on the validity of the hypothesis.

This procedure does not guarantee crosscultural comparability. Two questions still remain open: first, whether each auditory and visual test measures the same behavioral dimension or attribute in the two groups; second, whether cultural bias affects the difficulty of an auditory test more than the difficulty of a corresponding visual test.

In the first experiment to be reported here, Ss made absolute or category judgments on a loudness scale and on a brightness scale. The stimuli were 8 intensity values of a pure tone and 8 intensity values of a light spot 5 cm. in diameter. Ss were given

Table 1. *Group comparisons on loudness and brightness judgments*

		Mean	s.d.	t	Reliability
Loudness	Africans	25.60	8.39	} 2.05	.65
	Europeans	22.25	8.45		.58
Brightness	Africans	20.77	7.23	} .78	.58
	Europeans	19.40	8.48		.71

Statistics are based on the last 72 trials. Each reliability is a correlation of the last 72 trials with the first 72 trials of the third session.
$N = 40$ in each group.

432 trials on each scale divided over three testing sessions.

Most analyses were based on the last 72 trials. Table 1 shows that the Europeans performed somewhat better than the Africans in judging loudness; no significant difference was found on brightness judgments.

These results could be used for comparison only if certain conditions were satisfied. Two such conditions were investigated, viz.:

The relative level of difficulty of the items in a test should be the same for each group of Ss.

The sequential effects of the stimuli should be the same. It is known (Holland & Lockhead, 1968) that response to a certain stimulus is to some extent influenced by preceding stimuli.

To examine the first requirement the distributions of errors per stimulus for the two groups were compared. χ^2 tests showed no significant difference for either scale. The distributions of errors taken over all three sessions were less similar. The training obviously served its purpose of overcoming superficial cultural differences. The second requirement was tested by an analysis of variance. The interaction between sequence and culture of group was not significant.

In view of the lack of contrary evidence, both the loudness and brightness scales were taken as comparable. A formal statistical test was carried out by analysis of variance. The interaction between test and culture was not significant (see Table 1).

In the second experiment, choice reaction time (CRT) to auditory and visual stimuli were measured. The sounds originated from a Wundt hammer, a buzzer, a hooter, and a bell. The visual stimuli were easy to discriminate. In each of three testing sessions (with a total of 272 trials per session) 3 separate tasks were administered, i.e. a 4-choice auditory CRT, a 4-choice visual CRT and an 8-choice task during which auditory and visual stimuli were randomly presented in the same series of trials. Since the 4-choice and 8-choice tasks yielded essentially the same results, the latter will not be discussed further.

The Africans were considerably slower than the Europeans on both tests. For both groups there was a considerable improvement over training but there was little tendency to converge. The results of the last 60 trials in each test are presented in Table 2; they show a clear difference in speed between the two groups of *S*s for both types of stimuli.

Table 2. Group comparisons on choice reaction time

		Mean	s.d.	*t*	Reliability
Auditory	Africans	59.4	8.38	} 6.31	.90
stimuli	Europeans	49.6	5.09		.80
Visual	Africans	58.9	5.61	} 6.86	.79
stimuli	Europeans	50.4	5.49		.93

Statistics are based on the median performance on the last 60 trials. Each reliability is a correlation (corrected for length) of the last 40 trials with the next-to-last 40 trials. *N* = 40 in each group.

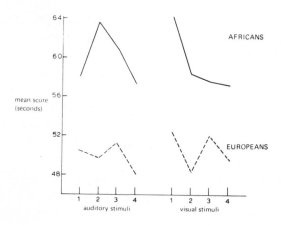

Figure 1. Choice reaction time with auditory and visual stimuli

A condition for comparability of results mentioned in the previous experiment is that the relative difficulty of the stimuli should be the same for the two groups of *S*s. Figure 1 indicates that this condition is not met. Analysis of variance showed a small but significant interaction between culture and stimuli for both tasks (P < .05 for the auditory and P < .01 for the visual task). This lack of comparability made the results of the experiment of doubtful value for testing the hypothesis. A formal test by analysis of variance did not support hypothesis H_1 (see Table 2).

No obvious explanations for the overall differences in response time between Europeans and Africans was found, but there are some indications that the African students were at a disadvantage in verbal identification of the stimuli. In an experiment reported elsewhere (Poortinga, 1971), no difference in simple RT between the same two groups of Ss was found.

To further check on the comparability of the experimental results, three intelligence tests were included in the testing program: the Mental Alertness test (measuring general reasoning ability), the Advanced Progressive Matrices, and the Blox test (a tests of spatial ability).

Table 3. Comparison of Africans and Europeans on three mental tests

	Africans			Europeans		
	Mean	s.d.	Split-half reliability	Mean	s.d.	Split-half reliability
Mental alertness	12.3	5.61	.72	23.2	3.60	.64
Raven matrices	9.2	5.66	.83	19.4	3.53	.71
Blox	17.4	7.39	.89	28.6	7.32	.88

Scores of Africans were considerably lower than those of Europeans (Table 3), but this does not *per se* deny that the test measure the same behavorial attributes in the two groups. It was expected that the intercorrelations between the intelligence tests and the perceptual scores would be low for the Europeans. If the experiments measured the same attributes or dimensions of behavior in both groups, low intercorrelations should also be found for the African Ss. The product-moment intercorrelations of the intelligence tests are quite different for the two groups (Table 4). These tests, then, are not comparable.

If it is assumed, however, that each of the mental tests measures *some* aspect of intelligence in both groups, the correlation matrices reveal the expected low correlations of each mental test

Table 4. Intercorrelations of scores in the African sample (below
diagonal) and the European sample (above diagonal)

	1	2	3	4	5	6	7
1. Loudness		.54**	.04	.16	.20	.20	.14
2. Brightness	.16		.19	.33	-.02	.03	.14
3. Auditory CRT	.23	.34*		.71**	-.24	-.45**	-.19
4. Visual CRT	.15	.40**	.64**		.00	-.16	.09
5. Mental alertness	.19	-.07	-.19	-.08		.29	.36*
6. Raven matrices	.22	.08	-.07	-.05	.73**		.42**
7. Blox	-.04	-.28	-.15	-.15	.59**	.64	

* P < .05; ** P < .01.

with perceptual scores for the Africans as well as the Europeans.
The difference in correlations between the loudness and brightness scales is probably due to sampling. If scores based on the last
144 trials instead of the last 72 trials are used, the correlation
between loudness and brightness was 0.26 for the Africans and
0.36 for the European students.

It was concluded that, despite shortcomings in the comparability of the data, the consistent absence of support for H_1
affects the status of the theoretical idea behind it.

REFERENCES

Biesheuvel, S. (1943) African intelligence. Johannesburg: South Afr. Inst.
   for Race Relations.
Holland, M. K. & Lockhead, G. R. (1968) Sequential effects in absolute
   judgments of loudness. Perception and Psychophysics, 3, 409-414.
Hudson, W. (1967) The study of the problem of pictorial perception among
   unacculturated groups. Intern. J. Psychol., 2, 89-107.
Oliver, R.A.C. (1932) The musical talents of natives in East Africa. Brit. J.
   Psychol., 22, 333-343.
Poortinga, Y. H. (1971) Cross-cultural comparison of maximum performance tests: Some methodological aspects and some experiments with
   simple auditory and visual stimuli. Psychol. Afr. Monogr. Supp., No. 6.
Verhaegen, P., & Laroche, J. L. (1958) Some methodological considerations
   concerning the study of aptitudes and the elaboration of psychological
   tests for African natives. J. soc. Psychol., 47, 249-256.

CHRISTOPHER G. M. BAKARE
University of Ibadan

40

Social-class differences in the performance of Nigerian children on the Draw-a-Man test

As a measure of general mental ability, the Draw-a-Man test (DAM, Harris, 1963) has a number of distinct advantages. Its ready appeal to children reduces differences in motivation which might otherwise increase error variance. Its ease of administration makes it usable even by testers who are unsophisticated with regard to psychometrics. And, because it is nonverbal in character, it can be administered in diverse cultures, even to subjects who would in other tests be handicapped by linguistic barriers.

The test has considerable resistance to differential instructional sets and to examiner effects; it can be scored reliably; and although it requires drawing, performance is not appreciably influenced by artistic talent ot by training (Phatak, 1959). Against this rather impressive list of assets must be weighed such shortcomings as low validity as judged by its correlation with other tests, with school grades, and with teachers' ratings of mental ability (Kellmer Pringle, 1963), and the existence of sex differences.

These shortcomings notwithstanding, it appears that the Draw-a-Man test has sufficient attraction to justify investigation of the possibilities of its large-scale use in developing countries such as Nigeria. Children are attending school in ever-increasing numbers, and these new school entrants have to be grouped and counseled. Also, research has to be done to find the most effective ways of helping them realize their potential. This calls particularly for tests of general mental ability. Such tests should be reliable, valid, easy to administer, and naturally attractive to young children, and they should be essentially nonverbal. The DAM test is known to fulfil most of these conditions.

This study was designed to investigate social-class differences in the performance of Nigerian children on the Goodenough-Harris test. The study was also aimed at examining the validity of the test for Nigerian children, and at providing local norms. If one holds an essentially environmentalist view he would expect children of differing social-class backgrounds to perform differently on the test, as such children would have unequal mastery of the cognitive and affective skills which adequate test performance requires. Social-class differences on the test could be regarded as evidence the construct validity of the test; it would be an essential quality in a test to be used in making classificatory (rather than predictive) decisions about children coming into school for the first time.

METHOD

Subjects

The Ss were 393 Nigerian children and 106 non-Nigerian children (American and English) attending school in Nigeria. 204 of the Nigerian children were from upper-class homes while 189 were from lower-class homes. There were 105 upper-class boys and girls ranging in age from 6 to 12; in the lower-class sample were 92 boys and 97 girls, of ages 6 to 15.

Social class was determined on the basis of parental occupation, which in Nigeria is closely related to the parents' educational level. Both occupation and education in Nigeria are highly related to the family's general style of life and especially to the environmental variables which one expects to influence the early cognitive growth of children. Fathers in the upper-class homes were senior civil servants or University administrators, lecturers, or professors. All had at least a university education. The mothers had at least a secondary-school education or the equivalent. Fathers in the lower-class homes were farmers, petty traders, taxi drivers, or office messengers; they typically had no more than a primary education. Mothers in the lower-class homes, mostly illiterate, were petty traders or housewives helping their husbands on the farms.

The upper-class families lived in modern houses supplied with electricity and running water and having spacious playgrounds; the lower-class families lived in crowded mud houses, often with no proper sewage system, and obtained their water from communal water taps. The upper-class children invariably had attended nursery school from the age of about 3 prior to entering the university staff school which they were attending; this had modern, well-equipped buildings and playgrounds and well-trained teachers. The lower-class children had not had the benefit of a nursery-school education and were attending a local-authority primary school which had dilapidated buildings with poorly trained teachers, bare playgrounds, and little or no equipment.

Procedure

The DAM test was administered to all children in their schools by the author in strict accordance with the instructions provided in the Harris-manual. This was done near the middle of the year; the youngest children would have been in school for at least 6 months. The drawings were scored according to the manual. Interscorer reliability was 0.92. On the day the test was given, teachers were asked to rate each child's mental ability on a 7-point scale. Cumulative midyear grades were obtained in each school subject, except for first graders, who had no regular marks.

Results

Upper-class children in every grade significantly outperformed their lower-class counterparts (Table 1). Scores of upper-class Nigerian children did not differ significantly from those American and English children going to the same school (Table 2).

Table 1. Comparison of upper-class and lower-class Nigerian children

Grade	Upper-class			Lower-class			t
	N	Mean	s.d.	N	Mean	s.d.	
1	83	20.05	6.84	35	9.63	2.81	11.74*
2	32	28.41	8.49	38	9.34	4.48	11.43*
3	34	32.91	7.70	40	12.38	5.36	13.08*
4	31	33.39	10.69	40	12.10	3.65	10.62*
5	24	38.04	11.12	36	18.72	7.81	7.38*

* $P < .01$.

Table 2. Comparison of upper-class Nigerian with American and English children in Nigeria

Grade	Upper-class Nigerian			American and English			t
	N	Mean	s.d.	N	Mean	s.d.	
1	83	20.05	6.84	39	21.95	9.12	1.16
2	32	28.41	8.49	14	29.21	8.87	.29
3	33	33.06	7.77	17	31.76	9.23	.50
4	32	33.06	10.54	22	33.82	9.04	.28
5	24	38.04	11.12	14	39.14	11.71	.28

In order to demonstrate further the effect of social class in performance, the mean score at each age was converted into a standard score on the basis of the Harris norms. Table 3 shows that, on the average, Nigerian upper-class boys were above aver-

Table 3. Deviation scores corresponding to means of Nigerian children

Age	Upper-class		Lower-class	
	Boys	Girls	Boys	Girls
6	102	98	78	75
7	116	99	75	64
8	110	105	75	61
9	116	95	67	64
10	111	98	70	63
11	106	95	76	58

age and upper-class girls just about average, while the lower-class boys and girls were much below the norms. Boys surpassed girls, which is inconsistent with previous findings of a difference in favor of girls (e.g., Alzobaie, 1965).

An examination of the content of the drawings revealed marked class differences. On the 73 Harris-Goodenough items, upper-class children performed significantly better than their lower-class counterparts on 60 items in Grade 1, 63 items in Grade 2, 58 items in Grade 3, 45 items in Grade 4, and 28 items in Grade 5. The number of these items is too large to permit discussion of specific items here, but classifying them into broad groups provides some insight into the nature of the social-class differences among Nigerian children. The two social classes did not differ with regard to the inclusion of the major body parts such as head, neck, eyes, ears, legs, etc.; the difference was in their elaboration and differentiation of these major body parts. The upper-class children were more likely to portray body parts in two dimensions, to show better proportion, to attach limbs more correctly, and to add clothing. Also, they were better in motor coordination. Both groups depicted movement poorly in their drawings.

Table 4. Intercorrelation among relevant variables for upper-class (above) and lower-class (below) Nigerian children

N		DAM	Rating	Paper
203 213	Draw-a-Man			
154 212	Teacher's rating	.22* .26*		
81 59	General paper	.10 .37*	46* .37*	
97 178	Total acad. perf.	.04 .00 ·	.59* .50*	.76* .89*

* $P < .01$. N varies from one correlation to another.
Value at left is number for whom data on a test were complete.

Table 4 provides information relating to the validity of DAM with Nigerian children.

There was a low but significant correlation between DAM and the teacher's rating of mental ability. There was, however, no correlation between the DAM scores and Total Academic Performance (average score on all school subjects). The General Paper (a general information test) correlated significantly with DAM only for lower-class children. One conclusion that could be drawn from these findings is that, with Nigerian children, DAM has low validity, if validity is defined as the correlation with teachers' rating of mental ability and with overall academic performance. Insofar as a valid test will discriminate between social class groups of Nigerian children, then the evidence argues for the test's validity.

DISCUSSION

In exploring the possible causes of class differences on DAM, perhaps it is best to begin by indicating the types of cognitive skills required for adequate performance on the test. According to Harris (1963), the child's drawing of a man represents his growth in conceptual complexity and in his discriminations about the human figure as an idea. For an adequate formation of this concept the following processes must occur. First, there must be sensory stimulation (the child must have seen men before), there must be perception (requiring that the child's sensory equipment be functioning well), there must be conceptualization (requiring that the child discriminate between this and other objects in his environment and that he make the resulting concept permanent with the aid of language), and there must be thinking (required, for example, for clarifying the relational aspects of the body parts whose concepts have been individually formed). Furthermore, the child also requires considerable visual-motor coordination for adequate performance on the test. The lower performance of lower-class Nigerian children on the test could therefore be ascribed to poorer functioning on some or all of these processes or skills.

Apparently, it is not in sensory stimulation or in perception that the lower-class children fall short, since their drawings show the major body parts. It is in the differentiation of these body parts that their performance becomes defective, indicating a failure to elaborate their concept of a man. Such a failure can only denote some malfunctioning in cognitive growth. If, as Piaget suggests, cognitive growth is a function of the environment to which the child is exposed, then it is reasonable to suppose that the causes of the poorer performance of lower-class Nigerian children on DAM lie in their less stimulating environment. This is supported by the finding that upper-class Nigerian children do not perform differently from American and English children living in the same type of environment, and are either average or better as compared with the Harris norms.

The lower-class Nigerian child receives little direct intellectual stimulation due to low levels of parental education and to the absence of books and toys; these are available to a greater extênt in upper-class Nigerian homes. To this must be added reboflavin difficiency, marginal thiamine intake, protein-calorie malnutrition, etc. Such health hazards undoubtedly take their toll on the child's cognitive growth. It is this type of reasoning that led us to anticipate a class difference on the DAM test in Nigeria.

Even if one takes the fact that the test discriminates between social-class groups as an evidence of its validity, one cannot ignore the implications of its low correlation with school grades and with teachers' rating of mental ability. The low correlations with school grades is hardly surprising since the test is nonverbal while school subjects are heavily weighted on the verbal factor. The teacher's rating of mental ability has a low correlation with DAM probably because these ratings have been largely based on the child's performance in class – an assumption partly confirmed by the much higher correlations between school grades and teachers' ratings of mental ability. Our findings have important implications for the use of the DAM test in Nigeria. When used alone, it would appear to be serving its best purpose as a screening device to learn the general mental status of a child or to classify children into broad groups at the start of schooling. It would be much less useful in predicting future performance in school since it is evident that, when it is so used, environmental factors and opportunities would decrease its predictive value. If, however, the test is included in a battery of tests with some verbal components, it would presumably serve some predictive function.

A much broader implication is that if there could be social-class differences on such a simple, nonverbal test as DAM, then one should begin to despair of ever finding a culture-free test. This would apply to Progressive Matrices, which is nonverbal and which is supposed to be highly loaded on g. The fact that Matrices presents several geometric shapes which have no names in most African languages makes it far from culture-free. It would therefore be improper to use such tests to measure the 'intelligence' of people in Africa or in other non-Western cultures. Such tests could measure their spatial ability, their perceptual speed, their visual-motor coordination and the like – but certainly not their 'intelligence', when the term is conceived as innate ability or cast in a slightly concealed form as 'educability' or 'adaptability'.

It would be more appropriate to drop the term 'intelligence' completely from psychological usage because of its associations. It is illogical to use scores on such tests to infer the level of innate ability possessed by people in non-Western cultures or as a basis for making judgmental statements of a superior-subordinate nature about their performance. It is equally illogical to put them into a factor analysis to find 'the factorial structure of African intelligence'. These tests could, however, be used to find the status of non-Western peoples on several cognitive abilities so as to train them on those abilities in which they are deficient, or to fit them into occupations for which they are most suited.

REFERENCES

Alzobaie, A. J. (1965) The validity of the Goodenough Draw-a-Man Test in Iraq. *J. exper. Educ. 33*, 331-335.
Harris, D. B. (1963) *Children's drawings as measures of intellectual maturity*. New York: Harcourt, Brace & World.

Kellmer Pringle, M. L. (1963) & Pickup, K. T. The reliability and validity of the Goodenough Draw-a-Man Test. *Brit. J. educ. Psychol. 33*, 297-306.
Phatak, P. (1959) A study of the revised Goodenough scale with reference to artistic and non-artistic drawings. Univer. of Baroda, India. (Mimeographed.)

PERIN UÇMAN
Haçettepe University, Ankara

41

A normative study of the Goodenough-Harris Drawing test on a Turkish sample

Various qualities of children's drawings have been the subject of research for many years. The aim of the present study is to investigate the intellectual component of children's drawings, applying the 1963 Goodenough-Harris Drawing Test to a Turkish sample.

The literature on children's drawings falls into three periods. During the first period (1885-1910), research was conducted which later helped to identify 'developmental stages' in children. The second period, starting in 1926, emphasized the psychometric use of children's drawings in assessing mental abilities. Goodenough demonstrated that the developmental aspects of human-figure drawings reflected a large intellectual component. During the period 1940-1955 such drawings were used to understand the personality structure and its deviations. Research data on the projective use of drawings present an empirical chaos and it has been difficult to establish a theoretical basis. On the other hand, the data on developmental and intellectual aspects of human-figure drawings has been more systematic and reliable.

The Goodenough Drawing Test, as revised by Harris in 1963, has been used as one of the tests in a battery. It is especially useful in establishing rapport with the client, and in assessing the intellectual level of deaf-and-dumb children and those with neurological deficits.

The views of the Goodenough and Harris were closer to the 'global intelligence' notion that to the notion of 'unitary intelligence'. Harris (1963, p. 5) stated that the abilities tapped by the drawing test could be described as 'intellectual maturity' or more specifically 'conceptual maturity'. Thus he replaced 'intelligence' with 'conceptual maturity', which was defined by three functions required for 'concept formation': perception (discrimination of likenesses and differences), abstraction (classification of objects according to these likenesses and differences), and generalization (assigning a newly experienced object to a correct class).

Harris (1963, p. 7) hypothesized that a child's drawing of an object will reflect his ability to classify that object as a 'concept'. It was also hypothesized that a frequently experienced object such as a human being generally becomes a useful index of the growing complexity of his concepts. The human figure is of universal popularity and is basically more important to the child than any other concept, both affectively and cognitively. Even a very young child is able to draw the outline of the human figure. Furthermore, there is little variability in the essential characteristics of the human figure, which makes evaluation more reliable.

In assessing children, the 1926 Goodenough Drawing Test used the mental age. One of the most important reasons for the revision by Harris, was to develop a deviation IQ. The deviation IQ made it possible to compare Goodenough-Harris scores with other tests of mental abilities. Harris tried to extend the test to the adolescent years but found that the test ceased to discriminate between ages at this period. He attributed this deficiency in discrimination to a developmental shift from what Piaget called 'concrete operations' to 'abstract or formal operations'.

New scoring rules ('items') were added to make a 73-item test. (The original test had 51 items.) The original Draw-a-Man (DAM) was augmented with alternate forms: a 'Woman Scale' (DAW) and a 'Self Scale'. There was an r of 0.75 between DAM and DAW, which was considered low for parallel forms. Although the 'Self Scale' was developed for projective purposes, attempts to find a theoretical basis for projective uses of the test have not been entirely successful. Harris also developed 'Quality scales', which were helpful in giving a rough estimate of intellectual maturity in cases where the point-score system was not appropriate.

The reliability and the validity reported in the manual are

fairly high (reliability 0.80-0.90, validity 0.60-0.70), but they are computed from the original Goodenough Test. Dunn (1967) and Strümpfer and Mienie (1968) later found even higher validity coefficients (<0.80) for the 1963 revision as compared to the 1926 test. Harris (1963, p. 199) stated that the test correlated highly with verbal abilities, and not so highly with performance. This was supported by further research (Byrd & Springfield, 1969; Dunn, 1967a; Strümpfer & Mienie, 1968). The reliability is almost the same as that of the 1926 edition. Dunn (1967b) obtained interrater and intrarater reliabilities of 0.88 to 0.93. Georgas and Papadopoulou (1968) reported even higher reliability coefficients ($r = 0.87$) for the 1963 revision. Strümpfer & Mienie (1967) calculated a Spearman-Brown reliability of 0.92 and a test-retest reliability of 0.73.

The test has been useful in the assessment of mental abilities for the American culture. There have been two fallacies in its application. The first was to use it as the only test to determine mental abilities, whereas the test should be used as part of a battery of tests. Secondly, it was thought to be culture-free, and was administered to children of different cultures. Later, Harris cautioned the test administrators about these important issues. He admitted that it was not culture-free.

The data from crosscultural studies using the drawing test generally lead to the following conclusions: there is conflicting evidence as to differences between boys and girls in various cultures; there is a tendency to underestimate the mental abilities of children coming from cultures outside the USA. Children in non-Western cultures differ from those in Western cultures.

Therefore, Harris (1963, p. 133) proposed that the test should be restandardized in cultures where the mode of living, clothing, and the quality and level of academic education differ from that of Americans.

The 1963 revision of the Goodenough test has not hitherto been the subject for investigation in Turkey, indeed, there are very few studies on the cognitive development of Turkish children. The writer had the opportunity of being trained and experienced in scoring both the 'Man' and the 'Woman' scales of the Goodenough-Harris Test.

The instrument was used as a means of evaluating the cognitive development of 180 Turkish children. Another purpose of the study was to collect information about the difficulties involved in standardizing the test in Turkey and to establish a basis for a comparative study.

METHOD

The study considers age and sex of the Ss, and their parent's SES. As an SES measure the level of father's education was employed, as there are no nationwide SES data available in Turkey. The educational levels chosen were: 1. elementary school (low SES), 2. junior high (middle SES) 3. *Lycée* senior high and university (high SES). *Lycée* and university graduates had almost the same opportunities for salary and promotion until recently, so these two were combined. Age levels 7, 8, and 9 were chosen.

Information on these variables was collected by questionnaires distributed to families. 180 Ss were chosen randomly within sex-age-SES classes, from two elementary schools in the city of Ankara. There were 60 S at each SES level, 60 Ss at each age level, and 90 Ss of each sex.

Only the 'Man' and 'Woman' tasks were administered. The test forms and instructions for group administration were translated into Turkish.

In order to minimize effects of motor coordination and manual dexterity in the lower grades, all tests were given towards the end of the academic year (May, 1970). The group administration was completed in 15 sessions, using 10 Ss in each. All testing was done by the investigator with the help of a proctor.

RESULTS

Drawings were scored by the investigator according to the instructions given in the 1963 manual.

Means and standard deviations are shown in Tables 1 and 2.

Table 1. Raw-score statistics for Draw-a-Man by SES, age, and sex

Age	Sex	Socio-economic status					
		Low		Middle		High	
		Mean	s.d.	Mean	s.d.	Mean	s.d.
7	Boys	21.2	6.2	19.7	8.2	33.5	11.1
	Girls	24.5	6.0	24.0	7.6	30.5	4.7
8	Boys	25.3	6.3	24.5	3.9	30.4	5.2
	Girls	24.7	7.6	26.8	2.9	31.8	6.3
9	Boys	27.1	7.2	33.0	4.2	36.8	8.5
	Girls	30.4	5.5	36.3	8.0	41.6	7.0

General means: Boys, 27.9; girls, 30.1
Low SES, 25.5; middle, 27.4; high, 34.1
Age 7, 25.6; 8, 27.3; 9, 34.2

Table 2. Raw-score statistics for Draw-a-Woman by SES, age and sex

Age	Sex	Socio-economic status					
		Low		Middle		High	
		Mean	s.d.	Mean	s.d.	Mean	s.d.
7	Boys	21.3	6.0	21.4	9.2	28.2	9.2
	Girls	24.5	7.2	24.9	9.5	32.1	5.3
8	Boys	25.2	7.2	24.0	4.4	30.6	6.8
	Girls	25.1	6.5	31.8	8.5	29.8	9.8
9	Boys	30.8	6.6	33.8	5.3	34.8	5.9
	Girls	32.5	11.3	42.8	10.3	39.8	5.8

General means: Boys, 27.9; girls, 30.1
Low SES, 26.6; middle, 29.8; high, 32.6
Age 7, 25.4; 8, 27.8; 9, 35.8

Mean scores increase with SES. There is a similar trend with age. The mean for girls is higher than that for boys, as in the USA. All these differences are significant.

The significant differences between the three SES levels confirm other studies.

The significant differences between boys and girls supports evidence obtained in the USA, Japan, Argentina, and Iraq (Harris, 1963, p. 130; Alzobaie, 1965). And significant differences between age levels indicate that the test discriminates among ages 7, 8, and 9 in the present sample.

REFERENCES

Alzobaie, A.J. (1965) The validity of the Goodenough Draw-a-Man Test in Iraq. *J. exp. Educ., 33,* 331-335.

Byrd, C. & Springfield, L. (1969) A note on the D-A-P test with adolescent retardates. *Amer. J. ment. Def., 73,* 578-579.

Dunn, J. A. (1967a) Validity coefficients for the new Harris-Goodenough D-A-M test. *Percept. mot. Skills, 24* 299-301.

Dunn, J. A. (1967b) Inter- and intrarater reliability of the new Goodenough-Harris Draw-a-Man Test. *Percept. mot. Skills, 24,* 269-270.

Georgas, J. G. & Papadopoulou, E. (1968) The Harris-Goodenough and the Developmental Sequence with five-year-old children. *Percept. mot. Skills, 26,* 352-354.

Harris, D. B. (1963) *Children's drawings as measures of intellectual maturity.* New York: Harcourt, Brace & World.

Strümpfer, D. J. W. & Mienie, C. J. P. (1968) A validation of the Harris-Goodenough Test. *Brit. J. educ. Psychol., 38,* 96-100.

JONATHAN SILVEY
University of Nottingham

42

Long-range prediction of educability and its determinants in East Africa

In Uganda, 2 per cent of the population of appropriate age are admitted to secondary schools. This paper is concerned with the long-range prediction of academic achievement from scholastic achievement and standard cognitive ability tests, and with possible determinants of secondary-school performance.

The secondary-school selection examination (SSE) is a very poor predictor of school performance, even though only 20% of candidates succeed (Somerset, 1968). Governmental records show that a candidate's chance of being selected is closely related to the quality of the junior school he attended in the previous two years. Entry to the junior schools is partly determined by a primary-school leaving examination, but junior-school entrants appear not to have been highly selected. It is not clear how far success in SSE is determined by the pupil's own ability, the quality of the school he is about to leave, and/or interaction. To what extent can secondary selection procedures be improved by using ability test scores along with attainment examinations?

In transplanting Western-style cognitive tests, even to select entrants for a British type of education, one cannot automatically interpret test results in the traditional manner. To remind us that the sources of variation in test results are unknown and to avoid the superstructure of intelligence test theory, this application of such tests is referred to as assessing 'educability'. This may be defined as that cluster of cognitive, affective, and biographical variables determining scholastic performance. We assume that the cognitive element will be the most significant.

PROCEDURE

Schools were stratified according to their record in the previous year's SSE. Junior schools in three provinces were randomly selected within strata. All pupils in their final year at 39 schools were tested on a verbal and a nonverbal intelligence test (N = 1567). Their SSE scores were also obtained. At the end of their first year in secondary school (S1), 264 of the successful entrants were tested on reading comprehension, English usage, and mathematics. At the end of the fourth year (S4), 211 of the original sample were retested and questioned, and a records of their performance in the Cambridge Overseas School Certificate (CSC) were obtained. The S1 and S4 attainment scores are our dependent variables.

The NIPR Mental Alertness Test is a 50-minute test designed for use with English-speaking African pupils with 8 to 10 years of education. It consists of number and letter series, simple codes, relational similarities, reasoning, and arithmetic problems. It is machine scored — in this sample, a disadvantage, as they took up to 40 minutes to understand how to indicate their answers. KR21 reliability in the present sample is 0.69.

Raven's 1938 Progressive Matrices was administered but not in the standard way, as it was impractical to test groups without time limits. Two pilot trials had shown that, although mean scores increased significantly, the rank order of pupils was similar for scores obtained after 30 and 50 minutes (median $\rho = 0.92$).

The variation in speed of working which these trials revealed suggested that with a fixed time limit, many candidates would not reach the later items. There are, in effect, five subtests; each of these was timed separately and generously. Matrices was included as a *less* educationally-biased test. It did prove empirically to be less associated with education than the other tests. Reports on matrix tests in African samples suggested that practice and coaching play a significant part in performance (Ombredane, 1959; Ramphal, 1962; Lloyd & Pidgeon, 1961).

Each of the separately timed subtests required a different principle for solution. Following the Congolese model, a new example for each subtest was devised to demonstrate the principle immediately before working that task. After a period of oral practice attempts, a standardized explanation was given. This served to show all candidates the nature of the task and the mode of response, and to offset any set that might be carried over from a previous subtest.*

As Irvine (1964) has pointed out, there is a curious homogeneity about the results for Progressive Matrices in African countries. Ten studies are available in the Congo, Rhodesia, and East African countries, in which PM38 was given to persons with six or more years of schooling in English, French, or an African language. The means range from 26 to 36, the larger means being for older, more educated, more select samples. For our two Uganda samples, the mean was 27.9 for eighth graders and 35.6 for eleventh graders, which agrees closely with means for similar ages in other countries.

Seven tests from the AIR-AID battery were given in the fourth year of secondary schooling.

RESULTS

Correlations of measures in Grades 8, 9, and 12 are shown in Table 1. All are significant ($P < .05$).

---

* A side experiment was conducted to examine effects of coaching and practice. Pupils in the second year of secondary school ($N = 66$) were randomly assigned to three groups. PM was administered twice to groups A and B on the same day, once to group C. Some testings involved instruction on the first problem set only, some involved instruction on each set. For the first test of Groups A and B, under first-set-only instruction, the mean was 33.6; for C, under all-set instruction, 36.0. For the second test Group A had first-set-only instruction and the mean score was 38.4. Group B had all-set instruction and the mean was 41.0.

The difference of A retest from A and B pretest of 4.8 was significant ($P < .05$); it estimates the practice effect. The difference of C pretest from A and B pretest estimates the effect of added coaching alone; the value of 2.4 was not significant. The difference of B retest from A and B pretest of 7.4 represents the combined effect of coaching and practice ($P < .01$). The two effects appear to be additive.

Table 1. Correlations for tests given at end of primary school with concurrent and later measures

Variable	Concurrent correlations at end of primary school		Correlations with criteria	
	Matrices	Mental alertness	Achievement, first year	CSC
Junior-school leaving exam	.13	.44	.58	.34
Matrices		.37	.20	.16
NIPR Mental alertness			.44	.39

$N = 264$ except in last column where $N = 211$

No test has much predictive value. The selction exam is the best predictor of scholastic performance over one year, but the educability test is best over four years. A combination of predictors that includes the educability scores correlates 0.63 with the one-year criterion; this compares with 0.58 for the best single predictor. Over the longer range, the multiple correlation using all tests is 0.43. The present selection procedure accounts for 11.4 of School Certificate variance. Adding a verbal ability test, weighted slightly more heavily than the current selection tests, would increase explained variance by only 7 per cent. Effective prediction of School Certificate standing still eludes us.

However stable its crosscultural factor content (Irvine, 1967), Progressive Matrices adds nothing to the prediction of achievement when used in conjunction with a verbal test. The same conclusion was drawn for the one-year follow-up.

It may be that this finding tells us more about the skills required for School Certificate than it does about the Matrices. It is widely believed that rote memory and an emphasis on formal learning characterize Uganda's schools. Where life-chances are effectively determined by the amount of education obtained, and where each student must survive highly competitive screening at regular intervals, this approach to education is understandable and perhaps rational. School Certificate subjects cluster into three groups demanding the ability to solve numerical problems and understand quantitative material, the ability to remember and communicate qualitative descriptive material, and an English language skill (Somerset, 1968). Somerset emphasizes how little attention is paid to judgments of value, or expression of arguments. If he is right, it would not be expected that PM — probably highly weighted towards *g* in Africa as elsewhere — would account for variance in CSC in a way which would differentiate it from a verbal reasoning test. Vernon (1967) has hypothesized that nonverbal matrices tests measure independent, resourceful thinking, and that East African schools tend to reinforce passivity rather than initiative.

Some evidence of the links between the tests used at the two stages can be seen in the correlational analysis of the four tests discussed so far, and the seven AID-AIR tests given concurrently with CSC. Table 2 shows the correlations between all tests obtained in Buganda (*N* = 136) and similar correlations obtained in Western Uganda, where the AID tests were not used (*N* = 73).

Table 2. *Intercorrelations between all tests in two samples*

	End of primary school					End of secondary school					
	1	2	3	4	5	6	7	8	9	10	11
1. PM38		.07	.07	.02	.05						
2. Mental alertness	.34		.28	.25	.27						
3. JLE	.11	.37		.15	.21						
4. English language	.12	.32	.27		.47						
CSC*											
CSC aggregate*	.11	.37	.33	.57							
AIR-AID tests											
5. Perc. flex.	.36	.24	.18	.10	.08						
6. Verbal reas.	.26	.14	.20	.27	.22	.28					
7. Reading. comp.	.22	.24	.29	.47	.50	.07	.30				
8. Sci.info.	.11	.12	.26	.12	.40	.17	.09	.29			
9. Current affairs	.08	.06	.04	.23	.30	.04	.22	.40	.34		
10. Clerical speed	.21	.21	.20	.08	.18	.29	.01	.11	.24	.07	
11. Graph reading	.11	.27	.26	.15	.31	.31	.19	.22	.18	.02	.45

* Reflected variable

Below diagonal: Buganda, *N* = 136. Above diagonal: Western Uganda, *N* = 73

Skill in the use of English and the ability to understand written materials are central to CSC attainment. Information tests (said by Schwartz to indicate an interest in the subject matter) are also relatively indicative, as is the Graph Reading test (claimed by Schwartz to assess a general ability to cope with multivariate problems). The concurrent verbal reasoning test is less related to CSC than a general verbal ability test four years earlier.

Insofar as higher education beyond SC increasingly demands less rote learning and more independent thinking, it may be that ability tests have an important role to play in selection at the highest levels. Even with regard to the CSC, verbal ability tests predict better than achievement in subjects.

In addition to examining the criterion we must examine the quality of the input to secondary schools, and the quality of the treatment there. To avoid 'regression to the mean' the sample has been divided into four categories according to whether their achievement relative to this sample, rose, declined, or remained at a similar level from S4 level to SSE. 59 pupils were above the median in both SSE and CSC and 67 were below both medians. These 126 can be said to have achieved about the level SSE predicted. 46 pupils improved their standing and 39 declined. To unravel possible causal influences of independent variables these latter groups are to be compared.

It might be argued that it is the function of the secondary schools to invalidate any correlation between SSE and CSC. The more a school can overcome the poorer pupils' handicap, the better is the school doing its job, and the lower will be the SSE-CSC correlation. If this were so, a higher proportion of the 46 'improvers' should be found in the better secondary schools than of the 39 'decliners'. Classifying schools by their overall CSC records in the year in which the sample took the CSC exam, virtually identical proportions of each group are found in the best schools. Furthermore, if the schools are classified according to the mean achievement in S1, more of the decliners than of the improvers are found in the best schools — the opposite of the expected trend. Although the difference is insignificant, the very lack of evidence makes it difficult to argue that the better schools are having over and above what is expected of them on the basis of the quality of their entrants.

What about the quality of the input? Again, the evidence is unclear: PM scores tend to be somewhat higher among those who will improve their performance, but the opposite holds for Mental Alertness. On concurrent cognitive performance (AIR-AID tests), the improvers score higher than the decliners on five of the seven tests, but the differences are insignificant.

Parental education has frequently been shown to be related to school performance in countries which had compulsory education when the parents were of school age. In countries without universal schooling, the greater variation in parental education should lead to an unusually strong relationship. In this sample, 22 per cent of fathers and 35 per cent of mothers had never been to school, while 6 per cent of fathers and no mothers had postsecondary schooling. Parental education was not associated with performance in a meaningful way.

This may be because of the generally low level of parental education, and because a little education had left no discernible trace on children's upbringing. Half the sample were farmers or cultivators; in Uganda they have little incentive to remain literate. It may be, then, that a little education is qualitatively no different later in life from no education.

Jobs can be crudely categorized according to whether they require some degree of functional literacy, such as shopkeeping or teaching. The father's job may also provide a more valid indicator of the educational climate of the pupil's background than amount of parents' education. It may take into account the extent to which the father, in addition to using his education in his job, has the resources to bring educationally stimulating materials into his home. Some support for this kind of explanation is suggested by the data. 44 per cent of improvers had fathers in jobs requiring some education, compared to 26 per cent of the decliners. Although not significant, the magnitude and direction of the difference is suggestive.

Finally we return to the opening argument that selection may be a function of the quality of junior school. There is a significant positive correlation between junior-school quality and CSC performance. This would suggest that a high proportion of the decliners should be found to come from the 'better' junior schools, owing to their selection into that school rather than to their own educability. Correspondingly, a high proportion of improvers would come from the 'poorer' schools, as the more borderline entrants whose success is achieved despite rather than because of their schools. These expectations are confirmed: while 72 per cent of the total sample came from the few 'best' schools, 80 per cent of the decliners and 56 per cent of the improvers did so.

Thus, with a small sample amd restricting ourselves to bivariate analyses, some hint of effective determinants of scholastic performance can be obtained. The next stage will be to use multivariate analyses.

REFERENCES

Irvine, S. H. (1964) A psychological study of selection problems at the end of primary schooling in Southern Rhodesia. Unpublished doctoral dissertation. Univer. of London.
Irvine, S. H. (1967) How fair is culture? Factorial studies of Raven's Progressive Matrices across cultures in Africa. Bristol: Univer. of Bristol. (Mimeographed)
Lloyd, F., & Pidgeon, D. A. (1961) An investigation into the effects of coaching on nonverbal test material with European, Indian, and African children. *Brit. J. educ. Psychol., 31*, 145-151.
Ombredane, A. (1959) *Etude sur le P.M. 1938 de Raven.* Brussels: Centre de Orientation Professionnelle.
Ramphal, C. (1962) A study of three current problems of Indian education. Unpublished doctoral dissertation. Univer. of Natal.
Somerset, H. C. A. (1968) *Predicting success in school certificate.* Nairobi.
Vernon, P. E. (1967) Abilities and educational attainment in an East African environment. *J. spec. Educ., 1*, 335-345.

Note: *Cronbach pointed out that the comparison of improvers and decliners does not avoid the artifacts commonly known to confuse studies that employ gain scores. Cronbach and Furby (see p. 423) offer alternative procedures.* (Eds.)

PART VII

Factor-analytic studies

While other conference papers use factor analysis incidentally to gain insight into a set of items or subtests, in only three papers is examination of a factor structure central. This in itself may bespeak a major trend in research.

Claeys starts within the concepts of Vernon and Cattell, and locates second- and third-order factors among Congolese teachers, but his final interpretation has several novel features. His two third-order factors are interpreted as 'historical fluid intelligence' (after Cattell) and 'adoption of a Western Attitude.'

Grant and Fatouros are both concerned with the long-lived controversy as to whether abilities become more differentiated with age, and both employ methods of factor analysis that permit integration of factor analyses from several groups. Grant drew rural and urban samples of Venda adult males and subclassified them on amount of schooling. The factors he found in NIPR performance tests intercorrelated higher in the educated groups, but this is interpreted as showing that their abilities are *more* differentiated. Fatouros dealt with 9- to 14-year-old Greeks, grouped by age, sex, and kind of school. Wechsler subtests were employed. The results are complex and not entirely in accord with expectations, but there is some indication of a stronger general factor at later ages. A maturational explanation is offered.

W. CLAEYS
University of Louvain

43

The factor structure of intelligence among teachers in the Congo*

PURPOSE OF STUDY AND HYPOTHESES

The *S*s were 101 Congolese first-grade teachers from Kinshasa, representative with respect to the geographical distribution and quality of their schools. They are a homogeneous sample with respect to profession and also with respect to education, most having completed 8 years of schooling. This report deals only with the tests of aptitude (Culture Free Test of Cattell, PMA, GATB, and Progressive Matrices 38), plus 9 tests of achievement in French and arithmetic.

Table 1 lists the test titles together with the abbreviations we shall use and traditional hypotheses regarding their factor composition.

With the aim of identifying the chief dimensions of aptitude and achievement in an adult population of the Congo, we correlated and factor-analyzed the tests. Several of the tests are virtually pure measures of the Thurstone 'primary abilities'. It follows that factors extracted from this battery are most likely second-order factors, and that the correlations among these factors yield third-order factors.

As a theoretical framework we took the Cattell (1963) model of 'fluid' and 'crystallized' intelligence, with the refinement of

* I thank R. Verbeke, head of the Department of Pedagogy at the University of Louvanium in Kinshasa, for having made available to me the data treated in this paper.

Table 1. Variables entering the factor analysis

Title of test	Abbreviation	Hypothetical factorial interpretation
Test of school achievement CM2 - Level 6		
Noun recognition	Nouns	
Adjective-pronoun distinction	Adj. Pron.	
Spelling	Spell.	
Unchanging words	Unch.	
Vocabulary	Voc.	
Knowledge of functions	Funct.	
Conjugation	Conj.	
Mechanical calculation	Calc.	
Arithmetic reasoning	Ar. Reas.	
GATB (Form B)		
Name comparison	Names	Thurstone P
Computation	Comp.	Thurstone N
Three-dimensional space	Space	Thurstone S
Vocabulary	Vocab.	Thurstone V
Tool matching	Tools	Thurstone P
Arithmetic Reasoning	Arith.	Guilford R
Form matching	Forms	Thurstone P, S
Copying of lines	Copy	
Thurstone PMA		
Numerical	Numer.	Thurstone N
Word fluency	Flu.	Thurstone W
Culture Free Intelligence Test of Cattell (Form 2A)		
Figure series	Fig. Ser.	Cattell gf
Classification	Class.	Cattell gf
Matrices	Mat.	Cattell gf
Conditions	Cond.	Cattell gf
Progressive Matrices (Standard form)	PM38	Spearman g

Horn & Cattell (1966). Starting with the conviction of Cattell regarding the 'culture-fair' character of his tests, and taking into account that our Ss are not located at the same point with respect to adoption of a 'Western attitude' (one favoring performance on tests that may be called 'culture-unfair'), we reached three hypotheses:

Table 2. *Loadings on 'second-order' factors after rotation to oblique simple structure*

Variable	1	2	3	4	5	h^2
Nouns	.56	22	.06	.09	−.43	.67
Adj. Pron.	.68	.12	.01	−.12	.00	.50
Spell.	.66	−.01	.21	.30	−.14	.72
Unch.	.73	.05	−.01	−.09	−.09	.55
Voc.	.84	−.15	−.15	.15	.17	.74
Funct.	.89	−.08	.19	.10	.05	.88
Conj.	.88	−.02	.07	−.18	−.08	.75
Calc.	.76	.19	−.12	.04	.11	.70
Ar. Reas.	.76	.03	−.19	.06	.02	.61
Names	.02	.67	.21	.12	.13	.68
Comp.	.08	.87	.04	−.20	−.12	.75
Space	.09	.17	.45	.33	−.21	.57
Vocab.	.17	.52	.11	.08	−.31	.58
Tools	−.18	.48	.32	.26	−.16	.60
Arith.	.22	.54	.08	.02	−.21	.52
Forms	−.05	.31	.80	−.09	−.11	.84
Copy	.03	.23	.49	.01	.21	.41
Numer.	.12	.47	.03	−.07	.11	.26
Flu.	.01	.56	.02	−.04	.27	.35
Fig. Ser.	.30	.44	.14	.18	.13	.57
Class.	.09	−.06	.09	.66	.02	.47
Mat.	.08	.27	.01	.48	.51	.73
Cond.	−.01	.28	−.25	.40	−.07	.31
PM38	−.04	.56	.05	.11	.01	.38
Latent root	5.43	3.51	1.47	1.31	.93	14.15

1 g_{scol}
2 Perception of relations
3 Analytic perception
4 Categorizing
5 Impulsiveness

1. There is not just a single second-order factor (which would be expected from the Thurstone position), but several oblique second-order factors comparable to the *gf, gc, gv, gs,* etc. of Horn & Cattell (1966).

2. The second-order factors have in their turn loadings on a third-order factor comparable to gf_{hist} (historical fluid intelligence; Cattell, 1967a).

3. Another third-order factor of 'Westernization' exists, independent of the first, loading all the intelligence factors of the second order with the exception of the one that explains the communality among CFT subtests. This factor can be found only among *S*s who have to compromise between adaptation to traditional culture and adaptation to Western culture.

RESULTS AND INTERPRETATION

Second-order factors

Principal-components analysis was used. Varimax rotation was applied, and also an oblique (Oblimin) rotation. Five factors explained 95.1 per cent of the communality among the tests, and 59 per cent of the total variance. The communalities stabilized after 7 iterations. The oblique rotation toward simple structure gave factors (Table 2) which we interpret as second-order factors that can be compared to those of Horn & Cattell (1966).

The most important factor can be labelled general academic achievement (*1*), since the achievement tests in arithmetic and French load highly on it. Among aptitude tests, only Reas. and FSer. had even modest loadings on *1*.

Subject-matter knowledge is an essential part of the professional competence of these teachers. One cannot exclude the possible influence of academic and professional motivation as a source of covariance among these tests; one could defend an interpretation of *1* as 'zeal', resembling the *X* factor of Alexander. We predicted that *1* would be influenced by both of the third-order factors.

Factor *2* is comparable to 'crystallized intelligence' (*gc;* Cattell, 1963), loading in all measures of Thurstone primaries save for S. Cattell equates this also with Spearman's g, with the restriction that the variance is strongly determined by educative and cultural experience. The aptitude enters those tasks that can be executed only after a long pretraining in which one acquires knowledge possessed by a culture. The large loadings of PM38 and FSer. on 2 in this study confirm the interpretation of it as 'perception of relations'.

Cattell's designation of this ability as 'crystallized' is less well founded, if that implies a large influence of experience on the application of perception of relations to certain tasks and materials, through making various techniques available. The high loading in PM38, FSer., Mat., and Condit. on this factor contradict this interpretation. Learning influences g through providing greater familiarity with the types of relations (e.g., causality, implication, etc.) which can exist among units of an item. Certain relations made explicit in the logic and mathematics of the West are not explicit in some other cultures. We recognize that the relations entering the items of tests that measure 2 were constructed in the West and reflect Western thought; hence they are 'culture-unfair' for African Ss even if the tasks are as novel for the European as for the African (which is the case in PM38 and FSer). Hence we predicted that not only the third-order intelligence factor but also the 'Westernization' factor would contribute to differences in 2 among our Ss.

Factor 3 is comparable to gv (general visualization; Horn & Cattell, 1966), entering primarily measures of S and P. We interpret it as 'analytic vs. global perception'. This accounts for the loading of Spell. and for negative loading of Condit. (where too minute an analysis of the figures reduces one's chance of solving a problem). In the Horn-Cattell study, 3 loaded on tests of 'flexibility of closure' (Witkin's 'field independence'). Witkin hypothesizes cultural differences in field independence and a small correlation between it and intelligence; hence we expect 3 to depend on both third-order factors.

Factor 4 coincides with Cattell's gf, loading strongly in this study on Class and somewhat less on Mat., Condit., and a spatial test. Cattell's eighth graders (1963) yielded loadings very similar to those we find for adult teachers. According to Cattell, *4* represents 'perception of relations and eduction of correlates', but it measures *g* only insofar as that ability is not affected by experience and cultural learning is not called upon. 'Fluid' ability is most clearly seen, according to Cattell, in tasks that are equally familiar to all *S*s (or equally novel to all) whatever their cultural backgrounds.

Cattell's interpretation is not convincing. It does not explain why Classification should systematically appear as the purest measure of the factor, in Cattell's studies (1963, 1967b) as well as ours, while FSer. shows little or no loading. The latter is a typical measure of inductive power (Thurstone's *I*) and it contains material just as 'culture-fair' as other parts of CFT. It does not explain why Raven Matrices should not load on *4*. It does not explain why measures of *S* regularly load on *4* in Cattell's studies (1963, 1967a) and ours.

If one considers *4* as a distinct aptitude — 'power of abstraction' or 'ability to categorize' — these questions can be given a more satisfactory answer. This aptitude is usually found when the examinee is to find a category to which elements (Guilford's 'units') belong, or when he is to judge the coherence of a given category. We now can understand why *4* loads strongly on tests of classification and selection of objects but weakly on tests where one must perceive a relation among a series of units as in FSer. or PM38. It is to be noted that the reasoning tests used by Cattell call primarily for grouping of units (letters, figures, or words), and that Guilford (1967) has shown that tests of grouping measure 'cognition of classes'; this, as distinguished from 'cognition of relations', is what Thurstone's letter-grouping test measures.

The loading of spatial tests on *4* becomes equally comprehensible; the tasks require not merely a spatial aptitude (that is, mental rotation of a figure) but equally an ability to abstract from the spatial position of the figures to find identical fgures among a series. This denies the interpretation of *4* as a mixture of Spearman's *g* and Vernon's *k*.

One must further question Cattell's opinion as to the 'fluid' character of *gf* (our *4*) if by that we mean that differences are not culturally determined. It is quite probable that any culture, traditional or Western, stimulates the classification of objects perceived and hence an abstract attitude. If tests of *4* are labelled 'culture-fair' it is not because the content and tasks are equally novel for all *S*s, European or African, but because the attitude of abstraction is probably stimulated to an identical degree in every culture. Thus we predicted that the third-order factor of intelligence and not the factor of 'Western attitude' would generate variance in *4*.

Factor *5* has to do with impulsiveness (or insouciance) vs. punctiliousness, loading in Flu. and Cop. (where obsessive verification wastes time) and negatively in a French test (hunting out all the nouns in a text) and in measures of *S*, *V*, and *R* which demand sustained accuracy. The heavy loading of Mat. probably reflects the insufficient difficulty of its earliest items. We suspect that *5* here replaces general-speed, fluency, and carefulness factors found by Horn & Cattell. *5* resembles the construct of Heymans and Wiersma − 'primary vs. secondary functioning' − and Cattell's 'harric assertiveness'. We expected that Westernization among our *S*s would lead them to replace traditional insouciance with the obsessiveness of Western man.

Third-order factors

We now sharpen hypotheses 2 and 3, predicting two third-order factors, one comparable to Cattell's gf_{hist} saturating all second-order factors save *5*; and one 'Westernization', saturating *1*, *2*, and *4* positively and *5* negatively. The factor intercorrelations appear in Table 3. (Note that *r (2, 4)* was 0.41, equal to the 0.47 that Cattell, 1963, finds between *gf* and *gc*.) Two principal components accounted for 91 per cent of the communality. Table 4 gives the result of the factor analysis, after five iterations. Varimax and Oblimin rotations produced almost no change.

It is possible to interpret Factor *I* as intelligence, as it did load on factors *1* to *4* and not on *5*. Factor *II* entered positively into *4* (categorizing) and *5* (impulsiveness), and negatively in *2* perc. rels.), hence it cannot be interpreted as 'adoption of a Western attitude'.

Table 3. Intercorrelations among the factors

	1	2	3	4	5
1. g_{scol}					
2. Perception of relations	.31				
3. Analytic perception	.14	.30			
4. Categorizing	.22	.41	.18		
5. Impulsiveness	−.04	−.08	.00	.08	

Table 4. Third-order factors

	Unrotated factors			Rotation to criterion*	
	I	II	h²	I $gf_{hist.}$	II West.
1. g_{scol}	.39	−.05	.15	.32	.22
2. Perception of relations	.78	−.17	.64	.63	.50
3. Analytic perception	.35	−.03	.12	.30	.19
4. Categorizing	.58	.29	.42	.65	.00*
5. Impulsiveness	−.03	.34	.11	.12	−.32
Latent root	1.23	.23	1.46	1.02	.44

* The rotation forced the loading of *4* on *II* to be zero.

Rotation to simple structure need not provide the best solution, as the hypotheses did not predict simple structure in the data. Using as a criterion the expectation that *4* would have no loading on *II,* we obtained axes which corresponded well to the remaining elements of hypotheses 2 and 3, see the last two columns of Table 4. Now *I* saturated strongly *2* (perc. rels.) and *4* (categorizing), and less strongly *1* (g_{scol}) and *3* (analyt. perc.), and so corresponded to gf_{hist}. Factor *II* had strong loadings in *2* (perc. rels.), weak loadings in *1* and *3,* and a negative loading in *5,* hence it can be interpreted as 'Westernization'.

DISCUSSION

We did not hypothesize a third-order factor simply of 'educative and cultural experience' because it is improbable that the *intra*cultural experience and learning that influence the variances of *1-5* would be the same for these several dimensions and so constitute a source of common variance.

We reinterpret gf_{hist} to indicate Factor *I* not only because it loaded chiefly *2* and *3* (akin to Cattell's *gc* and *gf*) but equally because we believe that differences in *I* reflect neurological and physiological differences that serve as the common base of the functions of abstraction and perception of relations. This common base is considered to be the product of hereditary influences and environmental factors other than educative experience and cultural learning.

The results appear to confirm the hypothesis concerning the culture-fair character of measures of *4* (abstraction) and the culture-unfair character of measures of *g*. They also give some support to the Witkin hypothesis regarding the influence of Western attitude on field independence, and to our hypothesis regarding its influence on punctiliousness and motivation.

We may compare our *4* (categorizing) with the 'ability to categorize and form concepts of wide generality' of Halstead (1951) or with the Goldstein-Scheerer (1941) 'abstract versus concrete attitude'. The latter is known to be reduced considerably by cerebral lesions; Cattell expects this also to be true of *gf.* Our distinction between *2* (perc. rels.) and *4* (categorizing) helps to clarify the relation between 'biological intelligence' – a concept arising from the study of cerebral lesions – and the traditional factorial notion of intelligence (Spearman's *g* or Thurstone's second-order factor). The distinction lends support to Guilford's distinction between factors associated with 'classes' and factors pertaining to 'relations'.

One might think – subject to confirmation by other studies – that there is some relation between the factors of abstraction and perception of relations, and the Piagetian notions of intelligence and formal operations. As for the conservation factor of Vernon, I do not see this as a necessary conclusion.

REFERENCES

Cattell, R. B. (1963) Theory of fluid and crystallized intelligence: A critical experiment. *J. educ. Psychol., 54*, 1-22.

Cattell, R. B. (1967a) La théorie de l'intelligence fluide et cristallisée, sa relation avec les tests 'culture fair' et sa vérification chez les enfants de 9 à 12 ans. *Rev. Psychol. appl. 17*, 135-154.

Cattell, R. B. (1967b) The theory of fluid and crystallized general intelligence checked at the 5-6 year-old level. *Brit. J. educ. Psychol., 37*, 209-224.

Goldstein, K. & Scheerer, M. (1941) Abstract and concrete behavior. *Psychol. Monogr., 53*, no. 2.

Guilford, J. P. (1967) *The nature of human intelligence.* New York: McGraw-Hill.

Halstead, W. C. (1951) Biological intelligence. *J. Pers., 20*, 118-130.

Horn, J., & Cattell, R. B. (1966) Refinement and test of the theory of fluid and crystallized general intelligences. *J. educ. Psychol., 57*, 253-270.

Note: *Claeys' identification of a factor as 'culture-fair' and strongly under biological influence is in marked contrast to the other papers in this meeting. One participant noted that 4 could be regarded as an 'instrument factor' arising from idiosyncratic features of the Cattell test or reflecting the Ss' states of mind on the day that test was given. The failure of Mat. and PM38 to load on the same factors is not readily explained in other terms.* (Eds.)

G. V. GRANT   44
University of the Witwatersrand

The organization of intellectual abilities of an African ethnic group in cultural transition*

Scholastic education and urbanization have frequently been mentioned (e.g., Doob, 1965; Andor, 1966) as variables which influence the performance of Africans on intellectual tasks. To date, there has been no systematic investigation designed to show how a change from a pre-literate rural culture to a literate urban culture affects both the level of intellectual performance and the structure of intellectual abilities.

Grant and Schepers (1969) critically appraised previous factoranalytic studies on intellectual tests of Africans and indicated some shortcomings of these studies. Their two main criticisms were that the finding of unitary factors in these studies was due to an adherence to the British factor analytic approach, and that since too few tests were used the factor structures obtained were more a comment on the status of test development for Africans

* This study was conducted while the author was employed at the National Institute for Personnel Research. It was part of South Africa's contribution to the International Biological Program during 1969. The study was subsequently submitted to the University of the Witwatersrand as part of a doctoral thesis.
The author thanks the Director of the National Institute for Personnel Research for the support afforded him while carrying out this study. The financial assistance of the Human Sciences Research Council and the University of the Witwatersrand is acknowledged. Opinions expressed or conclusions reached are those of the author and are not to be regarded as a reflection of the opinions and conclusions of the Human Sciences Research Council or the University of the Witwatersrand.

than a reflection of the structure of African intellectual abilities.

The analysis of Grant and Schepers yielded two intellectual abilities instead of the usual single factor. They drew attention to the possibility of two further group factors: perceptual speed *(P.S.)* and perceptual analysis *(P.A.)*.

Grant (1970b, 1971) followed up this initial investigation and identified three further group factors: perception of form relations (*P.F.R.*), conceptual reasoning (*C.R.*), and space (*Sp.*).

Five factors having been identified, it was judged possible now to investigate the differentiation of African intellectual abilities. Two theories on the differentiation of abilities are pertinent.

TWO THEORIES OF DIFFERENTIATION OF ABILITIES

Burt presented the first evidence for intellectual differentiation in his '1921 Report' (see Burt, 1954). He found that with an increase in age the influence of the general factor declined and the influence of group factors increased.

Garrett (1946), apparently unaware of Burt's findings, proposed that '. . . intelligence changes in its organization as age increases from a fairly unified and general ability to a loosely organized group of abilities or factors' (p. 373). To support his hypothesis Garrett quoted the results of a number of studies.

Guilford (1967), surveying the literature on the Burt-Garrett hypothesis, concluded that the findings reported were equivocal and the hypothesis untenable. He chiefly criticized the use of hierarchical models by those who claimed support for the hypothesis.

Ferguson's (1954, 1956) theory of the differentiation of abilities is attractive, and seems more tenable than that of Burt and Garrett. Of relevance here is Ferguson's remark that 'cultural factors prescribe what shall be learned and at what age; consequently different cultural environments lead to the development of different patterns of ability' (1956, p. 121). Ferguson (1954) refers to learning as an important process in the differentiation of abilities. He maintains that the process of differentiation is aided by the abilities which the individual already possesses. Thus an individual will learn more readily those activities which are facilitated by prior acquisitions and less readily those which are inhibited by prior learning. He regards abilities as overlearned skills or prior acquisitions which have attained a crude of state of invariance. These overlearned acquisitions have transfer effects on subsequent learning and the effects are differential. Different abilities are seen as having different effects at different stages of learning.

Ferguson's remarks on transfer are relevant in the methodology of factor analysis. Positive correlations between factors are explained in terms of the operation of positive transfer. Positive transfer, however, will only occur if the prior acquisitions have attained a state of invariance. Thus, if the abilities of individuals have reached a state of invariance they exert positive transfer effects on one another and in a factor analysis this will manifest itself in the form of positive intercorrelations among factors. Positive intercorrelations among factors therefore suggest the differentiation of abilities. Following Ferguson's reasoning we arrive at two hypotheses:

> As a result of the positive effects of literacy and urbanization, literate urban Venda males will perform significantly better on a battery of tests measuring intellectual abilities than illiterate rural Venda males.
> Literate urban Venda males, because they have been exposed to an enriched environment, will display greater differentiation in response to a battery of tests than illiterate rural Venda males, whose environment is, by comparison, impoverished.

METHOD

For purposes of this study two samples were drawn. A random sample of 199 Ss was obtained by area sampling from the domain of Chief Nelwomondo in Sibasa district in the Northeastern part of the Transvaal (rural), and 219 Ss were obtained from the township of Chiawelo, south of Johannesburg (urban). Persons were eligible for inclusion in the samples if they were Venda, male, between the ages of 17 and 55, without physical disability, and had no more than seven years of formal schooling. The urban *S*s were required to have been in an urban township for at least 6 months.

The two samples were further subdivided into those with no schooling and those with 1-7 years of schooling. The four groups thus constituted will be referred to as Rural Illiterate (RI, *N* = 94), Urban Illiterate (UI, *N* = 93), Rural Literate (RL, *N* = 105) and Urban Literate (UL, *N* = 125).

Sixteen tests were selected for administration. On the basis of pilot studies it was postulated that these tests measured five abilities. A brief description of these abilities and the tests which loaded on them in the pilot studies is presented below. Many of the tests are described briefly in the papers of Biesheuvel, Blake, and Reuning in this volume.

The Perceptual speed factor *(P.S.)* is characterized by the task of finding, in a mass of distracting material, a given configuration which is borne in mind during the search. *Tests:* Sorting I, Sorting II, Cube, Tripod (Biesheuvel, 1952). These tests constitute the General Adaptability Battery (GAB).

The Perceptual analysis *(P.A.)* factor is characterized by the task of analyzing perceptual material into its component parts. *Tests:* Fret Repetition, Fret Continuation, Pattern Reproduction, Circles (Grant & Schepers, 1969).

The Perception of form relations *(P.F.R.)* factor is characterized by the task of manipulating forms in such a way that when a correct relationship is obtained, it reproduces part of – or the whole of – a new form which is merely suggested by an outline. *Tests:* Formboards II, III, and IV, and Form Perception (Grant, 1970a).

The Conceptual reasoning *(C.R.)* factor is defined as the ability to discover or apply a rule by relating concepts to one another. *Tests:* Form Series, Symbol Series, Symco (Grant, 1971), Sorting I, Sorting II (Biesheuvel, 1952).

The Space *(Sp.)* factor represents the ability to perceive spatial patterns accurately and to compare them with each other. *Tests:* Tripod, Cube, Sorting I (Biesheuvel, 1952), and Squares Detection (Grant, 1971).

Sorting I and II, Cube Construction. Tripod Assembly, and the three formboards were administered by means of a silent 16 mm. film. The rest of the tests were administered verbally in Venda with the aid of demonstration posters. The first column of Table 1 indicates the sequence in which tests were administered. Tests 1-13 were administered during the morning of the first day and tests 14-17 on the afternoon of the second day. This procedure was followed to obviate fatigue. Groups of 15 or fewer were tested in each session. The Urban-Rural Scale was also administered (Grant, 1969). The range of the scale is 0 to 17.

Table 1. Means and standard deviations of variables for all four groups

Sequ- ence Variable	Rural illiterate $N = 94$		Urban illiterate $N = 93$		Rural literate $N = 105$		Urban literate $N = 125$	
	Mean	s.d.	Mean	s.d.	Mean	s.d.	Mean	s.d.
1 Sorting I	67.33	32.68	100.83	36.94	89.09	34.67	118.78	34.15
8 Sorting II	58.97	29.54	86.70	33.34	102.31	36.60	120.09	27.50
12 Cube Construction	20.11	13.24	25.84	12.97	24.44	12.67	31.22	15.44
16 Tripod Assembly	24.56	15.35	32.59	14.14	34.84	14.74	37.70	15.37
5 Form Perception	18.73	5.21	20.93	4.60	20.36	5.04	22.20	4.20
9 Formboard II	4.67	3.69	6.15	3.49	7.14	4.03	8.24	4.31
10 Formboard III	9.33	5.23	11.90	5.23	11.94	5.60	13.99	5.50
11 Formboard IV	7.00	4.86	8.43	5.28	8.11	4.78	9.42	5.50
2 Fret Repetition	6.53	3.05	7.68	2.44	8.81	1.74	8.91	1.86
3 Fret Continuation	5.17	3.56	6.42	3.03	7.73	2.60	8.21	2.37
6 Pattern Rep.	16.28	8.24	20.53	8.99	22.73	9.67	26.96	8.72
13 Circles	25.18	9.45	30.56	7.73	35.06	7.73	35.90	7.17
4 Form Series	5.30	4.73	7.27	4.60	9.89	4.47	11.00	4.52
7 Symbol Series	3.27	2.89	4.26	3.23	6.34	3.52	7.34	3.56
14 Squares Detection	14.43	7.09	16.16	7.10	20.04	6.24	19.78	7.83
15 Symmetry Compl.	7.12	5.08	9.12	5.41	11.27	5.37	11.61	5.38
Age	41.85	9.12	45.39	7.11	26.12	7.95	38.76	10.24
Schooling					4.34	1.73	4.76	1.52
Urban - Rural	1.85	1.25	5.33	2.60	2.73	1.38	6.39	3.26

RESULTS

Means and standard deviations are shown in Table 1. To compare group means, *t*-tests or Welch tests were performed, according to whether F ratios were significant or not. All differences between groups were significant ($P < .05$) except for the following:

RI vs. RL: Formboard IV
UI vs. UL: Formboard IV
UI vs. RL: Cube, Tripod, Form Perception, Formboards III and
            IV
UL vs. RL: Tripod, Fret Repetition, Fret Continuation, Circles,
            Squares Det., Symco.
For RI vs. UI and UL, all differences were significant.

For each group, covariance matrices were computed, and likelihood-ratio tests (Morrison, 1967) were carried out to test the equality of the covariance matrices. In the first, all four groups were compared; the asymptotic χ^2 was significant ($P < .01$). In the next step likelihood-ratio tests were performed to determine whether this difference was due to urbanization or scholastic education. For RI vs. UI the asymptotic χ^2 was not significant. Similarly for RL vs. UL the asymptotic χ^2 was not significant. It was concluded that the differences were due to education.

If a likelihood-ratio test is significant, the manifest-variable covariance matrices differ. This implies that factor matrices, and/or factor-covariance matrices and/or residual covariance matrices, are different.

The rationale underlying intergroup factor analysis has been formulated by Meredith (1964a, 1964b). Browne of NIPR formulated the mathematical procedure (cf. Grant, 1970b) and Barrett, also of NIPR, wrote the programme.

It is assumed that there is a single factor matrix common to all groups. The factor matrix common to all four groups was obtained from the factor matrices specific to each group. (Principal axis factor analysis, in which 5 factors were extracted, was previously performed on the intercorrelation matrix of each group). The matrix common to the four groups was rotated obliquely (Table 2), using the Promax procedure of Hendrickson and White (1964).

The factor correlations for each group were obtained by means of the intergroup procedure (Table 3).

Table 2. Factor matrix common to all four groups (Promax rotation)

Variation	P.F.R.	P.A.	C.R.	P.S.	Sp.
Sorting I	−.02	.01	.00	*.45*	*.33*
Sorting II	−.13	.12	.13	*.58*	.01
Cube Construction	.24	.03	.18	.13	*.31*
Tripod Assembly	.15	−.10	.06	.13	*.62*
Form Perception	.00	.13	.00	−.01	*.51*
Formboard I	.27	−.03	.01	*.53*	.00
Formboard II	*.70*	.06	−.02	.01	.06
Formboard III	*.41*	.00	.22	−.05	.07
Fret Repetition	.05	*.82*	−.06	−.02	.06
Fret Continuation	.02	*.67*	.12	.10	.00
Pattern Reproduction	.16	.04	*.41*	.28	.08
Circles	.08	.23	.12	*.30*	.29
Form Series	−.03	.05	*.83*	−.06	.04
Symbol Series	.11	−.03	*.66*	.09	.03
Squares Detection	.21	.19	.13	.05	*.34*
Symmetry Completion	.15	.16	.26	.07	*.34*

DISCUSSION

A clear trend in the means is discernible in the form of a continuum: Rural Illiterate (worst), Urban Illiterate, Rural Literate, Urban Literate (best).

When groups are matched in terms of education the urban groups perform better than the rural groups. It may be inferred that scholastic education and urbanization lead to better performance on intellectual tasks, eduaction being more important. The first hypothesis has thus been supported.

An important assumption in the intergroup procedure is that there is a factor matrix common to all groups. Table 2 largely confirms the factor structure which emerged from the pilot studies. Strictly speaking, *P.F.R.* and *P.A.* are doublets. It should be mentioned though, that if only three factors are extracted, a confusing picture of the factor structure is obtained. The fact that these two dimensions are doublets is a comment on the

Table 3. Factor correlation matrix for each group

	P.F.R.	P.A.	C.R.	P.S.	Sp.
Rural illiterate					
P.A.	.46				
C.R.	.37	.54			
P.S.	.59	.47	.53		
Sp.	.29	.49	.47	.50	
Urban illiterate					
P.F.R.					
P.A.	.53				
C.R.	.43	.55			
P.S.	.39	.38	.33		
Sp.	.63	.48	.51	.51	
Rural literate					
P.F.R.					
P.A.	.20				
C.R.	.20	.51			
P.S.	.30	.61	.69		
Sp.	.75	.67	.65	.80	
Urban literate					
P.F.R.					
P.A.	.47				
C.R.	.49	.69			
P.S.	.70	.60	.50		
Sp.	.52	.34	.54	.68	

composition of the test battery. Additional tests are required to overdetermine these factors.

In Table 3 the factor correlations for all groups are presented. If intercorrelations of 0.60 and above are take to indicate a strong relationship between factors, these is a distinct difference between the two illiterate groups on the one hand and the two literate groups on the other. In the UI group only one correlation exceeds 0.60 and in the RI group only one correlation approaches 0.60.

The significant χ^2 is also explained by these results. With greater literacy, fewer abilities are brought into play to solve an apparently 'diverse' array of intellectual tasks. Does this mean that abilities in the two literate groups are less differentiated in the two illiterate groups? On the contrary. The results show that literate subjects have attained abilities, which through learning have a crude stability or invariance. In this state, positive transfer between abilities occurs and this is reflected in the greater number of high intercorrelations among factors. It may therefore be concluded that since the two literate groups have attained certain abilities, measured by the tests in the battery they are likely to be more differentiated than their illiterate counterparts. This is not to say that illiterates have no overlearned acquisitions or abilities. It merely indicates that, in terms of the abilities measured by the present battery of tests, less differentiation was detected.

The second hypothesis is supported with regard to literacy but not with regard to urbanization. It should be mentioned, however, that although the urban sample was residing in an urban area the sample was still rural-oriented. (See results for the Urban-Rural Scale in Table 1.) Venda people are known to live in encapsulated societies characterized by a retention of tribal customs and mores. If a truly urbanized group had been included in the sample, the effects of urbanization as a differentiating variable might well have been demonstrated.

REFERENCES

Andor, L. E. (1966) *Aptitudes and abilities of the black man in sub-Saharan Africa 1784-1963: An annotated bibliography.* Johannesburg: NIPR.

Biesheuvel, S. (1952) Personnel selection tests for Africans. *So. Afr. J. Sc., 49*, 3-12;

Burt, C. (1954) The differentiation of intellectual ability. *Brit. J. educ. Psychol., 26*, 76-90.

Doob, L. W. (1965) Psychology. In Lystad, R. A., (Ed.) *The African world.* London: Pall Mall Press.

Ferguson, G. A; (1954) On learning and human ability. *Canad. J. Psychol., 8*, 95-112.

Ferguson, G. A. (1956) On transfer and the abilities of man. *Canad. J. Psychol., 10*, 121-131.

Garrett, H. E. (1946) A developmental theory of intelligence. *Amer. Psychologist, 1,* 372-378.

Grant, G. V. (1969) *The Urban-Rural Scale: A socio-cultural measure of individual urbanization.* Johannesburg: NIPR.

Grant, G. V. (1970a) Spatial thinking: A dimension of African intellect. *Psychol. Afr., 13,* 222-239.

Grant, G. V. (1970b) *The organization of mental abilities of an African ethnic group in cultural transition.* Ph. D. Thesis, Univer. of the Witwatersrand.

Grant, G. V. (1971) Conceptual reasoning: Another dimension of African intellect. *Psychol. Afr.* in press.

Grant, G. V. & Schepers, J. M. (1969) An exploratory factor analysis of five new cognitive tests for African mineworkers. *Psychol. Afr.,* 12, 181-192.

Guilford, J. P. (1967) *The nature of human intelligence.* New York: McGraw-Hill.

Hendrickson, A. E. & White, P. O. (1964) Promax: A quick method for rotation to oblique simple structure. *Brit. J. stat. Psychol. 17,* 65-70.

Meredith, W. (1964a) Notes on factorial invariance. *Psychometrika, 29,* 187-185.

Meredith, W. (1964b) Rotation to achieve factorial invariance. *Psychometrika, 29,* 187-206.

Morrison, D. F. (1967) *Multivariate statistical methods.* New York: McGraw-Hill.

MIKA FATOUROS
University of Thessaloniki

45

The influence of maturation and education on the development of mental abilities

It has been repeatedly suggested that the factor structure of intellectual abilities changes with time. Some investigators perceive a progression from general ability towards more differentiated abilities, but others perceive just the opposite. The evidence is far from conclusive. Even studies limited to the Wechsler tests disagree about factor structures at different ages.

Gault (1954) reported similar factor structures at ages from 10-6 to 13-6. Cohen (1959), analyzing results from the WAIS and WISC standardization samples, found the general factor contributing more to variance in the adult population than among children; that is, he observed progressive integration of abilities. Maxwell (1959), using the WISC standardization data, reported more integration of abilities at age 10-6 than at 7-6. He found differentiation, particularly of the spatial factor, at 13-6, but he did not observe further differentiation at later ages. Cropley (1964) reported larger general-factor variance among 12-year-olds than among 10-year-olds. As he points out, this may be due to the fact that the group was above average, so that the tasks might be too easy and fail to call upon specific skills for their solution. It has of course been argued that the Wechsler scales yield few factors and that differences in factor structures are unlikely to be adequately demonstrated using these subtests alone. Osborne (1966) overcame this difficulty by using reference tests.

One reason for the contradictory findings may be differences in experimental methods. The samples are sometimes much too small. The children may be chosen according to school class, not age. Tests may be too few or too limited to yield many abilities. Most important, differentiation is thought to appear at the beginning of adolescence, which usually is a time of considerable change in the person's education. This makes it very difficult to judge whether the changes in intellectual structure are due to maturational or to educational influence.

This study examines the strength of the general factor at age levels from 9 to 14, and attempts to study the influence of education by contrasting students receiving academic general education with a group receiving technical education. It was postulated that if loadings in a performance factor or something similar are higher among the students of technical schools these differences are largely due to education, since in Greece these students undergo no special selection. If, on the other hand, the two groups do not generate different performance factors, any increase or drop in the general factor would be due largely to maturation (provided of course that conditions like selectivity, intelligence, SES, etc. do not influence results). The study had yet another purpose; to test the validity and reliability of WISC in a Greek population.

SUMMARY STATISTICS

140 boys and girls, aged 13-6 to 14-6, were tested on WISC. They were randomly selected from the technical schools of Thessaloniki, the second largest Greek city. The analysis also sees scores obtained from a previous study on WISC with 260 schoolchildren of ages 9, 10, and 14, randomly selected from all the primary and high schools of Thessaloniki (Haritos-Fatouros, 1963). That study led to necessary corrections and alterations, in the verbal part of the test in particular — i.e., new vocabulary, alternative items, order of difficulty. The adapted version was applied in the present study. WISC was more difficult for the Greek sample than for the Wechsler standardization sample. This appears to be the case even if one makes some allowance for lack of test sophistication among Greek schoolchildren. In this sample boys tended to do better then the girls in all groups. Differences

Table 1. Means and standard deviations for WISC IQs by group
(B = Boys; G = Girls)

Group	Age	School	N	Verbal IQ Mean	Verbal IQ s.d.	Performance IQ Mean	Performance IQ s.d.	Full Scale IQ Mean	Full Scale IQ s.d.	Significance of difference from Wechsler means
9B	9	Primary	40	95.2	13.6	88.1	12.2	91.0	12.5	n.s.
9G	9	Primary	40	95.0	15.2	87.8	14.3	90.8	14.8	V, $P<.05$; P, F, $P<.01$
10B	10	Primary	40	95.8	13.8	88.3	12.5	91.5	12.6	V, $P<.05$; P, F, $P<.01$
10G	10	Primary	40	92.0	13.9	83.7	10.6	87.2	11.8	V, $P<.05$; P, F, $P<.01$
H 14B	14	High School	50	103.1[a1]	15.0	92.7[a2]	11.9	97.9[a3]	12.9	P, $P<.01$; V, F, n.s.
H 14G	14	High School	50	102.3[a4]	10.6	91.1[a5]	11.2	96.8[a6]	9.8	V, $P<.05$; P, F, n.s.
T 14B	14	Technical	68	91.4[a1, c7]	11.8	86.8[a2, b8]	12.4	88.2[a3, c9]	11.9	all, $P<.01$
T 14G	14	Technical	75	89.5[a4, c7]	9.0	82.7[a5, b8]	10.9	85.1[a6, c9]	9.1	all, $P<.01$

a, b, c Indicate differences significant $P<.01$, significant $P<.05$, and not significant, respectively.
Thus comparison 1, H 14B vs. T 14B on the Verbal scale is significant with $P<.01$.

reached significance in the technical sample (Performance Scale); also, in the 9 year olds, only girls' scores differed significantly from the Wechsler sample (Table 1). Similar results are reported by Seashore (1960).

Kuder-Richardson coefficients (Table 2) were higher among younger children than among older ones. The Performance Scale was less reliable than the Verbal Scale, and Object Assembly in particular was unreliable. The Performance Scale correlated less than the Verbal Scale with teachers' ratings. We believe that the Performance Scale is not as good a measure of intellectual ability as the Verbal or Full Scale.

Table 2. Reliability coefficients for WISC raw scores

Score	Boys				Girls			
	9	10	H14	T14	9	10	H14	T14
Inf.	.82	.79	.67	.68	.72	.49	.49	.70
Comp.	.66	.36	.71	.45	.71	.43	.43	.66
Arith.	.68	.73	.68	.67	.65	.42	.42	.73
Sim.	.67	.54	.70	.59	.81	.48	.48	.28
D. Span	.71	.62	.74	.45	.75	.70	.71	.55
Voc.	.80	.84	.85	.81	.86	.77	.77	.80
P. Comp.	.63	.56	.62	.70	.67	.65	.47	.37
P. Arr.	.66	.73	.66	.55	.70	.66	.45	.30
B. Des.	.78	.73	.58	.81	.74	.67	.73	.75
Obj. Ass.	.14	.44	.37	.09	.50	.59	.22	.24
Mazes	.66	.44	.21	.76	.77	.63	.45	.63
Verbal Scale	.78	.65	.76	.92	.73	.77	.65	.98
Perf. Scale	.77	.67	.67	.70	.71	.67	.57	.76
Full Scale	.86	.82	.80	.80	.79	.77	.63	.83

High-school and technical students had a smaller s.d. of IQ than younger groups (except for H14B, Verbal). Since this was not accompanied by a rise on the mean, it implies that selection was not based directly on ability. The drop in s.d. helps to explain the drop in reliability with age.

FACTOR ANALYSIS

In order to examine the influence of age and education on the structure of abilities, the scores obtained from all groups (primary, high school, and technical school), were factored by Tryon-Bailey (1970) cluster analysis. The computer program carries out two analyses. The first is based on the correlation matrix between subtests and factors within each group, and the second is based on the correlation matrix between groups and factors. That is, it finally pools all groups into a single analysis, thus permitting valid comparison of factor loadings between groups. The analysis is based on rotated factors. Factor loadings in excess of 0.30 were accepted as significant.

Table 3. Loadings of subtests on whatever factor, within the group, enters Cluster 1

Subtest	Boys				Girls			
	9	10	H14	T14	9	10	H14	T14
Inf.	.88	.72	.77	.80	.29	.92	.85	.71
Comp.	.72	.40	.79	.76	.29	.76	.48	.70
Arith.	.28	.53	.49	.38	.61	.60	.24	.13
Sim.	.70	.68	.68	.47	-.77	.66	.51	.53
D. Span	.26	.65	.38	.33	-.14	.43	.04	.13
Voc.	.93	.91	.96	.92	.84	.92	.85	.83
P. Comp.	.55	.45	.56	.73	.67	.62	.10	.25
P. Arr.	.68	.30	.64	.46	.85	.48	.30	.50
B. Des.	.67	.25	.50	.15	.42	.37	.12	.25
Obj. Ass.	.49	.15	.31	.45	.44	.26	.14	.24
Coding	.53	.41	.39	.44	.67	.28	-.16	.26
Mazes	.23	.17	.16	.29	.11	.19	.10	.11

Four oblique factors were obtained. The first (Table 3) seems to be a general factor; it accounted for 68 per cent of the total variance. All subtests except Mazes were significantly saturated with it, and it appeared in every group. In the spherical plot it formed a very tight cluster. It tended to have consistently higher loadings in Verbal than in Performance subtests, particularly among the older girls. It is probable that we are concerned here with a 'general-verbal' rather than a purely general factor.

The verbal-general factor tended to be stronger among older boys than among younger boys. Older girls did not differ consistently from younger girls, however. Loadings in the general factor were considerably lower for girls than for boys, regardless of kind of school. This may be due in part to the smaller variability of older girls. Had variability been held constant, we suspect that the older girls would have shown greater integration of abilities.

Table 4. Loadings of subtests on whatever factor, within the group, enters Cluster 2

Subtest	Boys				Girls		
	9	10	H14	T14	10	H14	T14
Inf.	.10	.27	−.15	.14	.16	.02	.20
Comp.	.00	.40	.01	.10	.10	−.06	−.04
Arith.	.15	.06	−.05	.24	.30	.24	.22
Sim.	−.13	.28	−.12	.16	−.20	.05	.10
D. Span	.53	.08	−.23	.16	.11	.41	.24
Voc.	−.11	-.03	.06	.25	−.01	.12	.08
P. Comp.	.25	.26	.28	−.25	.10	.43	.32
P. Arr.	.04	.42	.34	.24	.14	.26	.33
B. Des.	.23	.76	.31	−.22	.68	.63	.61
Obj. Ass.	.48	.64	.55	−.36	.25	.45	.67
Coding	.39	.13	.25	−.31	.61	.50	.28
Mazes	.63	.65	.62	.11	.71	.80	.58

The second factor (Table 4) accounted for 38 per cent of the total variance (somewhat higher than commonly reported). Usually the second factor is a performance factor but that is not clearly the case here. Some of the verbal subtests (D. Span, Comp.) had significant loadings on the second factor, whereas some of the Performance subtests had very small loadings (e.g., P. Comp.). This finding is by no means unique (see Lotsof et al., 1958). This may be a 'spatial' (k) factor, since the Mazes were heavily and consistently saturated with it.

We expected that with technical-school students more variance would fall into the performance factor owing to educational influence, whereas high-school students would show a stronger general-verbal factor. This was not the case. The boys' school is believed to offer a better educational program in technical subjects than the girls' school, but this presumed educational influence is not reflected in the Cluster 2 loadings, which were generally higher for girls.

This finding is contrary to what is usually reported on sex differences for the performance factor. Vernon (1961) observes that most studies report girls or women being poorer than boys or men on the k factor. He further points out that as intellectual ability drops, k is less differentiated from the general factor. In our study, although the technical-school girls scored significantly lower on WISC than the boys, the second factor (k?) tends to be better differentiated among them. We are therefore inclined to think that the sex differences in this study may be due to special cultural features of the Greek environment, with education playing a very limited role.

Table 5.   *Loadings of subtests on whatever factor, within the group, enters Cluster 3 or 4*

| Subtests | Cluster 3 | | | | | Cluster 4 | | | |
| | Boys | | | | Girls | Girls | | | |
	9	10	H14	T14	T14	9	9*	10	H14
Inf.	−.19	.19	.02	.11	.25	−.26	.11	−.01	−.15
Comp.	.13	−.004	.003	−.05	−.05	.58	.25	−.05	.47
Arith.	−.36	.06	.68	.23	.57	.39	.15	−.06	.24
Sim.	−.36	−.29	.36	.32	−.10	.03	−.23	.26	.19
D. Span	−.22	−.35	.32	.32	.28	.90	.07	.50	.51
Voc.	.09	.16	.04	−.18	−.02	−.37	.40	−.07	.11
P. Comp.	.31	.65	−.09	.20	−.07	.27	−.19	.18	−.07
P. Arr.	.15	.31	−.36	−.41	−.14	.03	.05	.16	.21
B. Des.	.05	.04	.28	−.001	.09	.29	−.27	.01	−.18
Obj. Ass.	.17	.11	−.18	.04	.07	.01	−.57	−.08	.17
Coding	−.20	.19	.05	.04	−.35	.58	−.20	−.10	−.20
Mazes	.08	.001	.002	.24	−.02	.26	.83	.10	.13

* Two dimensions from the analysis for the G9 sample entered Cluster 4

The third and fourth factors (Table 5) accounted for little variance (6 per cent and 4 per cent respectively). But they have some psychological interest.

The third factor loaded significantly in Similarities, Digit Span, Picture Arrangement, Arithmetic, Picture Completion, and Coding, Baumeister & Bartlett (1962) report similar trends; we are inclined to agree that this is probably an 'attention-concentration' or 'freedom from distractability' factor. It appeared more often in boy's groups, and its importance seemed to increase with age.

The fourth factor appeared only among girls, particularly younger ones. Digit Span and Coding were saturated significantly with it; this factor may be 'numerical facility', on which girls are known to be superior.

The last two factors in particular show what other studies have noted, that boys not only behave differently but also think differently from girls. One wonders whether this might not be the result more of cultural influence than of inherent tendencies, since education is very similar for the two sexes in both primary and high schools.

To return to the original hypothesis, the study has shown that there is a tendency toward integration of abilities, especially among boys of 14 years as compared to 9- and 10-year-olds of either sex. Better experimental procedures might yield similar results for girls at 14. The integration of abilities found among boys is probably maturational in origin, because it appears independent of educational orientation – indeed, in spite of it.

These findings are, we think, in accord with the views held by some developmental theorists, particularly Piaget (Inhelder & Piaget, 1958). He maintains that during the period of 'reflective' intelligence which begins to appear at age 11, the child 'gradually structures a formal mechanism (reaching an equilibrium point at about 14 or 15), which is based on both the lattice structure and the group of four transformations. This new integration allows him to bring inversion and reciprocity together into a single whole'. It is possible that the process of creating such a formal mechanism needs integration rather than differentiation in the abilities of the adolescent at that critical age.

REFERENCES

Baumeister, A. A. & Bartlett, C. J. (1962) A comparison of the factor structure of normals and retardates on the WISC. *Amer. J. ment. Defic.*, *66*, 641-646.

Cohen, J. (1959) The factorial structure of the WISC at ages 7-6, 10-6, and 13-6. *J. Consult. Psychol.*, *23*, 285-299.

Cropley, J. (1964) Differentiation of abilities, socioeconomic status and the WISC. *J. consult. Psychol.*, *28*, 512-517.

Gault, U. (1954). Factorial patterns of the Wechsler Intelligence Scales, *Austral. J. Psychol.*, *6*, 85-89.

Haritos-Fatouros, M. (1963) A study of the WISC applied to Greek school-children. Unpublished masters Thesis, Univer. of London.

Inhelder, B. & Piaget, J. (1958) *The growth of logical thinking.* Basic Books.

Lotsof, E. J., Comrey, A., Nogartz, W. & Arsfield, P. (1958) A factor analysis of the WISC and Rorschach. *J. proj. Techn.*, *22*, 297-301.

Maxwell, A. E. (1959) A factor analysis of the WISC. *Brit. J. Educ. Psychol.*, *29*, 237-241.

Osborne, R. T. (1966) Stability of factor structure of the WISC for normal Negro children from pre-school level to first grade. *Psychol. Rep.*, *18*, 655-664.

Seashore, H. G., Wesman, A. & Doppelt, J. (1950) The standardization of the Wechsler Intelligence Scale for children. *J. consult. Psychol.*, *14*, 99-110.

Tryon, R. C. & Bailey, D. E. (1970) *Cluster analysis.* New York: McGraw-Hill.

Vernon, P. E. (1961) *The structure of human abilities.* (2nd ed.) London: Methuen.

PART VIII

Technical issues and proposals

Cronbach introduces recently developed ways to analyze and present test data, including absolute scaling, regression analysis, search for interaction between aptitudes and instruction, multi-trait-multimethod validation, and regression estimation of aptitude profiles.

An invited paper by Irvine and Sanders considers the formal requirements that need to be met if the same construct is to be applied in interpreting the same instrument in different cultures. These requirements are not easily satisfied, hence the interpretations commonly made are open to question. They demonstrate the possibility of extending interpretations by considering cognition and affect simultaneously. Crosscultural comparison of indices of item difficulty and item-test correlation is suggested as a useful source of insight.

Mellenbergh reports an initial attempt to make a crosscultural comparison of item statistics derived from the Rasch model. The mathematics test used proved not to fit the model.

Van der Flier examines the concept of culture-reduced tests and proposes a partitioning of variance as a means of studying the environmental influence in any particular test.

Hürsch reviews a study in which he found factorial structure to vary as a function of experimental conditions of testing, and goes on to a further analysis on a subset of subjects who showed 'inconsistent' anxiety patterns. The results are seen as requiring an interactive model of factor analysis to augment the usual linear one.

LEE J. CRONBACH
Stanford University

46

Judging how well a test measures

New concepts, new analysis

Two lines of thought – psychological theory and statistical test theory – tell the test user how he should design and analyze his studies. This paper is concerned with innovations in test theory that have been taking shape in the last decade; the research that grows out of this conference should take advantage of these new concepts and procedures. The paper draws particularly on studies my colleagues and I have made of decision theory, generalizability or reliability theory, and construct validation. It is necessary to treat each topic briefly, without details of the mathematical models, formulas, and sources of illustrative data. The psychologist who sees one of these approaches as potentially useful will find a fuller treatment of it among the references. As few references can be given, I have listed secondary sources; many investigators not mentioned in this paper deserve better acknowledgement.

ABSOLUTE RATHER THAN DIFFERENTIAL MEASUREMENT

Practice and theory of measurement are moving away from preoccupation with individual differences, and toward an attempt to describe the individual on scales that have direct meaning. Forecasting rank on a criterion is generally insufficient; a test ought to describe the level at which a person can be expected to perform. This view leads to increased emphasis on regression lines in test validation and to reduced emphasis on correlations. While the regression function reflects the correlation, it embodies additional information about means and s.d.'s. Among other virtues, conclusions about regressions are more likely to generalize. Often, the relation between two variables can be described by the same regression surface in various cultures or subcultures, even though the two groups fall in different parts of the range or have different s.d.'s on the independent variable. *Per contra,* it is unlikely that a correlation will remain constant from group to group. The person seeking to establish a generalizable relation, or one that will be given a theoretical interpretation, is advised to evaluate the regression of the dependent variable on the predictor true score. The regression on observed score is not of basic interest (Cronbach & Snow, 1972, Chap. 2).

An absolute scale that describes what the person can do is more valuable than a scale that depends on norms, and more valuable than the number-right score which is affected by the test constructor's choice of items. Absolute measurement has been strongly encouraged by the attempts of Piaget, Gagné, and others to describe stages or processes in mental development. Absolute measurement is especially pertinent in assessing outcomes when a training program is intended to ensure that the graduate will perform a job adequately. When a company wants workers to reach a certain standard of production at the end of training, it does need to measure performance. The company often has no need to assess differences among the workers who meet the standard. If Negro workers can meet the standard they deserve a fair share of the jobs even though white workers might, on the average, outscore them.

In educational evaluation also, and in testing of readiness for schooling, one wants descriptive, absolute information rather than differential information. The old Ayres handwriting scale (Cronbach, 1970, p. 79) made descriptively meaningful reports; a display of standard specimens was at hand to show what was meant by the recorded statement that a certain child's writing was scored 60. Vocabulary can be described by listing representative words of whatever difficulty the child interprets with (say) 80 per cent success. Thus we can say that a child succeeds with words such as *pronounce, detail,* and *restless;* for a less able child the list might be *fence, appear,* and *ugly.* Piaget indicates that bead-chain performance progresses by stages. We can therefore use this kind of descriptive scale (Cronbach, 1970, pp. 347 ff.):

> Can copy a series of three colors onto a straight rod.
>
> Can copy a similar series when the copy is to be made on a rod that is fixed in position, distant from but within sight of the model.
>
> Can copy, onto a fixed straight rod, a series that is displayed on a circular rod.
>
> Can prepare a chain with colors in reverse order from those of the model.

If we had such scales for many tasks, we would learn, for example, that a certain child employs mediation in copying bead chains and not in an arithmetic task. This is psychologically significant, whereas the remark that he is at the 70th percentile on the first task and at the 40th on the second means almost nothing. (For a study elaborating the use of absolute scaling, with interest profiles as the example, see Cronbach, 1970, pp. 486 ff.).

CHECKING SELECTION TESTS FOR BIAS

Regression analysis needs to be used to investigate the charge, heard in nearly every nation today, that selection tests are biased. Among the many possible meanings of the accusation, one in particular ought to be verified or refuted in a factual basis. Suppose that applicants come from subcultures A and B, and that persons who score at and above score X* are hired. If criterion scores for persons at the borderline are distributed as in Figure 1, the test is truly biased against Group A. Members of Group A who score somewhat below X* and are therefore rejected deserve to be hired. On the average, they would have scored higher on the criterion than the persons in Group B who were barely accepted. The decision maker should regard a selection rule as biased if it tends to select relatively unproductive

Lee J. Cronbach

workers from one group while rejecting more productive workers from the other group. A similar definition of bias applies in selection of students, etc.

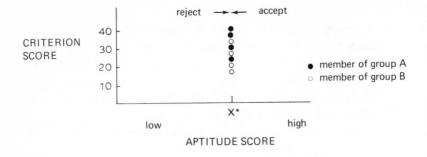

Figure 1. Distribution of criterion scores for persons having equal aptitude scores

To defend a selection procedure against the charge of bias one needs to examine the regression line for each group. The regression lines might coincide, as in Figure 2a. If so, the selection rule is not biased against Group B, by our definition. More members of the A group will be hired, to be sure, but only because they are better risks. Another possible result is shown in Figure 2b, where the lines are parallel. If the cutting score X^* is used for both groups, the selection procedure is biased against persons in Group A (even though more A's are hired than B's!) The only rule that can be defended on *statistical* grounds is the use of two cutting scores, X^*_A in Group A and X^*_B in Group B. The poorest workers selected in each group then have the same expected criterion score.

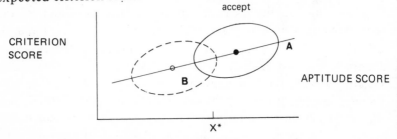

Figure 2a. Coinciding criterion-on-test regressions

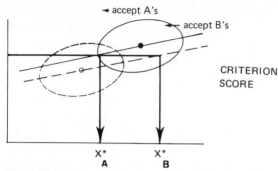

Figure 2b. Parallel criterion-on-test regressions

There have been a number of empirical studies of regression lines for black and white students in American colleges (Stanley, 1971). The findings are not entirely consistent, but the regression line for blacks often coincides with that for whites, as in Figure 2a, or lies slightly beneath it. These studies thus suggest the startling conclusion that when (on a typical test) a uniform cutting score is applied to both groups, any bias is bias against the whites.

There are three further comments to make about bias.

Using group-specific cutting scores to select workers of equal promise may be logical to the decision maker, but it will very likely not be politically acceptable. Group B will feel that it is discriminated against when the cutting score applied to it is higher. This feeling arises whenever high test scores are seen as conferring a benefit. The opposite is the case when a low score makes one eligible for remedial training. The low score then confers a benefit. The fact that some cultural group tends to perform badly on a mental test is a significant social indicator. It should lead to proposals for remedial social policies, just as evidence that a disease is prevalent in a certain population calls for a public-health program. It is when the psychological test is interpreted as an indicator of an unchangeable future that the implications of a low score may be biased.

When regression lines are compared to evaluate a charge of bias, test length is an important consideration. Suppose that group regression lines do coincide, but that the groups have different test means. Then one cannot generalize that this *kind* of test is unbiased, for the regression lines will not coincide when a shorter or longer version of the same test is used. A longer version, used with a single cutting score, will inevitably favor the group with the higher mean on the predictor. And a shorter version will favor the group with the lower mean (Linn & Werts, 1971).

The statistical defense of a selection method as unbiased is valid only if the criterion is unbiased. At least in the U.S.A., the usual industrial tests are good at predicting end-of-training criteria, and rather poor at predicting job performance. One likely reason is that the training and the tests assessing success in training demand verbal abilities that the job does not require. Many persons who are slow to respond to verbal training might make entirely satisfactory workers if they were allowed extra training time or if the verbal aspects of the training were simplified, or replaced by concrete training methods. The demand for social justice and the need to increase the number of excellent workers both call for the invention of modes of training that make only slight verbal demands, wherever the job itself is not highly verbal.

INTERACTION OF APTITUDE AND TREATMENT

This last comment moves us from consideration of selection to consideration of classification. To use tests simply for selection is unimaginative. Our readiness to regard a test as valid if it predicts success makes the test an instrument of social conservatism. The test identifies persons who will perform well in the system as it now stands, but it discourages persons who could perform well if the system were modified.

In our preceding comment we have envisioned two training programs; one is more verbal, more abstract, faster-moving; the other concrete and slow-paced. With these options, the testing problem becomes one of deciding which educational or training program each man will best respond to. The tests pertinent to such a decision are very likely not the ones that have the greatest validity in selection.

To verify the relevance of a test for classification one must carry out a predictive study within each treatment, and plot the criterion-on-test regressions. If the regression lines cross, there is an interaction between the aptitude and the treatment method. While the statistical ideal calls for an experiment with random assignment of persons to treatments, this is often inappropriate. It would make little sense to assign verbally competent trainees to a low-verbal treatment merely for the sake of collecting evidence. Fortunately, methods are becoming available that allow plausible inferences about interactions from nonrandom experiments (Cronbach & Snow, 1972, Chap. 2).

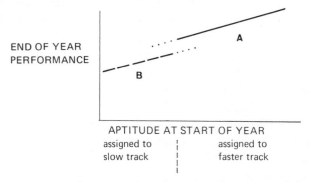

Figure 3a. Outcomes from screening when regressions are parallel

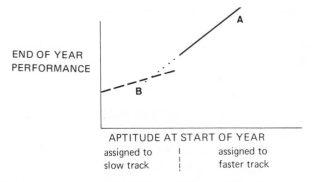

Figure 3b. Outcomes from screening when interaction is present

Pupils are often assigned to fast or slow streams on the basis of tests. An empirical defense of this requires a demonstration that the within-treatment regressions cross. When both groups are assessed on the same criterion one might find, not crossing, but a result such as appears in Figure 3a. This finding of parallel regressions implies that method B, used with the slow group, has no advantage; hence streaming is indefensible. In 3b, on the other hand, there is an interaction. Even though this test does not predict success in Treatment B well, there is a gain from streaming. The low scorers do better than they would in Treatment A. (Note that these results would suggest shifting the division point a bit to the left.)

Studies designed to detect interactions are needed whenever a school system attempts to serve a cultural group other than the group to whom the system was originally tailored. So far, no practically important interaction patterns have been thoroughly verified. Snow and I (1972, Chaps. 5-8) have tried to integrate the rather extensive literature, but the findings to date are conflicting and confusing.

Illustrations may be given of interactions that perhaps can be confirmed by further work.

General ability predicts success in most instruction, but it has little predictive value when the instruction relies on drill and reinforcement rather than meaning.

A work sample of ability to learn from films tends to predict success when instruction relies on visual demonstration, but it does not predict success when instruction is verbal.

The college student of independent character responds better to instruction that allows for much choice and self-direction. The docile student learns more from controlled, scheduled, monitored instruction.

Interactions of fluid and crystallized ability require study. There is especial need for invention of instructional methods that capitalize on fluid ability and depend little on crystallized verbal abilities. Traditional schooling serves best the pupils with high *v:ed* scores. The extensive research programs on culture-reduced, fluid-ability tests are incomplete and will remain so until treatments are invented in which the pupil with good fluid ability can do well if his *v:ed* abilities are low. Studies of response to alternative kinds of instruction have been sadly neglected in crosscultural research to date.

CONSTRUCT VALIDATION

Before leaving the topic of validation, mention should be made of two lines of work that are increasingly prominent in construct validation of theoretical interpretations (Cronbach, 1971).

It is useful to examine how test scores change under various experimental interventions. For example, Flavell and his colleagues (see Cronbach & Snow, 1972, Chap. 3) show that low scores of children on reasoning and classification tasks can often be raised by very simple orientation exercises that make clear to the child what is wanted. The child can solve much harder problems than he usually does, once the special introduction has cued him properly. Another kind of intervention goes a bit further and suggests an efficient strategy to the child. One can improve paired-associate learning, for example simply by advising the child to use mediation, i.e., to make up meaningful sentences combining the stimulus and response terms. Such prompting enables lower-class children to overtake middle-class children. Under ordinary conditions the latter have an advantage because they use mediation without prompting; this initial difference arises from a difference in strategy rather than from any true difference in ability to remember.

The valuable Campbell-Fiske paper (1959) provides a model for many current validation studies. You will recall that they described the multitrait-multimethod design, asking that the test under study be compared with three kinds of measures:

> Tests purporting to measure the *same trait*, by much the *same method* (Generalizability)
> Tests purporting to measure the *same trait* by a distinctly *different method* (Convergent validity)
> Tests purporting to measure *other traits* by much the *same method* (Discriminant validity)

To compare scores on operationally similar tests is to investigate generalizability; we return to that topic in a moment. To compare operationally different indicators thought to measure the same trait investigates convergent validity. When such indicators agree, the proposed interpretation is strongly supported. Thus Witkin reports that the Rod-and-Frame Test and the Embedded

Figures Test agree, as his theory of field differentiation requires.

The third step provides an important further control. Whenever a second trait can be mentioned as a plausible alternative interpretation for the test, an accepted measure of that trait ought to be included in any study. If the investigator's test diverges from the test representing a counterhypothesis, his view is sustained. Witkin made such a check, and showed that his tests diverge from conventional verbal tests. He failed, however, to check whether his tests diverge from established measures of *g*, or fluid ability. Embedded Figures correlates so strongly with Block Design and Matrices as to suggest to me that what Witkin calls 'field differentiation' is nothing but *g*, and he offers no evidence to dispel this criticism.

The typical crosscultural study compares groups on a single test. Such research will take on far greater significance if the future investigator carries along additional tests to represent the various rival interpretations for the test of central interest. Evidence on the convergence or divergence of these several indicators will raise the study from a descriptive one to one that can be given a theoretical interpretation.

GENERALIZABILITY

Generalizability theory is an extension and restatement of traditional reliability theory. An observed score is just one of a great number of observations, any one of which would be acceptable to the tester. The observation is a sample from a universe of admissible observations. The investigator would really like to know the person's universe score, i.e., the average the person would have over all test forms, examiners, etc. in the universe. The observed score is only a datum from which universe scores are inferred.

One gets better information about a person by regressing the observed score toward the mean of the person's cultural or subcultural group. The estimate very likely should be based on data in addition to the observed score. The theory therefore suggests making a multiple-regression estimate of the universe score.

Scale at age 7 and again at age 9. Subtest scores are recorded on the usual scale, which had a mean of 10 and an s.d. of 3 in the standardization group.

Ideally the Wechsler tester would like to obtain and interpret the universe score on each subtest.* Lacking that, he might use the observed score as if it were the universe score. Or he might make a simple regression estimate, or a multiple regression estimate.

Table 1. *Three estimators of the universe score on Comprehension*

Procedure	Formula	Root mean square error of estimate	Correlation with true value*
Unregressed	Est. = Comp.	2.25	0.63
Simple regression	Est. = 0.40 Comp. + 4.0	1.42	0.63
Multiple regression	Est. = 0.24 Comp. + 0.12 Arith. + 0.29 Vocab. + 0.12 Coding** + 2.23	1.07	0.82

* Analogous to square root of 'reliability coefficient'.
** Plus minor terms.

Table 1 gives three formulas for estimating the Comprehension score; these are derived form Osborne's 117 cases. It is evident that multiple regression is a powerful method, yielding a much improved estimate of the subtest score. Such improvement is likely whenever an observed score is somewhat unreliable. This technique is appropriate when scores of individuals are interpreted. It is unnecessary, however, when group means are interpreted as in Mittler's study (p. 341). In correlational research, an alternative technique should be used (Cronbach & Furby, 1970).

* The universe is conceived here as including all forms of the subtest and all occasions when a test might be given within a two-year interval. I.e., the investigator is interested in the standing of the subject over this period. Two occasions as a sample of a steady state have uncertain justification, as ability may be changing systematically over time.

The effect of multiple regression on profiles is striking. Consider this Wechsler profile:

	Inf	Com	Ari	Sim	Voc	DSp	PC	PA	BD	ObA	Cod
Mean of Osborne sample	11.6	11.0	11.2	11.8	11.6	10.9	10.9	11.5	10.9	11.0	11.7
Observed profile of one subject	10	6	6	10	10	10	12	7	10	7	6

One sees appreciable scatter. There are many differences within the profile that the psychologist would be tempted to interpret. When regression estimates are made, the profile changes to this:

$$9.2 \quad 7.9 \quad 9.9 \quad 10.0 \quad 8.4 \quad 10.2 \quad 10.3 \quad 8.6 \quad 9.3 \quad 8.9 \quad 8.2$$

The profile is very much flatter, because differences arising from errors of measurement are largely ironed out. The profile shape is changed in important ways: Arithmetic was low in the observed profile but there is no deficit in the estimated true profile; Picture Completion was distinctively high in the observed profile, but is only moderately high in the estimated true profile.

This procedure takes on even greater importance when one is dealing with persons from different subpopulations. Scores are regressed toward the subpopulation mean, hence two persons who have the same observed score are likely to have different estimated universe scores.

Our argument suggests that, for any construct, we get a better measure when we combine indicators than when we rely on a single operation to get the score. The procedure illustrated here is closely akin to that for estimating factor scores.

A good deal of exploration of details of the method will be needed before it can be widely used. Regression weights are undependable unless they are based on exceptionally large samples. It is uncertain whether regression equations ought to be calculated from current, local data, or should incorporate experience accumulated at other times and places. One could not have entertained the idea of multiple-regression estimates without computer scoring; as computer scoring technology becomes more widespread, the regression approach will merit attention.

Other features of generalizability theory have broad implications for mental testing. Our forthcoming monograph (Cronbach et al., 1972) may be consulted for details of the procedure and theory.

This paper has drawn attention to a variety of concepts and procedures, but through this variation runs an important unifying theme. Psychometrics has for too long been regarded as a set of routine statistical procedures, secondary to the scientific and practical aspects of test research. Any psychometric model, however, embodies a particular set of purposes or a particular scientific conception. Tradition sometimes leads an investigator to adopt a model or formula that does not truly fit his psychological problem; when he does so, his research is likely to ask the wrong question, or to reach an equivocal answer. The investigator who chooses a modern psychometric procedure that fits *his* purposes can expect to gain far more from his research effort.

REFERENCES

Campbell, D. T. & Fiske, D. W. (1959) Convergent and discriminant validation by the multitrait-multimethod matrix. *Psychol. Bull., 56,* 81-105.

Cronbach, L. J. (1970) *Essentials of psychological testing* (3rd ed.) New York: Harper and Row.

Cronbach, L. J. (1971) Test validation. In R. L. Thorndike (Ed.) *Educational measurement.* Washington, D.C.: Amer. Coun. on Educ. Pp. 443-507.

Cronbach, L. J. & Furby, L. (1970) How we should measure 'change' – or should we? *Psychol. Bull. 74,* 68-80.

Cronbach, L. J., Gleser, G. C., Nanda, N. & Rajaratnam. N. (1972) *The dependability of behavioral measurements: Theory of generalizability for scores and profiles.* New York: Wiley.

Cronbach, L. J. & Snow, R. E. (1972) *Aptitude and instructional methods. The search for interactions.* (In preparation).

Linn, R. L. & Werts, C. E. (1971) Considerations for studies of test bias. *J. educ. Measmt, 8,* 1- 4.

Stanley, J. C. (1971) Predicting college success of the educationally disadvantaged. *Science, 171,* 640-647.

Note: *Ortar expressed reservations about the use of absolute scales because teachers could too easily come to think that mental development is nothing but the mastery of the specific tasks chosen for tests, rather than acquisition of broad and transferable analytic skills of which a task such as bead stringing is one among many indicators. Cronbach accepted this characterization, and the risks of excessive operationalization. Analytic work with absolute scales, and planning of educational procedures, must use different models and different degrees of specificity. In this they are akin to molecular biology and public health – different in language, but mutually supporting.*

Irvine queried whether the technique that generated relatively flat Wechsler profiles was committed to emphasis on a predominant first factor. The answer was that Wechsler's tests provide little profile information; a more heterogeneous test could give a jagged profile under the new technique.

Levine wished to add a third variant to Figure 2, in which the leftmost regression line lies above the other one. The model acknowledges this possibility; Cronbach knows no data that take this form.

It was noted that recent and forthcoming work of Novick and Lindley on Bayesian methods extend the recommendations of the paper. (Eds.)

S. H. IRVINE and J. T. SANDERS   47
Brock University
University of Western Ontario

Logic, language and method in construct identification across cultures*

THE TACTICS OF CONSTRUCT MATCHING

By and large, the history of ability measurement and comparison across cultures has been one of unsuccessful attempts to compare 'similar' groups of people from different ethnic groups or 'different' subclassifications within the same ethnic group, on profiles derived from the 'same' tests. Attempts have been made to 'control' sample characteristic, while assuming that the test items have in fact tested the same things in the two different groups. Many studies have tried to match samples despite Biesheuvel's (1943) cautions as to the futility of such an attempt in a culture other than one's own. However, it was soon recognized that even if sample characteristics could be matched satisfactorily, some

* The authors acknowledge financial support for the preparation and presentation of this paper from the Canada Council and The Research and Development Fund, Althouse College, University of Western Ontario. They also thank Dr. Vincent D'Oyley of the Ontario Institute for Studies in Education, for the opportunity to present a draft of this paper to members of the Department of Educational Measurement and Evaluation. Ideas for this paper were formulated during the fall and winter of 1969-70, under the stimulus of the 1969 meeting of the British Association for the Advancement of Science, and the 1970 Kingston meeting of the Ontario Psychological Association. Much of the thought was initiated by the senior author as U.S. Public Health Service Visiting Scholar (1968-1969) at Educational Testing Service Princeton. He gratefully acknowledges the inspiration of his colleagues there.

tests measure different things from group to group or the same thing in a different way, and such tests were discarded as 'biased'.

Within cultures verbal tests have been much criticized because they appear to differentiate unfairly between socioeconomic groups. At one time it was proposed to 'reducing the culture loading' of the test, usually by reducing the verbal content and substituting some form of figural content. However, recent work (Irvine, 1969b) suggests that the Raven Matrices, the hardy annual of *g*-loaded tests, is highly susceptible to cultural influences. The cultural influences may be more difficult to identify, but they do exist. The results, particularly those showing cultural variation in item difficulties and individual variation in strategies of item solution, imply that the onus is on the experimenter to justify his tacit assumption that Test A is to Culture Group A as Test A is to Culture Group B.

Neither within nor across cultures have attempts to control the sample characteristics of the group, or to control the content of the test according to some assumption about functional relationship among test constructs, sufficed. One derives a set of numbers that seem to codify the interaction of a group of individuals within a set of stimuli; what the numbers mean remains to be determined.

THE LOGIC OF CONSTRUCTS

Few psychologists can resist the temptation to argue that a difference between means on a test of ability implies a difference in levels of a certain hypothetical construct the test is presumed to measure indirectly. The tendency is perhaps the direct outcome of the reliance of so much of measurement theory upon factor analysis. The logic behind the argument from operational mean differences to construct differences is that the test defines the construct to the satisfaction of the psychologist. In this context, for example, one might note how Witkin's construct of field dependence is now more often measured operationally by a paper-and-pencil Embedded Figures Test (EFT) than by the original Rod and Frame Test (RFT) which was used to generate the construct. Group means on EFT are offered as proof that groups differ in field dependence. Yet correlations between EFT and RFT in Western societies are often no greater than 0.50. Though this leaves 75 per cent of the variance unaccounted for, experimenters have been daring enough to take EFT into non-Western cultures as a measure of the construct. There is reason for unease over this kind of reasoning.

Royce's (1963) elegant essay on factors as theoretical constructs illustrates how persuasive our construct logic can become, but at the same time exposes its frailty when he illustrates that while matrix algebra may indeed 'identify' factors, their *functional* relationships are not at all deducible from the equations that identify them in the matrix. Investigators who compare group means on tests persistently endow these results with a functionalism that the original correlations do not justify. As soon as one implies association of the test with a construct by interpreting the 'levels of ability' of the groups, the construct is being used functionally to distinguish the two groups. The equation that will allow that construct to be used in such a way may not be available. Comparison of averages of tests that are supposed to 'tap' or 'represent' rather powerful explanatory concepts – Spearman's *g* or any current brand of intelligence: A or B of Hebb, C of Vernon (1967), or X of Irvine (1970), or any 'state' of intelligence crystallized or fluid (Cattell, 1963) – requires a great deal of caution across cultures and also within cultures.

We argue that if one wishes to use constructs to interpret the differences observed between the means of groups who interact with the same array of items, he makes several tacit assumptions:

> The test variance can be accounted for in each group by the same set of constructs.
>
> The same *number* of constructs will be required to account for all the variance in the test.
>
> The constructs in each group will be related to each other in the same way.

If one can satisfy these three assumptions, then discussion about 'levels of ability' or 'intelligence' in the context of traditional test theory might become fruitful. The first two conditions are necessary for *factorial invariance* of test content. The addition of the third gives rise to the notion of *construct congruence*. By this is implied that Royce's functional relationships are defined just as well as the factors are *identified*.

METHODOLOGICAL LIMITS TO SEMANTICS

Perhaps one can illustrate the problem involved by using the much-quoted studies by Lesser, Fifer and Clark (1965) and Stodolsky and Lesser (1968). These studies purport to show that the 'patterns' of abilities in children of Chinese, Jewish, Negro and Puerto Rican origin differ and that within the ethnic groups the 'levels' of abilities vary with SES, although the test mean profile for each SES level within each ethnic group remains the same. An examination of the correlations for the various ethnic groups, compared with the authors' estimates for the total group, yields the results in Table 1.

Table 1. Intercorrelations of tests for various ethnic groups (after Lesser, Fifer & Clark)

Tests	Population (estimate)	Chinese	Jewish	Negro	Puerto Rican
Verbal with Reasoning	.46	.42	.70*	.62	.62
Verbal with Number	.37	.38	.54	.58*	.58*
Verbal with Space	.32	.34	.48	.59*	.48
Reasoning with Number	.61	.64	.68	.71	.74
Reasoning with Space	.47	.64*	.49	.68*	.49
Number with Space	.35	.49	.40	.54*	.49

* Outside 95 per cent confidence limits for population estimate, $N = 80$ in each sample.

Seven of these correlations are above the 96 per cent confidence limits for samples from the population and four of the seven belong to the Negro sample. This result would make one hesitate to claim factorial invariance for the tests, or to apply to the Negro group the interpretations applying to the general population.

The measures do not appear to relate in the same way. If, as seems logical, test mean differences can be held to indicate differences at the construct level only when the three conditions have been satisfied, then the analysis-of-variance methods from which Lesser et al. assert differences in 'patterns' (a most unsatisfactory term) must be subject to some qualification. Only when the correlations suggest construct congruence (they will seldom prove it) can means be compared with any hope of legitimacy. Hence, when Lesser et al. assert that the tests do not relate together in the same way for different ethnic groups, they may be correct. But the comparison of means alone does not permit them to draw this conclusion. One might conclude, in fact, that as correlation patterns become more similar between ethnic groups, then it becomes more feasible to compare means. When the correlation patterns are different, interpretation of mean comparisons becomes very difficult indeed.

It becomes apparent, then, that when a writer speaks of 'patterns' of abilities, he is most often calling attention to one of two aspects of test results. He could be comparing two or more groups on the means of any number of tests and indicating that the differences between those means imply consistent differences in response to several arrays of items. Alternatively, he could be comparing the correlation matrices generated by a number of test scores from the same collection of items that constituted tests the different groups. Factorial invariance would probably produce the argument that the 'patterns' of abilities (in this sense the result of the application of matrix algebra to a correlation matrix) were similar. Previously, we asserted that means could not be compared nonoperationally unless the correlation matrices were examined at the same time.

Yet a third option, which is not the central concern of this paper, should be mentioned. 'Patterns' of abilities between groups have been traced, or suggested, when a number of measures have been regressed against a common criterion of success and the slopes of the regression lines compared. This technique has been used to examine the assumption that decision making procedures, based on the results of testing, are valid and fair for groups of different backgrounds. Admirable though this operationalism may be, one should point out, that the criterion now becomes the keystone of the argument, should one wish to press it into more than operational service. If this should happen it is subject to all the constraints already indicated which surround the meaning of constructs.

Yet it does not seem altogether impossible for future studies to be set up that at least recognize the differing emphases that these comparisons employ. Experimenters should now be self-consciously aware of the logical limits set by the techniques chosen. This paper has so far attempted to explore the limits of reasoning from two of these approaches — mean profiles and correlation matrix comparison. We now turn to empirical and theoretical examples of the consequences of observing those limits, in order to better interpret crosscultural data.

TEST BEHAVIOR AS A CLUE TO CONSTRUCT
IDENTIFICATION

So far we have voiced only the uneasiness experienced by many as they see tests, that are supposedly uncorrelated at the first order of factor analysis (a traditional transatlantic demand, ex-emplified, almost polarized by Guilford's work), undergoing mutation in subcultures and alien cultures. Such a logic of test selection makes very difficult the satisfaction of the three criteria of construct congruence. The search for construct validity has been overshadowed in recent years by the great stride forward in the technology of test administration in non-Western cultures. One has the feeling that in simply improving the test administration much may have been missed that would improve our insights into the functional linkages between constructs that were taken for granted.

In Nigeria, a reading test was administered to an extremely test-sophisticated group of fifth graders in the Kaduna-Zaria area ($N = 1095$, for the most part Hausa-Fulani).* Several items in the reading test had obvious informational content culture-specific to

---

* An evaluation study carried out on behalf of the Washington County Board of Education by Educational Testing Service in 1967.

North America. Nigerian responses to these items were predictably different from those of the original standardization group. One item, however, expected by us to present no great difficulty to the Nigerian children produced a response that was clearly culture-specific to the Hausa children (See Table 2).

Table 2.   *American and Nigerian responses to a reading test*

	Percentage of each sample giving response			
	1	2	3	
Sample	goat cow big	goat cow pig	boat cow dig	No response
American children, Grades 1 and 2	18	*58*	19	5
Nigerian children, Grade 5	12	27	*54*	7

These children, who were invariably Moslem, avoided the word *pig*. Their overwhelming endorsement of what was in the West an incorrect answer was indeed an ideological response, reflecting perhaps primary affect associated with early learning. No such ideology appeared to influence the responses in American Grades 1 and 2. But consider the WISC item that asks a child what he would do if he '. . . were sent to buy a loaf of bread and the grocer said he did not have any more.' This appears to take no account of what the consequence would be if the child had himself been taught to go to the only kosher grocery in the neighborhood; or if other groceries did not extend credit or encourage custom from minorities. Such a WISC item contains an implicit ideological component, and so do figural tests when standardized on the implicit assumption of mediation in English. Affect is one of the functional relationships of the nomological network of constructs that Royce illuminates for us.

The technology of testing African students, then, has raised logical problems concerning our use of theories, based on factor analysis, of what constitutes the domain of constructs with which it is appropriate to tackle problems in the measurement of intellect or intelligence. To explain the Nigerian children's answers, other factors or constructs would have to be introduced. One would have to say, following the logic of constructs, that those children who are high on ideological learning will get the answer 'wrong' and those who are low on ideological learning or conformity will get the item 'right'. The test constructor, seeking items that work, has little time to do other than discard those that do not, often without seeking reasons for the responses to the 'faulty' items. These responses are often among the most valuable theoretically since they represent, in communication terminology, the anti-environment to measurement theory. They show how the previous relevant experience of the respondents *overdetermines* their response to cognitive tasks. The study of 'faulty' test items becomes a check upon our assumptions about the nature of intellectual abilities and their possible relationships for any given cultural group. Perhaps one may be forgiven for speculating what our theoretical framework today would be like if all the 'faulty' items in test standardization procedures since Binet had been kept and then factor-analyzed.

One might surmise that the great issue in the theory of intellect would not be heredity-versus-environment, but perhaps the role of affect and feeling in determining what tasks are learned by each individual or group. The traditional division into cognition and affect, often polarized by varimax rotations of 'conglomerate' matrices, has perhaps systematically misled us in our quest for a better rationale within which to interpret group differences. The very technology of factor analysis has directed us largely into the pursuit of rather unprofitable hypotheses involving genetic and environmental differences in groups.

AFFECT AND COGNITION – A MULTIVARIATE EXAMPLE

The amount of work done on cognition in Africa is considerable. The amount of material on affect is negligible by comparison. Recent studies of secondary school graduates from a black elite group in Mashonaland, whose job aspirations were recorded and intercorrelated, gave an opportunity to explore avenues of liking or disliking for possible occupations (Irvine, 1969a). This study has been extended. Having identified the dimensions of as-piration by factor analysis, we could keep this factor structure (since we chose not to add other cognitive tests and re-factor) and calculate independent correlations of other nonaspirational variables (cognitive tests, education background of family, school subject biases) with the 8 factors.

The factors are labelled in Table 3 and the correlations with them are shown. Inspection of the table leads to the following broad conclusions:

> The number of correlations with the factors increases as the aspirations are related either to jobs that have arisen through cultural transposition or sex-role differentiation. Factors implying an emphasis on human relationships (political, social success motive, enterpreneur) show very little relationship to imported test measures or school or family background measures.

The political and entrepreneur factors bear an intriguing resem-blance to reported dimensions of tribal interaction (Irvine, 1969c) in which sociometric data yielded a dimension of ethnic identity, in which election to political office was the major item, and a dimension of social acceptance by peers where an in-dividual's success was measured by group approval. One is tempted to argue that this group of factors, having low correla-tion with imported Western tests, constitute a domain of affect with corresponding cognitive correlates that our present tests have been unable to measure. It would have been a mistake to isolate these factors as purely affective, without also asserting that to account for the performance on Western tests of the group of people identified by this aspiration factor pattern one might be required to posit first a functional relationship between the cognitive constructs and the affective domain. One might even venture to propose a causal framework.

Table 3. Correlations of cognitive, environmental and subject preference with primary aspiration factors (N= 324)

Variables	Primary aspiration factors							
	Teaching	High cognitive	Clerical	Adverse physical	Female preference	Entre-preneur	Political	Success motive
Primary sex loading	.71	.58	.24	.36 M	.70 F	—	.43	.44
Second-order loadings								
Cognitive	—	—	—	—	—	.59	.29	.48
Practical	—	—	—	.49	—			
Cognitive Measures								
Verbal analogies			-.17		-.13			
Reading	-.13		-.18		-.19			
Science information	.17	.20	-.30	.31	.31			
World information	.17		-.25	.34	-.43			-.20
Mechanical information	.12		-.15	.28	-.59	.12	-.12	-.13
Coding	-.16	.28	.17					
Embedded figures		.20						
Graph interpretation		.29			-.22	.12	-.16	
Name checking	-.21	.25		-.28		.13		
Table interpretation	-.21	.27						
Home background								
Father's occupation					.31			.13
Father's education				-.12				.13
Mother's education						-.19		
Subject preference								
Science bias	.19	.42	-.24	.37	-.40	.33	-.18	
Information bias		-.41	.13		.18			
Language bias			.14		.26			

A THEORETICAL ASSERTION – PRIMARY AND SECONDARY MODES

Having avoided a logical trap opened by the pursuit of con-structs, one still needs to justify the assertion that crosscultural work underlines the affect-cognition issue. One might proceed by pointing out that although Lévy-Bruhl's theory of primitive men-tality has been largely discounted, arguments for differences between groups in their 'approach to life', for example, are often advanced by different ethnic groups as evidence for their own uniqueness. It seems entirely plausible that if groups insist on differences in values, then this implies also differential emphasis upon the acquisition of skills. Whereas mankind's ability to adapt to almost every climate leaves little doubt that he will learn what he has to learn in order to survive, it is also a fact that he will sharpen specific skills in order to succeed better than his peers, within a socially sanctioned set of criteria for success. Society will value and devalue skills as they satisfy individual and group needs, which may be dictated by cultural, as well as biological, propensities. From this perspective, the word 'intelligence' is far more sensibly a cultural 'artefactor' than a derivation from matrix algebra. Whereas matrix algebra will identify a construct for us, it will not necessarily reveal the implicit substrates of cultural influence that have been subsumed by test standardiza-tion. For example, the standardization of so-called nonverbal tests of g assumes that the language of sub-vocalization or verbali-zation mediating test performance is the language of the test constructor and his standardization sample. When the language of the initial test-taker in another culture or subculture is from a different family of languages, this is often neglected in the interpretation of results.

Our concern is not simply for the logical consequences of encoding experience through languages that have different spe-cialized functions, appropriated through ecological reinforce-ment. The concomitant affective network that is established through learning in one's first language or sublanguage is of equal significance. Perhaps some examples might clarify the point. In Mashonaland, the Shona people have a rich heritage of sayings, omens, and beliefs governing conduct. From a number of these it was possible to deduce that children whose lives are built around the observance of them acquire a great fund of knowledge about the environment, much indeed of a sharply empirical nature. But a great deal of the knowledge implies an activity that might be termed 'associative-consequential' learning.

By this it is meant that the knowledge implies certain consequences in a special causal framework that relates through affect primarily to the kin group. Two of the sayings identify a cluster concerned with eating habits:

'Do not eat *guruumba* (small-winged flying termites): you might become deaf.'

'Do not eat the flesh or eggs of the nightjar; you may become habitually sleepy during the day.'

Knowledge of natural objects, animals, and insects clearly carries with it certain penalties. Such a system of causation is relatively unfamiliar to Western psychologists, but one should not label it pejoratively as superstition and leave it at that. Jahoda's (1968) most recent work on the persistence of what we call *associative-consequential learning* (i.e., learning that produces a classification of objects in terms of personal affective or physical consequences) even among science graduates from African universities, is too acute a reminder to allow us to neglect its heuristic implications for cognitive research.

Briefly, the argument, here and elsewhere (Irvine, 1969d, 1970) has been that early learning takes place essentially within a primary affective context and surely the steadfast legacy of Freudian theory is just that. Logical and formal operations emerge usually with adolescence. Our knowledge of what happens in this secondary mode of learning, through a kind of self-actualized logic, is limited. We suspect, from preliminary analysis of experiments conducted in Swaziland last year, that the averages of groups who are given the Raven Matrices by white testers are lower than the averages of those who are given it by black testers – even after re-testing. The key, the language of actual test instruction, must await further analysis.

Group differences in approach to reasoning tests are much more fruitfully observed at this point in our scientific development from assumptions of different values, affect, and language than from assumptions of different genetic interaction with environment. That assertion is not a specious argument invented to avoid the environment-heredity issue. That issue remains, but it must be carried beyond a theory of intellect that ignores affect as a mediator of cognitive structure. From this, we can then postulate that appreciable differences in cognitive test scores can be generated by creating positively reinforcing affective climates (see Schwarz (1963) on the 'climate' of testing). Second, we postulate that certain families of languages, through specialization that has occurred through the articulation of valued skills, will either be redundant or inhibitive for the learning of skills in other languages. Guthrie (1963) and Vandenberg (1959, 1967) already have provided examples to two 'verbal' families, one in English and the other in the vernacular language. This may be extended to dialects of a single language. (See Silvey, 1964, for an argument based upon Bernstein's notion of restricted and elaborated codes). Third, we postulate conflict in logical situations (for example if $A > B > C$ then $A > C$) when the ideology of primary thought process is threatened by acceptance of the argument, particularly when causation is involved. In such situations secondary learning would be under affective control from the primary mode of thought and we would posit different factorial dimensions according to anxiety or aggression levels. Fourth, group pressures toward the mode will tend to blunt individual differences when the secondary learning (particularly in schools) is not reinforced by the primary value system.

FROM TEST TO CONSTRUCT – TWO CHECKS

To establish these postulates in a theory of intellect that embraces affective and cognitive constructs in an interactive model is a technical task of some size. Nevertheless, to end this paper two insightful techniques are proposed that might help us clarify our thoughts about the limits of construct logic. These two suggestions use item-difficulty indices and item-test correlations. One of the simplest checks on the possibility that tests test different things in different cultures is to compare item difficulties by calculating the difficulty for each item of a single test in distinct groups within each culture. The difficulty values can be correlated, over items. Independent samples are necessary, of course. Table 4 gives an example. Item-difficulty intercorrelations are given for two black groups (*N* of each approximately 300 from a Nigerian Hausa-Fulani Grade-5 sample and two American groups (white Grade 1 and Grade 2) that constituted the original standardization sample for the test.

Table 4. Correlations of item difficulties from two Nigerian and two American groups (N = 50)

		Nigerian samples		American samples			
		1	2	1	2		
Nigerian	1	–	.96	.54	.59	}	average =
	2		–	.60	.65		0.60
American	1			–	.98		
	2				–		

N = 50 items

The correlations within ethnic groups are very high; within each culture the items have a nearly identical ordering on difficulty. But the crosscorrelations (average = 0.60) indicate that what was easy for white children was not necessarily easy for black children. Moreover, the confidence limits of the average crosscorrelations are exceeded by the within-group correlations. This seems to us to be an effective test for establishing that item difficulties across cultures are not the same as those within cultures. The null hypothesis would be rejected when the within-culture correlations come from the same population of correlations and all of these significantly exceed the average correlation across cultures. The implication of this finding for crosscultural test meaning is that many children scoring from zero up to around 50 per cent are earning the scores on different items in each culture group. This is perhaps a sobering thought for those who equate the names of omnibus reasoning tests with hypothetical constructs they are said to represent, and then interpret mean differences as differences in the level of these constructs. Indeed, one of the interesting empirical findings from comparison of the means of the Nigerian and American children on the same test was that the means were very similar. Nevertheless, if one tempted to interpret what these findings meant one would have to go much further in one's exploration of the comparability of the test-score meanings before these scores could be submitted to a *t* test. Such exploration would help define what differences on a *t* test would logically imply.

Item congruence. Assuming that one did find the result that we have illustrated above, namely that the item difficulties were distinctly different between two ethnic groups, one might then posit that the comparison of item difficulties raises the possibility of a different meaning for the test score. The model that we tentatively suggest below might lead to more detailed examination of items across cultures in order that one might get closer to the problems that we foresee.

Here is supposed an analysis of variance of a different family of item-indices where some previous tentative classification of items and marker tests have been made, presumably but not necessarily, of course, by correlation methods. As long as experimental independence of the rows of indices can be maintained through a sufficiently large initial sample, to permit random subdivision into smaller independent groups for the calculation of item indices, the analysis can proceed. This kind of analysis could take place both within and across cultures. Within cultures one might be able to examine the possibility of item congruence between socioeconomic groups or various other subclassifications of a given population, by comparing the results from two *separate* groups in a replication model. If the test items are given twice to the *same* group, and the first and second series of item indices are calculated with the external markers (or factor scores) with the groups for each row randomized on each occasion, one may get insights into the stability of test items under learning. Here a repeated-measure model is implied. The *crosscultural model* is identical for the two *separate* groups within a single culture. On all occasions interaction between replication and groups of items

Figure 1. Hypothetical model for item congruency

		Factor B Test items	Correlations (squared) with tests (or factor scores) considered to be stable factorially across groups		
			TA	TB	TZ
	Group 1	1 2 . . . N	R^2A	R^2B	R^2Z . . . . .
F a c t o r A	Group 2	1 2 . . . N	R^2A	R^2B	R^2Z . . . . .
	Group 3	1 2 . . . N	R^2A	R^2B	R^2Z . . . . .

This model implies two sources of variation: *Factor A,* between groups of items, and *Factor B,* between the tests or factor scores used to mark the construct. If one replicates *(Factor C)* the experiment with a separate group, either within or across cultures, then interactions are possible.

or replication and factor marker tests would give indication of item-construct instability. The model is recommended for trial. For all the labor of administering the measures to sufficient numbers of cases, the return in terms of insight into the behavior of specific items or groups of items may well be worth it.

The sources of variation that might be explored could also,

perhaps, be looked at from a null-hypothesis model. Assume an array of items homogeneous in difficulty and internally consistent that are validated against three factor-marker tests. The items could be randomly assigned to three groups, and correlations calculated with each of three marker tests. The null-hypothesis is, for any one sample of subjects, that there is only chance variation between groups of items (factor *A*) and also between marker tests (factor *B*). If one replicates the experiment with either (a) a separate group from the same culture, or (b) the same group, using only a *repetition of the original test* to generate a *second* set of correlations with the factor marker or (c) a separate group from *another* culture, one can look at interactions, since the replication of the experiment now becomes factor *C*. The null-hypothesis for two samples is that there is no difference between levels of *A*, *B* or *C*, nor are there interactions. This would place some confidence in the use of items across cultures.

One might gain considerable insight, however, should significant differences emerge. The following interpretations might accompany evidence of significant differences.

Factor A (between groups of items). The items do not behave consistently for the construct under examination. For this construct the grouping of items is not random. Had one hypothesized nonrandomness from a previous factor analysis of items and grouped them accordingly, one would expect the first factor-analytic finding to be confirmed by a difference in the levels of Factor A.

Factor B (between factor-marker tests). The factor-marker tests themselves are not consistent demonstrants of the construct if there are differences between the item indices for the various tests. This would raise the question of their use in factor-marker experiments in their present form.

Factor C (Differences between sets of indices generated from either (a) a different or (b) the same group). This would simply mean, *in conjunction with no significant differences in factor A or B*, that there was an average higher or lower correlation of the items with a marker tests. In short, for one group the items of the test were more closely identified with the theoretical construct than the other.

If interactions occur, they might tentatively be interpreted as follows:

$A \times B$ (Test items × marker tests). Neither the groups of items nor the factor marker tests show enough stability to merit much confidence in the intepretation of data for this test at the construct level for two different samples, since variations at one level are accompanied by variations at another.

$A \times C$ (Test items × replication). The test items, as they are grouped, generate consistently different correlations for each sample. This suggests that the items are not mediated by the two samples of respondents in the same way.

$B \times C$ (Marker tests × replication). The construct that the markers are said to represent operationally cannot be said to be represented in the same fashion by these markers for the two groups.

These two checks on the behavior of items in relation to their item difficulty and the factor markers that people use (one will recall how many times items and tests have been validated against the Stanford-Binet) have been made in attempt to alert test users and test constructors to check test behavior (which is the nearest datum in Royce's nomological net) with those measures that mark or demonstrate the construct (construct demonstrants). The ANOVA model, although open to refinement, at least offers checks on the variability of the test items and the construct demonstrants at one and the same time. It should indicate to the test user how secure the construct is and how consistently and under what conditions various items in the test he is examining relate to that construct. This kind of technology, it is argued, offers checks on the traditional construct logic that most of us employ. One feels certain that after going through these various operations the test user will be far more confident about the kind and nature of claims than he can make for any one test in any one culture.

The current view that new techniques and new methods are necessary for crosscultural research is implicitly shared in both parts of this paper. We have argued that our present factor-analytic model of cognition is insufficient, and that the nature-nurture controversy has been magnified out of all proportion by nonadherence to the logical limits of this model. By observing these limits we offer a rationalization that sees differential values as modal modifiers of cognition across cultures. In this we distinguish primary and secondary modes of thought. Formal operations are regarded essentially as a function of secondary mode learning under affective influence.

Our technical suggestions for insightful exploration of crosscultural test data center around the comparison of item difficulties and of item-external test correlations in a special analysis of variance design.

REFERENCES

Biesheuvel, S. (1943) *African intelligence.* Johannesburg: South Afr. Inst. for Race Relations.

Cattell, R. B. (1963) Theory of fluid and crystallized intelligence: A critical experiment. *J. educ. Psychol., 54,* 1-22.

Guthrie, G. M. (1963) Structure of abilities in a non-western culture. *J. educ. Psychol., 2,* 94.

Irvine, S. H. (1969a) The dimensions of vocational preference and prestige in an African elite group. In J. A. Lauwerys & D. G. Scanlon (Eds.), *The year book of education.* London: Evans. Pp. 319-332.

Irvine, S. H. (1969b) Figural tests of reasoning in Africa. *Intern. J. Psychol., 4,* 217-228.

Irvine, S. H. (1969c) Degrees and dimensions of social interaction in tribal grouping. *Intern. J. Psychol., 4,* 27-38.

Irvine, S. H. (1969d) Contributions of ability and attainment in Africa to a general theory of intellect. *J. biosoc. Sci., 1,* 91-102.

Irvine, S. H. (1970) Affect and construct: A cross-cultural check on theories of intelligence. *J. soc. Psychol., 80,* 23-30.

Jahoda, G. (1968) Scientific training and the persistence of traditional beliefs among West African university students. *Nature, 220,* 1356.

Lesser, G. S., Fifer, G., & Clark, D. H. (1965) Mental abilities of children from different social-class and cultural groups. *Child Develpm. Monogr., 30,* No. 4.

Royce, J. R. (1963) Factors as theoretical constructs. *Amer. Psychologist,* *18,* 522-538.

Schwarz, P. (1963) Adapting tests to the cultural setting. *Educ. psychol.* *Measmt., 23,* 673-686.

Silvey, J. (1964) Formal and informal learning in a second language. *Proc.* *East Afr. Acad., 1,* 57-63.

Stodolsky, S. S., & Lesser, G. S. (1968) Learning patterns in the disadvantaged. *Harvard educ. Rev., 38,* 546.

Vandenberg, S. (1959) The primary mental abilities of Chinese students. *Ann. N.Y. Acad. Sci., 79,* 257.

Vandenberg, S. (1967) The primary mental abilities of South American students. *Multiv. behav. Res., 2,* 175.

Vernon, P. E. (1967) Development of current ideas about intelligence tests. *Proc. Eugenics Soc. Conf.,* London.

HENK VAN DER FLIER

Free University of Amsterdam

Evaluating environmental influences on test scores

This paper discusses some theoretical problems in the evaluation of the culture-reduced character of a test. We encountered these problems in an attempt to develop a number of intelligence tests intended to be used as the nonspecific part of test programs for educational and industrial purposes in Surinam (Latin America). Surinam has a multiracial society. The groups vary greatly in the degree to which the members have maintained their traditional cultural environment, or have adopted a more Western way of life.

There are two major problems in using test scores for the allocation of jobs and of places in the educational system; the first is to prevent the selection from being biased against particular ethnic groups, and the second is to prevent it from being biased by intragroup differences. The application of separate norms for different ethnic groups solves the first but not the second problem; since environmental factors vary within these groups, selection may still be biased against certain subgroups. Moreover, one cannot be sure that such an approach will always be acceptable to the institutions involved, since its fairness may be more obvious to psychologists than to others. It was, then, necessary for us to look for relatively unbiased or culture-reduced tests in order to reduce the second kind of bias.

A comparison on formal characteristics such as the form of score distributions and the order of item difficulties can provide some information about the applicability of a test to different cultural groups. But when the culture-reduced character of a test has to be evaluated it is necessary to define what it is supposed to measure, and – equally important – what it is supposed not to measure.

In our discussion we shall speak about 'intelligence' as a concept that covers those mental abilities that predict success in more-or-less Western institutions. Of course one might prefer to use a less restricted definition, stressing the cultural specificity of intelligence and intelligent behavior, considering our concept to be something like 'adaptability'. But since the use of psychological tests for selection purposes in developing countries is mainly restricted to Westernized institutions like education, industry, and the army, there seems not to be much reason to use other definitions of 'intelligence' in discussing the cultural bias in selection. This does not imply however that always the same abilities are essential for a successful performance. Adaptation of an institution to a specific cultural environment in which some abilities are more strongly emphasized than others will bring about important changes in the relative importance of these.

Our definition allows for a certain influence of environmental factors on intelligence. To evaluate the culture-reduced character of a test we have to specify what kind of environmental influence on test scores is considered to be bias. The problem can be phrased thus: 'Reduced as to what influence? ' All intelligence tests depend on a number of skills that they do not intend to measure. Some of these skills will be mainly physiologically determined, like being capable of taking in oral instructions and of discriminating between colors. Others will be more strongly influenced by cultural and environmental variables, e.g., being able to use a pencil, comprehending the instruction, knowing how to work with numbers. In order to be able to draw conclusions about the capacities of examinees from their test scores, the test constructor has to make sure that (or to assume that) these skills are overlearned to such a degree that they do not produce substantial variance in test scores.

The influence of skill differences can be reduced in 3 ways: The first is to reduce the skill differences themselves by expanding the instructions and adding more practice items. (This does not apply to skills that take a long time to acquire, or to physiologically determined skills). The second is to restrict the interpretation of test scores to a selected part of the population. For instance, if the solution of test problems requires skills like discrimination between colors and knowledge of numbers, then a test for color-blindness and a number test can be used to identify the group in which no inferences from test scores may be drawn. Since in developing countries the size of this group will be relatively large, this method can only offer a partial solution. Sometimes the population to be tested will be restricted in such a way that one can assume certain skills to be overlearned. Thus, in testing sixth graders, there will generally be no need to select them in advance on skills which are relevant in schoolwork. In Western societies the educational system usually justifies assumptions like this, but in developing countries one can expect more variance in skill.

A third way to reduce the influence of skill differences on test scores is to develop a skill-reduced test. This applies to physiologically determined and to culturally determined skills; the Snijders-Oomen nonverbal test for hearing and deaf, and Ord's adaptation of Kohs' blocks can both be taken as examples. While we restrict ourselves to culture-reduced tests, the same sort of reasoning can be used with other skill-reduced tests as well.

In producing a culture-reduced test the objective is to reduce the number and level of culturally determined skills required to solve the test problem. This, like the extension of instruction and practice, can be seen as a way to enlarge the group in which inferences can be drawn from test scores. According to this line of reasoning it is not essential for a culture-reduced test to give similar score distributions in different cultural groups. Not every cultural environment will be equally effective in the fostering of 'intelligence' as defined above. The only condition for a completely culture-reduced test is that it not reflect *skill differences* determined by cultural factors.

It is possible to restrict this requirement to differences in skill between two or more cultural groups, and to call the tests that meet these requirements 'culture-fair'. If one can apply it to all culturally determined skills, then one might use the term 'culture-free'. It is more realistic, however, to assume that not all relevant skill differences can be detected, and to evaluate the culture-reduced character of a test in terms of a specified set of skills, or a finite number of environmental factors.

Two ways of doing this will be mentioned, the first construct-centered, the second criterion-centered. Although 'skill' is a construct and accordingly seems to fit best into the construct-centered orientation, it is very difficult to develop a meaningful skill index in this way. A construct cannot be measured directly. In order to find an index that reflects the degree to which, because of particular environmental influences, a test does *not* measure the intended skill-free construct, one has to specify in advance the degree to which the construct depends on environmental variables. Psychological theory generally does not provide the information necessary for making quantitative statements about constructs.

Of course we could define the construct we wish to measure as one completely independent of environmental variables, but this would depart from the original definition of 'intelligence' as including environmental influence, nor could this be done with terms like 'aptitude', as astitude need not be statistically independent from environmental variables either.

A 'negative' definition of the construct in terms of independence from a number of specific skill tests, reflecting aspects of the test procedure that should not produce substantial variance, does not solve the problem either. Such an approach would again imply that the construct has to be independent from environmental factors that produce variance in the predictor and skill tests.

A criterion-centered approach to the evaluation of the culture-reduced character of a test likewise requires some kind of measure of environmental factors that are important for the acquisition of the relevant skills. (Of course skill tests may be used.) This time one starts from a measurable criterion instead of a hypothetical construct. Since the major objective of the test is to predict this criterion as well as possible, the influence of environmental factors on test scores is unwanted only to the extent to which it reduces the correlation with the criterion.

The unwanted skill variance might accordingly be defined as that part of the environmental variance in the test which does not reflect the criterion. In order to isolate this part, one has to split up the predictor variance V_p, the criterion variance V_c and the variance of the measure of environmental factors V_o into a number of independent components:

$$V_p = V_x + V_{o1} + V_{o2} + V_{e1}$$
$$V_c = V_y + V_{o1} + V_{o3} + V_{e2}$$
$$V_o = V_{o1} + V_{o2} + V_{o3} + V_{o4} + V_{e3}$$

In this model, V_x and V_y indicate those parts of reliable predictor and criterion variance that are independent of environmental factors. Generally they will be interrelated. The environmental variance (V_o) is divided into

V_{o1} the part associated with the predictor and the criterion.

V_{o2} the part associated with the predictor only.

V_{o3} the part associated with the criterion only.

V_{o4} the part of reliable environmental variance that is independent of the predictor *and* the criterion.

V_{e1}, V_{e2} and V_{e3} indicate the error variance of the predictor, the criterion, and the environmental scores.

It will be clear that in the criterion-centered approach only V_{o2} (the part of environmental variance in the predictor which does not reflect the criterion) can be considered skill variance. As a skill index the ratio of V_{o2} to the total reliable test-variance – i.e. $V_{o2}/(1 - V_{e1})$ – can be used. This reflects the degree to which the test measures something other than the criterion, as a result of the measured environmental differences. This approach, however, is not without serious difficulties.

Even when their reliabilities are known, the scores on the predictor (p), the criterion (c), and the environmental measure (o) do not provide sufficient information to yield unbiased estimates of the variance components, since the number of independent components (or factors) to be distinguished exceeds the number of known variables. It is not difficult to derive from the inter-correlations of the three variables the part correlation between the predictor and the environmental measure, in which the criterion is partialed only out of the environmental measure. But to interpret the square of this coefficient as the part V_{o2} takes from the total test variance would be questionable. The part correlation can be seen only as an imperfect (and inverse) indicator of skill reduction.

This implies that in comparing different tests, or different versions of the same test, it will be necessary to make certain restrictions. One of these follows directly from the operational way in which we have used the term 'culture-reduced' – that comparisons can only be made with regard to the same criterion, and the same set of environmental measures. This means that the correlation between the criterion and the environmental measure (and consequently $V_{o1} + V_{o3}$) is kept constant across different tests. A second difficulty is that this approach assumes linear and homoscedastic relations between the predictor, the criterion, and the environmental measure. This may not always be realistic; especially when dealing with skills, one has to take seriously the possibility that environmental factors will act like 'threshold variables'.

If we are using environmental ratings or general indications of skill level to derive a skill index, it gives no direct suggestion for improvement of the test. To get this kind of information one will have to construct a number of skill tests closely corresponding to specific parts of the test procedure. Now the test-criterion correlation is kept constant across different skill tests, and the part correlations of the same test with different skill tests have to be compared. This second procedure will of course be less effective in comparing the skill-reduced character of different tests.

State University of Utrecht

Applicability of the Rasch model in two cultures

When psychological tests are used, the performance of a subject is usually compared with the performance of a specified population. (For example, 'the score of a subject is at the 60th percentile' or 'is one s.d. above the mean'). Difficulty indices of items vary with the average capacity of the persons tested. In the Rasch model, however, it is possible to estimate the ability level of the subject with respect to a certain domain of content using any set of items of that domain, and to estimate the level of item difficulty without reference to the particular subjects who take the test.

DESCRIPTION OF THE MODEL

Following Rasch (1960), we adopt the following model: N subjects have responded to k items of a test. The score of subject v on item i is denoted by s_{vi}. Each of the items is scored right or wrong ($s_{vi} = 1$ or 0). The probability that subject v gives a correct answer to item i can be written as a function of a variable e_{vi} (where $e_{vi} > 0$):

$$P(s_{vi} = 1) = \frac{e_{vi}}{1 + e_{vi}} \qquad (1)$$

Every subject is characterized by a parameter c for his ability and every item by a parameter d for its difficulty. It is assumed that e_{vi} can be written as

$$e_{vi} = c_v d_i \tag{2}$$

From (1) follows that the difficulty parameter *decreases* with *difficulty* and *increases* with *ease* of the items.

From (2) it is obvious that the model, just like the 'one factor model' used in factor analysis, is only useful for homogeneous tests.* Since only one item parameter ('difficulty') is used, the model will probably be most applicable if the items have about equal discrimination indices and are not strongly influenced by guessing.

Substituting (2) into (1) gives

$$P(s_{vi} = 1) = \frac{c_v d_i}{1 + c_v d_i} \tag{3}$$

In addition, it is assumed that a subject's scores on items i and j are independently distributed and a function of the item parameters:

$$P(s_{vi} = 1, s_{vj} = 1) = \{P(s_{vi} = 1)\} \ \{P(s_{vj} = 1)\} \tag{4}$$

Now, let two items i and j be given and let $P\{s_{vi} = 1 \mid (s_{vi} + s_{vj} = 1)\}$ denote when the conditional probability that subject v answers item i correctly when the sum of his scores for items i and j is equal to 1. From the assumption given above, it can then be shown that

$$P\{s_{vi} = 1 \mid (s_{vi} + s_{vj} = 1)\} = \frac{P(s_{vi} = 1, s_{vj} = 0)}{P(s_{vi} + s_{vj} = 1)} = \frac{d_i}{d_i + d_j} \tag{5}$$

In (5) the subject parameter c_v has been eliminated.

Let us suppose the two items i and j are administered to N subjects: N_1 is the number of persons answering just one of the two correctly. The probability that a of these N_1 subjects answer item i correctly (and thus answer item j incorrectly) is given by the binomial distribution:

$$\binom{N_1}{a} \left(\frac{d_i}{d_i + d_j}\right)^a \left(\frac{d_j}{d_i + d_j}\right)^{N_1 - a} \tag{6}$$

* A generalized model has been developed which makes it possible to analyse tests in terms of more than one parameter (factor) per test.

For the parameter $d_i/(d_i + d_j)$ of this binomial distribution, the maximum likelihood estimate is a/N_1. This estimate can be made in any group of subjects, whatever the distribution of the Ir ability.

Rasch (1960) has extended the model to consider k items simultaneously.

In a previous investigation, an achievement test in mathematics was administered to two groups of Dutch students differing greatly in ability. The model appeared to fit the data in each group separately, and the estimates of the d_i turned out to be very similar in both groups.

TESTING THE APPLICABILITY OF THE MODEL

The present project will investigate the applicability of the model in different cultures. The rationale for this project is that — if the model applies — the estimates of the parameters, derived separately from groups in different cultures, should be approximately the same. It is our intention to carry out a series of analyses of the model in different groups and with different tests. For each test the fit of the model to the data in different cultures will be examined. Tests for which the model holds within cultures will be selected for further analysis. For these tests estimates of item parameters derived separately from groups of different cultures will be compared. Further, the distribution of subject parameters in the different cultures will be compared.

For this investigation use can be made of data which will be gathered by the Psychology Department of the Free University of Amsterdam under Professor Drenth. This department is co-operating with the University of Bandung in adapting a battery of Dutch intelligence and achievement tests to Indonesia. In a tryout, the tests have been administered in February and March 1971 at several schools in Indonesia. The final collection of the data will be done early in 1972.

At the moment we can present only some results for an achievement test in mathematics. This test consists of 40 multiple-choice items with four options; this test has been administered to a group of Dutch pupils in Grade 7. The items were translated by an Indonesian teacher of mathematics. According to his judgment some items could not be used in Indonesia because the subject matter of these items was taught there. The translated version of the test consists of 35 items and has been administered to 329 pupils in Grade 9 of three schools in Java. It was supposed by the Indonesian school administration that these schools differ strongly with respect to the ability level of their pupils and the kind of instruction. For this reason a rather heterogeneous group of 369 Dutch pupils was chosen from the cases available. The sample was taken from schools drawing pupils from different ability levels, who had different kinds of instruction in mathematics.

For each group the mean, s.d., and KR20 reliability were calculated (Table 1).

Table 1. Statistics for the original and the selected sets of items in Dutch and Indonesian samples

	Original 35 items		Selected 22 items	
	Holland	Indonesia	Holland	Indonesia
Number of subjects	369	329	369	329
Mean score	18.23	14.88	13.85	10.69
s.d.	. 6.08	4.85	3.92	3.25
KR20 reliability	.82	.72	.73	.60

In each group separately the fit of the model for the total test was examined by the procedure of Wright and Panchapakesan (1969). The model *dit not* fit the data either in the Dutch group or in the Indonesian group. Especially for the Dutch group this fact is remarkable, because in a previous investigation the model appeared to hold in two different groups for a similar test of mathematics. We thought that in the present case two reasons might be important. Some items probably were badly constructed. Second the content of some items had not been treated in all schools. Due to a change in the school-system, many Dutch schools did not complete the whole curriculum.

It was decided to eliminate a number of items and to test the fit of the model in a subject of the items. First, an expert on teaching methods of mathematics in the Netherlands (who had written the items originally) was asked which items had not been treated in all Dutch schools; these items were eliminated. Second, use was made of item-analysis data for a new group of Dutch pupils from schools with a rather low ability level. Items answered correctly by fewer than 25 per cent of these pupils were also eliminated. Altogether 13 items were eliminated.

For the test composed of the remaining 22 items the mean, s.d. and KR20 reliability were computed (Table 1). Again the model *did not* fit the data either in the Dutch group or in the Indonesian group. Then it was examined which items did not fit at the 5 per cent level. In each group we found four items which did not fit the model at this significance level; the two sets of four had three items in common.

The Rasch model is probably not very appropriate for achievement tests where items are very dependent on the curriculum. In the Dutch group the model failed, while in a previous investigation the model appeared to hold for a similar test in two Dutch groups. A possible explanation is that there has been a substantial change in the curriculum of the Dutch schools during the last year. Many schools did not treat all topics of the curriculum. Items on topics not treated will test intelligence and not educational achievement; maybe a new factor — intelligence — has been introduced in the test by these items. When continuing the investigation a test of mathematics has to be carefully constructed: it should only contain well-constructed items about topics that will be treated in all types of schools in the Netherlands and Indonesia. Besides the test of mathematics we will also consider some intelligence tests in this investigation.

REFERENCES

Rasch, G. *Probabilistic models for some intelligence and attainment tests.* Kopenhagen: Pädagogisches Institut, 1960.
Wright, B. & Panchapakesan, N. A procedure for sample-free item analysis. *Educ. psychol. Measmt.*, 1969, 29, 23-48.

L. HÜRSCH
University of Bern

Cultural influence on the development of Number and Flexibility-of-closure factors

Factor analysis splits the variance of measures (or the reliable variance, or the shared variance) into linearly independent parts. Spearman tried to prove his general-factor theory by this method, but the usual correlation matrix is not one-dimensional. The number of factors reported has increased with the number of publications on factor analysis. The more variables analyzed simultaneously, the more factors found. Guilford developed a classification model in which tests are classified according to 5 kinds of operations, 6 kinds of products, and 4 kinds of contents, to imply 120 factors. In this structure common factors among tasks are thought to arise from similarities between problems, and hence between test achievements. This is not necessarily the only possible basis for classification. To defend it one would have to show why similar problems measure the same attribute, moreover, the conditions or processes leading to these achievements should be identified.

Differences in áchievement within a tested population are due to
a) the differences in aptitude and knowledge of the Ss;
b) the change in experimental situations from S to S. For instance, perhaps not all Ss have the same experimenter; and experimenters may introduce the test items in different ways.
c) Ss' attitudes towards the test. This depends on S's personality, experience, and cultural background, as well as upon his reaction to the test situation.
The achievement of the same S on two tests will (save for

random error) be identical if the tests are ideally parallel forms and (b) and (c) have no influence on the performance. Then the tests would covary up to the limit of their reliability and would show the same loadings on all factors. If, on the other hand, the tests measure entirely different attributes, they will not covary. A factor that loads in the first test may not load in the second. (This assumes that (b) and (c) have no influence. Only in that case can factors be explained solely by examining the content of test items).

As soon as there are covariances due to the objective situation (b) or attitude (c), the interpretation must take into account the behavior of the experimenter, and S's personality. Interpretations of this kind ought to be verified experimentally. This can be done by using a design which allows one to factor-analyze two different correlation matrices calculated from the same results of the same Ss. Attitude and objective situation ought not to be allowed to covary for the computation of the first kind of correlation; but they would be left free to covary for the computation of the second kind of correlation. The differences in factor patterns are to be used as a basis for interpretation of factors.

ANALYSIS OF TEST DATA COLLECTED UNDER EXPERI- MENTALLY VARIED CONDITIONS

The objective experimental situation cannot be a source of variance of all Ss take all tests under identical conditions. But differences will arise because of the fact that some Ss respond well to this condition and others do not. To cause such differences to vanish, conditions must be chosen for the individual S to suit his personality structure. Hence exactly the opposite of the objective experimental situation must be arranged (however impossible this may seem). The objective situation has to be varied in accord with the personality structure, so that differences in subjective attitude vanish. It is very hard to eliminate variance arising from attitude and personality by an experimental treatment, but one can imagine experiments that eliminate covariance

from this source. If the objective situation varies strictly randomly, error variance will be larger; but covariance will not be
increased. Furthermore, varying these aspects of the test situation
will cause reactions of *S*s to vary. Since personality types are
randomly distributed over conditions, the covariances relating
situation to attitude disappear.

Factor structures may be derived from the design with varying
objective test situations (and hence varying subjective attitudes),
and compared with structures derived where the objective situation is held constant. Then attitudes covary. It is not necessary to conduct a second experiment for this second factor
analysis. It is enough to compute the variance not influenced by
the changing objective situation and use it in place of the total
variance.

We obtained such a comparison of factor structures (Hürsch,
1970) by having 225 15-year-olds take 12 intelligence tests. We
altered the behavior of the experimenter (two levels, stern vs.
supportive), the reward for the number of correct answers (two
levels), and the difficulty of the introductory examples (three
levels). 12 different experimental situations resulted. *S* was confronted in each of the 12 tests with another of the 12 experimental situations. The sequence of situations was altered for every *S*
according to a random pattern, a sort of Latin square. This
eliminates covariance of tests arising from the behavior of the
experimenter, the reward, and the difficulty of the introductory
examples. We compared this factor analysis (FA 1, Table 1) with
a second (FA 2). In the scores for FA 2 there was no variance
associated with experimental conditions. Attitudes toward
achievement may covary. In both analyses we used the principal-
components method, the χ^2 test of Lawley, and Varimax rotation. The comparison showed marked differences.

Two of the six significant factors of FA 1 split in FA 2; tests for
which there was a large main effect for experimenter loaded
exclusively in the new split factors. In Number Analogies the
more severe experimenter produced higher scores. This test defined a new seventh factor, split from the numerical factor. In
Mutilated Words the 'nice' experimenter produced higher scores
(the difference being barely significant). This test defined a

Table 1. Factor matrix for the whole sample (FA1, 6 factors, N = 225)

	Numerisch/Schulisch Number	Ganzheit Speed of closure	Flüssigkeit Fluency	Komplexität General reasoning	Plastizität II Flexibility of closure II	Plastizität I Flexibility of closure I
Number operations	.86	−.12	.10	.08	.17	.12
Mutilated words	.06	.81	.08	−.07	.10	.25
Cattell sketches	−.07	.14	.84	.08	.21	.08
Number series	.48	.21	.00	.52	.25	.26
Food anagrams	.29	.18	.21	.04	.82	−.04
Street Gestalt	−.10	.79	.26	.19	.05	.05
Number analogies	.47	.16	.08	.54	.01	.38
Cattell words	.21	.18	.84	.04	.06	.14
Gottschaldt figures	.05	.20	.24	.07	.03	.84
Syllogisms	.05	.00	.08	.91	.12	.09
Domino	.34	.15	−.02	.26	.14	.68
Number blocks	−.01	−.03	.15	.33	.66	.46

The table header spans: *Factor, with identifications after Meili and Thurstone*

factor split off from Ganzheit (Meili, 1946; comparable with Speed of Closure — Thurstone, 1944). The remaining tests showed no significant effects of the experimenter and no marked differences in factor structure. Thus, if differences in Ss' attitudes covary, additional factors appear. Partial samples chosen according to type of school or sex showed almost the same factor structure as the total sample in FA 1 as long as the attitude toward the test situation could not covary.

AN INVESTIGATION WITH SELECTED CASES

Varying only three conditions (difficulty of introductory examples, reward, and behavior of experimenter) may not be enough to make all covariances caused by personality to vanish. Interdependence of tests caused by cultural or other lasting environmental influences are difficult to eliminate by variations of experimental conditions.

Kogan & Wallach (1964), using the AAS questionnaire (Alpert & Haber, 1960) 'for anxiety in academic achievement situations', selected extreme groups. The correlations of numerical and verbal tests were especially likely to differ from one group to the other. This investigation implies that Ss do not all show the same dependence in both kinds of achievements. School anxiety has a similar effect on achievement for only a part of the Ss, thereby creating a covariance. In order to obtain a factor matrix independent of anxiety we have to eliminate Ss of the first kind from our sample.

We translated the AAS questionnaire into German and altered it to fit 15-year-old Swiss students. The questionnaire has two scales. The Debilitating Anxiety scale consists of 10 questions related to inhibition by test anxiety; the Facilitating Anxiety scale contains 9 questions on stimulating effects. Each question could be answered 'always', 'sometimes', 'rarely', or 'never'. If S reported himself inhibited by anxiety, he was given 1 or 2 negative marks, otherwise positive marks. Answers related to stimulation were rated similarly. The two scales correlated 0.35, the means being approximately zero. We advanced the hypothesis that Ss with the same score in both scales will react similarly to examination situations. Ss for whom the two scores are discrepant presumably are without a consistent reaction to situations of this kind, or to tests; they do not have reliable judgments of themselves and hence obtain contradictory results.

We averaged the two scales, standardized the resulting mean, and chose Ss for whom this standardized score was in the range −.675 to +.675. The 108 Ss selected have a negative correlation between the two scales, i.e., they gave inconsistent reports of their frequency of anxiety towards examinations. If our hypothesis is correct they should react randomly to tests related to school. Factor analysis of this partial sample (FA 3) yielded only five significant factors ($P <$ .05 – only four at $P <$ .001). We conclude that part of the covariance which caused a splitting of factors in FA 1 vanished when the partial sample was used.

Table 2.   Factor matrix for the selected subsample (FA3, 5 factors,
N = 108)

	Factor, with identifications after Meili and Thurstone				
	Ganzheit Speed of closure	*Flüssigkeit* Fluency	*Plastizität* II Flexibility of closure II	*Plastizität* I Flexibility of closure I	*Komplexität* General reasoning
Number operations	−.58	.20	.37	.15	.43
Mutilated words	.61	.30	−.04	.06	.44
Cattell sketches	.06	.85	−.01	.16	.13
Number series	.06	.09	.82	.14	.18
Food anagrams	.01	.42	.18	.72	.01
Street Gestalt	.77	.29	.15	.07	.08
Number analogies	−.06	.11	.78	−.00	.27
Cattell words	.30	.82	.09	.12	.01
Gottschaldt figures	.24	.06	.25	.28	.73
Syllogisms	.07	.10	.77	.34	−.12
Domino	−.07	.04	.61	.10	.53
Number blocks	.02	.06	.19	.79	.36

The varimax rotation with 5 factors appears in Table 2. The
Number factor vanished and all tests which originally had load-
ings on the Number factor now had a higher loading on General
Reasoning. The reference test for the Number factor had a higher
negative loading on Speed of Closure and on Flexibility of
Closure. Therefore the Number factor is split off mainly from
General Reasoning.

Flexibility-of-Closure II vanishes from the analysis with four
factors. Food Anagrams, a verbal reference test for Flexibility II,
loads on Fluency in the four-factor result. The test Number Blocks
also has a significant loading on Fluency, but an even higher one on
Flexibility. The remaining factors are unchanged.

Table 3. Second factor matrix for the selected subsample (FA3,
*   4 factors, N = 108)*

	Factor, with identifications after Meili and Thurstone			
	Ganzheit Speed of closure	*Flüssigkeit* Fluency	*Plastizität* Flexibility of closure	*Komplexität* General reasoning
Number operations	−.42	.18	.50	.38
Mutilated words	.72	.21	.27	−.03
Cattell sketches	.17	.82	.13	−.01
Number series	.10	.11	.18	.83
Food anagrams	.03	.64	.37	.19
Street Gestalt	.77	.26	−.04	.15
Number analogies	.03	.06	.19	.79
Cattell words	.37	.79	−.03	.08
Gottschaldt figures	.41	.02	.69	.27
Syllogisms	−.02	.06	.07	.78
Domino	.08	−.01	.47	.63
Number blocks	.03	.27	.72	.21

As we used a χ^2-test to determine the number of significant factors – a test virtually independent of the number of Ss – the reduced number of significant factors cannot be a statistical artifact only. We remarked above that partial samples consisting of boys, girls, grade-school or high-school students had the same factor structure as the total sample of FA 1. The lesser degree of splitting in FA 3 is therefore not a necessary effect of using a more limited sample. The predicted effect has been confirmed and it remains to evaluate the result.

DISCUSSION

Tests which had high loadings on General Reasoning in FA 1 ask

S to recognize complex relational structures (several kinds of products according to Guilford). Problems are semantic as well as symbolic. Other investigations (Hedinger, 1965; Schädeli, 1961) confirm that tests of other product or material classes have high loadings in this 'Complexity' factor, as it was termed by Meili (1946). The common attribute of these tests seems to be the kind of cognitive operation involved. This cognitive operation is developed in school almost exclusively in connection with numerical problems. Anxious students, influenced by success or failure caused by their aptitudes, develop a certain attitude towards numerical problems.

Achievement in numerical problems tends to depend not only on aptitude but also on the security or insecurity feelings developed in school. *S*s free from school anxiety do not develop any specific attitude towards numerical tasks. Therefore numerical reasoning tests will covary more strongly with each other with other reasoning tests. This causes the numerical factor to split off from the more general reasoning factor. It is to be expected that in so-called culture-fair tests (which mostly comprise figural material; e.g. matrices, graphical series, figure analogies, picture series) achievement will be influenced by different attitudes, and that no additional covariance will be generated. It is not the material, but the necessary cognitive operations as well as the lack of a specific cultural influence on attitude which are responsible for the high loading on the same factors.

These results suggest that the factors defined by Meili seem to be more basic attributes of intellectual performance. A further investigation will try to decide whether there are even more fundamental but fewer attributes which split into these four factors.

I hope to have been able to show that interpretations of factors can be verified experimentally. The interaction model of intelligence structure which emerges is not necessarily in conflict with the linear model of factor analysis. But an interpretation of factors in this way seems to me a better, more parsimonious description of intellectual performances.

REFERENCES

Alpert, R. & Haber, R. N. (1960). Anxiety in academic achievement situations. *J. abnorm. soc. Psychol., 61,* 207-215.

Hedinger, U. K. (1965). Die Faktorenstruktur komplexer Denkaufgaben. *Z. exp. angew. Psychol., 9,* 1-57.

Hürsch, L. (1970) *Der Einfluss verschiedener Versuchssituationen auf die Faktorenstruktur von Intelligenzleistungen.* Bern: Hans Huber.

Kogan, N. & Wallach, M. A. (1964). *Risk taking: A study in cognition and personality.* New York: Holt, Rinehart and Winston.

Meili, R. (1946). L'analyse de l'intelligence. *Arch. de Psychol., 31,* 121, 1-64.

Schädeli, R. (1961). Untersuchungen zur Verifikation von Meili's Intelligenzfaktoren. *Z.f. exp. Psychol., 8,* 211-264.

LEE J. CRONBACH and PIETER J. D. DRENTH

Summary and commentary

TEST ADAPTATION AND TEST DEVELOPMENT

Great progress has been made in devising test procedures that enable unsophisticated subjects in remote cultures to respond appropriately to tests. Demonstration of tests by mime (often standardized through the medium of film) works well, and whole tests can often be presented in film (pp. 53, 185ff., 237). There are substantial difficulties in maintaining uniform procedures in mass testing programs for educational selection, especially in countries where there is little experience in testing. Two detailed handbooks have been developed to overcome these difficulties.

In testing unsophisticated subjects, practice exercises are vital; they clarify what is to be done and enable the tester to observe whether the examinee understands. Deliberate coaching is often advised (pp. 116, 212). Feuerstein (p. 265), indeed, gives extended clinical training on test tasks, both to obtain a more valid assessment and to raise the level at which the person regularly functions. It is clear that scores on tests like Matrices can be raised even by limited coaching.

Opinions differed as to the merit of coaching.* Biesheuvel wanted S's first exposure to Matrices to be 'a true lesson'; another discussant wished the tester to bring S to a relaxed state

* The past tense is used in reference to the conference discussion; the present tense is used in reference to content of papers in this volume, and also for beliefs of the editors.

and to make him familiar with the test, but to give 'no opportunity for learning' before assessment begins. There is insufficient formal evidence that the test that follows coaching is more valid than a test given after simple familiarization (p. 70). How the correlates and the meaning of the test change, as coaching extends from familiarization to elaborate instruction, remains almost entirely without investigation.

All the better-known Western tests have been translated for use in one culture or another. These translated tests may or may not serve well within a new culture. A translated test cannot be regarded as truly like the original and in the new setting it is necessary to establish whether one can give the traditional interpretation to scores. Often a straightforward translation produces too difficult a test, hence tests are modified in various ways to reduce their difficulty (e.g., pp. 129ff., 186). Thoughtful review not uncommonly shows that the 'intelligent' response to an item in the culture of origin is not the best response in a new culture (p. 433).

It is hazardous to interpret a test in its new setting as if it measured 'the same thing' as it did originally. Serious questions of comparability arise for translated performance tests as well as verbal tests. Culturally linked differences in carefulness and pacing cause mean scores of groups to differ. Nor can motivation for testing be standardized. In a less Westernized country there are differences even within an educated group in the degree to which Western work attitudes are adopted (p. 382). A particular incentive or technique of establishing rapport will not have the same significance in every culture.

Many participants spoke against investing further effort in test translation; they felt that the test developer may properly borrow ideas without trying to be faithful to the original. He should feel free to reject tasks or items on the basis of tryout. Thrane noted that a test is not uncommonly obsolescent in the country of origin by the time translation is undertaken (the Wechsler-Bellevue being an example), and argued that test development in a new locale should lead rather than follow the field. By the time translation is undertaken there should be enough information in hand to allow improvement on the original. Whether it is worthwhile to translate for the sake of obtaining 'comparable' data in a second culture is another issue, however (see below).

Norms from the locale where a test originated are useless elsewhere. It was suggested that in any new setting norms should be based on whatever population the test will be used with; this may be a select school population rather than a general one. There was some disagreement as to the importance of norms. In Cronbach's view (p. 413), if a test is to indicate readiness for schooling it is most important to describe what the child can do, without reference to norms.

Several participants noted the rarity within the conference of reports examining processes of thinking such as Rimoldi, Piaget, and others have worked on (though this theme appears in some papers, e.g., pp. 125, 272). Georgas spoke for many in criticizing an exclusively quantitative emphasis. Typically, test developers arrange individuals along a continuum that implies that one S 'has more of something' than others. But ability consists of acts, and is not a 'thing' that can be present to a greater or less degree. 'The psychologist who administers a test and finds that the person's IQ is 112 is left with the problem of inferring backward the thinking processes that led to this IQ. This is usually entirely subjective.' There was general agreement that a better research foundation for inference about process is needed.

Where the aim of testing is to make decisions within a culture, some conferees favor use of verbal tests in preference to nonverbal tests. Ortar and Kohan argued that verbal tests give more pertinent information about intellectual development and readiness for schooling. They stressed the central role of verbal and abstract thought in schooling and advanced work. This was supported by Fatouros, who had found performance tests rather unreliable, and more subject to cultural influence than is generally supposed. Nonverbal tests were advocated for various reasons. McElwain (p. 213) regarded the nonverbal but analytic task as a superior way to learn about S's ability to think verbally in his own language medium. Nonverbal tests often give a similar range of scores in different cultures. They are indispensable when applicants for school entry or employment who have to be compared come from diverse linguistic backgrounds (pp. 183ff.,

197ff., 143). The argument that verbal tests are superior because they correlate better with criteria was not accepted; the correlation may arise from verbal elements in the training or the criteria that are not inherent in the job itself (p. 245).

In test development there remains a role for statistical analysis, but the conference discussion seemed to favor reducing the emphasis on it. Some of the papers show constructive use of techniques such as item analysis and factor analysis, but very often the results are considered to be merely a starting point for further thought. This shift in attention, and indeed the rarity of traditional factor-analytic studies in the program itself, may reflect a change in psychology (Drenth, p. 31). The emphasis that formerly lay on the test and its characteristics has shifted towards the processes behind the scores, and the decisions to be based upon this information. One discussant spoke wistfully of the numerous informative items that must have been lost over the years, discarded because they did not satisfy some statistical criterion.

For the intellectual processes commonly studied in Western psychology, the conferees appeared to feel that an adequate range of tests have now been invented and put into forms applicable in non-Western cultures. The conferees appeared to be satisfied with the recommendations prepared for the International Biological Program (p. 142); these propose certain nonverbal tests for use in research that requires similar data from different locales.

The Western repertoire neglects aptitudes that may be highly developed in remote cultures. Lambert endorsed Berry's suggestion (p. 79) that the neglected aptitudes may have to be brought to attention by psychologists originating in remote cultures, since the intellectual frame of Western-reared psychologists may block them from perceiving alternative logics and cognitive skills. (A rare example of a test designed to fit an exotic culture is the NIPR Sand Drawing Test – p. 174.)

ENVIRONMENT AND ABILITY

Conferees agreed that test performance reflects a complex integration of social, emotional, and symbolic learning. The term 'ability' (also 'intelligence', etc.) causes trouble because it is used in two senses. One is operational – a performance, generated under somewhat standardized conditions, of a task on which the society values accurate (or speedy or persistent or . . .) performance. In the other sense, 'ability' is a construct that describes a property residing in the individual; test performance is only an *indicator* of ability in this sense. Conference members did not agree on a choice between these usages; our summary employs the more operational meaning insofar as possible. It makes sense to speak of 'capacity' (or 'potential') only if one refers to probable success under a specifically-mentioned training or supervisory condition. 'Capacity' as an unqualified term is undefinable.

A genetic base provides the raw material upon which culture and education work, but only that. Mittler (p. 339ff.) suggests that some kinds of performance are more affected by environment than others. Such a statistical statement refers to effects experience has had within the population tested. As Sanday (p. 90) notes, extending the variation among children in the richness of their environments will decrease the coefficient of heritability of most traits, and reducing the variation will increase the coefficient. Discussants seemed unready to endorse the suggestion of Claeys (p. 389) that certain tests rank Ss according to a more-or-less biological, culture-independent capacity for abstraction.

Differences in means of samples from various cultures are reported incidentally in a good many papers. (The differences very likely would be reduced by modifying test procedure – pp. 153ff., 211ff.). There is no point in dwelling on the observation that less-Westernized groups do less well on the commonplace verbal and nonverbal tests; the conferees saw this as a reflection of differences in child-rearing, symbol systems of the culture, and life styles. The score differences become much smaller when SES is held constant (pp. 324, 359). Control on duration of schooling is equally important (p. 396). There was a remarkable absence of interest in hypotheses about variations in development that occur among populations with different gene pools. Indeed, the discussion did not challenge two writers (pp. 92, 197) who took as a working hypothesis that any mean test-score difference *between* cultures is a reflection of environmental differences.

A much more discriminating view of 'culture' and its effects was called for. Such expressions as 'culturally deprived' do not stand up under analysis. Even so bleak an environment as that of the Bushmen provides plentiful stimulation and challange. Remarks about 'advanced' and 'traditional' cultures should give way, it was argued, to careful description of each ecology and social order (e.g., pp. 77ff., 171ff.). In another phrase: the significant dimensions of environments should be described (p. 101). Berry believes that an ability develops when the ecology surrounding a group demands and supports that ability. He is thus able to explain why certain groups are relatively weak in problem solving and perceptual discrimination.

The very idea that an ethnic group can be identified with 'a culture' proved to be oversimple. Reuning found that test results in one group of Bushmen differed radically from those roving a similar territory 25 miles away. The whole style of one community might differ from that of others, perhaps for no more basic reason than the emergence of a single vivacious woman as its moving spirit. Attempts to collect quantitative data with standard instruments may miss the influence of dynamic factors in the community (p. 291).

Opinions differed about the ease with which intellectual performance can be improved. Practicing personnel workers including Belbin and Rimland recalled the difficulty psychologists have had in producing changes in the adaptability of adults, and warned that practical techniques for bringing about change may be long in coming. Failure and ultimate demoralization may occur if a student or employee is given work beyond his reach. Honzik and Ortar stressed the influence of events during infancy and early childhood on mental development. But Feuerstein argued against the implication that there is an age after which it is 'too late' to improve mental ability; his clinical work (see pp. 265ff.) is one of the few thoroughgoing attempts to improve functioning of below-average adolescents and adults, and he considers his results a reason for optimism.

TESTS IN SELECTION

Correlations of nonverbal tests with criteria of school success differ remarkably from study to study. Appreciable positive relationships are found in the Pacific region (esp. pp. 188ff.) and in South Africa (pp. 41ff., 54) for both school and job criteria. Matrices and DAM correlate with school marks in Greece (p. 219). But reports of low correlations of nonverbal tests with school performance are commonplace in the psychological literature; many authors here report additional low correlations of this type. Various explanations for the contradictions can be offered. Perhaps the South African and Pacific batteries are better instruments than other performance tests. Perhaps there is an extreme range of performance within some of these populations so that the test detects many persons scoring at a very low level. Perhaps, as Vernon has suggested (see p. 53; also p. 375), the nature of schooling in some places calls for a different kind of aptitude than schooling in London or New York. Clarification can come only from meticulous application of comparable tests to comparable samples in different places. The samples ought to be homogeneous in social class. The investigator should give close attention to the style of instruction and he should report the regression surface rather than the correlation alone (p. 414). Unless studies are so systematic, they produce only a welter of empirical findings for particular schools in scattered localities.

Results with industrial criteria are equally discordant. Ghiselli's summary of Western experience (see p. 246) shows that verbal tests predict success in training but that tests – whether verbal or nonverbal – only sporadically predict on-the-job criteria. Rimland reports additional discouraging experience in the US Navy. NIPR, however, has had great success in predicting job criteria with performance tests (pp. 42, 41; see also p. 189). Again, differences in samples, in testing technique, in job demands, and in criteria require close examination.

Local criterion-oriented studies will still be needed every-where. The conferees believed, however, that if crosscultural generalization or comparison is the aim, isolated correlational studies ought now to give way to studies planned to facilitate causal explanation.

There was much discussion of fairness and bias of tests. It was agreed that no test is 'culture-free', and few participants wished to endorse the promise that 'culture-fair' tests are possible. This term proved to be highly ambiguous; some writers use it to refer to tests based on abstract drawings, some apply it to any test on which different groups achieve similar scores, and some introduce complex statistical considerations (pp. 415, 427ff.). Tests that are 'culture specific' need not be condemned as biased, in San-day's view; they do indicate which persons are most likely to fit into that specific culture (at least in the short run), be it a middle-class urban society or a factory in a nation where trans-culturation has barely started.

Participants engaged in personnel selection defend tests that predict criteria (pp. 24ff., 37ff., 142). Tests, including those that reflect education and Westernization, raise productivity when used to select workers. Equity and practicality are served by testing, when applicants vastly outnumber vacancies and when in the absence of tests the selection will be based on irrelevant characteristics. The *sine qua non* is locally-demonstrated validity; the test must predict criteria that the policy makers consider to be important. Drenth (p. 29) argues that the psychologist has a responsibility for making sure that the outcome the firm seeks to maximize is a proper choice of criterion. Managers may be shortsighted or uncritical in defining the standards for good work.

Implicit in several papers (pp., 15ff., 29ff.) and much of the discussion is the criticism that tests that predict criteria set by 'the Establishment' have a conservative effect. Cieutat, however, took the position that psychologists ought not to set policy but ought to make a country's policy work. Some African countries are devoting a quarter or more of the national budget to educa-tion; even so, the number of school places is very limited. 'The procedures used for selection in those countries before we got there had validities close to zero. With our tests we are able to predict which of the prospective students will do well on *the country's* criteria of success in its educational system. We increase the number of people who get through the system; we reduce the dropout rate; the people who get through get higher grades. To me that seems a contribution. To use as criterion anything other than what the country sets involves dabbling in educational policy.' Biesheuvel added: 'I think we psychologists ought to have the guts to stand up for the instruments which we have produced which we know will do a better job [than other methods] of sorting out those people who can take advantage of the very limited educational opportunities that are available.'

Tests and selection rules must be acceptable to the local public and the individuals tested. Tests serve interests of able members of cultural outgroups by opening chances for them. This may or may not be appreciated. When the average score of a group farther from the cultural mainstream is relatively low, the test is likely to be challenged as 'unfair' to them no matter how real their disadvantage is. In both the East Indies and Africa, it has been necessary to adopt tests that would yield not-too-disparate distributions in the various regions of the country, and hence assure roughly equal chances for employment (p. 143). This puts a premium on nonverbal tests.

There was agreement that testers must take seriously the resistance to tests among applicants. To make testing acceptable and more legitimate, it was suggested that a greater part of the decision in educational placement or employment be left with S. He would be given a frank picture of his prospects and left free to take up a high-risk option. Institutional decisions cannot continue to be independent of individual decisions in Drenth's view (p. 31ff.). The recommendations in this vein of the Commission on Tests of the College Entrance Examination Board (1970) were noted. Wickert suggested (p. 258) that self-estimates of abilities by workers may serve some of the institutional purposes of tests.

The legitimacy claimed for tests with verbal and scholastic content on the basis of their predictive validity was challenged by those who suspect bias in present educational criteria. Levine in particular felt that in the USA the grade-point average embodies the prejudices of white teachers who do not expect black students to do well, and that this leads to a spurious validation of biased tests.

COMPARATIVE STUDIES WITHIN CULTURES

Many of the empirical papers include a comparison of males with females. Reports of no difference were usual, but comparisons on the same test vary from culture to culture (e.g., see results for Draw-a-Man — pp. 217ff., 365ff.). What is known about male and female roles in the several cultures sometimes seems to explain such facts, but some of the findings are surprising.

A number of studies document age differences, and these trends sometimes differ for the two sexes. In studies of such matters, a major difficulty is that samples taken from schools are systematically affected by school admissions policy and by dropouts. The probability of dropping out differs with sex, SES, and ethnic group, and one ordinarily has little basis for judging how much this biases comparisons. A partial solution is the repeated-measures or longitudinal design (p. 102). This is coming more into use. Another advance is the use of systematic community-wide sampling to obtain out-of-school subjects. Thus Grant used an aerial photograph of a rural district in the Transvaal to map a strict probability (area) sampling plan.

Of correlations between test scores and SES there is no end. No matter what the region and no matter what the test, a correlation is found. (But note Gitmez' intervention — p. 156 — that wiped out the difference in one sample.) Repeatedly, discussants urged a shift in the style of research on SES. Present studies almost invariably select a gross index of home background and correlate it with scores. Honzik and others recommended separating data on various characteristics of the home. Research ought to determine which characteristics have effects, on what aspects of child development, and at what age. It was urged that, beyond the obvious separation of father's education from family income and mother's education, there be close attention to the style of parent-child interaction. Ortar expressed dissatisfaction with any source of data less valid and less detailed than direct observation in the home.

This discussion was one more manifestation of the demand for movement from description. toward theory. Harrold's (pp. 317 ff.) multifaceted inquiry into categorizing behavior illustrates one way in which research can probe for causes.

CROSSCULTURAL TEST INTERPRETATION: LOGICAL RESTRICTIONS

While these Proceedings include a number of reports on score differences between populations on one or another test, there was very little enthusiasm for further studies in this style. Some insisted that efforts to compare peoples on the same instrument should be abandoned because translation alters the instrument, and motivation can never be held constant. To quote one speaker at the height of the debate: 'Everything that has been said in this conference has demonstrated that it is meaningless to make comparisons in different cultural environments of even so-called culture-free tests'.

Others judged it important to collect comparative data but proposed stringent restrictions as to admissible kinds of data. Several papers (p. 103, 351, 429ff.. 453ff.)' call for 'functional equivalence' in tests to be interpreted crossculturally. The papers appear to be calling for all of the following in combination: The test should be homogeneous within each culture, according to some statistical criterion of unidimensionality; the indices representing the difficulties of the items should have the same order in the cultures considered; the test should have the same factor loadings when the same battery is applied in each culture, and factored; with many external variables, the test should have the same relationship in each culture. Similar demands are made when two tests, each adapted to a different culture, are to be given the same interpretation.

Such strong demands are not likely to be satisfied; relations usually change from one culture to another (e.g., p. 453). Discussion of this conflict between ideal and reality brought out the fact that at least some of those who propound strong models (specifically, Irvine and Mellenbergh) advocated them primarily as a strategic way to force the investigator to challenge conventional test interpretations. While tests are likely fully to satisfy such demands only in limited and trivial cases, the departures from the model can have considerable value in reshaping interpretations. The models also serve as a warning against taking seriously the convenient, familiar language that speaks of a test as a measure of some one construct.

Test interpreters have the habit of speaking of Test X as 'a measure of g' and Test Y as 'a measure of practical-mechanical ability'. Much writing on construct validation had incautiously encouraged such thinking, but the conference called it sharply into question. A construct interpretation can be verified only in one particular culture or subculture at a time. There is no more justification in carrying an interpretation across cultural lines – without confirmatory studies in the second culture – than there is in assuming the validity of a predictor test for all mechanical jobs on the basis of studies in some one factory.

The heart of the difficulty in carrying interpretation across cultural lines is that performance on a test calls for many attributes in combination. All must be present for good performance. To quote Irvine: 'It is like cricket or baseball – you can be "out" in a great number of ways.' Attributes universally present among Ss in the culture where the test originated, hence not a source of variance, may vary greatly in another culture (p. 449). The added variance is quite often related to S's attitude, motivation, or social response to the test. One implication is that factor analysis can go only a small distance toward clarifying a 'structure of abilities'. Claeys finds a factor among Congolese that he interprets as the degree to which S's have adopted a Western attitude; this perhaps would not vary within a Western, test-wise group.

Skepticism regarding the likelihood of finding universal generalizations or universally applicable constructs does not make cross-cultural comparisons pointless. So long as the *operations* of data collection are near to identical, replication of studies in different settings will give thought-provoking results. Most likely, no standard instrument will 'mean the same thing' in different cultures; it is precisely for this reason that the crosscultural comparison holds an interest.

The idea of operational comparability is reasonably obvious so far as test stimuli are concerned. It is not so obvious that holding incentives and administrative procedures constant is the best way to get comparable data. If a standard procedure is to be used, it should be one likely to elicit a fully adequate effort from each *S*. But the familiarization that benefits persons in one culture may make the test tedious for those in another, and the incentive that makes an appeal in one culture may be worthless elsewhere. Whether it makes sense to optimize the procedure within each culture, thereby making the testing operations somewhat dissimilar, is an unresolved issue. A paper that became available following the conference (Cole & Bruner, 1971; see also Cole et al., 1971) strengthens concern with this issue. The writers cite work by the linguist Labov on the American black child, and Cole's own data from Liberia, to defend the proposition that a person may possess verbal competence even though his verbal performance is poor on the 'alien' task set by the psychological tester. A single instance of successful performance, elicited in a social interaction that is natural within *S*'s culture, is sufficient to justify the inference that he possesses a degree of competence far greater than his test score suggests. 'By the use of such a methodology, Labov demonstrated that culturally deprived black children, *tested appropriately* for optimum performance, have the same grammatical competence as middle-class whites.' (p. 874). If the investigator's best efforts to elicit evidence of some competence fail, this is still not evidence that the competence is absent; perhaps he just has not found the situation where *S* finds it appropriate to use that competence. This implies that attempts to hold operations constant in crosscultural comparisons will be misleading rather than helpful.

This view of research strategy would have been more prominent if more of the conference members had been anthropologists and ethnographers. The present volume may well be considered alongside the report of a conference on 'transcultural studies in cognition' (Romney & d'Andrade, 1964), where a distinction is made between developing theory to describe a culture in its own terms and developing transcultural theory. This comment by Romney and d'Andrade gives some indication of the way the two conferences are related:

'[A] characteristic of the ethnographic approach is the feeling that the only proper data consist of samples of culturally appropriate behaviors occurring in "natural" situations. The subject's behavior should not, it is felt, be delimited by tests or other "arbitrary" devices. The contrast . . . [with] the testing procedures of the psychologist . . . is especially sharp. The psychologist who describes cognitive process with respect to a specific test situation assumes that the behavior which occurs in the test situation will be similar to the way in which subjects respond to a large class of other situations. The ethnographer . . . assumes that whatever rules he constructs . . . may have to be changed to describe behavior in other classes of situations.'

This characterization of the psychologist's work applies to interpretations of performance in terms of traits or constructs rather than to sheer operational statements. But these too have to be interpreted in the end to rise above the descriptive level, and it became increasingly questionable, as the conference proceeded, whether psychologists possess constructs that can be successfully used to explain diverse cultures within a single theoretical frame.

ADAPTABILITY – TO WHAT?

'Adaptability' is offered by Biesheuvel, Dague, and others as a solution to the psychologists' need for an integrating and goal-setting term. The proposal has obvious merits, the first of which is that it is intended to push the outworn word 'intelligence' into the discard. It is substantially broader than 'intelligence', making a place for the affective component of performance.

Among the empirical papers of the conference, explanations of results on 'cognitive' tasks are often couched in terms of 'affective' concepts: self-confidence, preference among rewards, conditioned attitudes, etc. Conference discussion tended toward the verdict that the traditional separation of the cognitive from the affective in psychological theory is unwise and should be abandoned. There is good precedent for seeing performance as an amalgam of the cognitive and the affective; Binet's own characterization of intelligence put substantial weight on mental set and self-criticism. The subsequent emphasis on task content and on the logical structure that would regulate a perfect performance, among writers from Spearman to Guilford and Piaget, has led to a neglect of the affective component that generally makes performance less than perfect.

Some statements seem to emphasize the culture-specific or job-specific character of 'adaptability'. What constitutes adaptability for the African in the bush may not constitute adaptability for the one taking a job in the gold mines. Given this point of view, an adaptability test would consist of whatever correlates with success in learning the performances the environmental setting calls for. But the tests recommended by Biesheuvel to measure adaptability are intended to be relevant in all settings, and most have hitherto been regarded as measures of general ability. Hence it is not certain that the proposal liberates us from a monolithic general factor.

Discussion brought out Biesheuvel's interest in the level of proficiency the person can attain on a task or in a life style, when given all the help he needs to reach his best level. This seems to define adaptability in terms of what one can do in a situation that has been made thoroughly familiar, not what he can do in a surprising situation. Ortar criticized this shift in emphasis from independent problem solving to trainability. The idea that 'adaptability' may consist in large measure of ability to learn only adds to its ambiguity, since no one knows how many different 'abilities to learn' there may be, or how much they have in common with reasoning abilities, vocabulary, etc. There is need for clearer thought about the construct of 'learning ability'; Irvine in particular was unwilling to stop with mere operationalization. He argued that operations available in coaching and transfer experiments are flexible enough to lead into an infinite regress of 'learning-to-learn-to-learn-. . .'. It is to be remembered also that no one in the conference had appreciable evidence that tests of 'learning rate' are correlated with practical criteria.

The term 'adaptability' can easily be interpreted as echoing a desire to shape the person to conform to the *status quo* in society or the work setting. Many conferees felt that the times demand instead an emphasis on how men can reshape the society to conform to human needs. Any attempt to reshape society will call for a high level of intellectual functioning, but very likely the intellectual style of the reformer will not be identified and encouraged if successful conformity to the requirements of industrial society is the criterion of what tests should measure.

There is a dilemma: Admittedly, a transitional culture cannot make the transition unless it identifies persons competent to take part in industry; but in moving toward a replica of Western culture it may be sacrificing its own indigenous forms of adaptability. Lambert saw this as a risk even in advanced cultures, noting some American evidence that independent 'productive' thinking becomes weaker during adolescent years because the system in the USA does not reward independent thought.

Whether a person fails to show a certain competence in a certain situation may or may not be important, according to Cole and Bruner, depending on how large that situation looms in the subject's own ecology. 'Cultural differences reside more in differences in the situations to which different cultural groups apply their skills than to the differences in the skills possessed by the groups.' (p. 874). Problems arise less in assessing the person's ability to function within his own culture or subculture – a question the psychologist from an outside culture rarely poses – than in assessing the ability of the person to fit into a middle-class or Westernized culture that wishes to employ his skills and offers inducements and pressures to get him to make the transition. As Cole and Bruner see it, the problem is one of designing instruction in which the person who seeks to fit himself to the 'alien' culture can transfer the skills he has already built up. The argument puts the burden of adaptation on the agents transmitting the new culture, rather than on the learner.

The conferees were critical of any hint that superiority on tests arising out of Western logic is more meritorious than superiority on tests where Westerners do badly. The Bushman provided a prime example of adaptability, as he copes with an environment in which the Westerner could not survive. It is a major difficulty for psychologists to escape the automatic assumption that the kinds of problems Western man sets for himself in this century define what should be credited as mental ability (p. 107).

Taken as a whole, the conference seems likely to mark a watershed in applied psychology. The participants were highly sensitive to resistance to testing and to the worldwide distrust of productivity as the sole criterion of the good society, and sensitive also to the inadequacy of purely descriptive, factual studies as a way of understanding how experience affects intellectual development. The papers and discussion called insistently for greater attention to the assumptions underlying psychological research and practice, and for a redirection of research effort. While the conference originally set out to take a crossnational perspective, it became apparent that the questions discussed are equally pertinent to research and practice within any one nation, and even within its mainstream culture.

The questions turned a skeptical eye on most the psychologist's long-sacred beliefs. Are we measuring the right things? Are we defining too narrowly the kind of intellect to be valued? Are we sacrificing valuable indigenous cultures in the drive to increase productivity? Are we giving adequate thought to the dignity and right to self-determination of the examinee? Are we to accept correlations of ability with home background as inevitable, or are we to learn how to remove the limiting effects some homes have? Are we to continue to certify abilities only after they have been developed, or are we to return to the original problem, of detecting capabilities that could be developed if we changed childrearing or education or industrial training? Can the diversity that exists within and between societies be made into a resource for human progress by cultivating multiple styles of expression and adaptation?

To capture the issues in a single query: Are tests to be used to adapt people individually and collectively to the presently dominant model of Western industrial society, or are they to uncover human potentialities to which cultures can be adapted?

A 1972 report of unusual interest to readers of this volume has just been prepared by P.H. Liederman and others at the Department of Psychiatry, Stanford University, California. Sixty-five Kikiyu infants were given the Bayley Scales at two-month intervals from one month to 15 months. For both mental and motor performance the Kikiyu children were superior to USA whites and blacks (by about two months at age 10 months). Performance was correlated with family economic status.

REFERENCES

Cole, M. & Bruner, J.S. (1971) Cultural differences and inferences about psychological processes. *Amer. Psychologist,* 26, 867-876.
Cole, M. et al. (1971) *The cultural context of learning and thinking.* New York: Basic Books.
Commission on Tests. (1970) *Report.* (2 vols.). New York: College Entrance Examination Board.
Romney, A.K. & d'Andrade, Roy G. (Eds.) (1964) Transcultural studies in cognition. *American Anthropologist, 66,* No. 3, Part 2.

Roster of Conference Participants

Abul-Hubb, Dhia M. (Dr.) Assistant Professor of Psychology, Baghdad University, Baghdad, Iraq.

Ahumada, Isabel. National University of Mexico, Mexico City, Mexico.

Ahumada, Rene (Dr.) Professor of Psychology, National University of Mexico, Mexico City, Mexico.

Akeju, Simon S.A. (Dr.) Head, Aptitude Testing Department, Test Development and Research Office, West African Examinations Council, Lagos, Nigeria.

Akyüz, Riza. Supervisor, Elementary Education, Millî Egitim Müdürlügü, Samsun, Turkey.

Alam, Suzan. Higher Technical Teacher Training School for Girls, Ankara, Turkey.

Angelini, Arrigo L. (Dr.) Director, Institute of Psychology, University of Sao Paolo, Sao Paolo, Brazil.

Arıcı, Hüsnü (Dr.). Associate Professor of Psychology, Haçettepe University, Ankara, Turkey.

Arkun, Nezahat (Dr.) Professor of Psychology, Istanbul University, Istanbul, Turkey.

Ataman, Işık (Dr.) Clinical psychologist, Department of Psychiatry, Haçettepe University, Ankara, Turkey.

Bakare, Christopher G.M. (Dr.) Lecturer in Educational Psychology, University of Ibadan, Ibadan, Nigeria.

Balkır, Belkıs. Vefa High School, Istanbul, Turkey.

Baycan, Gülçin. Clinical Psychology Laboratory, Istanbul University Medical School, Istanbul, Turkey.

Belbin, Eunice (Dr.) Director Industrial Training Research Unit. Cambridge, England.

Belbin, R. Meredith (Dr.) Consultant, 8 Lansdowne Road, Cambridge, England.

Berry, John W. (Dr.) Assistant Professor of Psychology, Queens University, Kingston, Ontario, Canada.

Beuchelt, Eno (Dr.) Lecturer at the University of Cologne, Cologne, Germany.

Beyhan, Solmaz. Department of Child Psychiatry, Istanbul University, Istanbul, Turkey.

Biesheuvel, Simon (Dr.) Psychologist, Box 1099, Johannesburg, South Africa.

Blake, R. Hilton (Dr.) Head, Division of Personnel Selection and Vocational Guidance, National Institute for Personnel Research, Johannesburg, South Africa.

Bozzo, Maria Teresa. Assistant, Institute of Psychology, University of Genova, Genova, Italy.

Calin, Bahar. Istanbul Tip Fakültesi, Capa Psikiyatri Klinigi, Istanbul, Turkey.

Cantez, Esin (Dr.) Assistant, Institute of Experimental Psychology, University of Istanbul, Istanbul, Turkey.

Cassie, Alexander. Head, Psychology Division, Army Personnel Research Establishment, Farnborough, Hants., England.

Cho, Sam (Dr.) Research Scientist, American Institutes for Research; Director of Training, West African Examinations Council, Lagos, Nigeria.

Cieutat, Linda (Dr.) Child Consultation and Education Service, 1811 Ottard St., Pittsburgh, Pa., USA.

Cieutat, Victor J. (Dr.) Director, International Studies Institute, American Institutes for Research, Pittsburgh, Pa., USA.

Claeys, Willem (Dr.) Professor of Differential Psychology, Catholic University of Louvain, Louvain, Belgium.

Cook, Paul F. (Dr.) Deputy Director, Regional Testing Resource and Training Center, Gaborone, Botswana.

Coumoutsakos, Spiridon. Director, Experimental Center for Vocational Guidance, Ministry of Labor, Athens, Greece.

Cronbach, Lee J. (Dr.) Professor, School of Education, Stanford University, Stanford, Calif., USA.

Crowell, Doris C. (Dr.) Assistant Researcher, Center for Research in Early Childhood Education, University of Hawaii, Honolulu, Hawaii, USA.

Dague, Pierre C. (Dr.) Professor of Special Education, National Center for Open Air Education, Suresnes, France.

Dede, Saban. Head, Measurement Section, Planning, Research, and Coordination Office, Ministry of Education, Ankara, Turkey.

Delin, Ayla. Planning, Research, and Coordination Office, Ministry of Education, Ankara, Turkey.

Drenth, Pieter J.D. (Dr.) Professor and Director, Psychology Laboratory, Free University of Amsterdam, Amsterdam, Netherlands.

Eckensberger, Lutz H. (Dr.) Assistant, Psychological Institute, University of the Saar, Saarbrücken, Germany.

Fatouros, Mika (Dr.) Senior Assistant, Psychological Laboratory, University of Thessaloniki, Thessaloniki, Greece.

Felipe, Abraham I. (Dr.) Associate Professor of Psychology, University of the Philippines; Resident Consultant in Test Development, Fund for Assistance to Private Education, Makati, Rizal, P.I.

Feuerstein, Reuven (Dr.) Director, Hadassah Wizo Canada, Research Institute, Jerusalem, Israel.

Frost, Barry P. (Dr.) Associate Professor and Head of Division of Clinical Diagnosis and Special Education, University of Calgary, Calgary, Alberta, Canada.

Geirnaert, W.R.B. Psychologist, Military Neuro-Psychiatric Center, Antwerp, Belgium.

Georgas, James G. (Dr.) Research Associate, Athenian Institute of Anthropos, Athens, Greece.

Gitmez, Ali S. (Dr.) Lecturer in Psychology, Haçettepe University, Ankara, Turkey.

Grant, Gerard V. (Dr.) Senior Lecturer in Psychology, University of the Witwatersrand, Johannesburg, South Africa.

Harrold-Stroebe, Margaret. Postgraduate student, Department of Psychology, University of Bristol, Bristol, England.

Hesse, Hermann. Student, Psychological Institute, University of Heidelberg, Heidelberg, Germany.

Honzik, Marjorie (Dr.) Research Psychologist, Institute of Human Development, University of California, Berkeley, Calif., USA.

Hürsch, Luzius (Dr.) Lecturer, Psychological Institute, University of Bern, Bern, Switzerland.

Irvine, Sidney H. (Dr.) Dean of Education, Brock University, St. Catharines, Ont., Canada.

Johnson, Richard T. (Dr.) Senior Research Scientist, American Institutes for Research, Regional Testing Centre, Limbe, Malawi.

Kagıtçıbaşı, Cıgdem (Dr.) Assistant Professor of Psychology, Middle East Technical University, Ankara, Turkey.

Kalay, Hale. Planning, Research, and Coordination Office, Ministry of Education, Ankara, Turkey.

Kepçeoglu, Muharrem. Head, Guidance and Counseling Division, Planning, Research, and Coordination Office, Ministry of Education, Ankara, Turkey.

Knook, Arie I.C. Chief Psychologist, Vocational Guidance Division. Ministry of Social Affairs & Public Health, The Hague, Netherlands.

Kodanaz, H. Altan. Chairman, Division of Clinical Psychology, Department of Psychiatry, University of Ankara, Ankara, Turkey.

de Kohan, Nuria Cortada (Dr.) Professor of Statistics Applied to Psychology and Sociology, Buenos Aires University, Buenos Aires, Argentina.

Kyöstiö, Oiva K. (Dr.) Dean, Teachers College, University of Oulu, Oulu, Finland.

Lambert, Wallace E. (Dr.) Professor of Psychology, McGill University, Montreal, P.Q., Canada.

Lavoegie, Madeleine. Director, Center for Applications of Psychology in Industry and Commerce, Paris, France.

Le Maitour, Louis-Marie (Dr.) Director, Regional Psychotechnical Center; Professor of Industrial Psycho-sociology, University of Toulouse, Toulouse, France.

Levine, David (Dr.) Professor of Psychology, University of Nebraska, Lincoln, Nebraska, USA.

Lévy-Leboyer, Claude (Dr.) Professor of Industrial Psychology, University of Paris, Paris, France.

Lienert, Gustav A. (Dr.) Professor of Psychology, University of Düsseldorf, Germany.

Lynn, Richard (Dr.) Professor of Psychology, Economic and Social Research Institute, Dublin, Ireland.

Machado, Fernando F. (Dr.) Director, Lyceum Garcia de Orta, Porto, Portugal.

Mannekens, Georges J. (Dr.) Director, Psychological-Medical and Social Center of Ghent, Ghent, Belgium.

Mansueto-Zecca, Graziella (Dr.) Professor of Psychology, University of Genoa, Genoa, Italy.

Martin, Maurice A. (Major) Deputy Assistant for Personnel Research, Canadian Forces Headquarters, Ottawa, Ont., Canada.

McDaniel, Ernest D. (Dr.) Co-director, Purdue Educational Research Center; Professor of Education, Purdue University, West Lafayette, Ind., USA.

McElwain, Donald W. (Dr.) Professor of Psychology, University of Queensland, Queensland, Australia.

Mellenbergh, Gideon J. (Dr.) Associate Professor, Psychological Laboratory, University of Utrecht, Utrecht. Netherlands.

Mittler, Peter J. (Dr.) Director, Hester Adrian Research Centre for the Study of Learning Processes in the Mentally Handicapped, University of Manchester, Manchester, England.

Ord, I. G. Reader in Psychology, University of Waikato, Hamilton, New Zealand.

Ortar, Gina (Dr.) Professor of Education, The Hebrew University, Jerusalem, Israel.

Öktem, Öget. Assistant, General Psychology Department, Edebiyat Fakültesi, Istanbul, Turkey.

Ormanlı, Mücellâ. Assistant, Institute of Psychology, University of Istanbul, Istanbul, Turkey.

Pauker, Jerome D. (Dr.) Professor, University of Missouri, Columbia, Missouri.

Piyamada, Mantana. Testing Section, Thai Civil Service Office, Bangkok, Thailand.

Poortinga, Ype H. (Dr.) Senior Research Officer, National Institute for Personnel Research, Johannesburg, South Africa; Free University of Amsterdam, Netherlands.

Prien, Borge (Dr.) Head, Test Department, Danish Institute for Educational Research, Copenhagen, Denmark.

Reuning, Helmut (Dr.) Head, Temperament and Personality Research Division, National Institute for Personnel Research, Johannesburg, South Africa.

Rimland, Bernard (Dr.) Director, Personnel Measurement Research Division, U.S. Naval Personnel and Training Research Laboratory, San Diego, California.

Samuel, John A. Chief Psychologist, Post Office Central Headquarters, London, England.

Sanday, Peggy R. (Dr.) Assistant Professor of Anthropology and Urban Affairs; Director of Research, Carnegie-Mellon Action Project, Carnegie-Mellon University, Pittsburgh, Pa., USA.

Schmitz, Georges (Dr.) Professor of Psychology, Pädagogische Hochschule Westfalen-Lippe, Hüttental-Weidenau, Germany.

Şemin, Refia (Dr.) Director, Institute of Pedagogy, Istanbul University, Istanbul, Turkey.

Silvey, Jonathan. Lecturer in Applied Social Science, University of Nottingham, England; Research Associate, Makerere Institute of Social Research, Uganda, Africa.

Smith, Louis M. (Dr.) Professor of Education, Washington, University, St. Louis, Mo., USA.

Solstad, Karl Jan. Assistant Professor, Institute for Educational Research, University of Oslo, Oslo, Norway.

Stavrianopoulo, Vassiliki. Director, Vocational Guidance Bureau, Manpower Employment Organization, Athens, Greece.

Suben, Müjgân. Clinical Psychology Laboratory, Istanbul University, Medical School, Istanbul, Turkey.

Sümbül, Oral. Middle East Technical University, Ankara, Turkey.

Tan, Hasan (Dr.) Professor of Psychology, Middle East Technical University, Ankara, Turkey.

Tan, Naime. Namik Kemal High School, Ankara, Turkey.

Thrane, Vidkunn Coucheron. Senior Research Associate, Institute of Applied Social Research, Oslo, Norway.

Togrol, Beglân B. (Dr.) Chairman, Department of Experimental Psychology, Istanbul University, Istanbul, Turkey.

Tsakalos, Panayotes. Department of Primary Education, Curriculum and Research Department, Ministry of Education, Athens, Greece.

Turgut, Fuat (Dr.) Associate Professor of Psychology Institute of Education, Haçettepe University, Ankara, Turkey.

Uçman, Perin. Technical Assistant, Department of Psychology, Haçettepe University, Ankara, Turkey.

van der Flier, Henk. Research Fellow, Laboratory for Psychodiagnostics and Industrial Psychology, Free University of Amsterdam, Amsterdam, Netherlands

Vingopoulos, Ilias (Dr.) Professor of Education, Academy de Lamia, Athens, Greece.

Wahl, Izak Rousseau (Dr.) Assistant Director, Institute for Psychometric Research, Human Sciences Research Council, Pretoria, South Africa.

Wickert, Frederic R. (Dr.) Professor of Psychology, Michigan State University, East Lansing, Mich.. USA.

Yanık, Rukiye. Planning, Research, and Coordination office, Ministry of Education, Ankara, Turkey.

Yerasimos, Athene. Private Psychologist, Istanbul, Turkey.

Yurdagül, Yüksel. Sişli Terakki High School, Guidance Service, Instanbul, Turkey.

Zamantılı, Fatma. Psychiatry Clinic, Istanbul University, Medical School, Istanbul, Turkey.

Index